Screening the Crisis

Screening the Crisis

US Cinema and Social Change in the Wake of the 2008 Crash

Edited by
Juan A. Tarancón and Hilaria Loyo

BLOOMSBURY ACADEMIC
NEW YORK • LONDON • OXFORD • NEW DELHI • SYDNEY

BLOOMSBURY ACADEMIC
Bloomsbury Publishing Inc
1385 Broadway, New York, NY 10018, USA
50 Bedford Square, London, WC1B 3DP, UK
29 Earlsfort Terrace, Dublin 2, Ireland

BLOOMSBURY, BLOOMSBURY ACADEMIC and the Diana logo are
trademarks of Bloomsbury Publishing Plc

First published in the United States of America 2022
Paperback edition published 2024

Volume Editor's Part of the Work © Juan A. Tarancón and Hilaria Loyo, 2022, 2024
Each chapter © of Contributors

For legal purposes the Acknowledgments on p. xi constitute an extension
of this copyright page.

Cover design: Eleanor Rose
Cover image: Jennifer Lawrence in *Winter's Bone* (2010), Dir. Debra Granik © Film
Company Roadside Attractions / Alamy

All rights reserved. No part of this publication may be reproduced or transmitted
in any form or by any means, electronic or mechanical, including photocopying,
recording, or any information storage or retrieval system, without prior
permission in writing from the publishers.

Bloomsbury Publishing Inc does not have any control over, or responsibility for, any
third-party websites referred to or in this book. All internet addresses given in this
book were correct at the time of going to press. The author and publisher regret any
inconvenience caused if addresses have changed or sites have ceased to exist,
but can accept no responsibility for any such changes.

Library of Congress Cataloging-in-Publication Data

ISBN: HB: 978-1-5013-8812-5
PB: 978-1-5013-8816-3
ePDF: 978-1-5013-8814-9
eBook: 978-1-5013-8813-2

Typeset by Deanta Global Publishing Services, Chennai, India

To find out more about our authors and books visit www.bloomsbury.com and
sign up for our newsletters.

CONTENTS

Foreword: Crisis and Critique Timothy Corrigan viii
Acknowledgments xi

Introduction: Cinema and the Age of Crisis *Juan A. Tarancón and Hilaria Loyo* 1

PART I US Cinema in the Age of Crisis

1. It's Always Been Crisis: Hollywood History *Toby Miller and Bill Grantham* 15

2. Independent Films in an Age of Crisis: Illuminating the Lives of Outsiders in Neoliberal America *Cynthia Baron* 31

PART II Labor Crisis and the Neoliberal Subject

3. Limitless?: Neoliberal Femininity in the Post-recessionary Chick Flick *Beatriz Oria* 53

4. Screening Recessions through a Gendered Lens: Nostalgic and Critical Revisions of the Past from the Post-2008 Crisis Perspective *Elena Oliete-Aldea* 68

5. Screening Neoliberalism in *Nightcrawler* and *The Wolf of Wall Street* *Stephen Felder* 83

PART III Technology and the State of Surveillance

6. The Shock Doctrines of *The Social Network*: Zuckerberg, Trump, and Surveillance Capitalism in Big-tech Cinema *Ian Scott* 99

7 "I Figured You Were Probably Watching Us": Performing Gender and Citizen Surveillance in *Ex Machina* Kayla Meyers 113

PART IV The Housing Crisis and the Home Question

8 Stand Your Ground: Neoliberal Horrors, *The Purge* Franchise, and the Allegorical Moment of US Trauma Tony Grajeda 131

9 Horror, Race, and the Economics of Interiority: Homeownership in the Blumhouse Universe Leah Pérez and William J. Simmons 148

10 Resignifying the National Home: Gendered Domopolitics and Neoliberal Geographies of Exclusion in Debra Granik's Cinema Hilaria Loyo 163

PART V Politics, Affect, and the Crisis of Public Values

11 White Identity, Great Replacement Politics, and Auteurism: The Cinema of S. Craig Zahler Carlos Gallego 183

12 A Crisis of Confidence: Fracture and Malaise in the US Polity in *Dragged Across Concrete* Fabián Orán Llarena 198

13 "I Guess It Comes from Being Poor": Inequality, Affect, and Point of View in *The Florida Project* Juan A. Tarancón 213

PART VI Ecological Crisis and Visions of the Future

14 Who the Earth Is For: Reframing Rural Landscapes as Collective Polities in *Leave No Trace* and *Beasts of the Southern Wild* Tim Lindemann 231

15 Turning Over a New Leaf: Exploring Human-Tree Relationships in *The Lorax* and *Avatar* Virginia Luzón-Aguado 245

PART VII Crisis and Violence in the Borderlands

16 "No One to Call Around Here. These Boys Is on Their Own": The Postindustrial Frontier in *Hell or High Water* and the Western as a Landscape of the Crisis *Luis Freijo* 265

17 Bad Hombres at the Border: Masculinity and Mexico in *Rambo: Last Blood* *Gregory Frame* 279

18 We're No Longer Here: *Ya no estoy aquí* as an Example of Neoliberalism and Economic Crisis in the US-Mexico Borderlands *Roberto Avant-Mier* 293

Notes on Contributors 309
Index 314

FOREWORD

Crisis and Critique

Timothy Corrigan

Two years after the massive US banking collapse of 2008 and the shattering economic recession that followed, James Cameron's blockbuster *Avatar*, with a theatrical gross of approximately $2.85 billion, would replace his 1997 *Titanic*, with its $2.2 billion gross, as highest box-office success in US film history. The irony embedded in the contrast between the hardships of that economic recession and those movie profits is hardly new or surprising in US film history, but there is another, more revelatory irony in these different narratives, a dark and prophetic irony that would rattle US life and films for more than a decade. The earlier film looks back at a historic disaster that pitted the luxuries of the wealthy against the struggles of an underclass, as a background to romanticize a love that would transcend class and time. The more recent *Avatar* fantasizes a future in which an interstellar colonialization brutalizes an indigenous people who are harmoniously part of their magical natural world and who must overcome the violence of a US military attempt to decimate them. As cinematic signposts of the movement from the twentieth to the twenty-first centuries, these two cultural landmarks become themselves markers of the not unusual bond between excessive movie financial investments and mainstream popularity. They also become allegorical shadows of the larger crises that would define the transition into a new century, including the social and political critiques that would permeate the 2000s: about massive financial and racial inequities (from Occupy Wall Street to Black Lives Matter), about pervasive traumas of individual and social loss (from the home evictions to the opioid addictions), about military, political, and sexual violence and displacements (from Iraq to #MeToo), and about the deterioration and destruction of the natural and social environments (from massive oil spills and global warming to mass murders and famine).

Let's keep in mind, however, that crises often lead to changes. Indeed, counterpointing the blockbuster narratives of those two Cameron films are the subsequent successes of Kathryn Bigelow's 2008 *The Hurt Locker* and 2012 *Zero Dark Thirty*. In contrast to the films of her then-husband/partner, the two Bigelow narratives graphically return the US social crises from high seas and distant planets of the Cameron films to the *terra firma* of the US earth and its fraught politics. In both films, the violence that has traditionally, according to Richard Slotkin, regenerated America becomes exposed as a kind of degeneration: on the one hand, as the revenge plot of individuals still in the grips of the 9/11 trauma and, on the other, as the disintegration of a domestic sphere and its masculine underpinning traumatized by never ending wars. As an extra-filmic version of related gendered changes and shifts, the success of Bigelow's two films, as winners of Oscars and other awards, might also, retrospectively, be seen as signs of an industrial critique and change, whereby the visions and voices of women and women directors would begin to gain significant momentum in Hollywood and in the sexual politics of US culture at large. Between these four Cameron and Bigelow films, the social and cultural upheavals of the last fifteen years in the US become double-edged, suggesting perhaps that what these upheavals share is a fundamental and acute turbulence, a turbulence that can be destructive, productive, or both.

Amid this turbulence and the changes it has demanded, crisis opens the door for productive critique. Across the many films released during this period, engagements with this spectrum of transformative events have been, as this volume of essays demonstrates, the source for numerous symptomatic representations, such as in *The Wolf of Wall Street* (2013) or *Rambo: Last Blood* (2019), and conversely the source for cinematic exposures and critiques which bring reality of those crises and issues into a sharp and glaring light. Not surprisingly, economics, race, violence, technology, class, drug addiction, war, and the houseless loom in the foreground and background of many of these films. More or less outside the mainstream blockbuster path of *Avatar* or *Zero Dark Thirty*, many so-called smaller films offer direct critiques of those central crises permeating US culture. Rattling a perspective of the US on and off the screen, these movies include remarkable new subjects and perspectives, across a range of films that includes *Winter's Bone* (2010), *Beasts of the Southern Wild* (2012), *Ex Machina* (2014), *American Honey* (2016), *Hell or High Water* (2016), *The Florida Project* (2017), *Get Out* (2017), *Leave No Trace* (2018), *Us* (2019), and *Nomadland* (2020).

Many of these films, it is important to note, spring from another crisis and contemporary transformation, an industrial crisis in the US movie making during the last fifteen years. Part of a trend that is several decades old but accelerated by the Covid-19 pandemic, new patterns of movie making and movie going have now shifted their framework significantly from theatrical screenings to domestic streaming sites, and these have in turn tended to better accommodate the edginess of those crucially alternative visions. As venues such as Netflix, Amazon, Hulu, and Mubi have become more and more central to the film experience, so has the expanding possibility, I believe, of those alternative critiques of the crises that permeate the United States. What Hollywood and its mainstream has often seen as a dangerous and critical threat to the traditional movie industry has become a vehicle for topics and stories more aggressively presenting where the United States is now.

As direct and indirect articulations of various breakdowns and flashpoints that bind the cinematic to the larger US culture, this capacity for cinematic critique points to a second articulation of that critique that is luminously mapped in the essays in this volume. Responding to the social and personal turmoil represented on films of the last fifteen years, these essays deftly articulate engagements with a spectrum of movies as ways not only to look critically at contemporary movies but, perhaps more importantly, to look through these films at a cultural landscape which has been subject to dramatic and constant change in the 2000s and which, as these essays and the films they discuss demonstrate, needs to use the wave of that turbulence as the momentum for continual social and cinematic change.

ACKNOWLEDGMENTS

Research toward this book was partly funded by the Spanish Ministry of Economy, Industry, and Competitiveness through the research project "Film and Crisis: Social Change and Representation in the Cinema of the New Century" (FFI2017-82312-P) and by the General Council of Aragon through the research project "Cinema, Culture and Society" (Ref. H33_17R).

The editors would like to thank all our stalwart contributors for sharing their inspiring and provocative work. We appreciate their patience and their positive responses to our comments and suggestions. Most particularly, we would also like to thank Chantal Cornut-Gentille D'Arcy, Timothy Corrigan, Katie Gallof, Lawrence Grossberg, Annette Kuhn, Ana M. López, Chon Noriega, Edward Schwarzschild, Ulrike Spree, Kathleen Staudt, and Billiwald Steinmetz. Special thanks are due to all the members of our research group with whom we have debated these ideas during the last four years.

Introduction

Cinema and the Age of Crisis

Juan A. Tarancón and Hilaria Loyo

The start of a new century does not mark a fundamental change of course in history or the beginning of a new mindset. Rather, as Stuart Hall observed, "what drives history forward is usually a crisis, when the contradictions that are always at play in any historical moment are condensed" (Hall and Massey 2010, 57). The 9/11 attack on the World Trade Center was one of those historical moments. It carried a massive impact on our worldview and, as a society, set the United States on a different course. Sadness and anger ignited a sense of community and the George W. Bush Cabinet used the near total consensus as an occasion to shift power further away from the people to the Executive and the Pentagon and to initiate a global "war on terror" in connivance with the corporate class. In Hollywood, somber war films, dark thrillers, border dramas, and so-called torture porn registered government corruption and the distrust in the imperialist presidency of George W. Bush. As Douglas Kellner illustrated (2010), films like *Syriana* (2015), *Michael Clayton* (2007), the *Bourne Conspiracy* trilogy, and the *Saw* and *Hostel* series articulated these concerns.

Barely seven years later, also on George W. Bush's watch, the 2008 financial crash marked another moment of crisis that unsettled our convictions about society. It revealed a historical process (the dismantling of the welfare state and the transfer of wealth to the economic elites) that had been unfolding for a long time but that the anxieties caused by 9/11 and the calls for unity in the war against terrorism pushed off the public debate. The films produced in the aftermath of the crisis attempted to make sense of an economic catastrophe that was too complex to understand and its consequences too severe to fathom. The intricate and disconcerting ramifications of the crisis posed such representational challenges that led filmmakers to reconceive the potentialities and the limits of cinematic storytelling. The creative effort that followed was an attempt to analyze the multiple consequences of the economic downturn. In general, there was a shift from global to domestic concerns and films—from so-called financial crisis movies like *The Company Men* (2010) to class warfare dystopias like *The Purge* franchise, from Southern gothic stories like *Winter's Bone* (2010) to cop dramas like *Dragged across Concrete* (2018)—became more introspective and inward-looking.

Economic crises, as theorists and economists from Marx to Minsky recurrently noticed, may be inherent to the functioning of capitalism, but each crisis is distinctive to a particular social formation and demands "not an already-discovered general law but an analysis sensitive to its particularities" (Ginding 2014). On this occasion, the collapse of the financial institutions brought the world economy to a halt and caused a crisis of an unprecedented magnitude that cascaded through all areas of society. The impact of the financial meltdown on the real economy led to a recession that revealed complex social ramifications. Four decades of culture wars and neoliberal policies have led to a reconceptualization of all aspects of life from the perspective of the market and have transformed how we think about social life in a "stealth revolution" (Brown 2015) of devastating consequences. When the financial crisis morphed into a political one, governments worldwide endorsed extreme austerity measures that advanced the interests of corporate capital ahead of the interests of the people. It's not just that we are caught up in a crisis that does not move towards a resolution. Worse yet, in a context marked not so much by old notions of consistent political and moral positions as by cultural polarization and visceral responses, the state of crisis turned out to be the perfect scenario for conservatives and neoliberals to pursue their policies more aggressively. However, these crises have also unleashed forces that may forge a different political consciousness, transform how we think about society, and counteract the impact of market fundamentalism. As Stuart Hall observed (Hall and Massey 2010, 57), "[c]rises are moments of potential change, but the nature of their resolution is not given."

The ongoing economic, political, and social crises have exposed the damaging impact of neoliberalism. The increasing rates of unemployment, homelessness, poverty, violence, drug use, perpetual wars, displaced populations, and premature deaths are just some indicators of a global humanitarian crisis that has inspired research on the impact of neoliberalism on all spheres of society. Neoliberalism, a political project conceived by the corporate class in the aftermath of Second World War "to curb the power of labor" (Harvey 2016) and insulate the market against "the threat of democracy" (MacLean 2017), has proved extraordinarily resilient over time. During the past decades, it has received increasing scholarly attention in numerous disciplinary fields and from different theoretical perspectives. Not surprisingly, Marxian and neo-Marxian thought has been recovered as a critical method to better understand the complex ramifications and the repercussions of neoliberalism and to appraise the political responses to the manifold crises of global capitalism (Robinson 2019). Revised elaborations on the contradictions of capitalism (Harvey 2010) have also framed numerous works about the rising inequality of wealth distribution (Therborn 2013) and the emergence of a new class, the precariat (Standing 2011), whose low wages and unstable working conditions push them into a cycle of poverty. The assault on the public sector, the shrinking of the state, the trampling of fundamental civic values, and the rise of totalitarianism and extreme-right groups pose a real threat to liberal democracies worldwide. Equally important in Marxian thought is the connection between capitalism and the ecological crisis, which has inspired new works on the destructive impact of neoliberal globalization on the environment and on extreme weather events (Klein 2014) and which calls for effective policies to curb pollution and reverse climate change. The Green New Deal, a class-based environmental program that rests on public policies, requires political commitment and decisive action, and all the signs are that in the current climate of political confrontation we are still far from achieving a consensus that takes us forward. From the same materialistic perspective, other studies have centered on the impact of new digital technologies and the fourth industrial revolution and on the way these are transforming social and political relations into new models such as so-called surveillance capitalism (Zuboff 2019) and runaway capitalism (Hill 2015).

Public discourses and the vast crisis literature have turned the term "crisis" into a ubiquitous catchword in the analysis of contemporary political, social, and cultural phenomena. Its fuzzy and "overburdened" meaning has stimulated scholarly interest in untangling its manifold and complex semantics (Freeden 2017). The flexibility of the term is in itself "the symptom of a historical crisis that cannot as yet be fully gauged" (Koselleck 2006, 399). Particularly illuminating have been the theories of crisis deriving from the field of conceptual history and, in particular, Reinhart Koselleck's account of the concept of crisis, its historical development, and its resulting ambiguities. As a temporal concept, crisis is not only used to demarcate historical turning points, epochs, and their structures, but it also involves "its diagnosis of time" (Koselleck 2002, 239). It has long served to elicit moments of reflection on a particular period, this being a powerful force since it "disposes one to both a knowledge of the entire past and a prognosis of the future" (239). The term "crisis" indicating the end of a period may also have a political function as it offers a perspective from which events are interpreted and judged, thus setting the range of expectations that orients future decisions (Koselleck 2002; 2006). The twofold nature of the term "crisis"—referring both to specific events and to their interpretations—has led some intellectuals to warn about its "socially constructed" dimension (Walby 2015, 14–34; Roitman 2016). In her examination of the rhetorical function of the term, Janet Roitman, drawing upon Koselleck's work, has unveiled how crisis has come to serve as "a non-locus" that enables claims concerning access to and knowledge of history. Roitman thus urges us to make "this blind spot visible" (2016, 19), a denaturalization of crisis narratives already advocated by French sociologist Edgar Morin in 1976 when he encouraged us to "put the concept of crisis in crisis" (in Strolovitch 2013, 168). This is a call to give special attention to the ways narrative frames serve as particular lenses through which events are construed and political decisions justified.

One example of the political and social repercussions of crisis narratives can be seen in the account of the crisis that focuses on "fiscal rather than financial matters." This narrative shifts the focus of the political debate from the failures and contradictions of neoliberalism to one centered on government's excessive expenditure on welfare and social programs, which justifies the implementation of harsh austerity measures (Waltby 2015, 18). The control over crisis narratives seems to have played a key role in neoliberalism's resilience and malleability, accelerating and intensifying previous social and political trends with undesired and fatal outcomes (Callison and Manfredy 2020). The consequences of the current Covid-19 pandemic, with its unprecedented global economic paralysis, are still too early to determine but it might set off a chain reaction of economic, social, and political disasters at global scale, aggravating historical processes already underway. One of the earliest observations noted how the virus epidemic led to a rise in the epidemic of "fake news, paranoiac conspiracy theories, explosions of racism" (Žižek 2020, 39), which in turn revealed the dangers of corporate media and social networking sites and the need to regulate them (Ferguson 2021). Other intellectuals have identified an acceleration of already existing trends, such as the disappearance of the public spirit and the emergence of some forms of barbarism in the struggle for survival (Caron 2021; Žižek 2020).

In the public terrain of contesting rhetorical invocations of crisis, the corporate media bears a large part of the responsibility for their reckless and sensationalist use of the term and for the role this plays in the construction of affective formations and collective identities. The concept of crisis, Koselleck argued, "which once had the power to pose unavoidable, harsh and non-negotiable alternatives, has been transformed to fit the uncertainties of whatever might be favored at a given moment" (2006, 399). For instance, as Dara Z. Strolovitch (2013) has noted, the dominant crisis narratives privilege some groups as particularly affected by hard economic times, while they normalize the economic hardships of others. These narratives not only avert questions of structural inequalities and systemic failures in capitalist societies but also perpetuate them. Intellectuals—as well as artists—need to enter into the struggle about the political and the social consequences of the crisis, and assemble different contexts against which to evaluate the repercussions of the crisis. In brief, we need to change the dominant narratives and offer alternatives to the economic common sense that holds that self-interest and market values are the primary means of achieving the public good.

In the struggle for the control of crisis narratives, cinema has played a crucial role. In the wake of the financial collapse, a myriad of productions, from documentaries like *American Casino* (2009), *Capitalism: A Love Story* (2009), and *Debtocracy* (2011) to fiction films like *The Company Men* (2010), *Wall Street: Money Never Sleeps* (2010), and *Margin Call* (2011), just to mention but a few, competed with other media in an effort to make a diagnosis of the banking collapse, most often in the muckraking tradition (Boyle and Mrozowski 2013, xii–xx). In a pioneering survey on these films about the financial crisis, Jeff Kinkle and Alberto Toscano (2011) already paid attention to the key question of representation and the textual strategies adopted to describe the onset of the crisis. One of the challenges cinema faced, they noticed, was to make visible aspects of capitalism that are by definition invisible and systemic. In this first cycle of financial crisis films they denounce a tendency "to *personify* systemic and impersonal phenomena," persistently eschewing systemic critique (Kinkle and Toscano 2011, 39; Negra and Tasker 2014, 15). This observation led them to famously conclude that "representations of the crisis need not be crises of representation" (39). We believe this observation urges film studies scholars to pay special attention to the narrative and aesthetic devices deployed in the cinematic representations of the many crises that impacted US society in the years following the financial collapse of 2008 *and* to the ways these devices determine how films articulate into concrete historical processes. Rigorous formal analysis, then, is most pressing to understand how films engage viewers in a reconstruction of the relation of forces that characterize the current moment of crisis. But to assess the role of films in the construal of the crisis, film scholars must first put these representations of the crisis in crisis. That is, we need approaches that pursue an analysis of the ongoing multiple crises in the context of questions about changes in representation; we need strategies that situate the films as part of a struggle over the construction of the context within which we make sense of the crises and that regard the film's formal specificity not as a consequence of social change but, rather, as one more element in the contention for meaning.

Although the term "crisis" brings with it a sense of apocalypse, it actually conveys both failure and opportunity. This redemptive dimension, Koselleck notes (2002, 245), provides "a perspectival illusion" that Kinkle and Toscano identified in some of the cinematic representations of the financial crisis. Intersecting with other terms like "catastrophe" or "disaster," the notion of crisis as "final decision" has undergone a semantic shift that, according to Eva Horn, has come to denote "a process instead of an event" (2018, 21). Crises as catastrophes are perceived "not just as a break from a given reality but rather a revelation of underlying structures" (2018, 28). Thus, the recent crises have exposed hidden truths about societies under stress. Both Žižek (2020) and Ferguson (2021) have noticed, for example, how the virus epidemic has revealed even more failures of the global capitalist system and has served to identify other looming catastrophes. Although these revelations are taken as great opportunities for radical political changes, Žižek also points at the pressing need to retrieve a true sense of politics and seriously consider "*how* we change it" (Žižek 2020, 94). In a similar vein, Antonio Y. Vázquez-Arroyo (2013, 738) has remarked that our "response to the 'catastrophization' of political life" should be "the politicization of catastrophe." Contemporary representations of catastrophe often mediate and strengthen a narrative that has depoliticizing effects by "misrecognizing," or "rendering invisible," "the catastrophic nature of capitalism" (Vázquez-Arroyo 2013, 747). The designation of the financial crisis as catastrophe, for example, justified the bailout of Wall Street and the auto industry with taxpayer money, but there was no similar relief package for workers who lost their jobs, their savings, and their homes.

Cinema has contributed to the pervasive apocalyptic tone in the popular imagination and to the emergence of what Lawrence Grossberg calls an "organization of passive nihilism" (2018, 93). In the last two decades, cinema has offered multiple narratives of catastrophe that show the collapse in the social order, the end of the world, and the extinction of humanity: *Wall-E* (2008), *The Road* (2009), *Melancholia* (2011), *Contagion* (2011), *4:44: The Last Day on Earth* (2011), and *World War Z* (2013) are just a few examples in a surprisingly long list of films that adopt a pessimistic attitude toward the future. Fredric Jameson, for example, has argued that the future frame in these narratives is a "strategy of indirection" that allows for meditations on the effects of capitalism on everyday life at the present (287), thus disclosing a contemporary incapacity to imagine utopian worlds (289).

Another central question in the study of crisis narratives is the role of emotions, which are as "multi-layered and ambiguous" as the concept of crisis (Koselleck 2006, 375). It is imperative that we identify how they work in all their complexity and address how people orient themselves within crises in a culture that, as Lawrence Grossberg puts it (2018, 108), is "dominated by affect rather than politics." How we position ourselves in relation to the multiple crises we face at the moment is determined, not by objectivity and evidence—not even by self-interest—but by affective formations in which political issues and cultural projects intertwine. Most importantly, these affective formations determine the conditions and the limits of possibility, what is considered allowable and what is deemed unacceptable. It is thus not surprising that affect theory has also become a central theoretical framework to analyze how film aesthetics engages with circulating affects and provide alternative ways to meditate on our present historical time (Berlant 2011, 16). This perspective has produced, for example, remarkable studies on the experiences of the underprivileged segments of society in these precarious times (Sticchi 2021). The study of the role of emotions in crisis narratives has also prompted film studies scholars to examine recent reconfigurations of generic conventions—mainly in melodramas and horror films—as cinematic expressions of anger and resentment. These emotions have been lately registered in films pivoting around the housing crisis and around homes as sites of violence, fears, and anxieties about the nation-state's capacity to perform its protective function (Snelson 2014).

Robert Sinnerbrink (2012) has recently identified a crisis in film theory and has called for a reconsideration of the core objectives of film studies as a discipline. This volume takes up the challenge and explores theoretical approaches that inquire into the role of films in fostering critical thought about the present conjuncture and about the ways to cultivate a democratic ethos. Furthermore, in this regard, we wish to make it clear, first, that we believe our work is about agendas as much as it is about films, and second, that only through a rigorous analysis of the ways the narrative and aesthetic specificity of films engage with the context of crisis can a given agenda be pushed forward.

The chapters in this anthology seek to offer a complex picture of how the many crises that have occurred in recent years are transforming social relations in the United States by examining the ways cinema articulates into the assemblage of forces that characterizes the present conjuncture. It provides a broad critical framework for understanding the complexity of the present social context by covering a wide range of issues and contributing to the debate about the textual strategies adopted in contemporary cinema to examine the social challenges facing the United States as a consequence of the multiple, ongoing crises. This volume is by no means exhaustive, but the chapters included here represent a variety of theoretical and methodological approaches to cinema and provide different insights into the many forces that characterize the current moment of crisis. The chapters have been arranged by topic. We believe the thematic affinity structuring the volume will help the reader grasp the complexity and the interconnections of the issues addressed in the films under study. This volume also covers a wide spectrum of films, from mainstream US cinema to the works of independent filmmakers. Although it is a small sample of an almost encyclopedic topic, we believe the methodological approaches adopted and the ideas developed here will offer valuable insights into many other films.

To begin with, the first section of this volume, "US Cinema in the Age of Crisis," provides general overviews on the Hollywood film industry and on contemporary US independent cinema. Toby Miller and Bill Graham survey the history of Hollywood and conclude that the film industry has always capitalized on past crises and has always managed to reinvent itself and continue to make big profits. In addition to providing an account of how contemporary US independent cinema has represented the impact of the crisis on marginalized groups, Cynthia Baron identifies an emergent naturalistic aesthetics and considers its potentialities to analyze the ordeals faced by vulnerable workers.

The three chapters in the section "Labor Crisis and the Neoliberal Subject" examine different aspects of labor relations and individual aspirations in different work sectors in a context marked by economic instability and the ascendancy of the neoliberal subject. Taking her cue from Negra and Tasker's work on the "gendering of the crisis," Beatriz Oria's contribution examines the trope of the working woman in the chick flicks of the post-crash decade. Also from this perspective, and with a special focus on the "mancession" myth, Elena Oliete-Aldea analyzes Todd Haynes's *Mildred Pierce* (2011) as a nostalgic revision of Michael Curtiz's eponymous original. Stephen Felder centers on male aspirational subjects, and his analysis of *The Wolf of Wall Street* (2013) and *Nightcrawler* (2014) exemplifies two distinct ways of rendering visible workingmen's psychic investment in the promises of "the neoliberal fairy tale."

The third section, "Technology and the State of Surveillance," deals with the impact of new technologies on the transformation of capitalism and politics. Ian Scott explores the role of social media technology as a surveillance tool in his analysis of David Fincher's *The Social Network* (2010), a film that tackled the impact of big-tech in the development of surveillance capitalism and anticipated its role spreading fake news. Also concerned with the social impact of surveillance technology, Kayla Meyers analyzes Alex Garland's *Ex Machina* (2014). She draws on performativity to explore the ambivalence of surveillance and how it is experienced as a mechanism of self-subjugation.

The three chapters in the fourth section, "The Housing Crisis and the Home Question," offer different perspectives on how cinema has addressed the politics of housing—in its conflation with home and homeland—after the housing crisis that led to the financial crash. Tony Grajeda examines *The Purge* franchise. Focusing on the trope of home invasion and drawing on Walter Benjamin's work on allegory, his analysis reads the series' reformulation of horror conventions as an allegory of an age in which fear and violence jeopardize the fragile sense of nationhood in the US. Leah Pérez and Williams J. Simmons draw upon a different cinematic tradition of horror films and use the concept of home as the central trope to analyze Jordan Peele's *Get Out* (2017), a film that resonates with the housing crisis and the fear of homelessness in the context of rising racial violence. In a chapter that examines the home trope in the three films of independent filmmaker Debra Granik, Hilaria Loyo draws on the notions of gendered domopolitics and slow cinema to frame the analysis of the struggles of the poor female protagonists to save their homes. Loyo delineates the narrative trajectories that expose the neoliberal mechanisms that exclude the poor from the nation-home.

The fifth section, "Politics, Affect, and the Crisis of Public Values," includes three chapters that expand the political issues addressed in the previous section by centering on the growth of inequality, the undermining of public values, and the rise of ethnopopulisms. The chapters by Carlos Gallego and Fabián Orán Llarena offer different perspectives on the films of S. Craig Zahler, whose (apparently) reactionary stories and expressive aesthetics have been surrounded by controversy. While Gallego sees Zahler's films as vehicles that foreground the core ideological tropes of conspiracy theories like the "Great Replacement," Orán Llarena analyzes *Dragged Across Concrete* (2018) and identifies the elements that configure the affective regime of ordinary workers in the current precarious time to reinforce the film's ideological ambivalence. Juan A. Tarancón offers a contextualized analysis of how the textual strategies deployed by Sean Baker in *The Florida Project* (2017) circulate affects that counter the common sense about inequality in contemporary society and challenge spectators to think through the ways we make sense of poverty.

The ecological crisis is addressed in the sixth section, "Ecological Crisis and Visions of the Future," in which two chapters provide very distinct—but hopeful—analyses of films depicting rural landscapes, commonly presented as shorthand metaphors for economic, ecological and political crises. Tim Lindemann analyzes how the notion of landscape as place in two films, *Beasts of the Southern Wild* (2012) and *Leave No Trace* (2018), allows for social mechanisms of solidarity against the atomization and marginalization endorsed by neoliberalism. A similar hopeful theme is identified by Virginia Luzón in her examination of human-tree interactions in *The Lorax* (2012) and *Avatar* (2009). Luzón adopts an ecocritical perspective to trace the possibilities for the avoidance of an environmental catastrophe.

The final section, "Crisis and Violence in the Borderlands," deals with the question of how the crisis has reconceptualized the notion of the border as an abstract political space demarcating both national and foreign identities. The chapters in this section focus on three different types of border films. In his analysis of *Hell or High Water* (2016), Luis Freijo examines how the economic violence of neoliberalism has inflected the Western genre. An opposite ideological role of violence is identified by Gregory Frame in his analysis of *Last Blood* (2019). Frame argues that the fifth installment in the *Rambo* series retrieves the regenerative use of violence of the classic Western in line with the vigilante movement against immigration at the US-Mexico border. The focus of Roberto Avant-Mier's chapter is an inventive Mexican-US coproduction, *Ya no estoy aquí/I'm No Longer Here* (2019). He locates the film as part of a cinematic trajectory traced by other Mexican filmmakers who had previously dealt with US-Mexico relations against the backdrop of globalization. Like the two previous chapters, Avant-Mier's contextualized analysis registers the devastating violence on both sides of the frontier, but posits music as the ultimate nation-home. Taken together, the chapters included in this volume provide us with a complex picture of how neoliberalism is transforming social relations in the United States. By examining the different ways in which contemporary cinema articulates into the multiple crises facing the country, these contributions not only reveal the contradictions inherent in the current social formation but also open up the possibility of transforming how we think about society and of imagining other futures.

References

Berlant, L. (2011), *Cruel Optimism*, Durham, NC and London: Duke University Press.
Boyle, K. and D. Mrozowski (eds.) (2013), *The Great Recession in Fiction, Film, and Television: Twenty-First-Century Bust Culture*, Lanham, MD and Plymouth: Lexington Books.
Brown, W. (2015), *Undoing the Demos: Neoliberalism's Stealth Revolution*, New York: Zone Books.
Callison, W. and Z. Manfredy (eds.) (2020), *Mutant Neoliberalism: Market Rule and Political Rupture*, New York: Fordham University Press.
Caron, J-F. (2021), *A Sketch of the World After the COVID-19 Crisis: Essays on Political Authority, the Future of Globalization, and the Rise of China*, eBook, Singapore: Palgrave Macmillan.
Ferguson, N. (2021), *Doom: The Politics of Catastrophe*, eBook, New York: Penguin Press.
Freeden, M. (2017), "Crisis? How Is That a Crisis? Reflections on an Overburdened Word," *Contributions to the History of Concepts* 12 (2), pp. 12–28.
Ginding, S. (2014), "Clarifying the Crisis," *Jacobin*, 2 January. Available online: https://www.jacobinmag.com/2014/01/clarifying-the-crisis/.
Grossberg, L. (2018), *Under the Cover of Chaos: Trump and the Battle for the American Right*, London: Pluto Press.
Hall, S. and D. Massey (2010), "Interpreting the Crisis: Doreen Massey and Stuart Hall Discuss Ways of Understanding the Current Crisis," *Soundings* 44, pp. 57–71.
Harvey, D. (2010), *The Enigma of Capital and the Crises of Capitalism*, Oxford and New York: Oxford University Press.
Harvey, D. (2016), "Neoliberalism Is a Political Project: An Interview with David Harvey," *Jacobin*, 23 July. Available online: https://www.jacobinmag.com/2016/07/david-harvey-neoliberalism-capitalism-labor-crisis-resistance/.
Hill, S. (2015), *Raw Deal: How the "Uber Economy" and Runaway Capitalism Are Screwing American Workers*, New York: St. Martin's Press.
Horn, E. (2018), *The Future as Catastrophe: Imagining Disaster in the Modern Age*, trans. V. Pakis, New York: Columbia University Press.
Kellner, D. (2010), *Cinema Wars: Hollywood Film and Politics in the Bush-Cheney Era*, Malden, MA and Oxford: Wiley-Blackwell.
Kinkle, J. and A. Toscano (2011), "Filming the Crisis: A Survey," *Film Quarterly* 65 (1), pp. 39–51.

Klein, N. (2014), *This Changes Everything: Capitalism vs. the Climate*, New York: Simon & Schuster.
Koselleck, R. (2002), *The Practice of Conceptual History: Timing History, Spacing Concepts*, trans. T. S. Presner, et al., Stanford: Stanford University Press.
Koselleck, R. (2006), "Crisis," trans. M. E. Richter, *Journal of the History of Ideas* 67, pp. 357–400.
MacLean, N. (2017), *Democracy in Chains: The Deep History of the Radical Right's Stealth Plan for America*, Melbourne and London: Scribe.
Negra, D. and Y. Tasker (eds.) (2014), *Gendering the Recession: Media and Culture in an Age of Austerity*, Durham, NC and London: Duke University Press.
Robinson, W. I. (2019), "Global Capitalist Crisis and Twenty-First Century Fascism: Beyond Trump Hype," *Science & Society* 83 (2), pp. 155–83.
Roitman, J. (2016), "The Stakes of Crisis," in P. F. Kjaer and N. Olsen (eds.), *Critical Theories of Crisis in Europe: From Weimar to The Euro*, London and New York: Rowman & Littlefield, pp. 17–34.
Sinnerbrink, R. (2012), "Sea-change: Transforming the 'Crisis' in Film Theory," *NECSUS. European Journal of Media Studies* 1 (1), pp. 67–84.
Snelson, T. (2014), "The (Re)possession of the American Home: Negative Equity, Gender Inequality, and the Housing Crisis Horror Story," in D. Negra and Y. Tasker (eds.), *Gendering the Recession: Media and Culture in an Age of Austerity*, Durham, NC and London: Duke University Press, pp. 161–80.
Standing, G. (2011), *The Precariat: The New Dangerous Class*, New York and London: Bloomsbury Academic.
Sticchi, F. (2021), *Mapping Precarity in Contemporary Cinema and Television: Chronotopes of Anxiety, Depression, Expulsion/Extinction*, London and New York: Palgrave Macmillan.
Strolovitch, D. Z. (2013), "Of Mancession and Hecoveries: Race, Gender, and the Political Construction of Economic Crises and Recoveries," *Perspectives on Politics* 22 (1), pp. 167–76.
Therborn, G. (2013), *The Killing Fields of Inequality*, Cambridge and Malden: Polity Press.
Vázquez-Arroyo, A. Y. (2013), "How Not to Learn from Catastrophe: Habermas, Critical Theory and the 'Catastrophization' of Political Life," *Political Theory* 41 (5), pp. 738–65.
Walby, S. (2015), *Crisis*. Cambridge: Polity Press.
Žižek, S. (2020), *Pandemic! COVID-19 Shakes the World*, New York and London: OR Books.
Zuboff, S. (2019), *The Age of Surveillance Capitalism: The Fight for a Human Future at the New Frontier of Power*, London: Profile Books.

PART I

US Cinema in the Age of Crisis

1

It's Always Been Crisis

Hollywood History

Toby Miller and Bill Grantham

Introduction

The last century and a half of capitalism has been characterized by the military, cultural, and commercial power of the United States. Some say those times are over, because we occupy a multipolar world with equally powerful economic actors, while new media technologies are breaking down old forms of dominance. This chapter argues against those positions. But that is not to disavow a profound reality. Crisis is ever-present in Hollywood, as it is in the country more broadly.

Robert Wilson's neo-*noir* novel *The Vanished Hands* finds Inspector Jefe Javier Falcón of Sevilla suggesting to expatriates Maddy and Marty Krugman that US society has been driven by fear since September 11, 2001. He is quickly rebuked: 'It's *always* been fear' (2004, 41). And the US population indulges in catastrophically risky conduct: 50 percent of people participate in the irrationality of the stock market. But US residents also fear the consequences of such choices: in 2005, they spent $1.1 trillion on insurance—more than they paid for food, and over a third of the world's total insurance expenditure (Miller 2008). These tendencies represent the acceptance and incorporation of crisis into lifelong and posthumous planning. Such wagers on hopelessness and fear bring crisis into the home as an everyday ritual.

And over the last fifty years, the United States does appear to be perennially in crisis. For example, the country's sense of economic and constitutional superiority was challenged, if not subdued, in the 1970s by oil shocks, Watergate, Vietnam, and urban revolt. An unremitting pessimism was animated by rising unemployment and inflation, booming interest rates, and failed generational change. Capital took this as an opportunity for governmental action to control wage increases and redistribute wealth upward. It has been thus ever since, further stimulated by the waning of state socialism in Eastern and Central Europe from 1989 and the emergence of a massive reserve army of labor in the People's Republic of China since 2000, when the global pool of workers doubled virtually overnight. Yet through a transition from a quarry, farm, and factory to a copyright and finance economy, the nation's extraordinary influence on world affairs is unabated.

Consider the 2008 financial crisis. It certainly rocked the nation. But the crisis was resolved via a familiar formula: socialism for the wealthy and capitalism for the poor. Huge bailouts of major capitalist enterprises by the state restored the system, at the same time as treasuries plunged into debt and subsequent reductions in social services and tax hikes for ordinary people were legitimized. Bankers were bankrolled, homeowners evicted, accountants acquitted, and neoclassical economists pardoned (by themselves). When one of us asked the editor of a glossy magazine for the super-wealthy of Southern California how his readers were responding, and what impact the crisis was having on advertising revenues, he replied, "They don't know there's a crisis. And advertising is holding up just fine, thank you" before turning firmly on his heel.

The state is everywhere and nowhere in US capitalism, ready to ameliorate crises, whatever the prevailing rhetoric. Post offices, telephone exchanges, public schools, airports, bus stops, freeways, and railway stations are created and sustained through the socialization of risk by governments. Even the Internet is a product of anxieties about Soviet missile attacks, which led to the packet system of communication, developed by research schools with Pentagon subvention. In addition, one is never physically far from the long arm of the state in the United States. Military bases proliferate, college towns dot otherwise barren landscapes, ubiquitous police forces detain people on the grounds of DWB (driving while black), prisons controlled by private corporations incarcerate nonviolent offenders by the score, and on it goes.

Everyone seems certain that an Asian Century is succeeding the American one. Yet it is worth remembering that tens of millions of Asians and Asian-Americans choose to live in the United States; many Asian countries regard Washington as their protector against China; US ties to massive and growing economies in Latin America are profound and deepening; its links with Europe continue to develop; it has massive new military bases across Africa and the Arab world; its currency is the world's reserve; it has most of the world's wealthy and powerful people; and what *goes on* in the United States remains the topic of governmental, military, commercial, financial, academic, media, and popular fascination elsewhere in a way that is not true of any other country. The reality is that the military might, economic power, cultural influence, and environmental impact of the United States have never been greater.

Hollywood is also said to be diminishing in importance (more money is made in electronic games, and more films are made in Nollywood and Bollywood). Really? The Motion Picture Association of America (2014), the peak body representing the major studios, notes that Hollywood receipts around the world "reached $36.4 billion in 2014"—a record. China has been moved effortlessly into the center of the industry's overseas sales, its reserve army of productive labor now matched by a reserve army of audience labor: "more middle-class movie-goers are being minted every day." Hollywood box office in China increased 34 percent in 2013, "the first international market to exceed $4 billion" ("Split Screens").

So far, this has been a second American Century. Hollywood both indexes and perpetuates the fact it's always been laden with crises. We'll show this with reference to institutional history, labor, technology, and geopolitics.

Institutional History

Flux—change—is an unavoidable constant of the world, as Heraclitus pointed out 1,500 years ago (in Plato 1892, 402). But the *consequences* of change are less predictable. Hollywood frequently depicts itself as being in crisis, to the point of that becoming a self-referential cliché. Frank O'Hara's 1955 poem "To the Film Industry in Crisis" declaims, mock-heroically, that "In times of crisis we must all decide again and again whom we love / And give credit where it's due." This plays with both the film industry as a site of perpetual crisis and its function as a corrective to the rest of the world's crises (O'Hara 1979, 232).

The essential features of the US film (and later television) industries—vertical integration of development, production, distribution, and exhibition and horizontal international implantation—were established as early as 1908 (Grantham 2000, 43–4). It's the stability and continuity we should notice. The more things change in Hollywood, as the French journalist Alphonse Karr almost pointed out in the nineteenth century, the more they seem the same (Karr 1862, 305). That said, Hollywood's sense of itself often seems one where it is required to move from stability and certainty to some new, existential event that threatens its very existence. It's as if nobody has noticed that the system has remained predictably secure in its shape and institutions for 120 years or so.

In one sense, any new model of business will experience extreme difficulties at its onset. Even though we're now well familiar with the prehistory of cinema—music halls, magic lantern shows, public presentations of the *camera obscura*, and so on—that should not take away from the fact that what emerged from 1895 was quite new and took time to settle down. The nascent US film industry suffered "problems with technological standardization, patent and copyright problems, audience boredom with predictable subject matter, stagnant demands, and cutthroat competition" in its first decade (Musser 1990, 297). These difficulties were resolved quite quickly by the entities that survived the crisis.

A greater threat was the Motion Picture Patents Company, an attempt by the Edison and Biograph companies in 1908 to drive out foreign competition (Thomas 1971, 34). They pooled their various patents on film production and exhibition technology, but were struck down by emerging US antitrust laws (Thompson 1985, 1–15). The claim that the creation of "Hollywood" in Los Angeles was due to the cartel's driving rivals who failed to comply away from the East Coast has been substantially qualified, although stirring stories such as Cecil B DeMille's claim that he was shot at by a cartel operative while riding home on a horse may be true (Eyman 2010, 71). Some foreign companies were admitted to the cartel, but their role in the US market was progressively reduced. Other factors may have contributed to this—the move toward feature-length films, developments in narrative approaches, the impact of the First World War, and poor management. By 1921, Hollywood had triumphed over the onetime market leaders from Europe. This "crisis" of cutthroat competition—undoubtedly real for Lumière, Star Films, and Pathé—did not change the fundamental shape of the industry, which continued to be vertically integrated and horizontally implanted (Grantham 2000, 44–5). The more things changed, the more they stayed the same.

The big existential challenge to Hollywood was the Progressive-era legal apparatus that brought down the patent cartel. As early as 1921, the Federal Trade Commission (FTC), using antitrust laws, began investigating studio practices, particularly "block booking"—renting films in blocks, often unseen, and hence removing exhibitors' ability to choose what to screen. The wheels of government can grind slowly, and it took until 1927 for the FTC to attack block booking in a lawsuit against the studios, and another three years of tortuous legal proceedings for the Commission to win in the Supreme Court (*Paramount Famous Lasky Corp. vs. United States* 1930). But by that time, the Depression had taken grip of the country, and there was reluctance to police the film business, which was already an adept lobbyist against federal policies of which it disapproved. The new Roosevelt administration developed various mechanisms to regulate the economy, but key provisions were struck down by the Supreme Court (*A.L.A. Schechter Poultry Corp. vs. United States* 1935). Following this setback, the FTC renewed its antitrust efforts against the studios in 1938, attacking block booking, blind showing, and the concentration of theater ownership. A 1940 settlement did not satisfy Hollywood's antagonists, and in 1945, the Commission resumed its lawsuit. This worked its way once more to the Supreme Court, which issued a landmark 1948 decision penalizing the studios (*United States v. Paramount Pictures Inc.* 1948; Schatz 1997, 326–8). The major studios were found to have:

- Fixed ticket prices;
- Limited reruns in geographical areas to benefit first-run cinemas;
- Operated pools of theaters to keep out competitors;
- Made deals with owned or affiliated cinemas to exclude others;
- Block-booked, packaging major films with less lucrative ones; and
- Discriminated against small cinemas.

The "bust" of the late 1940s caused by this Decree has to be seen in the context of the "boom" that preceded it. In fact, total studio profits in 1949, after the huge blow of the *Paramount* decision, were about the same as 1941, and substantially greater than in 1940 (Schatz 1997, 465). And the same companies ruled the business. They showed a similar solidity even as Hollywood's labor process changed.

Labor

Los Angeles talks about crisis all the time. US film and television drama workers seem haunted by it, because they operate as part of the cognitariat or precariat, depending on whether their jobs lie above or below the line of accounting for labor skills and costs.

Fordist assembly-line production characterized Hollywood between about 1920 and 1970. But while films were made en masse, the routinization, de-skilling, and invigilation that manufacturing machinery and scientific management forced on factory workers did not occur. Many studio employees participated in the labor process at various points rather than being restricted to a single task, and their work was not easily undertaken by others. In addition, they experienced social interaction across class barriers through face-to-face connection (Powdermaker 1950, 69). Ironically, these differences from classic working-class *anomie* helped open the way to intensive networking as a substitute for factory discipline when Hollywood post-Fordism eroded from the late 1940s as a consequence of vertical disintegration, suburbanization, and televisualization.

These three transformations occurred thanks to a mixture of state action and demographic change. Trust-busting by the Department of Justice (as earlier), returning white GIs clutching preferential housing deals, and the spread of TV combined to turn urban moviegoers into suburban homebodies.

That conjuncture gradually transmogrified Hollywood workers from studio staff, with regular, long-standing relations of subordination and opportunity, into transient, irregular employees working for small, short-lived firms (Miller et al. 2005). At the top level, the studios of the classical Hollywood era had to deal with legal challenges to their suzerainty over above-the-line employees, notably Olivia De Havilland's successful lawsuit in 1944 against Warner Bros., which fractured the studios' power over stars (*De Haviland* [sic.] *vs. Warner Bros. Pictures* 1948; Schatz 1988, 318).

Hollywood pioneered the flexible model of employment beloved of contemporary management, with jobs constantly ending, starting, and migrating. The New International Division of Cultural Labor has seen it delight in subsidies, skills, and pliancy across the world. After the Second World War, international location shooting became a means of differentiating stories and cutting costs as color and widescreen formats grew fashionable, portable recording technology became available, and technical skills proliferated. Studios purchased international facilities to utilize cheap, docile labor. They were further encouraged to set up production companies overseas by tax incentives, avoiding the cost of studio space and pension and welfare-fund contributions in Los Angeles. By investing abroad, which it has done ever since, Hollywood sidesteps foreign-exchange drawback rules that prevent the expatriation of profits, simultaneously benefiting from host-state subvention of "local" films. Other nations' screen industries, mostly built on policy responses to external cultural domination, enable that domination by commodifying and governmentalizing locations.

Today, Hollywood workers and bosses strike complex, transitory arrangements on a project basis via temporary organizations. Small or large numbers of diverse hands are involved at different stages, sometimes functioning together and sometimes semi-autonomously; "independent contractors coalesce for a relatively short period of time around one-off projects to contribute the organizational, creative, and technical talents that go into the production of a film" (Ferriani, Cattani, and Baden-Fuller 2009, 1548). Those deals depend on evolving technology.

Technology

New media are routinely regarded as signs of progress that move history toward a common humanity, transcending nation-states and industries. In 1935, Rudolf Arnheim predicted that television would bring world peace. By enabling viewers to share simultaneous global experiences, from railway disasters, professorial addresses, and town meetings to boxing bouts, dance bands, carnivals, and aerial mountain views—a spectacular montage of Athens, Broadway, and Vesuvius—TV would surpass the limitations of linguistic competence and interpretation to show each spectator that "we are located as one among many" (Arnheim 1969, 160–3).

This reads remarkably like today's neoliberal prelates celebrating the boundless potential of new as opposed to middle-aged media to undermine Hollywood hegemony. New technologies supposedly allow us all to become simultaneously cultural consumers and producers (prosumers) without the say-so of media gatekeepers. The result is said to be a democratized media, higher skill levels, and powerful challenges to established expertise and institutional authority. And indeed, Hollywood sometimes trembles in the face of what has happened over the last twenty years to middle management in the recorded music industry, thanks to file sharing and so-called social media (remember Artist & Repertoire [A&R] people who used to hang around music venues looking and listening for hipness to describe next day in the office? They're mostly on the scrapheap, displaced by direct marketing to corporations by artists).

In cybertarian fantasies, everyone and no one is a cultural producer in the traditional, quasi-institutional sense, just as everyone is simultaneously an unpaid worker and a paying customer. Cybertarians have more or less forgotten the bursting of the so-called dotcom bubble between 2000 and 2002, when the NASDAQ Composite stock market index—which included most significant high-tech stocks in the United States—declined by more than $5 trillion (Gaither and Chmielewski 2006). Capitalist crises such as that one may be euphemized as "adjustments," but other crises are systemic: the cost of broadband in the Global South is 40.3 percent of average individual gross national income (GNI). In the Global North, by comparison, the price is less than 5 percent of GNI *per capita* (International Telecommunication Union 2012, 4). Not everyone can become a producer-distributor under those conditions.

And even cybertarian utopias hold the key for Hollywood surviving and prospering. Fans write zines that become screenplays. Interning grad students in New York and Los Angeles read scripts for producers, then pronounce on whether they tap into audience interests. Precariously employed part-timers spy on fellow spectators in theaters to see how they respond to coming attractions and report back to moguls. End-user licensing agreements ensure that players of corporate games online sign over their cultural moves and perspectives to the very companies they are paying in order to participate. Hollywood hegemons gain from reduced costs of film duplication and distribution. According to the Organisation for Economic Co-operation and Development, new film technology integrates production and postproduction, redefines and relocates duplication, offers new means of distribution, and integrates film and TV (2008, 10).

Here's the historical reality. Hollywood weathers its seemingly perpetual technological crises because what really matters is worldwide content and distribution. There may be changes in players—RKO disappears, Netflix arrives—but the overall picture remains the same.

That said, new technologies really cause disruption. The introduction of talking pictures in the late 1920s involved substantial investment. The studios had to spend money on insulated sound stages, advanced recording equipment, upgraded cameras, and the like. Cinema owners (who often included the studios and their affiliates) needed to rewire movie theaters. This was greatly complicated because the arrival of commercial sound pictures in 1927 was briefly overtaken by the Great Depression, which is conventionally tied to the 1929 stock-market crash. The global economy went into extreme decline. *Pace* claims that the movie business was countercyclical, it experienced the same crisis as everyone else, possibly exacerbated by introducing sound. Production costs had escalated, while cinema attendance and ticket prices fell precipitously. RKO, Fox, Paramount, and Universal sought protection in the bankruptcy courts. Other studios imposed deep cuts (Balio 1993, 15–18). Even at MGM, the most successful studio, staff experienced the sight of its boss, Louis B. Mayer, red-eyed and unshaven, appealing desperately to them to accept huge pay cuts (Eyman 2005, 178–80). But after a couple of turbulent years, the studios, including those that had been forced to shelter behind bankruptcy laws, were booming again, even in a Depression economy with high unemployment. The leaders remained the same: RKO, Fox, Paramount, MGM, Warner Bros., Universal, Columbia, and United Artists (Balio 1993, 30–2). No matter how devastating the Depression was for individuals, for Hollywood the twin crises of the introduction of sound and the crash turned out to be just a business blip—as was the next big technological innovation.

> What's happening all over?
> I'll tell you what's happening all over
> Guy sitting home by a television set
> That used to be something of a rover (Loesser 1950)

As early as 1950, television was regarded as having changed gendered existence, transmogrifying "guys" from an outdoors life to domestication via the box. US cinema audiences declined substantially from their peak of 1945, impacting studios revenues. Although there are several reasons for this decline in income—among them, the *Paramount* decree, suburbanization of the postwar audience, the impact on revenues of foreign limitations on Hollywood, and persistent political and moral attacks on the institutions of cinema themselves—the "key factor" was TV (Lev 2003, 7–9).

Many film historians downplay the impact of Hollywood's attempts to respond (Lev 2003, 107–25) but today's cinema, in color, with widescreen formats and high-quality sound recording, was implanted in the 1950s, even if some versions of these changes—such as Cinerama or 3D—were transitory (their progeny still exist, in IMAX cinemas and continuing gestures to the third dimension). More importantly, Hollywood learned to co-opt television, initially as a major supplier of programs, whether as a producer of network shows or as a seller of films to the new medium. As early as 1958, TV contributed 30 percent of Warner's revenues and 25 percent of Columbia's (Wasko 2003, 139). And repertory cinema, once the province of second-run or vintage theaters, found a new and profitable home—old movies screened on TV.

Something similar happened with the arrival of VHS, Betamax, and Philips 2000 home video in the 1970s (World Intellectual Property Organisation 2006). Hollywood catastrophized over the advent of video cassette recorders, as witnessed by the offensive rhetoric of the then-president of the studios' trade association, Jack Valenti, before a congressional hearing: "I say to you that the VCR is to the American film producer and the American public as the Boston strangler is to the woman home alone" (Valenti 1982). The reality was that the studios cleaned up on home video. By 2001, its domestic video revenues had hit $16 billion (Vogel 2004, 103).

Subvention

When confronted by crisis, the studios can always rely on the federal government. It has a long, if obscure, history of participation in film production, control, and industry policy based on attempts to harness domestic, immigrant, and foreign populations. The racist epic *Birth of a Nation* (D. W. Griffith 1915) was given military support and endorsed by the president. From the moment the United States entered the First World War, theaters across the country saw speakers and movies testifying to German atrocities, while films imported from the Central Powers were banned. Paramount Famous Lasky studio executive Sidney R. Kent joyously referred to cinema as "silent propaganda" (Miller et al. 2005).

As a quid pro quo, Hollywood lobbyists of the 1920s and 1930s treated the US Departments of State and Commerce as "message boys": State undertook market research and shared business intelligence, while Commerce pressured other countries to grant cinema open access and favorable terms of trade. The crisis of liberalism produced by the Depression was met with Keynesian policies and institutional instruments that deepened and solidified the relation of Hollywood and the state. Propaganda and business aims merged.

Hollywood also benefits from domestic film commissions run by regions, cities, and states. Their incentives are said to generate investment in new infrastructure—sound stages and skilled workers, for example—that provide ongoing attractions beyond temporary direct subvention ("The Money Shot"), and encourage "a 'clean' or 'environmentally friendly' industry" (Rollins Saas 2006, 3). These schemes compete for producers and crews to visit, thanks to eviscerated local taxes, *gratis* policing, and the closure of putatively public wayfares (Maxwell and Miller 2011; Cantrell and Wheatcroft 2018). Between 1997 and 2015, the cost was almost $10 billion. In 2010, for instance, forty-three states sought to "attract" Hollywood, to the tune of $1.5 billion. The past decade has seen a massive overall increase in subsidies. Initially stimulated by Louisiana and New Mexico upping the ante, Georgia became a front-runner, providing $800 million in certified credits in 2017 ("Unilateral Disarmament"; Foster, Manning, and Terkla 2013).

Support for film production has moved from minimal credits against income tax, deductions based on losses, loan guarantees, free access to public services, and exemptions from hotel taxes, to expansive transferrable tax credits. A new business has sprung up in trading such giveaways: tax credits from governments to producers are sold to wealthy people who don't feel like paying their share of tax so producers get their money faster than they would via refunds. What began in 2009 is now a multimillion-dollar business (Verrier 2013).

There is no evidence that these subsidies pay for themselves in terms of private-sector expenditure during production or infrastructure. Such prospects are jeopardized by the fact that the major talent and corporations reside in Los Angeles and New York, while bidding contests between states simply ratchet up the terms they offer California-based producers. Evaluations of the incentives suggest that transferrable tax credits have a derisory impact on film employment and none on wages; refundable credits offer no employment benefits and only contingent ones for wages; and no programs have clearly positive effects on local media employment or the wider economy (Foster, Manning, and Terkla 2013; Tannenwald 2010; Thom 2018). But the system persists.

Other countries are also sucked into the game. For decades, Los Angeles producers have filmed in the UK, Australia, Mexico, the former Soviet sector, and other locales to take advantage of government incentives, advanced technology, and compliant labor. German financing of Hollywood films early this century was frequently stimulated by tax breaks for lawyers, doctors, and dentists. French money came from firms with state subvention in other areas of investment, such as cable or plumbing, which then subsidized US studios. In the early twenty-first century, TV shows shot in Canada rely on provincial welfare to attract Hollywood. Again, the benefits are oft-trumpeted but rarely proven (Miller et al. 2005). It's free money for Hollywood to mitigate risk.

Geopolitics

There can be no greater crisis for Hollywood than a war: markets are decimated, lives are endangered, and censorship increases. Really?

The Great War saw the destruction of the German and French industries, which had been dominant around the world. Enter Hollywood. The United States opened an Office of the Coordinator of Inter-American Affairs (OCIAA) to gain solidarity from Latin Americans for the Second World War. Its most visible program was the Motion Picture Division, headed by John Hay Whitney, co-producer of *Gone with the Wind* (Victor Fleming 1939) and future secret agent and front man for the CIA's news service, Forum World Features (Stonor Saunders 1999, 311–12). The Office had at least one Hollywood film reshot because it showed Mexican children shoeless in the street, and was responsible for getting Hollywood to make *Saludos Amigos* (Jack Kinney et al. 1942) and *The Three Caballeros* (Norman Ferguson et al. 1944) and distribute *Simón Bolívar* (Miguel Contreras Torres 1942). Some production costs were borne by the OCIAA, and prints were distributed by US embassies and consulates across the region. Whitney accompanied Walt Disney and Donald Duck to Rio de Janeiro (Powdermaker 1950, 71; Kahn 1981, 145).

During the invasion of Europe in 1944 and 1945, the military closed Axis films, shuttered the industry, and insisted on the release of US movies. A quid pro quo for the subsequent Marshall Plan was the abolition of customs restrictions, among which were limits on film imports (Miller et al. 2005). In the case of Japan, the occupation immediately changed the face of cinema. When theaters reopened after the United States dropped its atomic bombs, all films and posters with war themes were gone. Previously censored Hollywood texts dominated screens. The occupying troops established an Information Dissemination Section in their Psychological Warfare Branch to imbue the local population with guilt and "teach American values" through cinema (High 2003, 503–4).

The film industry's peak body at this time referred to itself as "the little State Department," so isomorphic were its methods and ideology with US policy and politics. This was also the era when the industry's self-censoring Production Code appended to its bizarre litany of racial, sexual, and narcotic prohibitions and requirements two items requested by the "other" State Department: selling the US way of life around the world, and avoiding negative representations of any "foreign country with which we have cordial relations" (Powdermaker 1950, 36).

And the Cold War? Around the same time as he shot a romantic rival with a gun, producer Walter Wanger trumpeted in a scholarly journal the meshing of "Donald Duck and Diplomacy" as "a Marshall Plan for ideas . . . a veritable celluloid Athens," concluding that the state needed Hollywood "more than . . . the H bomb" (1950, 444, 446). Industry head Eric Johnston, fresh from his post as Secretary of Commerce, saw himself dispatching "messengers from a free country." President Harry Truman referred to movies as "ambassadors of goodwill" (in Johnston, 1950). The CIA's Psychological Warfare Workshop employed future Watergate criminal E. Howard Hunt, who clandestinely funded the rights purchase and production of George Orwell's anti-Soviet novels *Animal Farm* (1954) and *1984* (1956) (Cohen 2003).

The US Information Service spread its lending library of films across the globe as part of Cold War expansion. John F. Kennedy instructed the Service to use film and television to propagandize, and his administration funded 226 film centers in 106 countries. The title of a Congressional Legislative Research Service 1964 report made the point bluntly: *The U.S. Ideological Effort*. That impulse has been renewed. Four decades later, union officials soberly intoned that "although the Cold War is no longer a reason to protect cultural identity, today US-produced pictures are still a conduit through which our values, such as democracy and freedom, are promoted" (Ulrich and Simmers 2001, 365).

For a century, the Department of Defense has provided motion pictures with money, diplomacy, technology, soldiers, and settings, in return for a jealously-guarded right to veto stories that offend its sensibilities. The Pentagon provides the studios with open access to locations, technologies, and extras—all for free. This support does not normally occur through overt subvention, but it's impossible to imagine films such as *Top Gun* (Tony Scott 1986) being made minus citizens' tax dollars to underwrite producer Jerry Bruckheimer and his fun-filled storytellers and hell-raisers using *matériel* and labor provided by their admiring and admired friends over at Defense (Galloway 2016). Film thereby acts "as a tool for recruitment, military public relations, and commercial profit" (Löfflmann 2013).

In addition to providing scenery, soldiers, and sidearms to "authenticate" action-adventure masculinity, the Department of Defense also pays for research that assists film and television. Today's hybrid of SiliWood (Silicon Valley and Hollywood) articulates technology to storytelling through military funding. The interactivity underpinning this hybrid has evolved since the mid-1980s thanks to connections between Southern and Northern California semiconductor and computer manufacture and systems and software development (a massively military-inflected and military-supported industry that thrived throughout the Cold War). Hollywood stepped in to exploit the detritus of the post-1989 recession, as disused aircraft-production hangars became entertainment sites. The links are as much about technology, personnel, and collaboration on ancillary projects as stories. Steven Spielberg wears the Pentagon's Medal for Distinguished Public Service; Silicon Graphics designs material for the empire; and virtual-reality research veers between soldierly and audience applications, subsidized by the Federal Technology Reinvestment Project and Advanced Technology Program. Defense sends scientists to film school to produce positive images of violent technocracy, while educrats and Hollywood elites reciprocate: they invite the military to town to explain its needy hopes for friendly ideological representations. The state of Virginia, so proximate to the Pentagon, offers the usual raft of tax credits, grants, and in addition, easy access to key military personnel and locations, from naval shipyards to the Pentagon itself ("Virginia Offers").

Conclusion

Today's members of the Motion Picture Association are Disney, Netflix, Paramount, Sony, Universal, and Warner Bros. (Motion Picture Association 2021). Disney controls the ABC television network, most of the old 20th Century Fox studios, and the streamer Hulu. Paramount is part of the ViacomCBS group, which also runs the CBS network, MTV, and Showtime. Sony includes Columbia Studios. Universal is part of Comcast, which also controls the NBC network. WarnerMedia, as well as running the old studio, controls the pay-television channel HBO, its new streamer HBO Max, and much else besides. At the time of writing, it appears likely to become a junior partner of Discovery. Of the six current MPA members, in various incarnations five were founding members of the Association's predecessor a century ago. Only Netflix is a genuinely new player, supplanting companies such as RKO, MGM, and United Artists. Other streamers like Amazon Prime may join the club. But although there may be changes in the business, the leading players remain amazingly constant, seemingly impervious to the many crises—some would merely call them challenges—that they encounter. As the noted motion-picture analyst Pete Townshend put it in 1971: "Meet the new boss / Same as the old boss." But this time, those pesky antitrust mavens have been defanged; back to vertical integration as the studios own whichever parts of production, distribution, and exhibition they wish.

Here's a likely future for the crisis posed by the putative Asian twenty-first century: Hollywood will make a few textual concessions to China's censors and markets, thereby also potentially satisfying segments of its Asian-American audience in the quest for dollars-through-diversity. China may buy segments of the industry, perhaps even a studio. It will be resumed—perhaps easily, perhaps not—to US business and cultural norms and regulation, as Japan was in the 1990s. Hollywood observers will sit back, relax, and watch history take its usual course through the ensuing material conflict between fractions of capital and state. Crisis? Always. Survival? Always.

References

Arnheim, R. (1969), *Film as Art*, London: Faber and Faber.
Balio, T. (1993), *Grand Design: Hollywood as a Modern Business Enterprise, 1930–1939*, Berkeley: University of California Press.
Cantrell, G. and D. Wheatcroft (2018), *Film & TV Tax Incentives in the U.S.: Courting Hollywood*, London: Taylor & Francis.

Cohen, K. (2003), "The Cartoon That Came In from the Cold," *The Guardian*, 7 March. Available online: https://www.theguardian.com/culture/2003/mar/07/artsfeatures.georgeorwell.

Eyman, S. (2005), *Lion of Hollywood: The Life and Legend of Louis B. Mayer*, New York: Simon & Schuster.

Eyman, S. (2010), *Empire of Dreams: The Epic Life of Cecil B. DeMille*, New York: Simon & Schuster.

Ferriani, S., G. Cattani, and C. Baden-Fuller (2009), "The Relational Antecedents of Project-Entrepreneurship: Network Centrality, Team Composition and Project Performance," *Research Policy* 38 (10), pp. 1545–58.

Foster, P., S. Manning, and D. Terkla (2013), "The Rise of Hollywood East: Regional Film Offices as Intermediaries in Film and Television Production Clusters," *Regional Studies* 49 (3), pp. 433–50.

Gaither, C., and D. Chmielewski (2006), "Fears of Dot-Com Crash, Version 2.0," *Los Angeles Times*, 16 July. Available online: https://www.latimes.com/archives/la-xpm-2006-jul-16-fi-overheat16-story.html.

Galloway, S. (2016), "Galloway on Film: As 'Top Gun' Turns 30, Jerry Bruckheimer Reveals Secrets of the Film's (and His Own) Success," *Hollywood Reporter*, 20 June. Available online: https://www.hollywoodreporter.com/news/top-gun-at-30-jerry-bruckheimer-looks-back-his-career-as-a-mega-producer-904291.

Grantham, B. (2000), *"Some Big Bourgeois Brothel": Contexts for France's Culture Wars with Hollywood*, Luton: University of Luton Press.

High, P. B. (2003), *The Imperial Screen: Japanese Film Culture in the Fifteen Years' War, 1931–1945*, Madison: University of Wisconsin Press.

Johnston, E. (1950), "Messengers from a Free Country," *The Saturday Review of Literature*, 4 March, pp. 9–12.

Kahn, Jr., E. J. (1981), *Jock: The Life and Times of John Hay Whitney*, Garden City: Doubleday.

Karr, A. (1862), *Les Guêpes*, Paris: Michel Lévy Frères.

Lev, P. (2003), *Transforming the Screen 1950–1959*, Berkeley: University of California Press.

Löfflmann, G. (2013), "Hollywood, the Pentagon, and the Cinematic Production of National Security," *Critical Studies on Security* 1 (3), pp. 280–94.

Loesser, F. (1950), *Guys and Dolls*, Shubert Theater, Philadelphia.

Maxwell, R. and T. Miller (2011), "'For a Better Deal, Harass Your Governor!': Neoliberalism and Hollywood," in J. Kapur and K. B. Wagner (eds.), *Neoliberalism and Global Cinema: Capital, Culture, and Marxist Critique*, New York: Routledge, pp. 19–37.

Miller, T. (2008), *Makeover Nation: The United States of Reinvention*, Columbus: The Ohio State University Press.

Miller, J. L. (2011), "Producing Quality: A Social Network Analysis of Coproduction Relationships in High Grossing Versus Highly Lauded Films in the U.S. Market," *International Journal of Communication* 5, pp. 1014–33.

Miller, T., N. Govil, J. McMurria, R. Maxwell, and T. Wang (2005), *Global Hollywood 2*, London: British Film Institute.

"The Money Shot: Why Government Handouts to Hollywood are Growing" (2009), *The Economist*, 15 August. Available online: https://www.economist.com/business/2009/08/13/the-money-shot.

Motion Picture Association (2021), "Who We Are," Available online: https://www.motionpictures.org/who-we-are/#our-members.
Motion Picture Association of America (2014), *Theatrical Market Statistics 2014*. Available online: http://www.mpaa.org/wp-content/uploads/2015/03/MPAA-Theatrical-Market-Statistics-2014.pdf
Musser, C. (1990), *The Emergence of Cinema: The American Screen to 1907*, Berkeley: University of California Press.
O'Hara, F. (1979), *The Collected Poems of Frank O'Hara*, ed. D. Allen, New York: Alfred A Knopf.
Organisation for Economic Co-operation and Development (2008), *Remaking the Movies: Digital Content and the Evolution of the Film and Video Industries*, Geneva: Organisation for Economic Co-operation and Development.
Plato. (1892), *The Dialogues of Plato*, vol. 1, trans. B. Jowett, Oxford: Clarendon Press.
Powdermaker, H. (1950), *Hollywood: The Dream Factory: An Anthropologist Looks at the Movie-Makers*, Boston: Little, Brown and Company.
Rollins Saas, D. (2006), "Hollywood East? Film Tax Credits in New England," *New England Public Policy Center at the Federal Reserve Bank of Boston*, October. Available online: https://core.ac.uk/download/pdf/6707057.pdf.
Schatz, T. (1988), *The Genius of the System: Hollywood Filmmaking in the Studio Era*, New York: Pantheon Books.
Schatz, T. (1997), *Boom and Bust: American Cinema in the 1940s*, Berkeley: University of California Press.
"Split Screens: A Tale of Two Tinsel Towns" (2013), *The Economist*, 23 February. Available online: http://www.economist.com/news/business/21572218-tale-two-tinseltowns-split-screens.
Stonor Saunders, F. (1999), *Cultural Cold War: The CIA and the World of Arts and Letters*, New York: New Press.
Tannenwald, R. (2010), *State Film Subsidies: Not Much Bang for Too Many Bucks*, Washington: Center on Budget and Policy Priorities.
Thom, M. (2018), "Lights, Camera, but No Action? Tax and Economic Development Lessons from State Motion Picture Incentive Programs," *American Review of Public Administration* 48 (1), pp. 33–51.
Thomas, J. (1971), "The Decay of the Motion Picture Patents Company," *Cinema Journal* 10 (2), pp. 34–40.
Thompson, K. (1985), *Exporting Entertainment: America in the World Film Market 1907–1934*, London: British Film Institute.
Townshend, P. (1971), "We Won't Get Fooled Again," *Who's Next*, Track Record, LP.
Ulrich, P. C. and L. Simmers (2001), "Motion Picture Production: To Run or Stay Made in the U.S.A.," *Loyola of Los Angeles Entertainment Law Review* 21, pp. 357–70.
"Unilateral Disarmament: After a Decade of Escalation, a Stupid Trend May Have Peaked" (2011), *The Economist*, 9 June. Available online: https://www.economist.com/united-states/2011/06/09/unilateral-disarmament.
Valenti, J. (1982), "Testimony," *Hearings before the Subcommittee on Courts, Civil Liberties and the Administration of Justice of the Committee on the Judiciary*, 12 April, Washington, DC: U.S. Government Printing Office.

Verrier, R. (2013), "Hollywood's New Financiers Make Deals with State Tax Credits," *Los Angeles Times*, 26 December. Available online: http://www.latimes.com/entertainment/envelope/cotown/la-et-ct-hollywood-financiers-20131226,0,5151886.story.

"Virginia Offers Producers Multiple Locations, Tax Credits and Grants" (2018), *Variety*, 20 April. Available online: https://variety.com/2018/artisans/production/virginia-production-incentives-2-1202756546/.

Vogel, H. L. (2004), *Entertainment Industry Economics: A Guide for Financial Analysis*, 6th ed., Cambridge: Cambridge University Press.

Wanger, W. (1950), "Donald Duck and Diplomacy," *Public Opinion Quarterly* 14 (3), pp. 443–52.

Wasko, J. (2003), "Hollywood and Television in the 1950s: The Roots of Diversification," in P. Lev (ed.), *Transforming the Screen 1950–1960*, Berkeley: University of California Press, pp. 127–46.

Wilson, R. (2004), *The Vanished Hands*, Orlando: Harcourt, Inc.

World Intellectual Property Organisation (2006), "Timeline of the Video Cassette Recorder," *WIPO Magazine*, November. Available online: https://www.wipo.int/wipo_magazine/en/2006/06/article_0003.html.

2

Independent Films in an Age of Crisis

Illuminating the Lives of Outsiders in Neoliberal America

Cynthia Baron

Twenty-first-century US independent cinema includes a collection of low-key naturalistic films about people whose manual labor is integral to contemporary society but who bear the brunt of the externalized social and economic costs generated by neoliberal policies and a transnational corporate system in which financial services and biotech research occupy the top tier of the "global postindustrial hierarchy" (Curtin and Sanson 2016, 7). Characters in the films represent a precarious group that includes food service workers, drivers, maids, janitors, childcare providers, "retail clerks, day laborers, landscape workers, … [and] migrant workers" (Zaniello 2020, vi). Today, precarity is "a common condition for workers all over the world, from the low-end service sector in developing nations to white-collar elites in centers of capital" (Curtin and Sanson 2016, 5). Yet as the films reveal, narratives about unskilled workers in the United States who are women, immigrants, Black, Indigenous, or other people of color can illuminate the effects of neoliberalism *and* salient cultural forces in America, some coalescing after 9/11, some crystalizing in the 1970s, and others entwined in the country's formation (see Roediger 2008).

Illustrating the importance of social identity, the films show that disenfranchised people in the contemporary United States face challenges that are manifestations of entrenched social hierarchies and contemporary neoliberalism shaped by the late-eighteenth-century "liberal revolution" that sought to limit "state intervention into the economy and society on the assumption that this would enable forms of market and individual 'freedom'" (Grieveson 2018, 9). From the outset, liberalism has proposed that "the state's principal remit is to enable economic growth, and [that] it should do this by protecting property rights while removing regulatory restraint" on property owners (Grieveson 2018, 9). Moreover, the liberal revolution dramatically "broke with hitherto largely dominant traditions in thought and practice that viewed people as fundamentally social beings" (Grieveson 2018, 10). Unburdened by those traditions from the 1770s forward, liberalism has aligned personhood with men, linked property rights to "the power of unlimited appropriation," and claimed that these rights entail "the freedom to *exclude* others" (Grieveson 2018, 10). After a brief era of social democratic capitalism, the 1979 US Federal Reserve decisions to increase interest rates and trigger a recession ignited contemporary neoliberal practices that "restored profitability to capital" by excluding workers from profits; the intended rise in unemployment generated an oversupply of labor and thus falling wages (Basu 2018, 12). Securing the revitalized liberal agenda in the United States and the world, employers and governments coordinated efforts "to roll back union power, labour rights, wages, benefits and conditions of work" (Basu 2018, 12).

Thomas Austin, Angelos Koutsourakis, Leshu Torchin, Tom Zaniello, and others have shown that fiction and documentary films worldwide shed light on the experiences of people negatively affected by neoliberal policies and corporate rapaciousness. This chapter's delimited study analyzes six low-budget, critically acclaimed US independent films that illuminate the lives and labor of people from myriad backgrounds who are disenfranchised outsiders in twenty-first-century neoliberal America. The selection of films includes *Man Push Cart* (Ramin Bahrani 2005), which takes audiences into the world of a Pakistani immigrant who works in New York City as one of many cart vendors selling coffee and baked goods to white-collar workers as they bustle to their offices. *August Evening* (Chris Eska 2007), set primarily in rural environments near small-town Gonzales, Texas, a few hours from the US-Mexico border, focuses on a hardworking undocumented farm laborer and his family after his Anglo boss abruptly replaces him with a younger Latino worker. Filled with images of their characters' thoughtful faces and skilled hands, *Man Push Cart* and *August Evening* draw memorable portraits of immigrants who provide the invisible manual labor still essential in postindustrial America.

Frozen River (Courtney Hunt 2008), a border story involving the St. Lawrence River separating Quebec and New York State, illuminates the hardscrabble lives of two capable, but marginalized, women. One is a young Mohawk woman who sometimes works at a local bingo parlor, and the other is a white, middle-aged mother kept to part-time employment at a dollar store. *Wendy and Lucy* (Kelly Reichardt 2008), about an unemployed white woman passing through Portland, Oregon, on her way to Alaska in hopes of finding work in fish canneries, reveals the vulnerability of manual laborers in postindustrial United States, and the film presents Portland as an industrial-era relic now little more than a cargo transit point. Placing ordinary-looking women at the heart of the films' visual and narrative designs, *Frozen River* and *Wendy and Lucy* create an enduring counterpoint to neoliberal visions of human laborers as little more than pieces in the supply chain.

Middle of Nowhere (Ava DuVernay 2012) explores the life of an African American woman who navigates a maze of bus routes to work as a nurse in Los Angeles hospitals and a web of emotional and financial challenges to support her husband incarcerated in a Victorville prison in the California desert west of the metropolis. Like other films in the study, *Middle of Nowhere* slows its narrative pace to give audiences time to understand the central character's experience; rather than present the couple's story through a sociological lens, it reveals that incarcerating one person also imprisons their loved ones because audiences "spend sympathetic time with Black people in a narrative where the most significant meaning lies within *them, not* within the gaze of some idealized White observer" (Taylor 2015, xxii). Also, like other films in the study, *Middle of Nowhere* illustrates the profoundly negative effect of "rational" neoliberal practices that determine the types of labor and laborers important to the contemporary economy.

Spa Night (Andrew Ahn 2016) is also set in Los Angeles, this time in Koreatown near the city center. The film brings audiences into the world of a young Korean man and his parents after the family is forced to close the small restaurant that has been their livelihood. Like *August Evening*'s story about people of Mexican heritage, *Spa Night* shows how manual labor figures into the relationships between first- and second-generation immigrants. In *Spa Night*, this relationship is complicated by the son's growing embrace of his queer sexuality and his parents' assumption that he will go to college, marry a Korean girl, and give them grandchildren. Like other films in the study, *Spa Night* uses settings as multidimensional spaces that disclose character, contribute narrative and metaphoric meaning, and contribute to "discourses about those real places" (Deleyto 2016, 7). Spas reflect the son's interest in sexual intimacy yet are also a space for familial bonding, and despite the father's view that his son should do something other than unskilled labor, a spa gives the son a chance to do the kind of (manual) labor he enjoys.

Whether considered singly or as a group, these finely crafted, slow-paced productions offer nuanced portraits of characters whose situations highlight the subjective experiences of people who belong to postindustrial society's invisible labor force and grapple daily with the US neoliberal economic-legal system and its entrenched white (male) supremacist social hierarchy.

Yet the films do more than show the toxic effects of contemporary United States. Using images of the characters in their daily lives and scores of scenes featuring ordinary people traveling by foot or using public transportation to traverse urban and rural environments, the six films make visible the presence and even remarkable gracefulness of invisible laborers. Through repeated close-ups of the actors' attractive, expressive faces and point-of-view shots that present settings from the characters' perspectives, the films momentarily reorder the hierarchies that shape socioeconomic realities in twenty-first-century New York City, rural and urban south Texas, upstate New York, south Los Angeles, downtown Los Angeles, and Portland, Oregon.

US Independent Cinema and Naturalistic Aesthetics

Going against a twenty-first-century trend of close connections between independent and Hollywood filmmaking, the films sustain the tradition of *Matewan* (John Sayles 1987) and other 1980s productions with progressive cultural politics and independent distribution. They reflect a continuity with 1980s filmmaking by using "the classic independent recipe of low-resource production and traditional smaller-scale release" (King 2014, 170). Moreover, their "sincere engagement with social issues" distinguishes them from contemporary independent films associated with "designer quirky" and what some audiences see as the "shallow superficiality of mumblecore" and its economically secure white protagonists (King 2014, 170). Discussing independent film's "resurgence in . . . documentary-style social realist features," Linda Badley finds that this "post-postmodern return to realism" is marked by "minimalist, on-location shooting, indigenous, non-professional or relatively unknown actors, and a *cinema vérité* effect" (2016, 121; 123). As she notes, the cycle of naturalistic filmmaking includes *George Washington* (David Gordon Green 2000), *The Dead Girl* (Karen Moncrieff 2006), *Chop Shop* (Ramin Bahrani 2007), and Debra Granik's *Down to the Bone* (2004), *Winter's Bone* (2010), and *Leave No Trace* (2018).

The six naturalistic films featuring manual laborers continue the tradition of regional cinema integral to 1980s independent cinema. They also build on documentary and fiction work exemplified by films such as *Union Maids* (Julia Reichert 1976) and *Bless Their Little Hearts* (Billy Woodberry 1983). Some show the influence of films in world cinema: *Man Push Cart* draws on work by Robert Bresson and Abbas Kiarostami; *August Evening* is influenced by the films of Satyajit Ray and Yasujiro Ozu. *Man Push Cart* also builds on films by US independents John Cassavetes and Lodge Kerrigan, just as *August Evening* recalls the Chicano characters in *Fast Food Nation* (Richard Linklater 2006) and evokes Chicano cinema productions that highlight the lives of laborers, such as *Raíces de sangre* (*Roots of Blood*, Jesús Salvador Treviño 1975) and *El Norte* (*The North*, Gregory Nava 1983). *Frozen River* continues the cultural work of *The Exiles* (Kent MacKenzie 1961) and anticipates *Songs My Brothers Taught Me* (Chloé Zhao 2015); all three films reveal ties between perennial job insecurity and the vulnerability of Indigenous people in the United States. *Wanda* (Barbara Loden 1970), *Alice Doesn't Live Here Anymore* (Martin Scorsese 1974), and *Gas Food Lodging* (Allison Anders 1992) precede *Wendy and Lucy*'s depiction of a woman left behind by US society. *Killer of Sheep* (Charles Burnett 1978), which shows the stress racialized labor has on Black families, anticipates *Middle of Nowhere*. *Hito Hata: Raise the Red Flag* (Robert Nakamura and Duane Kubo 1980) and *Chan Is Missing* (Wayne Wang 1982) set a precedent for *Spa Night*'s story of how Asian Americans' cultural outsider status makes them socially and economically vulnerable in (white) US society.

Naturalism is just one aesthetic approach filmmakers use to illustrate the effects of twenty-first-century socioeconomic crises. Boots Riley's *Sorry to Bother You* (2018) and Terrence Nance's *Random Acts of Flyness* (HBO 2018–present) show that films shaped by postmodern aesthetics can effectively critique social and economic hierarchies in neoliberal United States. Identifying another path, Juan Sebastián Ospina León and others see twenty-first-century filmmakers using melodrama to make "the global downtrodden visible" (2020, 53). Analyzing Alejandro G. Iñárritu's *Amores perros* (2000), *21 Grams* (2003), *Babel* (2006), and *Biutiful* (2010), Ospina León finds that the films reveal "social inequalities on a global scale [by] connecting individual melodramas to larger sociopolitical problems" (2020, 48).

Other scholars show how American genre films disclose social anxieties arising from contemporary socioeconomic crises. James D. Stone proposes that *Paranormal Activity* (Oren Peli 2007) and *Paranormal Activity II* (Todd Williams 2010) are "tales of the recession" because they dramatize "the gradual collapse of consumer capitalist dreams" (2013, 51). Analyzing disaster movies that "couch economic collapse in ecological terms," Kirk Boyle finds that the independent film *Take Shelter* (Jeff Nichols 2011) "captures the traumatic effects of a worldwide recession hitting the American heartland" (2013, 5). Discussing films that use the horror genre to convey the type of critique that emerges from the naturalistic films in the study, April Miller shows that Sam Raimi's *Drag Me to Hell* (2009) and Steven Soderbergh's *Contagion* (2011) use "the specter of economic collapse . . . to highlight the recession's augmentation of gender and class divisions and the failure of financial and governmental institutions to protect citizens from this spreading horror" (2013, 30).

Taking a different aesthetic path to generate candid appraisals of neoliberalism *and* sympathetic depictions of people who move through the world in caring, intelligent ways, the naturalistic films from *Man Push Cart* to *Spa Night* depict characters who have complex subjectivities and are social types defined by specific environments. As such, they are distinct from ahistorical characters in classical-realist Hollywood productions that feature ostensibly unique individuals caught in moments of dramatic crisis or fictional types associated with genres. Notably, the films in the study show the influence of what Raymond Williams calls "authentic naturalism," which differs from romanticism and realism because it is "a critical movement, in which the relation between [people] and their environments [is] not merely *represented* but *actively explored*" (in Naremore 1988, 200–1).

The naturalistic films' active exploration of socioeconomic environments depends not only on their socially grounded conception of character; it also emerges from their de-dramatized pace and narrative design. Describing *Wendy and Lucy* as a "beautiful and gutting film [that] offers a deeply human and close up view" of its central character, Leshu Torchin articulates an insight that applies to all six films (2020). Highlighting *Wendy and Lucy*'s narrative design, she proposes that the "slowness of the film is a needed counter to the speed of capitalism, which forces [comfortable, white-collar workers] to move past people and their stories" (2020). Like other independent productions lacking "the strong dramatic conflict of the classical Hollywood style," the naturalistic films share common elements with art cinema (Murphy 2007, 16). They explore "dedramatized, apparently trivial everyday moments" and sometimes have "a drifting episodic quality rather than a single linear narrative development" (Buckland 2017, 408). The open-ended, character-centered narratives also convey "the intrusion of an unpredictable and contingent daily reality" (Bordwell 2008, 154).

In the slow-paced, de-dramatized narratives, "the momentum of action gives way to the moment of gesture and the body" (Elsaesser 2004, 292). Consequently, the naturalistic films provide incomparable opportunities for audiences to feel the presence and emotions of the ordinary people at the heart of the stories and the center of images. The six films amplify the effect of their narrative design by often casting first-time or little-known actors. This naturalistic choice eliminates extratextual associations surrounding major stars and makes the performers' physical appearances especially significant; the social types suggested by the actors' ordinary looks and culturally specific physical-vocal expressions give the characterizations a resonance that reaches beyond the fiction. Featuring various performers with physiognomies that carry associations with identities underrepresented or misrepresented in Hollywood movies, the films about invisible laborers shed light on the xenophobia bound into neoliberal practices.

Immigrant Stories: *Man Push Cart* and *August Evening*

In *Man Push Cart*, a worker, whose laboring body is his only resource, pulls a massive vending cart through New York City every weekday in the predawn hours to reach his assigned corner in midtown Manhattan. Later, he hauls the cart back to its warehouse, casually sells bootleg DVDs as he travels city streets, goes by subway to a rented room an hour away in Brooklyn, sleeps a few hours, and then makes the hour-long trip into the city to drag the heavy cart back to its assigned spot. Noting that the character's labor supports little more than "his ability to keep on working," Roger Ebert finds that he is like "so many Americans who work low-wage jobs, sometimes two or even three of them" (2006). The film provides additional evidence for seeing connections between the fiction and contemporary United States; with its images of shop keepers and garbage collectors who also inhabit Manhattan in the predawn hours, *Man Push Cart* illuminates a world of non-white workers who do backbreaking, but invisible, labor in a society dominated by white financial elites.

For Ahmad (Ahmad Razvi), who had been a pop star in Pakistan but now does manual labor in the States, it is a lonely, grueling existence. Cut off from his young son by in-laws who blame Ahmad for their daughter's untimely passing, his dream is to make enough money to recreate a home life with his son. In contrast to Mohammad (Charles Daniel Sandoval), a Pakistani businessman in New York who recognizes Ahmad from photos on CDs that he owns, romance is not something he can even consider. Thus, when Noemi (Leticia Dolera), a Spanish immigrant who works at a nearby newsstand, becomes interested in him and encourages him to write and perform music again, he candidly assesses the social isolation that comes with his economic status, telling her, "I'm just a Pakistani guy, you know, selling coffee and donuts, that's all."

The film's slow-paced narrative, actor-centered shot selections, and spare, elegiac score make Ahmad's thoughts and feelings legible. It orchestrates these elements to focus audience attention on the gestures, movements, and facial and vocal expressions of first-time actor Ahmad Razvi, whose performance "never strains for effect [but instead] embodies the bleakness and exhaustion of his character" (Ebert 2006). Discussing Razvi's nuanced portrayal, Dana Stevens explains that "he conveys more in 10 seconds of stillness than many actors do in entire careers" (2006). Echoing Leshu Torchin's point that unhurried naturalistic films can interrupt elites' habit of moving "past people and their stories," Stevens, writing for other white-collar workers, notes, "you may never see your doughnut vendor in the same way again" (2006).

Razvi's physiognomy and subdued performance lend plausibility to the disparate aspects of Ahmad's life, for he is handsome enough to be a rock star (the "Bono of Lahore"), while his thoughtful countenance, quiet demeanor, and relaxed, graceful, and purposeful movements suit a laborer. The film enhances Ahmad's humanity by continually placing him in a dark, mechanical world of trucks, buses, and jammed Manhattan streets. Repeatedly enclosed by metal frames in a monochromatic setting, Ahmad is a vivid sign of human life. The film generates interest in Ahmad by placing Razvi in essentially every shot. With sparse dialogue, the film delays conventional information about the character. Audiences are fifteen minutes into the film before there is exposition and a long take that focuses on Razvi's well-lit face. By then, they have become attentive to every shift in Razvi's facial and vocal expression, so that when he turns to the camera, his steady gaze conveys Ahmad's frustration about being kept from his son, just as the rapid flow of Razvi's words and intermittent breaths reveal Ahmad's underlying desperation (Figure 2.1).

Razvi's restrained expression of emotion here and elsewhere conveys the character's isolated existence as a young widower and an immigrant who has lost all social status. It also reflects Ahmad's need to remain as invisible as possible in post-9/11 United States; as a Pakistani neighbor reminds him, he must be careful because "it's getting harder for people like us these days." In the months following 9/11, "the number of hate crimes against Muslims jumped: In 2000, there were just 28 recorded hate crimes; in 2001, there were 481" (Belle 2020). Additionally, the US National Security Entry-Exit Registration System required male noncitizens from twenty-four predominantly Muslim countries to register with the Department of Homeland Security. The Special Registration program hit Brooklyn's Pakistani

FIGURE 2.1 *Ahmad Razvi in* Man Push Cart *(Ramin Bahrani 2005)*.

and Bangladeshi neighborhood hard; "poverty-stricken and marginalized before 9/11," the community collapsed socially and economically due to the disproportionate immigrant enforcement (Kampf and Sen 2006). *Man Push Cart* tacitly captures these realities. Using the subdued, evocative details of an ordinary person's portrayal to illuminate the subjective experiences of a Pakistani outsider in post-9/11 New York, the film offers a culturally specific critique of neoliberal practices that exploit immigrant laborers.

August Evening, a US independent film in Spanish with English subtitles, explores the daily lives of people in the migrant labor workforce, which Western economies have depended upon "in agriculture, care work, factories, sex work, construction and other low-status jobs" both before and after the Great Recession (Austin and Koutsourakis 2020, 17). Focusing on undocumented poultry-farm worker Jaime Esparza (Pedro Castaneda) and his widowed daughter-in-law, Lupe (Veronica Loren), *August Evening* "is likely to stand as one of the most memorable films to dramatize the painful experience" of Latinx people negotiating white US society, which sees them as little more than cheap and reliable laborers (Farber 2007).

The film's opening seven minutes, which features just a few lines of dialogue, establishes the central characters as manual laborers, corralled into destinies by larger outside forces. It begins with images from the industrial poultry farm where Jaime works: chickens in a packed factory-farm coop; eggs traveling down a shoot, covered with flies, feathers, and chicken droppings; Jaime scrubbing chicken wire, putting eggs in wholesale cartons, and tossing broken eggs into a fly-covered bucket; live chickens trampling dead ones on the coop floor; Jaime carrying dead chickens, scrambling to catch a loose one, wiping his brow. A pickup, with Jaime in the back, takes him to his living quarters, a tiny adobe house on a dirt road. Once inside, there are images of his wife, Maria (Raquel Gavia), and Lupe cooking as Jaime whittles a piece of wood. Audiences see Lupe walking along a rural road, leaving flowers at a roadside cross, scrubbing dishes in a restaurant kitchen, giving children a guitar lesson; they see Jaime walking a stretch of rural road and later boxing egg cartons coming down multiple conveyor belts. There is a brief pause in their labor: Jaime places a bracelet on Maria's wrist (an early birthday present); they hold hands and watch television. Then Jaime, Maria, and Lupe attend an informal dance in town. The respite is short-lived: in the first moments of dancing with Jaime, Maria feels dizzy and has a sharp pain in her chest. She passes away (off-screen) the next morning.

Jaime and Maria's married son and daughter make the hour-and-a-half-drive from San Antonio to attend the small funeral but leave shortly after. With his children absorbed in their middle-class lives, Jaime is now as isolated as Lupe. Six years earlier, her mother had held a "kind of a funeral" for her when she left her hometown in Oaxaca, Mexico, knowing they "would probably never see each other again." Two years later, Lupe's husband is killed in a car accident, leaving the young bride with no family other than Jaime and Maria. Cut off from other family and isolated in the English-speaking, white-dominated country, Jaime and Lupe contend with Jaime losing his job and housing, their rejection by Jaime's children when they travel to San Antonio to seek assistance, and their day-to-day survival when they move back to Gonzales.

By centering the mundane realities of Jaime and Lupe's lives and placing Castaneda and Loren in almost every frame, *August Evening* illuminates the kind of subjective experiences that millions of Latinx workers in the United States face in ways that perhaps even compelling documentaries like *Food Chains* (Sanjay Rawal 2014) do not. Reviews highlight the resonance of the first-time actors' performances, noting that "their faces tell the story" (Rainer 2008). Finding *August Evening* to be "masterful in its depiction of the realities of daily life on the fringes of American Society," Marc Savlov observes: "as in reality, it's often the enormously eloquent silences between people, events, and generations that speak the loudest and mean the most" (2008). Arguing that the "performances are first rate," Stephen Farber proposes that the film "combines perfectly honed, naturalistic acting and visual lyricism" (2007).

August Evening depicts Jaime and Lupe's quiet friendship and their evolving connections with other characters; its title derives from Jaime's fond memory that evening had been Maria's favorite time of day. The characters communicate exclusively in Spanish, which also reflects their subjectivities. The film deepens its characterizations and establishes ties between the fiction and socioeconomic reality by making images of Jaime laboring or looking for work the most frequently repeated element in the visual design. Moreover, *August Evening* conveys that Jaime and other undocumented workers in the United States have a candid awareness of the system's inequities. During an uncharacteristic night of drinking, Jaime's childhood friend reminds him, "All this shit goes back to losing the war with America . . . If we hadn't lost, all the whites would be pouring across the border into the Mexican state of Texas. Their gringo kids would be singing Mexican folk songs and they'd be cooking for us, man." Reflecting the humor and sage perspective that has helped him survive, Jaime chuckles and replies, "Then it's lucky we lost."

Women's Stories: *Frozen River* and *Wendy and Lucy*

Just as *Man Push Cart* and *August Evening* were first features for Ramin Bahrani and Chris Eska, respectively, *Frozen River* was the first feature of writer-director Courtney Hunt. Yet in contrast to their do-it-yourself budget films, *Frozen River* was made for one million dollars, employed thriller genre conventions, and co-starred character actor Melissa Leo and rising ingenue Misty Upham, who transformed her appearance for the role. Still, it shares common ground with the study's other films by focusing on two women without access to a living wage. Penniless after her gambling-addicted husband leaves the week before Christmas with the money she had saved for the family's new trailer home, Ray (Melissa Leo) agrees to use her car to smuggle people across the frozen St. Lawrence River at the US-Canada border. Her dour, but knowledgeable, partner is Lila (Misty Upham), an outsider in white United States and in her own Mohawk community after her husband dies during a smuggling mishap. Condemned to social isolation, she cannot even visit their young son now living with her mother-in-law.

Frozen River includes formulaic thriller elements such as the ill-fated one last trip. Moreover, the characters' brazen smuggling efforts to "attain financial independence and self-worth" and the film's happy ending, in which Lila reclaims custody of her son and cares for Ray's two children while Ray is in prison, might reinforce neoliberal visions of individual autonomy (Frame 2020, 261). Yet scene by scene the narrative remains focused on the characters' economic survival, bringing attention to the "obscured underclass" of America's working poor (Gilbey 2009). The film's naturalistic approach not only emphasizes the characters' punishing physical environment but also provides intimate access to the portrayals of the now ordinary-looking performers.

The film introduces Ray and her wretched situation in a tightly framed moving shot revealing Leo's chipped fingernail polish, messy hair, irritated skin, and teary eyes. The drab setting in surroundings shots convey Ray's inner experience and suggest that, for someone like her, the prospect of a better life is unlikely. Embodying a character weighed down by responsibility and disappointment, Leo maintains a slightly bent posture that conveys her determination and exhaustion. The varied pitch in her voice and irregular rhythm of her words as she goes from one confrontation to the next communicate her desperation. In counterpoint, Upham maintains a guarded stance, conveying Lila's hurt and bitterness over experiences that have made her wise beyond her years.

Throughout the film, the terse verbal exchanges between Lila and Ray are most often distinguished by Upham's even, controlled tone, with its slight variations to convey impatience, distain, appeals to reason, and varied degrees of threat. By comparison, in Lila's encounters with other members of the Mohawk community, Upham reveals Lila's vulnerability, her voice more expressive and girlish as it changes pitch and volume. By creating a multidimensional character, Upham not only illuminates the subjective experiences of a person who belongs to the US working poor, she also crafts one of cinema's only complex depictions of a young Indigenous woman.

Like *Man Push Cart* and *August Evening*, *Frozen River* gives audiences time with characters rarely seen in US cinema. Critics note that audiences "come to understand how much these exhausted women, both tired of being on the short end of the stick, have in common" (Turan 2008). Yet this "is not a story of bonding. It is a story of need" (Ebert 2008). The film makes this point by repeating moments of the women quickly counting their money or using few words to handle travel and even childcare logistics. The characters "hardly have a conversation that isn't practical and immediate" because their anger and desperation, brought on by economic peril and social isolation, have left them with no time or energy for casual conversation (Ebert 2008).

The actors' naturalistic performances coordinate with the film's focus on the characters' material conditions. The film grounds character motivations and actions in a specific socioeconomic setting. This includes problems stemming from neoliberal policies such as the difficulties of securing affordable housing, management's refusal to pay workers a living wage, and the complete lack of community or state support for people who need it. The film also captures the reality that even before the Great Recession, women in neoliberal society have been especially vulnerable due to "fraught and contingent financial arrangements, lower amounts of savings and more dependent obligations" (Negra and Tasker 2014, 22).

Despite its $300,000 budget, *Wendy and Lucy* is the study's best-known film, perhaps because it represents one of several collaborations between recognized independent filmmaker Kelly Reichardt and Oscar-nominated actor Michelle Williams. Yet like *Frozen River*, it sees the world from a woman's perspective and takes a naturalistic approach to depicting the experiences of an "unskilled" worker left behind by neoliberal United States. Moreover, like Lila in *Frozen River*, Wendy (Michelle Williams) is "a woman whose last tear was cried some time ago [and her] resolve seems less a matter of tenacity than reflex; she keeps moving forward because she has nowhere else to go" (Adams 2008). However, Wendy is even more isolated. Whereas Lila finds a coworker and eventually a friend, Wendy's only companion is her dog, Lucy—and they are together for only the first twenty minutes of the film. Caught stealing food for Lucy, Wendy is arrested. Wendy is released later that day, but Lucy is no longer where she left her, so Wendy spends the rest of the film searching for her. Eventually finding Lucy at a nice foster home, she realizes the dog is better off there. The film ends with Wendy continuing alone to Alaska, dwarfed by the size of the boxcar in the train that will take her to the next uncertain stop along the way.

Upon its release, critics saw *Wendy and Lucy* as "a lucid and melancholy inquiry into the current state of American society" and "uncannily well suited, in mood and manner, to [the] grim, recessionary season" (Scott 2008). In its depiction of postindustrial Portland, the film suggests that Wendy and the handful of people she encounters "haven't dropped out of life; they've been dropped by life. It has no real use for them, and not much interest" (Ebert 2009). Her main source of assistance is "a security guard of retirement age (Wally Dalton) whose job is to stand and look at a mostly empty parking lot for 12 hours and guard against a nonexistent threat to its empty spaces" (Ebert 2009). Like characters throughout the study's films, he and Wendy reveal their astute understanding of socioeconomic realities. During a pause in Wendy's search, their brief exchange includes the following lines:

> **Wendy:** Not a lot of jobs around here, huh?
> **Guard:** I'll say. I don't know what the people do all day. Used to be a mill, but it's been closed a long time now. Don't know what they do.
> **Wendy:** Can't get a job without an address anyway, or a phone.
> **Guard:** You can't get an address without an address. You can't get a job without a job. It's all fixed.

As these lines suggest, the characters in *Wendy and Lucy*, like those in *Man Push Cart*, *August Evening*, and *Frozen River*, know full well how neoliberal United States works. Further, in this short exchange and elsewhere, by slowing down the narrative to explore the mundane realities of Wendy's stop in Portland, the film plainly illustrates how the lives of unskilled laborers "are grounded in an unyielding material reality" (Scott 2008).

Los Angeles Stories: *Middle of Nowhere* and *Spa Night*

Middle of Nowhere is another film by a woman director who uses a naturalistic approach to illuminate a woman's experience and socioeconomic realities. In this instance, the central character's story is emblematic of a society that imprisons massive numbers of Black men in part because they belong to "a population deemed disposable" in neoliberal United States (Alexander 2012, 18). The film takes the time to follow Ruby (Emayatzy Corinealdi) as she works through the emotional and practical challenges of putting her life on pause to better support her husband Derek (Omari Hardwick), who is in prison for illegal weapons activities he undertook to support the middle-class lifestyle he thought suited her aspiration to be a doctor.

Seeing the film as exemplifying independent cinema's return to realism, Linda Badley highlights its use of "sustained close-ups and moments of stillness to immerse spectators in Ruby's emotional interiors" (2016, 123, 126). As she observes, just by "focusing on the everyday interior life of a young black woman, *Middle of Nowhere* is experimental and quietly political" (2016, 126). Effectively using its modest $200,000 budget, the film gives audiences time to appreciate this ordinary character's quiet despair and resilience, in part because Corinealdi is in every scene. This approach, which parallels that of *Man Push Cart*, makes even slight changes in her physical and vocal expressions significant. *Middle of Nowhere* allows audiences to witness Ruby's evolving perspective and the emotional connection she has with her husband despite being separated from him. Letters between them, read in voiceover by Corinealdi and Hardwick, convey the couple's closeness.

Yet prison is the characters' reality, and the film opens with a scene between Ruby and Derek in a penitentiary visiting room. Corinealdi and Hardwick speak in hushed, intimate tones as he tells her to go on with life and she replies that she cannot, saying, "You are me. Remember?" During the next visit shown, four years later, Ruby and Derek hash out their different responses to his upcoming parole review and Ruby's discovery that Derek has been involved in "street shit" while in prison. Their bond momentarily disrupted, the couple reestablish their connection after Derek gets Ruby to remember moments from their honeymoon six years earlier. Importantly, the film suggests that both the couple's affection and struggle to remain close are not unique. During prison visits, there are other couples in the space, and when Ruby travels by bus to and from the prison, she is surrounded by other inmates' wives. Derek's incarceration also affects Ruby's family, heightening tensions with Ruth (Lorraine Toussaint), who had wanted Ruby and her sister to have better lives than she had as their single mother.

As of the film's release, African American men comprised 6.5 percent of the US population but 40.2 percent of the prison population. Thus, Derek, Ruby, and Ruth are characters who must contend with the material and emotional effects of being outsiders in a socioeconomic system shaped by a white supremacist backlash against the civil rights movement. The 1970s backlash led to the rise of mass incarceration involving disproportionate imprisonment of Black men and ongoing racial disparity in the "larger web of laws, rules, policies, and customs that control those labeled as criminals both in and out of prison" (Alexander 2012, 13). Further, reinvigorated white supremacist ideology fueled the "opposition to the 'overreach' of the federal government in terms of busing and affirmative action [and this] was fundamental in building the appeal of a return to an uncompromising laissez-faire economics" (Gomer 2020, 12). With civil rights programs dismantled, the "neoliberal notion of individual colorblind freedom" ascendant, and the United States in a supposedly post-racial era (Gomer 2020, 12), Derek, Ruby, and Ruth see themselves, rather than the system, as failing, and they contend with their shame in different ways. Denied access to middle-class status, Derek takes shortcuts that Ruby pretends not to notice. After Derek is imprisoned and Ruby drops out of medical school, Ruth seethes with bitterness, blaming the young people for their situation. Yet the film suggests that they are not inherently lazy or criminal but instead caught in a caste system in which Black men are often "barred by law and custom from mainstream society" (Alexander 2012, 13). Slowing down the narrative to explore the daily existence of someone with a loved one in prison, *Middle of Nowhere* illuminates key aspects of US neoliberal society, which consigns all but exceptional African Americans to chronic outsider status because Black men are so often unable to make a living wage before, during, or after incarceration, and their families are pushed further into debt as they struggle to cover the exorbitant legal fees inherent to the prison industrial system.

Spa Night is another Los Angeles story about outsiders in white, neoliberal United States. The Kickstarter- and grant-funded film follows David (Joe Seo), his mother (Haerry Kim), and his father (Youn Ho Cho). An immigrant story and coming-of-age narrative, the film "is as much about the surrounding social context as it is about David's sexual awakening" (O'Malley 2016), since audiences learn about the Korean tradition of family spas, the socioeconomic role of the Korean Christian church, and the hardships of people with shops and restaurants in Koreatown, which police used as a buffer between South Los Angeles and white midtown neighborhoods during the 1992 Los Angeles Riots. Financially ruined by the devastation of the 1990s, David's parents are also among the working-class shopkeepers evicted from spaces that became valuable when gentrification transformed the neighborhood in the 2010s.

To tell its story of unskilled Korean Americans excluded by white neoliberal schemes, *Spa Night* employs an unhurried pace that allows audiences to focus on the actors' subtle portrayals. At a church social, David's mother responds to a member's inquiry about the family's recently closed restaurant; she glibly lies that they sold it, then gracefully solicits and accepts a job at the woman's restaurant. Meanwhile, her husband and son remain silent, and during the women's conversation, Cho registers the husband's mounting shame by incrementally slowing his movements until he becomes immobile. Later, David's mother wistfully recalls her arrival in Los Angeles as a young woman, recalling that David's father had a Cadillac when he met her at the airport. Two small moments at a child's traditional Korean birthday party convey the sense of failure that permeates the family. Ashamed to tell David that his first-birthday ritual foretold poverty, his parents awkwardly pretend to forget what happened when he turned one. Then, when David sees them happily playing with the young child destined for success, a long take of Joe Seo lets audiences absorb the subtle expression of emotion as his eyes well up with tears (Figure 2.2).

Spa Night illustrates that neoliberal United States will accommodate Korean Americans able to support the financial sector. David's uncomfortable campus visit to nearby University of Southern California shows that Korean Americans who major in business at private universities have promising futures; David and his father's failed stint as day laborers for a furniture moving company reveals that Korean Americans possessing white-collar skills can live in spacious, nicely decorated homes in beautifully landscaped neighborhoods like Beverly Hills. By comparison, first-generation manual laborers and unskilled second-generation Korean

FIGURE 2.2 *Joe Seo in* Spa Night *(Andrew Ahn 2016)*.

American workers are vulnerable in neoliberal United States, consigned to dislocation and uncertainty. David's father blames himself, rather than the riots or gentrification, for David's working-class status, and David feels the pain of failing to realize his parents' dreams. Yet by the close of the film, he has become estranged from his parents' Korean vision of success, even though he has little idea how to live another way. *Spa Night* thus illuminates David's compounded alienation; his sexuality makes him an outsider in Korean American society, and his unapologetic embrace of manual labor makes him a vulnerable outsider in postindustrial United States.

Concluding Thoughts

Without offering "reassuring vignettes of individual agency as compensation" for crises created by financial elites (Negra and Tasker 2014, 2), the naturalistic US independent films from *Man Push Cart* to *Spa Night* convey the dignity of human labor and show that physical labor might not require official certification but does require attention and skill. With intelligent, reflective, and goal-directed characters at the center of the narratives, the six films provide evidence that people who do manual or unskilled labor are hardly inept, incompetent, or ignorant. From the isolated characters in *Man Push Cart* and *Wendy and Lucy* to the characters bound closely to family in *August Evening*, *Frozen River*, *Middle of Nowhere*, and *Spa Night*, they all recognize and understand the power dynamics that shape the larger socioeconomic system. Fully aware that it favors elites, the characters work with the options available to them while doing right by those closest to them, whether a family member, pet, or partner in crime.

The films about unskilled laborers clarify the toxic combination of neoliberalism and the US history of white male supremacy in ways that films about white-collar greed like *Margin Call* (J. C. Chandor 2011), *Too Big to Fail* (Curtis Hanson 2011), and *The Big Short* (Adam McKay 2015) perhaps do not. These fast-paced, dialogue-heavy, and pictorially realistic films make the neoliberal adventure seem exciting. The white male characters driving the narratives also mask the reality that neoliberal practices and a social system built on white male privilege carries far greater negative consequences for everyone else. By comparison, the films in the study illustrate the consequences of financial crises in contemporary United States.

Across the globe, neoliberalism has fostered deregulation, privatization, and austerity measures to minimize health, education, and welfare programs that could reduce the suffering of disenfranchised people. As the films from *Man Push Cart* to *Spa Night* demonstrate, US neoliberalism not only places a premise on individualism but also sustains socioeconomic practices that have *excluded* women, immigrants, African Americans, Indigenous Americans, and other people of color. The neoliberalism that coalesced in the 1970s in response to the civil rights movement and economic downturn was expanded in the Reagan era and 1990s dot-com boom and took a virulent form in the wake of 9/11 when it was accompanied by a surge in white Christian nationalism. In the twenty-first century, dominant socioeconomic forces have framed financial crises as a wound to US pride (meaning white male pride) and a threat to the US family (code for white, heterosexual families), despite the crises affecting women, people of color, and LGBTQ people far more profoundly.

To make those realities visible, *Man Push Cart*, *August Evening*, and *Spa Night* explore immigrant experiences in a country that needs, but is hostile to, manual immigrant labor. *Spa Night* also highlights the perspective of an outsider in Korean and (white) queer communities. In *Wendy and Lucy*, the isolated white woman represents millions in the United States perpetually out of work in the postindustrial period. *Frozen River* illustrates the financial peril faced by the millions of underemployed people in the country's service industries and illuminates the disparate justice meted out to white and Indigenous people and the ongoing practice of human trafficking in a neoliberal world. *Middle of Nowhere* not only reveals the emotional toll on the families of incarcerated people but also points to the social, political, and economic systems that have created the prison industrial complex and "a stigmatized racial group locked into an inferior position by law and custom" (Alexander 2012, 12).

During the increased emphasis on financialization and deregulation since the 1970s, economic downturns have been "an opportunity to deepen neoliberalism under the rubric of austerity as a necessary 'balancing of the books'" (Austin and Koutsourakis 2020, 8). Yet *Man Push Cart, August Evening, Frozen River, Wendy and Lucy, Middle of Nowhere,* and *Spa*

Night balance the moral ledger by taking time to explore ordinary lives affected by the freedom elites enjoy in postindustrial United States. These films reveal the competence required for "unskilled" labor. Filmed in loving detail, afforded ample screen time, and presented as the *living* figures in often formidable urban and rural settings, the characters also have an indelible human presence, which challenges the naturalized prejudices that continue to fuel neoliberalism in the United States.

Dedicated to Misty Upham (1982–2014), a member of the Blackfeet Nation and an actress known for *Frozen River*, *August Osage County*, Chris Eyre films, and other productions. Sexually abused as a child, Upham was then raped by a Weinstein Co. executive at the 2013 Golden Globes ceremony. In 2014, after police in Auburn, Washington, refused to investigate their missing person report, Upham's family and other Muckleshoot Tribe members found her dead at the bottom of a cliff. Her off-screen life reflects the disenfranchisement of Indigenous women, who experience the highest levels of sexual violence in the United States. One in three Indigenous women is sexually assaulted; 67 percent of these assaults are perpetrated by non-Natives.

References

Adams, S. (2008), "Review: 'Wendy and Lucy'," *Los Angeles Times*, 12 December. Available online: https://www.latimes.com/entertainment/la-et-wendy12-2008dec12-story.html.

Alexander, M. (2012), *The New Jim Crow: Mass Incarceration in the Age of Colorblindness*, New York: The New Press.

Austin, T. and A. Koutsourakis (2020), "Introduction," in T. Austin and A. Koutsourakis (eds.), *Cinema of Crisis: Film and Contemporary Europe*, Edinburgh: Edinburgh University Press, pp. 1–24.

Badley, L. (2016), "Neo-neorealism and Genre in Contemporary Women's Indies," in L. Badley, C. Perkins, and M. Schreiber (eds.), *Indie Reframed: Women's Filmmaking and Contemporary American Independent Cinema*, Edinburgh: Edinburgh University Press, pp. 121–37.

Basu, L. (2018), *Media Amnesia: Rewriting the Economic Crisis*, London: Pluto Press.

Belle, E. (2020), "Yes, 9/11 Did Cause an Increase in Islamophobia," *Refinery 29*, 11 September. Available online: https://www.refinery29.com/en-us/2020/09/10019797/islamophobia- after-911-september-11-hate-crimes.

Bordwell, D. (2008), *Poetics of Cinema*, New York: Routledge.

Boyle, K. (2013), "The Imagination of Economic Disaster: Eco-catastrophe Films of the Great Recession," in K. Boyle and D. Mrozowski (eds.), *The Great Recession in Fiction, Film, and Television: Twenty-first Century Bust Culture*, Lanham, MD: Lexington Books, pp. 3–27.

Buckland, W. (2017), "The Craft of Independent Filmmaking: Editing in John Sayles' *Return of the Secaucus Seven* and *Baby It's You*," in G. King (ed.), *A Companion to American Indie Film*, Malden, MA: Wiley-Blackwell, pp. 407–29.
Curtin, M. and K. Sanson (2016), "Precarious Creativity," in M. Curtin and K. Sanson (eds.), *Precarious Creativity: Global Media, Local Labor*, Berkeley: University of California Press, pp. 1–18.
Deleyto, C. (2016), *From Tinseltown to Bordertown: Los Angeles on Film*, Detroit: Wayne State University Press.
Ebert, R. (2006), "Sisyphus in New York," *RogerEbert.com*, 19 October. Available online: https://www.rogerebert.com/reviews/man-push-cart-2006.
Ebert, R. (2008), "Smuggling Humans as a Part-time Job," *RogerEbert.com*, 14 August. Available online: https://www.rogerebert.com/reviews/frozen-river-2008.
Ebert, R. (2009), "A Girl and Her Dog on the Lonesome Road," *RogerEbert.com*, 28 January. Available online: https://www.rogerebert.com/reviews/wendy-and-lucy-2009.
Elsaesser, T. (2004), "The Pathos of Failure: American Films in the 1970s: Notes on the Unmotivated Hero," in T. Elsaesser, A. Horwath, and N. King (eds.), *The Last Great American Picture Show: New Hollywood Cinema in the 1970s*, Amsterdam: Amsterdam University Press, pp. 279–92.
Farber, S. (2007), "Empty: Review of *August Evening*," *The Hollywood Reporter*, 9 July. Available online: https://www.hollywoodreporter.com/movies/movie-reviews/august- evening-157969/.
Frame, G. (2020), "The Cultural Politics of Jennifer Lawrence as Star, Actor, Celebrity," *New Review of Film and Television Studies* 18 (3), pp. 345–68.
Gilbey, R. (2009), "Film of the Month: *Frozen River*," *Sight and Sound*. Available online: http://old.bfi.org.uk/sightandsound/review/5056
Gomer, J. (2020), *White Balance: How Hollywood Shaped Colorblind Ideology and Undermined Civil Rights*, Chapel Hill, NC: University of North Carolina Press.
Grieveson, L. (2018), *Cinema and the Wealth of Nations: Media, Capital, and the Liberal World System*, Berkeley: University of California Press.
Kampf, L. and I. Sen (2006), "History Does Not Repeat Itself, but Ignorance Does: Post-9/11 Treatment of Muslims and the Liberty-Security Dilemma," *Humanity in Action*. Available online: https://www.humanityinaction.org/knowledge_detail/history-does-not-repeat- itself-but-ignorance-does-post-9-11-treatment-of-muslims-and-the-liberty-security- dilemma/.
King, G. (2014), *Indie 2.0: Change and Continuity in Contemporary American Indie Film*, London: I. B. Tauris.
Miller, A. (2013), "Real-to-Reel Recessionary Horrors in *Drag Me to Hell* and *Contagion*," in K. Boyle and D. Mrozowski (eds.), *The Great Recession in Fiction, Film, and Television: Twenty-first Century Bust Culture*, Lanham, MD: Lexington Books, pp. 29–49.
Murphy, J. J. (2007), *Me and You and Memento and Fargo: How Independent Screenplays Work*, New York: Continuum.
Naremore, J. (1988), *Acting in the Cinema*, Berkeley: University of California Press.

Negra, D. and Y. Tasker (2014), "Introduction: Gender and Recessionary Culture," in D. Negra and Y. Tasker (eds.), *Gendering the Recession: Media and Culture in an Age of Austerity*, Durham, NC: Duke University Press, pp. 1–30.

O'Malley, S. (2016), "Spa Night," *RogerEbert.com*, 19 August. Available online: https://www.rogerebert.com/reviews/spa-night-2016.

Ospina León, J. S. (2020), "(In)visibilities: Iñárritu's Cinema and the Melodramatic Regime," *Journal of Cinema and Media Studies* 59 (2), pp. 43–61.

Rainer, P. (2008), "Review: 'August Evening'," *The Christian Science Monitor*, 6 September. Available online: https://www.csmonitor.com/The-Culture/Movies/2008/0906/p25s02- almo.html.

Roediger, D. R. (2008), *How Race Survived US History: From Settlement and Slavery to the Obama Phenomenon*, New York: Verso.

Savlov, M. (2008), "August Evening," *The Austin Chronicle*, 10 October. Available online: https://www.austinchronicle.com/events/film/2008-10-10/683291/.

Scott, A. O. (2008), "This (New) American Life: Movie Review: 'Wendy and Lucy'," *New York Times*, 9 December. Available online: https://www.nytimes.com/2008/12/10/movies/10wend.html.

Stevens, D. (2006), "Sob Stories: The Quiet Beauty of *Man Push Cart* and *Le Petit Lieutenant*," *Slate*, 7 September. Available online: https://slate.com/culture/2006/09/man-push-cart- and-le-petit-lieutenant-reviewed.html.

Stone, J. D. (2013), "Horror at the Homestead: The (Re)Possession of American Property in *Paranormal Activity* and *Paranormal Activity II*," in K. Boyle and D. Mrozowski (eds.), *The Great Recession in Fiction, Film, and Television: Twenty-first Century Bust Culture*, Lanham, MD: Lexington Books, pp. 51–65.

Taylor, C. (2015), "Preface: Once Upon a Time in the West … L.A. Rebellion," in A. N. Field, J. C. Horak and J. N. Stewart (eds.), *L.A. Rebellion: Creating a New Black Cinema*, Berkeley: University of California Press, pp. ix–xxiv.

Torchin, L. (2020), "Themed Playlist: Embodying Capitalism and Its Abuses," *Playlist Initiative: Resources*, Scotland: Centre for Screen Cultures, University of St. Andrews, 27 March. Available online: https://screenculture.wp.st-andrews.ac.uk/2020/03/27/themed-playlist- embodying-capitalism-and-its-abuses/.

Turan, K. (2008), "Acting, Storytelling Warm 'Frozen River'," *Los Angeles Times*, 1 August. Available online: https://www.latimes.com/archives/la-xpm-2008-aug-01-et-river1- story.html.

Zaniello, T. (2020), *The Cinema of the Precariat: The Exploited, Underemployed, and Temp Workers of the World*, New York: Bloomsbury.

PART II

Labor Crisis and the Neoliberal Subject

3

Limitless?

Neoliberal Femininity in the Post-recessionary Chick Flick

Beatriz Oria

"Look at me: I'm limitless." This is what Jennifer Lopez sings during the end credits of *Second Act* (Peter Segal 2018), in which she also stars.[1] The lyrics of this song ("Limitless") encapsulate some of the key ideas put forward in the movie and describe a very specific model of aspirational femininity for the twenty-first century: to succeed, a woman has to be resilient ("I'll never give up"), self-sufficient ("I am a woman who roars, nobody opened my doors"), ambitious and assertive ("I am a woman saying I want more, so give me what I'm asking for"), and ready to tailor her identity to the circumstances ("I told myself I had to be a different someone"). These lyrics are remarkably similar to Daya's "Forward Motion," the closing credits theme of *Late Night* (Nisha Ganatra 2019), which also deals with topics of perseverance ("Keep pushing ahead . . . keep moving in forward motion"), adding an element of competitiveness ("Leave them under your wheels, kick them all to the curb"), and positive thinking ("Don't let the negative ever get in your way"). Tellingly, this song also includes the line "Know you got no limits," which basically sums up both films' main message.

Second Act and *Late Night* both feature women succeeding in the workplace against all odds. They offer a fantasy of empowerment in which the female individual can achieve any professional goal if she sets her mind to it because she is "limitless," regardless of systemic constraints. This chapter will consider how the trope of the working woman is represented after the economic crisis of 2008. More specifically, it will explore how the genre of the chick flick has adapted to a post-recessionary context by leaving aside concerns that have traditionally occupied a central position in the genre—such as romance—to focus on the individual project of the self. This dovetails with the individualistic and self-investing ethos of neoliberalism, thus constructing a new model of aspirational femininity for the twenty-first century based on a discourse of unfettered professional ambition, but also on an ideal of authenticity and emotionality often connected to female bonding.

Before the Great Recession female work onscreen was often trivialized and minimized. It was usually portrayed as a choice from which (white, middle- to upper-class) women could opt out if needed, and frequently subordinated to marriage, which was still presented as women's greatest achievement (Leonard 2007; Negra 2009). However, after the crisis, the depiction of female labor as a mere lifestyle choice was no longer plausible and women could not be unproblematically detached from their jobs anymore.

Still, the cinematic representation of the recession's impact on the genders is far from equal. While melodrama is commonly used to portray men as tragic victims of a crisis that provides them with opportunities for reinvention and personal growth, women's struggles are often comically approached, with work not being regarded as an issue of identity in the same way (Negra and Tasker 2013, 347). In general, the chick flick has maintained an escapist attitude in the face of economic hardship, refusing to acknowledge the reality of millions of people who do not have access to a decent paycheck, let alone to the high-flying jobs and hyper-consumerist lifestyles routinely featured in these films. On the other hand, as Negra and Tasker point out, those movies that do acknowledge the impact of the crisis for women tend to downplay it, as happens in *Bridesmaids* (Paul Feig 2011) or *What's Your Number?* (Mark Mylod 2011). These films present professional struggles as a manifestation of the characters' relationship failures and solve them through heterosexual coupling as a means of economic and ideological stabilization (Negra and Tasker 2013, 351). The problem of female unemployment is thus framed by the conventions of romantic comedy, while films depicting men's redundancy carry more serious undertones and give more prominence to the reconstruction of male identity in the professional sphere.

While I agree with the idea that the recession-era chick flick has often ignored economic concerns or foreclosed them altogether through couple formation, I would like to argue in this chapter that the 2010s have witnessed a considerable output of chick flicks in which the development of female identity in connection with professional and personal accomplishments has grown in importance irrespective of romance. As Betty Kaklamanidou points out in her book *Genre, Gender and the Effects of Neoliberalism*, the success of the romantic union started to become directly associated to financial security in the romantic comedy of the 2000s (2013, 152). However, from the 2010s onward, the genre seems to have strengthened its commitment to the neoliberal values of personal achievement and accumulation of wealth, to the point of taking romance out of the equation almost completely in some cases. There is an increasing number of films in which romantic attachments play second fiddle to the characters' professional and personal goals, including titles such as *Morning Glory* (Roger Michell 2010), *In a World . . .* (Lake Bell 2013), *The Intern* (Nancy Meyers 2015), *How to Be Single* (Christian Ditter 2016), *Second Act, I Feel Pretty* (Abby Khon and Marc Silverstein 2018), *Late Night, Long Shot* (Jonathan Levine 2019), *Isn't It Romantic?* (Todd Strauss-Schulson 2019), *Always Be My Maybe* (Nahnatchka Khan 2019), *The High Note* (Nisha Ganatra 2020), and *Like a Boss* (Miguel Arteta 2020). If the happy endings of the chick flicks considered by Negra and Tasker can be regarded as "neoliberal manoeuvres that emphasize the social security of coupledom" (2013, 352), most of the movies mentioned here seem to go one step further in their promotion of neoliberal ideology, downplaying intimacy as a source of fulfillment for the individual and emphasizing professional achievement as their characters' raison d'être instead. This is presented as an attainable goal for all women, no matter their race or socioeconomic background, as these films tend to feature greater diversity in the representation of their characters, thus moving from the postfeminist "white 'chick' backlash that denies class, avoids race, ignores (older) age, and 'straight'-jackets sexuality" (Holmlund 2005, 117) to an apparently more inclusive era.

Of course, the trope of the independent working woman has been present in the chick flick for a long time. Films like *Nine to Five* (Colin Higgins 1980), *Baby Boom* (Charles Shyer 1987), *Broadcast News* (James L. Brooks 1987), or *Working Girl* (Mike Nichols 1988) opened the scope of representation for women in the genre, deploying the workplace as more than a mere backdrop for their quest for happiness. Much has been written about this in the past (Tasker 1998; Levinson 2012), but the figure of the post-recessionary working woman is yet to be examined. This chapter explores how this trope is portrayed in post-2008 chick flicks, considering the impact that neoliberal ideology has had on cinematic representations of femininity and intimacy. This new cycle of films is arguably related to the surge of the "self- centered rom-com" (Oria 2021a), a recent trend in contemporary romantic comedy in which romance is subordinated to the development of the protagonist's self-identity and individual potential. This chapter will analyze this new generic inflection in connection with a post-recessionary context characterized by the infiltration of neoliberal rationality in all aspects of society. It argues that the contemporary chick flick's retreat into the self and away from the couple can be partly explained by the intensification of a neoliberal discourse that has permeated the intimate realm. In a context in which individualism runs rampant, there is a growing number of chick flicks veering toward a less romantic paradigm, constructing a female subject partially or fully imbued with a self-investing ethos that puts personal interest ahead of couplehood in the name of self-realization.

These films are increasingly numerous and, obviously, they are not all the same. Many of them include a romantic interest whose centrality varies in importance depending on each particular case. However, all the aforementioned movies tend to place most of the narrative weight on their characters' careers and self-realization as individuals. To illustrate this, I have chosen two movies that I consider representative of this cycle: *Second Act* and *Late Night*. The former tells the story of Maya (Jennifer Lopez), a forty-year-old Latina woman of poor upbringing working as an assistant manager at a supermarket. Maya has been striving for a promotion during the last six years but she is finally rejected because she does not have a college degree. Devastated, she quits her job and starts a successful corporate career thanks to the fake online persona her godson creates for her. Despite her bogus credentials, Maya proves to be deserving of the job, gaining everyone's love and trust in the process, including Zoe's (Vanessa Hudgens), one of the company's vice presidents, who turns out to be the daughter she gave up for adoption when she was sixteen.

Late Night, on the other hand, follows Molly (Mindy Kaling), an Indian woman working at a chemical plant whose dream of becoming a comedy writer comes true when she gets a position at the acclaimed Katherine Newbury's (Emma Thompson) late-night talk show. Being a diversity hire, the film focuses on Molly's struggle to prove her worth in a hostile, white, all-male environment. She also faces another challenge: rescuing the show from cancellation. Initially disliked by Katherine, Molly will manage to bond with her and help her save her career.

Second Act and *Late Night* have been selected for analysis because of their many points in common: both feature a dyad of female characters as protagonists, one of whom is non-white and manages to succeed professionally against all odds despite her gender, race, and humble socioeconomic background. Both movies downplay romance in favor of professional accomplishment, propose the idea of reinventing the self through good choices and hard work, and put forward a discourse of authenticity and emotional disclosure linked to female bonding as the road to success.

"The Only Thing Stopping You, Is You": The Neoliberal Subject

Both *Late Night* and *Second Act* revolve around the promise of success through personal drive. In *Late Night*, Molly is presented as a goal-oriented, tireless worker. Her personal motto, "Never give up," hangs from the wall of her otherwise impersonal office. With no friends or romantic partner, she is entirely devoted to her dream of becoming a comedy writer. *Second Act*'s protagonist, on the other hand, does have a boyfriend and is integrated in a close-knit community of female friends. Despite this, the movie hinges more prominently on the individualistic ethos of self-responsibility to reach one's goals.

Maya comes from a poor background. Her parents died when she was young, and she was raised by her grandmother. She got pregnant at sixteen and, being homeless, she was forced to give up the baby for adoption a few months after she was born. She did not even get to graduate from high school. For the last fifteen years she has been working at a big-box store, first as a checker and later as assistant manager. When she fails to get the promotion she deserves because of her lack of formal qualifications she is distraught. The comfort provided by her friends and the news that her boyfriend, Trey (Milo Ventimiglia), is about to propose are not enough to cheer her up. So, unlike previous recession-era chick flicks in which heterosexual coupling makes up for the heroine's economic precariousness, Maya's successful personal life does not compensate for her lack of professional advancement. In this way, the beginning of the film seems to criticize a system in which the cards have been dealt from the start, but it will end up providing a fantasy of upward social mobility fueled by the neoliberal idea of self-responsibility.

Second Act explores what it is that defines the individual and, more importantly, how the self can be changed and "optimized." Determined to prove she is "more than a title" (or lack thereof), we follow Maya in her quest for an identity upgrade. Remarkably, this does not include marriage or children. When her partner finally proposes she rejects him because he wants a family and she does not, arguing it is not the right time. After the breakup, she will go on to thrive professionally, becoming a consultant for the skincare line of an international company thanks to the fake online self her godson, unbeknownst to her, has created.

During the rest of the movie we see Maya rise to the top thanks to her talent, hard work, and determination. She succeeds because she takes active control of her life and makes the right decisions (as opposed to the poor choices she made when she was younger). She reinvents herself through a self-entrepreneurial ethos, going from "irredeemable" subject as economically deprived single mother to "responsible" capital-enhancing individual (Rottenberg 2018, 96). Catherine Rottenberg uses these terms to refer to the two types of women created by neoliberal feminism, qualifying them as "a small class of aspirational subjects who self-invest wisely and augment their capital value, and a large class of women who are expendable" (2018, 103–4). *Second Act* tells the story of Maya's transformation from the latter, a drag to economic growth, to the former, a valuable asset for the market in general and her company in particular.

This idea of becoming a "responsible" woman dovetails with Foucault's concept of *Homo oeconomicus*, a responsibilized citizen "who appropriately self-invest[s] in a context of macroeconomic vicissitudes" (Brown 2015, 84). *Homo oeconomicus* is apparently non-gendered, but, according to Wendy Brown, in practice it is usually male because "only performatively male members of a gendered sexual division of labor can even pretend to the kind of autonomy this subject requires" (2015, 103). *Homo oeconomicus* thrives thanks to the "care work" (Tronto 1993) provided by (paid or unpaid) domestic workers who take care of others in "households, neighborhoods, schools, and workplaces" (Brown 2015, 105). This task is mostly undertaken by women, whose role goes unacknowledged by the system while becoming *Homo oeconomicus*'s stepping stone and the invisible infrastructure upon which capitalist societies are built.

Maya did not have the personal freedom to become *Homo oeconomicus* when she was younger because she was tethered to a child and burdened by her dire socioeconomic circumstances, but now she is determined to become a responsibilized neoliberal subject. This implies rejecting motherhood because it would thwart her project again, which suggests that in the postrecessionary chick flick, economic autonomy takes prevalence over romance and family. The result is a grim prospect for traditional configurations of intimacy and family. As Brown argues, when—instead of becoming *femina domestica*—women choose to align themselves with the conduct of *Homo oeconomicus*, "the world becomes uninhabitable" (2015, 104) because the invisible infrastructure of care work that sustains it disappears.

But how does this gloomy idea fit in with the chick flick's lighthearted spirit? This conundrum is "magically" solved in *Second Act* by displacing the solution both onto the future, through Maya's promise about the possibility of a family next to Trey (which does not hinder her present professional prospects); and onto the past, through the reunion with her long-lost daughter. In this way, Maya is free to pursue the neoliberal feminist ideal of "balance" between personal and professional life (Rottenberg 2018, 72) in the present thanks to both her past and future motherhood, which grants her a family and a romantic relationship without having to renounce her present career. *Second Act* therefore offers a fantasy solution for a very real dilemma faced today by contemporary professional women.

Through the movie we see Maya surmount all kinds of difficulties to complete a quasi-impossible assignment: to create a profitable, fully organic skincare product from scratch in a very limited time. Molly also faces a formidable task in *Late Night*: saving her boss's career while proving her own professional worth. In both cases, it is these goals that take precedence in the narrative, with their achievement playing the greatest role in the characters' happy endings. Also, in both cases, these tasks are presented as individual endeavors that can be accomplished only by means of self-determination, regardless of other factors. The idea that the key to happiness lies in the individual constitutes a comforting discourse in times of uncertainty. As Cabanas and Illouz (2019, ch. 2, sec. 5) argue, people are encouraged to withdraw into themselves in times of crisis. The consequences of the financial crisis still endure—many of them having become chronic—creating a sense of precariousness that fuels insecurity, powerlessness, and anxiety in the individual, who is faced with a situation whose underlying forces escape their control. The post-recessionary chick flick offers a fantasy of empowerment through a discourse of self-sufficiency that calls on individuals to look into themselves to find the self-discipline needed to weather the storm on their own in the face of economic turmoil.

This individualistic discourse may give hope to the viewer in a context of instability, but it also dispossesses the films of significant political potential. By proposing individual solutions to structural problems, the possibility of systemic change is diluted. Together with many other chick flicks, *Second Act* emphasizes the idea that it is the female individual that needs to change, not the status quo, and that she is responsible for her success or failure. The movie provides a fantasy of female empowerment via neoliberal ideals, disavowing the evidence that the gender imbalance is actually intensified by neoliberal policies (Brown 2015, 105–6). Maya's predicament is repeatedly shown as the product of her bad choices. In a letter she writes to her daughter she remarks: "I believe we create our own fate, that our lives are shaped by a series of choices . . . In the end it's up to us. We get to write our own story." The movie seems to disregard the fact that she probably did not have much of a choice as a homeless sixteen-year-old Latina single mother. She is punished by the film for this and redeemed only when she breaks down her old identity to create a new, more "productive" self.

Neoliberal feminism posits that it is by working through internal—not structural—obstacles that "women will then be able to muster the self-confidence necessary to push themselves forward toward their professional goals" (Rottenberg 2018, 65–6). This discourse is fully supported by the movie, which quickly forgets its initial critique of the status quo to endorse a neoliberal ideology explicitly voiced by Maya in the film's closing lines: "Every day you wake up and have a second chance to do whatever you want, to be whoever you want. The only thing stopping you, is you." This idea that success can be attained through willpower and self-monitoring replaces the need for collective struggle with personal agency, recasting issues of social justice as individual affairs and foregoing any critique of underlying structures of power.

The Real Self

The neoliberal idea of achieving personal goals through the active reshaping of one's individual self is common in many popular culture texts and genres.

This section will highlight what is specific about the aspirational female identity constructed by the post-recessionary chick flick, focusing on two interconnected discourses: authenticity and emotionality.

Second Act explores what it is that defines the individual and whether this identity is fixed and tethered to gender, class, race, and age, or whether it is something fluid that can be altered at will. As previously explained, the film leans toward the latter, but—unlike male-centric recessionary corporate dramas (Oliete-Aldea 2020, 8)—it also questions the ethics of certain choices. Maya's rise to the top is originally based on a lie. Her godson gives her a new identity and, despite her initial misgivings, she decides to go along with the deception. Through the movie, we see Maya slipping into her new self: "cross-class dressing" (Tasker 1998, 39) and faking upper-class skills, such as rowing and speaking Mandarin. However, in the second half of the film it is suggested that reinventing yourself professionally is acceptable, but lying about your true self to your loved ones constitutes a red line. Maya's personal relationships suffer because of her scheme: it sets her apart from her best friend, who accuses her of confusing her new self with who she really is, from her ex-partner, who puts down the end of their relationship to her dishonesty about her daughter, and from Zoe, who severs their bond when she learns the truth.

In the end, Maya comes clean in an emotional speech during the presentation of the organic skincare product she has created, revealing her identity is a fabrication:

> Maybe I did get where I am today because I wasn't afraid to tell the truth. Even if it hurts. And the truth is a lie . . . I thought it was what I had to do to get in to those doors . . . I gave you a version of me. But for better or for worse, I have to be who I really am, and I'm Maya Davilla, from Queens, New York. That's the real me. I'm sorry.

In this speech the film suggests that deception is not the right path to success if it entails hurting others, but it also highlights the idea that anyone can make it to the top despite their background if they reshape themselves wisely in the professional realm because, as "the truth is a lie" line suggests, there is room for reinvention. Tellingly, the result of Maya's hard work is a product called All in One, whose name alludes to her multifaceted individuality, while its all-natural composition points to Maya's will to reveal her true self.

Maya losing her job and her daughter on account of her deception implies that self-investment is encouraged in a context of fierce professional competitiveness but the individual's real essence and emotional self should never be completely erased. This entails a shift from previous representations of successful women in the workplace, who were forced to separate their real identity from their "public face" (Traube 1992, 103). This is not the case in the post-recessionary chick flick, in which the merging of the private and public selves is not only allowed but also actively promoted, becoming the neoliberal worker's main asset.

This discourse of authenticity and the blurring of the personal and the professional are also pivotal ideas in *Late Night*. They are personified by Molly, but they are even more clearly realized through the character of Katherine, who has been a renowned comedienne and talk show host for twenty-eight years. Having no family or friends—except for her aging and sick husband—she is successful, driven, and completely focused on her work. However, she is also portrayed as cold, ruthless, and out of touch with her feelings. On the brink of cancellation, she resorts to her writers—who she has never bothered to meet before—to give the show a makeover.

Despite her lack of experience, Molly holds the key to save her career: dealing with topics that are personal and more engaged with current events, including thorny subjects. At first Katherine rejects the idea, her self-righteousness preventing her from learning the lesson both Molly and a young YouTuber have to teach her: that "the best comedy comes from truth." Katherine will undergo a learning process in which her reluctance to show her true self onscreen will be slowly overcome. The turning point comes in a cathartic impromptu stand-up comedy performance she gives at a charity event hosted by Molly; when her impersonal jokes about social media are met by cold silence she turns to the topic of aging women in Hollywood and her painful coming to terms with the dawn of her career. The resounding success of her act opens her eyes to the fact that, to regain the audience's favor, she needs to reveal more of herself. From then onward, with Molly's help, her comedy gets more personal and she becomes more humane—both for the audience and for those around her. Her efforts are rewarded with higher ratings, but she is still bound to be replaced by a younger male comedian. She publicly resists the layoff and retaliation comes in the shape of a sex scandal in which she is slut-shamed for having a brief affair with one of her writers. Unwilling to address the issue in the show, Molly complains and Katherine criticizes the self-centered millennial obsession with catharsis.

This is followed by an emotive scene in which Katherine is forgiven by her husband. She is therefore not punished ideologically by the film for her misstep. Nor is she punished for her ambition either. When she regrets her lack of children or friends, her husband reminds her she never wanted them and that her true passion had always been her career. He encourages her to fight for it and, interestingly, this part of the conversation feels more relevant and emotional than the one about the affair. In this way, *Late Night* legitimizes Katherine's choices and her career-oriented personality as a valid blueprint of femininity for the contemporary working woman.

As happens in *Second Act*, the movie ends with an emotional speech in which, following Molly's and her husband's advice, Katherine addresses the scandal, admitting her infidelity. She fully discloses herself and, on the brink of tears, she makes a public declaration of love, not for her husband, but for her work: "This show is my source of energy. It's my life. It's my blood. Entertaining you has been the joy of my life." She also acknowledges her husband as being her only family, but the lines about the show seem much more poignant. Her true crime is having lost her passion for her craft, thus betraying her audience more seriously than her husband. Unexpectedly, her honesty is rewarded with her continuation in the show, because the public wants to keep on hearing "her take on the world." The film thus suggests that in a highly competitive job market, the key to success for women lies in baring the self and revealing one's true personality, rather than hiding it in the workplace.

This idea is present in other post-recessionary chick flicks (*Long Shot, I Feel Pretty, Isn't It Romantic?*) which also end with a cathartic speech that puts forward the idea that to attain success, women need to reveal their true (emotional) self. This identity has to be, not only authentic, but also self-made (reinvented if necessary as in Maya's and Katherine's case), and completely focused on one's career, untethered if necessary from family, lovers, and friends. These films also share the idea that confession brings redemption. Despite Katherine's mockery of millennials' need for catharsis, by proving Molly right and Katherine wrong, *Late Night* actually displays a millennial sensibility in its support of a discourse of emotional openness and self-disclosure realized through public acts of confession (Twenge 2014, 48), such as Maya's and Katherine's.

Finally, it should be highlighted that the post-recessionary chick flick's validation of women's professional ambition should not be equated with a disconnection from their "feminine" emotional side. Unlike contemporaneous corporate dramas, in which female characters are usually divided into successful professionals that are vilified, "masculinized," and coded as "anti-natural" in their heartless competitive conduct; and traditionally feminine women that are relegated to positions of inferiority with respect to their male colleagues (Oliete-Aldea 2020, 7), the chick flick offers a postfeminist ideal of balance that juggles both professional drive and emotionality.

Katherine is not punished by the film for rejecting family and friends over her career, not even for cheating on her husband. She is punished for her general emotional disconnection from the world around her. She is eventually redeemed when she finally gets in touch with her feelings, even if these feelings are for her job mainly. On the other hand, Maya and Molly seem to represent the right model of neoliberal femininity from the onset: focused on themselves and passionate about their careers but also in contact with their emotions, which shows mostly in Molly's commitment with social causes and Maya's close bond with those around her. As the next section will show, another important feature of the post-recessionary chick flick's protagonist lies in this emotional connectedness.

"I Need Your Talent": Happy Endings

As previously mentioned, the happy ending of the post-recessionary chick flick lies mostly in professional fulfillment: Katherine gets to keep her show, Molly becomes head monologue co-writer, Zoe leaves the company to pursue her true vocation, and Maya achieves success with her own business. Even though both Molly and Maya end up in a relationship, romance is conspicuously downplayed through the films, as happens in other examples of the genre like *Morning Glory*, *The High Note*, and *Like a Boss*.

Molly has no friends or partner; she is completely focused on her work. She briefly dates one of the writers (the one Katherine had the affair with), but he is depicted as a womanizer and the relationship never holds actual potential. The complications brought by this character to both Molly and Katherine suggest that romance represents a hindrance in women's quest for happiness rather than its cornerstone. Molly's and Katherine's happy endings are encapsulated in a coda that shows us a glimpse of their lives one year after Katherine's moving speech. The show is still on air, but things have changed: the atmosphere is more relaxed, Katherine smiles at people now, and the staff is more diverse. In this respect, it is worth noting that, by acknowledging the need for more diversity at the workplace, unlike *Second Act*, *Late Night* seems to display a certain awareness of the shortcomings in the discourse of individualism, as it tries to provide a feel-good fantasy of systemic change that has not taken place in reality yet. Still, the biggest change is of an individual nature and it concerns Molly, with the movie highlighting her personal achievement. When Katherine walks into the set, she is there with Tom (Reid Scott), one of the writers, which means that she has been promoted. A romantic relationship between them is implied by a casual kiss he plants on her shoulder. This is a blink-and-you-miss-it moment, quickly followed by Katherine stepping onto the stage to thunderous applause, with her husband conspicuously absent from the crowd. Both women's happy endings thus lie mainly in their professional achievement, with heterosexual coupling being completely de-emphasized.

Interestingly, it is the characters' eventual bonding that makes this denouement possible. Katherine and Molly's relationship goes through the same motions typically present in traditional romantic comedy, including the characters' initial antagonism, negotiation of positions, transformation, breakup, and reconciliation (Mernit 2000). After Katherine rejects Molly's idea of addressing the scandal on the show they have a fight, which ends up with Molly's dismissal. However, the narrative has made it clear that these two characters are meant to be together. Molly is offered another job, with a friendlier boss, but she still thinks about Katherine despite her meanness, and speaks about her as she would of a crush. The climactic reconciliation comes after Katherine's successful monologue. In a scene reminiscent of *Pretty Woman* (Garry Marshall 1990), Katherine goes all the way to Molly's humble neighborhood in her chauffeured car to get her back. Her apology is heartfelt and is interpreted by Molly—and by the rom-com connoisseur—as a declaration of love: "I need your pushiness and lack of boundaries. I need the annoying way you light up every time I walk into the room. It makes me feel like I'm not a fraud. But mostly, I need your talent." This can be read as an intense moment of female bonding that fills the void left by heterosexual coupling in the genre, but it also brings closure to Molly's quest, with her individual worth being finally validated by one of the highest authority figures in the business. She has managed to prove she is more than a racial quota.

With their focus on the self rather than on the couple, *Late Night* and *Second Act* deploy the conventions of the "self-centered romantic comedy" (Oria 2021a), a new cycle of films in which romance is subordinated to professional and/or personal fulfillment. The increasing number of chick flicks that participate in this trend may be connected with the context of economic precariousness in which the movies are inscribed. Romantic comedy experienced a creative slump during the 2010s, which is reflected on its poor output during this decade. This can be partly attributed to the lack of real obstacles keeping the lovers believably apart in the present. In the era of online dating and hook-up culture, finding a partner seems easier than finding a job. Therefore, in the "post-romantic era" (Oria 2021b) the quest for professional fulfillment comes across as a much more engaging subject matter for the cynical—and impoverished—millennial generation than the endlessly repeated boy-meets-girl plot.

Millennials' apparent lack of engagement with romance may be partly explained by the precarious living conditions many of them experience. As Jennifer M. Silva argues, "feeling overburdened by the task of taking care of themselves in a precarious labor market and unable to meaningfully plan for the future, for them commitment becomes yet another risk" (2013, 78). In a context in which the individual is left to fend for herself in the turbulent waters of the risk society, intimacy "is simply one demand too many on top of the already excessive demands of the post-industrial labor force" (66). In this context women embrace neoliberal ideals of self-sufficiency and personal responsibility that put the self on a pedestal: as Beck and Beck-Gernsheim (1995) argue, the more uncertain living conditions become, the more individualistic we become, and the greater our need for self-realization.

The post-recessionary chick flick's dwindling interest in romance does not mean its characters are cut off from their feelings, though. As previously highlighted, emotion is a key defining factor for its heroines, but it is channeled differently: first, through their passion for their job, and second, through sorority. These two ideas are often intertwined: I have pointed out how in *Late Night*, it is Molly and Katherine's eventual bond that makes possible the continuation of the show, and therefore, their careers. Something similar happens in *Second Act*: Maya's corporate success is greatly indebted to Zoe, who helps her with the development of her product. Significantly, her support comes before they learn of their family connection, when they are still rivals competing to create a profitable product for the company. When Maya comes clean, she is fired and Zoe leaves for London to finish her degree, cutting her off. Maya's happy ending does encompass her reconciliation with Trey, but the emphasis lies mostly on getting Zoe's affection back, and also on reinventing herself professionally once more. In a coda reminiscent of *Late Night*, we see Maya one year later, having started a new successful business based on her years of experience in sales. She is the head of the company, but she has partnered with her girlfriends. Having Maya finally achieve success through entrepreneurship feels like the ultimate expression of individuality and neoliberal self-responsibility: being her own boss, she is entirely self-reliant now. And equally important, she no longer has to pretend to be what she is not. Dressed in casual clothes, her attire matches that of her business partners, who are coded as working-class, just like her. Maya is a self-sufficient subject now, but she is integrated in a solid network of female friends, whose support has been crucial for her individual accomplishments.

In this way, even if these films' individualism seems to be at odds with communal values, their positive portrayal of relationships among women distinguishes them from previous chick flicks set in the workplace, such as *Working Girl* or *The Devil Wears Prada* (David Frankel 2006), in which female characters are pitted against each other in their climb of the corporate ladder. In 2009 Angela McRobbie argued that feminism was being replaced by an "aggressive individualism" (2009, 5) and its empty discourse of empowerment, which actually disempowers women (2009, 45). I do not dispute this claim; it is obvious that feminism is still under vicious attack from the individualist values of neoliberalism—among other fronts—but the positive view of sisterhood displayed by films such as *Second Act*, *Late Night*, *Like a Boss*, *How to Be Single*, or *In a World...* could hopefully point at a timid beginning for the blossoming of a more feminist chick flick in the mainstream market, even if still subsumed by the values of neoliberalism.

Conclusion: Truly Limitless?

This chapter has analyzed two movies of the late 2010s that I consider representative of the post-recessionary chick flick. By the end of the decade the 2008 economic crisis is allegedly left behind, but its impact is still deeply felt. One of its most obvious effects has been the re-entrenchment of neoliberal rationality, which permeates most aspects of everyday life, including the intimate realm. The chick flick has responded to this new climate by reworking its conventions, shifting the spotlight from the couple to the self: in a context of economic instability, some of these films choose to present romance as a safe haven of security for the individual, but there is a significant group of chick flicks that seem to go a step further in their glorification of the individualistic values of neoliberalism by presenting professional achievement as women's true locus of self-fulfillment in the face of precarity.

The strengthening of the neoliberal ethos in the chick flick breeds a model of identity for aspirational women that is self-made, self-reliant, and goal-oriented, and therefore perfectly in tune with a context of increasing competitiveness. However, it is not completely detached from traditional blueprints of femininity, as it relies on emotional disclosure and—equally important—on a discourse of authenticity that sets the female worker apart from the herd. Paradoxically, it also leans on sisterhood for the achievement of success. This seems to be at odds with neoliberalism' individualistic ethos, but the positive view of relationships between women might point to a more feminist turn in a genre that had often sowed dissension among female characters in the workplace. On the other hand, the assumption that willpower equals success regardless of gender, race, age, and class factors, together with the individualistic discourse of hard work and self-responsibility, often make these films oblivious to systemic constraints, proposing individual solutions for structural problems and therefore defanging them of any real oppositional potential. By presenting their heroines as role models the post-recessionary chick flick naturalizes the neoliberalization of female identity, an identity that does not easily translate to the everyday economic reality of millions of women all around the world. Maya and Molly may be limitless, but their audiences will probably need more than a catchy tune in the face of precarity.

Note

1 This research was supported by the Spanish Ministerio de Ciencia e Innovación (Grant PID2020-114338GB-I00) and Gobierno de Aragón (Grant H23_20R).

References

Beck, U. and E. Beck-Gernsheim (1995), *The Normal Chaos of Love*, Cambridge: Polity Press.
Brown, W. (2015), *Undoing the Demos: Neoliberalism's Stealth Revolution*, New York: Zone Books.
Cabanas, E. and E. Illouz (2019), *Manufacturing Happy Citizens: How the Science and Industry of Happiness Control Our Lives*, Cambridge: John Wiley and Sons.
Holmlund, C. (2005), "Postfeminism from A to G," *Cinema Journal* 44 (2), pp. 116–21.

Kaklamanidou, B. (2013), *Genre, Gender and the Effects of Neoliberalism: The New Millennium Hollywood Rom Com*, London and New York: Routledge.

Leonard, S. (2007), "'I Hate My Job, I Hate Everybody Here.' Adultery, Boredom, and the 'Working Girl' in Twenty-First-Century American Cinema," in L. Spigel (ed.), *Interrogating Postfeminism*, Durham and London: Duke University Press, pp. 100-31.

Levinson, J. R. (2012), *The American Success Myth on Film*, New York: Palgrave Macmillan.

McRobbie, A. (2009), *The Aftermath of Feminism: Gender, Culture and Social Change*, London: Sage.

Mernit, B. (2000), *Writing the Romantic Comedy*, New York: HarperCollins.

Negra, D. (2009), *What a Girl Wants? Fantasizing the Reclamation of Self in Postfeminism*, London and New York: Routledge.

Negra, D. and Y. Tasker (2013), "Neoliberal Frames and Genres of Inequality: Recession-Era Chick Flicks and Male-Centred Corporate Melodrama," *European Journal of Cultural Studies* 16 (3), pp. 344-61.

Oliete-Aldea, E. (2020), "Transnational Representation of a Gendered Recession in Corporate Dramas," *European Journal of Cultural Studies*, 27 May, pp. 1-16.

Oria, B. (2021a), "'I'm Taken … by Myself': Romantic Crisis in the Self-Centered Indie Rom-Com," *Journal of Film and Video* 73 (1), pp. 3-17.

Oria, B. (2021b), "We Found Love in a Hopeless Place: Romantic Comedy in the Post- Romantic Era," in M. San Filippo (ed.), *After "Happily Ever After": Romantic Comedy in the Post-Romantic Age*, Detroit: Wayne State University Press, pp. 27-46.

Rottenberg, C. (2018), *The Rise of Neoliberal Feminism*, New York: Oxford University Press.

Silva, J. M. (2013), *Coming Up Short: Working-Class Adulthood in an Age of Uncertainty*, Oxford: Oxford University Press.

Tasker, Y. (1998), *Working Girls: Gender and Sexuality in Popular Cinema*, London and New York: Routledge.

Traube, E. G. (1992), *Dreaming Identities: Class, Gender, and Generation in 1980s Hollywood Movies*, Boulder: Westview.

Tronto, J. (1993), *Moral Boundaries: A Political Argument for an Ethic of Care*, New York: Routledge.

Twenge, J. M. (2014), *Generation Me—Revised and Updated: Why Today's Young Americans Are More Confident, Assertive, Entitled—and More Miserable Than Ever Before*, New York: Atria.

4

Screening Recessions through a Gendered Lens

Nostalgic and Critical Revisions of the Past from the Post-2008 Crisis Perspective

Elena Oliete-Aldea

The first decades of the new millennium have witnessed an extensive use of the buzzword *crisis* to describe the current conjuncture. Inaugurated by the 9/11 terrorist attacks, and followed by the 2008 global financial crash, the twenty-first century has been characterized by a series of globally intertwined, political, democratic, environmental, migratory, health, and social crises. This "all-embracing crisis," as Lawrence Grossberg (2015) described it, has actually revealed a crumbling system whose cracks had originated a few decades ago and has also entailed a series of competing discourses in the socioeconomic, political, and cultural domains.

David Runciman identifies some problems to the temporal tension of the concept of crisis as, on the one hand, an "acute moment of change" and, on the other, an "ongoing state of uncertainty" (2016, 4). The time frame of the crisis will depend on who is experiencing it—"experiential problem"—and the extent to which individuals are suffering its effects—"perspectival problem": "the further one is from a crisis, the shorter it is likely to appear" (6). Janet Roitman also points out that crisis is a signifier for a decisive moment which designates a historical conjuncture while, at the same time, it has been constructed as a "condition" (2016, 18). This idea of ongoing crisis, also described by Bauman and Bordoni as a "state of crisis" (2014), seems to be an oxymoron which construes crisis as "a non-locus from which to signify contingency and paradox" which, according to Roitman (2016, 19), may enable a "blind-spot for the production of knowledge."

As sites of (re)production of cultural discourses, cinematic texts may also include personal and social experiences of the conjuncture into which narratives are articulated; hence, the analysis of cinematic texts may provide alternative ways to which the multilayered 2008 crisis was understood and experienced or even constructed by certain groups. In this chapter, I propose to give first an overview of the articulation of class and gender in cinematic productions of the Great Recession in order to subsequently analyze Todd Haynes's *Mildred Pierce* (2011) as a TV product that cleverly links the Great Depression and the Great Recession. Through the critical lens of what Fred Davies has called "reflexive nostalgia" (1979), the miniseries challenges twenty-first-century discourses on recession and mancession by highlighting the "experiential" and "perspectival" aspects of crises.

In the aftermath of the 2008 crisis, a series of films reenacted the traumatic crash of financial markets in an attempt to understand its causes and consequences. Apart from documentaries, fiction films attempted to provide the viewer with an accurate representation of the economic meltdown. Some of these "Financial Crisis Films" (Oliete-Aldea 2018) raised critical views on an economic system that had allowed the accumulation of wealth and power in the hands of the financial elite.[1] Nonetheless, by focalizing the events through financial executives, these films also allowed spectators to empathize with them. With an almost all-male cast, many of these corporate dramas were male melodramas that focused on men's troubles. On the one hand, these films depicted competitive *male* cultural values and criticized the so-called *bro culture* of Wall Street as one of the causes of the crisis (Ho 2018). On the other hand, the lack of alternatives other than saving the too-big-to-fail banks actually tied the narratives to a perpetuation of the neoliberal-cum-patriarchal system. What is more, the dim recessionary future actually encouraged a nostalgic return to an idealized past when capitalism was based on tangible production instead of volatile speculation. Such nostalgic discourses tended to be accompanied by a yearning for the traditional heterosexual family structure, with a male partner as the provider and a supportive wife creating an emotional shelter at home.

While the subprime mortgage crisis left many people without a place to live in, most executives in these financial crisis films did have houses, but lacked homes, unless female characters embraced their roles of supportive wives and mothers to provide a happy ending to the movie.[2] Films such as *The Company Men* (John Wells 2010) and *Wall Street: Money Never Sleeps* (Oliver Stone 2010) nostalgically opposed what was regarded as stable societies in the past, based on productive Fordist capitalism, to the instability of present times due to the speculative dimension of twenty-first-century late capitalism (Bauman 2007, 3). According to Kinkle and Toscano (2011, 45), such harking back to the booming years of the US economy went hand in hand with a longing for a traditionally patriarchal social structure in which the family was a pillar and refuge from any economic problem. Many films depicting the Great Recession actually reinforce this contrast with lighting and mise-en-scène: homely spaces are usually tinged with warm colors, while workspaces tend to appear in cool shades of grey and blue.

The gender backlash implicit in the nostalgic ingredient of these films went hand in hand with the "mancession" discourses that proliferated during the post-2008 crisis years (Rosin 2010; Coonz 2012). Mancession referred to white- and blue-collar male suffering and precarity due to high unemployment rates, which was interpreted as an unequivocal sign of the failures of the current economic system. Other less favored groups, such as women, ethnic minorities, and immigrants, also suffered from the consequences of the economic crisis, yet that was taken for granted. When visible, these groups were actually blamed for the lack of work for the white, working, and middle-class man and for the debt crisis caused by public spending. As Negra and Tasker (2014) point out, many popular culture texts actually naturalized gender inequality, dismissing women's experience of the recession. Therefore, the term "mancession" privileged the white male perspective and experience of the crisis.

Following Runciman and Roitman's critique of the overuse of the term "crisis," Strolovitch questions the political construction of the mancession, which disregards racialized and gendered inequalities (2013). According to the National Bureau of Economic Research, the Great Recession started in December 2007 and employment started to recover in March 2011. This perspectival and experiential time span of the recession clearly privileged a white male standpoint. Ethnic minorities and women had already experienced the mortgage crisis evictions long before 2007, and cuts in public sector employment (with posts mostly held by women and African Americans) went on long after the so-called hecovery (Strolovitch 2013, 167). Structural inequalities and persistent economic problems based on race and gender are, however, not to be considered as crises but normalized "bad things" within the system (169). The proliferation of mancession discourses in the United States were mainly due to the fact that it was the first time in history since the Great Depression that unemployment increased dramatically in the group of college-educated white men and they were unable to find another job anytime soon. As job losses occurred mainly in male-dominated sectors, many newspapers repeated the idea that female employment could surpass men's (Mulligan 2009). The fact that the terms "mancession" and "hecovery" were coined and overused in the media points to the normalization of female unemployment and job precarity.

Mancession talk focused not only on the *unexpected* failure of the economic system but also on the devastating psychological effects on middle-class white males who had grown up in a patriarchal capitalist socioeconomic system in which "this wasn't supposed to happen" (Marin 2011). Male unemployment problematizes male identity as breadwinner; hence, the economic crisis went hand in hand with the masculinity crisis of the "bread-loser" (Marin 2011).³ Instead of questioning the system, the fact that neoliberalism shifts the blame exclusively on the individual increased the devastating psychological effects of male unemployment. Consequently, the reversal of traditional socioeconomic gender roles caused resentment in many heterosexual couples and marriages. Mancession discourses were challenged by other critical voices which argued that not only the causes of the recession but also the measures implemented to overcome it were actually gendered and that the new scenario of precarity and vulnerability was hitting women and other minorities even harder (Peterson 2012; Griffin 2015; Walby 2015).

Todd Haynes's miniseries *Mildred Pierce* was broadcast in HBO in 2011, within this context of competing discourses in culture and the media. Departing completely from the immediacy of the financial crisis films released in those years, this production does question contemporary discourses on crisis and mancession, as well as the nostalgic longing for traditional gender roles, by establishing a dialogue between the Great Depression and the post-2008 recessionary period. In line with Haynes's previous films, *Mildred Pierce* offers a revision of bygone times. With an aesthetically appealing mise-en-scène, the series brings to the fore the inconsistencies of gender discourses of the 1930s, which are actually intertwined with the gender backlash of the 2010s. This five-episode miniseries, based on the 1941 homonymous novel by James M. Cain, tells the story of a divorced woman who, amid the Depression era, strives to provide a better life for herself and her daughters, but who ends up failing in both her business and family life due to her troubled relationship with Veda, her eldest daughter. With a carefully constructed mise-en-scène and an acclaimed performance by Kate Winslet as the main character, the series carefully depicts the contradictory feelings of Mildred as a woman, mother, and entrepreneur torn between her own desires and the demands of 1930s US society in terms of gender and class.

Having been considered an exponent of the New Queer Cinema, Haynes's aesthetics and narrative mode convey the perspective of the other, depicting the story from the margins, with characters whose gaze is enclosed within frames and glass panes. As Cook explains (2013), Haynes's contemporary adaptations of other literary and filmic sources are not mere reproductions or remakes but complex critical comments on an intertextual pastiche of memories from the past. Depicting a visually appealing past, based on collective cultural memories from the visual arts—cinema, painting, and photography—Haynes's narratives actually depart from the visual pleasures of the mise-en-scène in order to show the melodramatic suffering of characters that do not fit the social conventions of the time. It could be said that Haynes's miniseries *Mildred Pierce*, together with the films *Far from Heaven* (2002) and *Carol* (2015), allows the viewer to indulge in the nostalgic visual pleasures of an aesthetically appealing past while the melodramatic narrative crudely exposes the conflicts of the characters. Haynes uses the melodramatic mode of the novel not just as an aesthetically excessive portrayal of the classical conflict between the individual and society but as a revision of what was silenced in the past and still resonates in the present. In so doing, Depression-era *Mildred Pierce* establishes a dialogue with the twenty-first-century recession to open up the viewers' eyes to the tricks of selective memory and the dangers of an uncritical harking back to the past. *Mildred Pierce*'s explicit return to the past seems to be complicit with the nostalgic discourses of financial crisis films; however, the narrative events and the evolution of the main character contradict mancession discourses by privileging the perspective of a woman struggling against an invisible and silenced "shecession."

As a TV product, *Mildred Pierce* appears to be a period drama set out to indulge the spectator into the visual pleasures of an aesthetically beautiful women's picture set in the past. Haynes, nevertheless, prevents the audience from lingering on nostalgic escapism, constantly undermining any longing for safety and stability. The miniseries proposes a constant blurring of boundaries, which accounts for a critical portrayal of the past when intersected with discourses on contemporary crises at the time when it was broadcast. Haynes offers a transmedia narrative in which novel, film, and critical theory intersect, questioning the nature of the cinematic text itself from the very credit sequence.[4] Despite being a miniseries broadcast on television, the credit sequence presents it as a *film* by Todd Haynes, thus requesting the audience to watch it through the lens of auteur cinema, placing it in relation with Haynes's filmography. Furthermore, as an HBO production, audiences are reminded of the well-known slogan "it is not TV, it is HBO." It is therefore a miniseries which questions its very nature by claiming that it is not television but a kind of elongated film which enables spectators to explore the evolution of characters and events. By contradictorily pointing out what it is *not*, Haynes's miniseries creates a distancing effect in spite of its realistic style. Cook (2013, 379) draws attention to the fact that such *Verfremdungseffekt* is reinforced by the use of frames within frames, mirrors, and translucent glasses which mediate the gaze of the spectator and give a sense of opacity in its portrayal of the events.

Also, the credit sequence juxtaposes, in similar font, Kate Winslet's name with that of the eponymous main character. If anything, Mildred Pierce epitomizes the female version of the American Dream, a persistent, practical woman who does not mind to "get her hands dirty" in order to earn a living. This character is ironically played by a well-known British actress. On the other hand, the US actors Morgan Turner and Evan Rachel Wood play the role of Mildred's daughter Veda (as a child and a young woman respectively), who is presented as an embodiment of European high-class tradition in terms of class and gender. Veda's first appearance in the miniseries resembles that of a character in a British heritage film, as an affected upper-class child using French words to explain what she did in her music lessons in the afternoon. For all the realist and careful depiction of the mise-en-scène, accurate psychological portrayal of the characters, and excellent performances of the cast, the audience is constantly reminded of the artificiality of the miniseries as a cultural product, the events portrayed being the result of memories of the past stemming from the intersection of intertextual sources that shape the perception of past experiences.

The miniseries starts with lively non-diegetic swing music as the screen shows extreme close-ups of a pair of hands kneading dough, soon to be transformed into mouth-watering cakes. The haptic visuality of the image creates the illusion that TV spectators can even smell and try a piece. Those hands, adorned with a ring and a bracelet, do not belong to a professional cook but to an idealized 1930s wife and mother cooking homemade food. The carefully arranged and beautiful mise-en-scène, recalling idealized vintage postcards, fuels feelings of nostalgia for suburban homely bliss and *authentic* homemade cakes in times of yore. The camera then shows a man—the husband—gardening the front yard, creating an image of cozy and traditional family life. He is seen through a translucent glass, therefore blurred, creating the impression of an old painting or photograph. As Hastie explains (2011, 28), those images of domestic bliss, enhanced with the music, are therefore filled up with the spectators' potential feelings of nostalgia for idealized happy family times.[5]

Mildred is shown, for the first time, through the glass window, with an expression that is far from happy. Her sweaty face shows her tired and concerned as she is making several cakes at the same time. Suddenly, Mildred's husband, Bert (Brian F. O'Byrne), enters the house and the noise of the slamming door startles Mildred. Then, the lively music fades away as the couple starts their conversation. The illusion of homely happiness is suddenly interrupted and spectators soon learn that, far from domestic bliss, the narrative starts with financial trouble and a marriage breakup. The nostalgic feeling of past safety and stability is thus abruptly stopped. Similarly to *Far from Heaven*, *Mildred Pierce* also opens up a window to an aesthetically beautiful past to immediately prevent spectators from indulging in that illusion of idealized past times that are evoked in people's minds from childhood memories or from images created by the media. The five episodes revolve around this double sense of reconstruction and deconstruction of the past.

When Bert comes inside the house, he says, "Well, don't think there's much else I can do around here." He has been working outdoors, in the garden, but his domestic duties end there. We will learn that he is unemployed due to the 1929 crash and, in spite of the fact that the family needs money and that he could have helped Mildred bake more cakes to be sold to their neighbors or even do household chores, working inside the house is out of the question. The gendered separation between public and domestic realms is clearly established from the very beginning. Yet, this strict division proves to be a source of distress for all the characters. Not only is Mildred trapped within the home, but the shot showing Bert in the front yard through the distorting glass traps him within the discourse of mancession: his jobless situation and consequent loss of his status as breadwinner cause psychological distress and damage his family relationships. Actually, after their separation, Bert visits his family on some occasions and enjoys moments of happy family life inside the house with Mildred and the children. It seems, therefore, that what separate the couple are precisely the rigid gendered socioeconomic structures. Bert resents Mildred in her role as provider, and Mildred resents Bert in his lack of action and his need to boost his masculine ego by taking a lover. As Hilton Als explains (2011, 4), the miniseries replicates Cain's novel by introducing this subplot:

> What ever happened to the white American male? The Depression has emasculated the cowboy, and his powerlessness has made him callow. Women like the resourceful Mildred have taken over as "man of the house." Indeed, when we first meet Mildred, she's working—making a cake for a neighbor—in order to put food on the family's table.
>
> Herbert resents her for this, and, in an effort to upstage her, he flaunts a kind of "bad boy" elusiveness:
>
> "You going to be home for supper?"
>
> "I'll try to make it, but if I'm not home by six don't wait for me. I may be tied up."

In spite of the almost eight decades that separate the Great Depression and Great Recession eras, the mancession discourses that resonate in this scene are but too similar to those uttered in the media at the time this miniseries was broadcast: Bert's frustration and Mildred's resentment actually mirror the situation many heterosexual couples endured in the 2010s.

This first scene cleverly depicts a twisted reversal of gender roles under the apparent image of a traditional socioeconomic family structure. While the main characters occupy their corresponding spaces according to their gender—the wife is placed inside the house while the husband is working outside—they are actually performing socioeconomic roles which subvert that traditional order: the man is performing unpaid domestic chores, as he is taking care of their front yard, while the woman is cooking cakes to make money. The ideological adjustment of the inversion of socioeconomic gender roles is what causes the main characters frustration and resentment. It is the constant effort of adapting themselves to the precarious economic situation while keeping up appearances in terms of class and gender that psychologically erodes their relationship.

In this very scene, while the main characters start an argument that leads to their divorce, the camera pans around the living room, showing the main sources of conflict that will spur the melodramatic dynamics: drawings and pictures of a failed construction plan of suburban houses called "Pierce Homes." The camera also shows photographs of the couple's wedding and of their daughters, Ray (Quinn McColgan) and Veda, the former shown in the beach and the latter in a significantly bigger portrait. The picture with the real estate firm establishes a house-home dichotomy and connects the main characters' context of the Great Depression with that of the Great Recession, as Bert's failed property business is what led the family to bankruptcy, recalling the 2007 subprime mortgage crisis.

Fiction films and documentaries addressing the Great Recession, such as *99 Homes* (Ramin Bahrani 2014) and *Capitalism: A Love Story* (Michael Moore 2009), have focused on an imagery of empty houses, evictions, and landscapes of buildings in decay while enhancing the importance of the family and the community. In contrast, Haynes portrays an apparently nostalgic image of the family home which is visually appealing, but which reveals itself as a source of conflict and unhappiness due to the ideological constrictions, paradoxes, and contradictions of neoliberal discourses. This tension actually contests the twenty-first-century mancession discourses that frequently evoked an idealized view of traditional families and homes in the past. The miniseries does not follow the contrast that other films have depicted in presenting workspaces in cold, bluish colors and cozy homes in warm hues. In *Mildred Pierce* both spaces have a continuum of greenish and reddish tones that actually highlight the melodramatic dimension of the film, by enhancing the emotions experienced by Mildred in both public and private spaces: red as a symbol of repressed trouble and dim green symbolically representing both death and renewal. The miniseries does offer a contrast between light and darkness as an intertextual reference to the film noir component of Michael Curtiz's 1945 adaptation, which also problematized the home as a place of safety and happiness. Lighter scenes are often associated with Mildred's brief happy moments outdoors or with spaces where she might find freedom as opposed to the social constrictions she finds as a woman in both public and private spheres. Furthermore, in comparing the Great Depression and the Great Recession, the miniseries refuses to focus on mancession by actually drawing attention to the "shecession." Mildred embodies the economic hardship and psychological trouble women have always undergone in trying to succeed in a capitalist and patriarchal society. As Mildred's friend, Lucy (Melissa Leo) tells her:

"You just joined the biggest army on earth. You're the great American institution that never gets mentioned on the Fourth of July: grass widow." With Mildred as the main character, Haynes, therefore, makes the "grass widow" visible and leaves Bert to play the role of a secondary character, thus leaving aside the mancession discourse embodied by Mildred's husband.

The picture of the Pierce Houses, which represents the economic crisis that spurs the family drama, is, by no chance, placed next to the pictures of the Pierce children. Showing different personalities, both Ray and Veda symbolically represent opposing ways of facing life: while the younger daughter, Ray is free from the ideological constrictions of gender and class, Veda is deeply imbued with them. The predominance of Veda's portrait anticipates the importance that this character will have in the narrative, symbolically erasing Ray's innocent principles of freedom and imposing her reactionary ideological discourses which will cause the main conflicts in the plot.

Ray is introduced as a lively happy child who has not yet been fully socialized in the gender and class norms of 1930s America. When she first appears, she proudly shows her mother the roller skates she has fixed up. While wearing comfortable clothes to be able to play outdoors, she jumps and moves freely, as opposed to the restrained movements of her elder sister. She shows her autonomy in fixing up her skates, without needing any older person—or man—to do it. This *free* movement outdoors, which her skates symbolize, recalls Mildred's need to get the car in order to move around the city to work and provide for the family. Actually, Mildred's first concern after Bert leaves the house is that he took the car, and she soon plots to get it back.

Ray brings happiness and conciliation in the scenes she appears. She likes dressing up, performing and singing for its own sake, not as part of a commercial transaction, as is Veda's case. In the scene when her father comes to visit, she is the one that brings domestic bliss by actually releasing the rest of the characters from their troubles. Veda, in an apparent act of politeness, offers a drink to her father. Mildred feels quite uncomfortable with the situation, as Veda's true intention is to imply that her mother keeps alcoholic drinks at home because she may also receive other male visitors. In contrast, Ray brings laughter by faking to be drunk—making fun of those social conventions her sister tries to impose. While Veda tries to behave as an adult, asking her father about the economic situation with pompous, artificial language, Ray's laughter is contagious, truly creating domestic happiness. Interestingly enough, Veda asks her father, "Can't you control her?" and Bert, driven by Ray's joy, abandons Veda's conversation to play with Ray, experiencing one of the few happy family moments in the series.

In another scene, Ray is dressed up combining a ballerina suit with a hat, with moustache painted on her face and using a banana as a gun, clearly defying gender roles. She says, "Look mum, I'm the public enemy!" and plays lively with the music coming from a radio in the background. Mildred stops the music abruptly and has an argument with her elder daughter, who has discovered her waitress uniform and tries to humiliate her. Ray mocks Veda's sophisticated manners, but she later asks her mother not to be mad at Veda in a conciliatory tone; "She just likes pretending," she adds. As a child, Ray is the only character that speaks overtly the truth. She regards social conventions as a performance, in the same way she may perform a drunkard or a gangster in her games. While bathing, she sings, "I'm always chasing rainbows," a song which will gain symbolism in subsequent episodes, as it will be sung by Mildred and Veda in different contexts. Ray is perhaps the only character that performs the lyrics with honesty. It would therefore not be too far-fetched to state that Ray is a challenging queer character. As opposed to Veda's sophistication, Ray's name, clothes, and attitudes are genderless; she disregards class and gender rules and, by so doing, brings moments of joy and freedom to the rest of the characters.

She, however, will die and, with her, any possibility of freedom and true happiness in social transgression. After her death, Veda's ideology will be imposed. The hope of "chasing rainbows" thus fades away. Even after her death, Ray's remembrance makes her parents embrace each other honestly and emotionally. In contrast, when Veda arrives from the funeral, she embraces her father while asking her mother again where she was when Ray became ill, with an accusing tone. Veda points out that Mildred was not at home, as a *good* mother should have been. Bert, Veda, and Mildred embrace, but Veda stands in the middle, symbolically separating them.

When Mildred comes back home after Ray's death, she embraces Veda in her bed, almost fusing with her. The camera is placed outside the room with the door ajar, and, as it slowly tracks back, the image of mother and daughter is framed more and more narrowly within a small space between the door and the wall, almost suffocating the characters, until only the wall is visible and the screen fades to black. Without Ray, Mildred remains stuck with Veda, who will impose her rules, demanding money from her mother while despising her for her work, trapping Mildred in a class and gender paradox. Veda's relationship with her mother reflects the double standards against which women were measured: Mildred has to be at home to take care of their daughters, yet, having become the breadwinner, Veda also demands expensive presents and an elitist education from her. In contrast, she celebrates her father's scarce appearances or less expensive presents. Cook points out that the miniseries downplays Mildred's incestuous sexuality and turns it into maternal love and sacrifice, which makes the spectator sympathize with her while shifting the blame onto Veda (2013, 383). This fact reinforces Haynes's deconstruction of the nostalgic backlash in the 2010s, when mancession and recessionary discourses advocated for a return of traditional gender roles. The home is presented as a troubled space for Mildred, and her maternal love actually brings her to her failure as a mother and downfall as a businesswoman.

Veda and Mildred represent opposite socioeconomic values. Mildred symbolizes the capitalist mode of production. She embodies the practical spirit of the American Dream: no matter how hard the times are, hard work will help overcome any difficulty. It is true that a bit of luck also helps, as she appears to be in the right place at the right time (a waitress is fired in the café where she is having lunch and she replaces her); but the series devotes several scenes to Mildred's search for a job and also to the physical and emotional difficulties she has to endure in order to earn a living. Mildred is practical and, even though she is careful with money, she is not obsessed about it. She enjoys other perks of her job: to please her customers and to have a good relationship with her employees and business partners. She does not pursue a life of luxury; she will go bankrupt because she will spend her money in pleasing Veda as well her lover Monty (Guy Pearce), who will become her second husband.

Veda, in contrast, is a self-centered, money-oriented character that represents the values of late capitalism: not only does she embody the unbridled individualist ethos promoted by neoliberalism, but also the speculative logic of finance-led capitalism; rather than making a profit through business activities that could also satisfy the needs and wants of consumers, speculation creates money for its own sake, for greed, or for power. This is what Veda stands for: instead of earning a living through work, she prefers to commodify her art and her body to reach the social status she longs for. Her role model is not her mother but Monty, a rent-seeker. The 1929 crash exposed the ills of speculation by showing the consequences of creating artificial bubbles in the market by manipulating the value of money. The 2008 meltdown exposed the volatility of leveraged global financial markets. Both the Great Depression and the Great Recession showed the devastating social consequences of speculation and the lack of opportunity and the vulnerability of hardworking individuals as opposed to parasitic rent-seekers, whose privileged position shielded them from the consequences of the economic crisis. *Mildred Pierce* clearly favors the perspective of Mildred, the working woman, as opposed to Veda and Monty, the money-obsessed, emotional speculators.

In terms of gender, Mildred defies the neoliberal patriarchal structures by transforming the traditional unpaid labor of housewives into a business venture (Wilson and Chivers Yochim 2015). She is happy as a businesswoman and also wants to enjoy family relationships, but the home will not be a source of bliss, rather the opposite. Although she briefly enjoys moments of happiness, matrimony and motherhood will become sources of grief for her. She can have a good relationship with Bert only after their separation and subsequent divorce, which legally frees her to set up her business. She is also able to enjoy sexual pleasure outside marriage with Monty (Hastie 2011, 30); nevertheless, once she and Monty get married, their relationship will become a nightmare, both emotionally and financially. The miniseries constructs Mildred as a female character that wants to be free both sexually and economically, move freely around the private and public spheres as men do, thus contravening the dominant values of her suburban environment. Even though she does find support in some of her male and female friends, it will be her daughter Veda the one that condemns her behavior. Veda is at ease with the traditional vision of women as sexual objects: she has no problem in faking a pregnancy to achieve her ends. The fact that the younger generation represents both a class and, especially, gender backlash as opposed to the more transgressive views of the older generation not only engages in the social changes of the 1930s and 1940s but also recalls the twenty-first-century mancession discourses.

The miniseries has a circular structure, as the ending places Mildred back where she started: she loses her business and remarries Bert. Apparently, she is trapped by her traditional gender role, which prevents her from having the linear narrative of the American Dream fulfilled. Nonetheless, the ending also presents a clear departure from Mildred's circumstances at the beginning of the narrative; it is in the last scene that Mildred is finally liberated from Veda's oppression. Mother and daughter have their last argument in Mildred and Bert's welcome party after their remarriage and honeymoon. After realizing Veda's commodification and speculation with her own voice, Mildred tells her to leave. Instead of seeking refuge and comfort at home with their friends, Mildred runs toward her former restaurant—where she has been offered to work again. Bert follows her and stands briefly under an older sign of "Pierce Homes," but moves away from it toward the sign "Mildred's." It is not in the home but in Mildred's workspace where husband and wife comfort each other. In contrast to his anger and resentment in the first scene, Bert plays now the role of an emotionally supporting husband who also rejects the values embodied by Veda—"To hell with her," he says. This reversal of traditional gender roles—Mildred is associated with the public realm of work and business while Bert is the caring and comforting spouse—provides an alternative vision of women's melodrama as opposed to the male melodramas of financial crisis films. The ending thus presents a clear departure from the beginning: the couple is reunited in terms of equality, as gender roles are now allowed to be reversed and they are freed from the socioeconomic patriarchal discourses that had split them apart. As Amber Jacobs states, Haynes exploits the genre of women's melodrama to allow female characters to experience "alternatives to dominant, oppressive, gendered psychological norms" (2012, 9). In spite of Mildred's apparent defeat, Haynes's miniseries remains "on the side of the alternative," rather than forcing the main character to return to the status quo (9). The circular narrative of the series may symbolically mirror history as moving in circles resembling a spiral rather than linear progress, thus contrasting the wishes and ambitions of a woman in the post-Depression years with the gender backlash and mancession discourses of the post-2008 crisis. For all the criticism of the system, male corporate dramas of the Great Recession remained paralyzed in a "state of crisis" and offered only a nostalgic harking back to an idealized past that reinforced the neoliberal there-is-no-alternative discourse (Bauman and Bordoni, 2014). In contrast, by revisiting the past, Haynes offers the twenty-first-century spectators several moments of resistance and opens up the ending with possible alternatives for the future.[6]

Notes

1. Films and TV movies that belong to this cycle are *Too Big to Fail* (Curtis Hanson 2011, HBO), *The Big Short* (Adam McKay 2015) and *The Wizard of Lies* (Barry Levinson 2017), *The Last Days of Lehman Brothers* (Michael Samuels 2009, BBC), and *The Guarantee* (Ian Power 2014), among others. See Oliete-Aldea (2018).
2. See Oliete-Aldea (2012, 2020).
3. See Mulligan (2009), Banerjee (2010), and Ostrowski (2011).
4. Pam Cook points at the indirect references to Michael Curtiz's version, as well as to the subsequent feminist criticism of the film, which Haynes was very much acquainted with. It is actually a "palimpsest [. . .] rewritten by multiple authors," which accounts for its intertextual and intersectional complexity (2013, 387).
5. Digital media such as Pinterest, Facebook, or Instagram have displayed both vintage and contemporary pictures of women creating domestic "havens" in times of precarity, which are set to sustain neoliberal social order by relying on the feminized domestic unpaid care work. These images "stabilize the happy family, as a myth, an inheritance, and a duty"; yet the unattainability of such a happy life recalls Berlant's "cruel optimism" (Wilson and Chivers Yochim 2015, 245).
6. I would like to thank the editors for their helpful comments and suggestions on this chapter. Research toward the writing of this chapter has been funded by the Spanish Ministry of Economy, Industry and Competitiveness, project no. FFI2017-82312-P.

References

Als, H. (2011), "This Woman's Work," *The New Yorker*, 28 March. Available online: https://www.newyorker.com/magazine/2011/03/28/this-womans-work.

Banerjee, P. (2010), "Feeling Our Way Out of the Mancession," *The Globe and Mail*, 8 December. Available online: https://search.proquest.com/docview/2385146356?account id=202933.

Bauman, Z. (2007), *Liquid Fear*. Cambridge and Malden: Polity Press.

Bauman, Z. and C. Bordoni (2014), *State of Crisis*, Cambridge and Malden: Polity Press.
Cook, P. (2013), "Beyond Adaptation: Mirrors, Memory and Melodrama in Todd Haynes's Mildred Pierce," *Screen* 54 (3), pp. 378–86.
Coontz, S. (2012), "The Myth of Male Decline," *New York Times*, 29 September. Available online: https://www.nytimes.com/2012/09/30/opinion/sunday/the-myth-of-male-decline.html.
Davis, F. (1979), *Yearning for Yesterday: A Sociology of Nostalgia*, New York: The Free Press.
Griffin, P. (2015), "Crisis, Austerity and Gendered Governance: A Feminist Perspective," *Feminist Review* 109, pp. 49–72.
Grossberg, L. (2015), *We All Want to Change the World: The Paradox of the U.S. Left (A Polemic)*, Creative Commons.
Hastie, A. (2011), "Sundays with Mildred," *Film Quarterly* 65 (1), pp. 25–33.
Ho, K. (2018), "Finance, Crisis and Hollywood: Critique and Recuperation of Wall Street in Films about the Great Recession," in C. Parvulescu (ed.), *Global Finance on Screen: From Wall Street to Side Street*, London and New York: Routledge, pp. 89–104.
Jacobs, A. and R. White (2012), "Todd Haynes's 'Mildred Pierce': A Discussion," *Film Quarterly*, 23 February. Available online: https://filmquarterly.org/2012/02/23/todd-hayness-mildred-pierce-a-discussion/.
Kinkle, J. and A. Toscano (2011), "Filming the Crisis: A Survey," *Film Quarterly* 65 (1), pp. 39–41.
Marin, R. (2011), "Can Manhood Survive the Recession?," *Newsweek*, 17 April. Available online: https://www.newsweek.com/can-manhood-survive-recession-66607.
Mulligan, C. B. (2009), "The 'Mancession'," *New York Times*, 30 September. Available online: https://search.proquest.com/docview/2219816489?accountid=202933.
Negra, D. and Y. Tasker (2014), "Introduction: Gender and Recessionary Culture," in D. Negra and Y. Tasker (eds.), *Gendering the Recession: Media and Culture in the Age of Austerity*, Durham and London: Duke University Press, pp. 1–30.
Oliete-Aldea, E. (2012), "Fear and Nostalgia in Times of Crisis: The Paradoxes of Globalization in Oliver Stone's *Money Never Sleeps* (2010)," *Culture Unbound* 4, pp. 347–66.
Oliete-Aldea, E. (2018), "Global Financial Crisis in Local Filmic Scenarios: Transnational Cinema of the Great Recession," in C. Parvulescu (ed.), *Global Finance on Screen: From Wall Street to Side Street*, London and New York: Routledge, pp. 179–97.
Oliete-Aldea, E. (2020), "Transnational Representation of a Gendered Recession in Corporate Dramas," *European Journal of Cultural Studies* 24 (2), pp. 514–29.
Ostrowski, J (2011), "Florida Can't Escape 'Mancession' as Women Face Easier Job Search," *Tribune Business News*, 11 July. Available online: https://search.proquest.com/docview/875703183?accountid=202933.
Peterson, J. (2012), "The Great Crisis and the Significance of Gender in the U.S. Economy," *Journal of Economic Issues* 42 (2), pp. 277–90.

Roitman, J. (2016), "The Stakes of Crisis," in P. F. Kjaer and N. Olsen (eds.), *Critical Theories of Crisis in Europe from Weimar to the Euro*, London and New York: Rowan and Littlefield, pp. 17–34.

Rosin, H. (2010), "The End of Men," *The Atlantic*, July/August. Available online: https://www.theatlantic.com/magazine/archive/2010/07/the-end-of-men/308135/.

Runciman, D. (2016), "What Time Frame Makes Sense for Thinking about Crises?," in P. F. Kjaer and N. Olsen (eds.), *Critical Theories of Crisis in Europe From Weimar to the Euro*, London and New York: Rowan and Littlefield, pp. 3–16.

Strolovitch, D. Z. (2013), "Of Mancessions and Hecoveries: Race, Gender and the Political Construction of Economic Crises and Recoveries," *Perspectives on Politics* 11 (1), pp. 167–76.

Walby, S. (2015), *Crisis*, Cambridge and Malden: Polity Press.

Wilson, J. and E. Chivers Yochim (2015), "Pinning Happiness? Affect, Social Media and the Work of Mothers," in E. Levine (ed.), *Cupcakes, Pinterest, and Ladyporn*, Champaign: University of Illinois Press, pp. 232–48.

5

Screening Neoliberalism in *Nightcrawler* and *The Wolf of Wall Street*

Stephen Felder

So ridiculous. Greta must work on her Anger Management problem, then go to a good old fashioned movie with a friend! Chill Greta, Chill!

PRESIDENT DONALD J. TRUMP, TWITTER, DECEMBER 12, 2019

L'écran n'est pas seulement ce qui cache le réel, il l'est sûrement, mais en même temps il l'indique.

JACQUES LACAN, *SÉMINAIRE XIII. L'OBJET DE LA PSYCHANALYSE* (MAY 18, 1966)

I have seen that dream all my life. It is perfect houses with nice lawns. It is Memorial Day cookouts, block associations, and driveways. The Dream is treehouses and the Cub Scouts. The dream smells like peppermint but tastes like strawberry shortcake.

TA-NEHISI COATES, *BETWEEN THE WORLD AND ME* (2015, 11)

In response to Greta Thunberg's speech to the United Nations' Climate Action Summit where she accused world leaders of being able to talk only about "money and fairytales of eternal economic growth" (Thunberg 2019), Donald Trump told her to "chill" and "go to a good old fashioned [sic] movie." This was very perceptive on his part. If by "chill," he meant for her to stop worrying about the climate crisis and sink back into the comforting reality of fairytales about money and eternal economic growth, a movie might be a good idea. Of course, it depends on the movie. Some movies sustain those fairy tales, but others subvert them.

Perhaps the most pernicious fairy tale of our era is that of neoliberalism. This fairy tale is the defining reality for billions around the world today. There are plenty of films which confirm that reality while critiquing the financial system, corporate power, and excess associated with such crises. Such films often point to the excesses of some at the top, blaming our crises on a cabal of greedy "bad actors." However, many of these movies that overtly criticize current economic conditions nevertheless bolster our psychic investment in the neoliberal fairy tale. *The Wolf of Wall Street* (Martin Scorsese 2013) is an example of an excellent film that falls into this category. On the other hand, *Nightcrawler* (Dan Gilroy 2014) subverts the neoliberal order not by critiquing the excesses generated by capitalism but by subverting the neoliberal fairytale and our psychic investment in it.

The Neoliberal Ethic in *Nightcrawler* and *The Wolf of Wall Street*

Neoliberalism is a fraught category. Some have wondered if it can be used meaningfully at all. Often deployed simply as a generic slur, it is difficult to find any self-proclaimed neoliberals today, and while there have been many definitions given, they often fail to distinguish it from classical "liberalism" (Kostko 2018, 11).[1] One of the more helpful conceptualizations of neoliberalism is Michel Foucault's. In a series of lectures given in 1978–9—right at the moment of neoliberalism's political ascendance (i.e., the beginning of we might call "actually existing" neoliberalism)—Foucault could already see that this new kind of liberalism had aims and tactics distinct from its classical liberal antecedents. He identified a shift in the mid-twentieth century from the liberal emphasis on exchange to the neoliberal emphasis on *competition*. Foucault put it bluntly: "not equivalence but on the contrary inequality" is the objective. For Foucault, the neoliberal goal is to create "a society in which the regulatory principle should not be so much the exchange of commodities as the mechanisms of competition" (Foucault 2008, 105; 116–17; 118; 120; 145; 147). For Foucault, neoliberalism saw the market (characterized by competition) as the only valid legitimation for the state.

But Adam Kotsko has shown that neoliberalism is, itself, a strategy of legitimation that is best understood as a kind of "theodicy." He shows that in typical theodicies, human freedom is prioritized over good outcomes. In the Christian tradition, freedom is the precondition of guilt: God allowed the angels the freedom they needed in order to rebel, then he provided humans the freedom they needed in order to sin. In this way, the Christian theodicy reconciles the contradictions between the belief that God is good and all-powerful with the contradictory experience we have of evil in the world by transferring responsibility for evil onto rational creatures who misuse the divine gift of free will. Thus, Kotsko argues, in Christian theology freedom does not function as a venue for ethical action, but as the very means by which all humans are rendered blameworthy (2018, 34–6; 49; 73; 80–1; 89).[2] In this way, neoliberalism can be seen as a theodicy for capitalism that claims: capitalism and neoliberal policies are unarguably good, yet inequalities, crises, and so on persist; therefore, it is the free choices of human beings that cause these negative results. These results cannot be eliminated without eliminating freedom.

Extrapolating from these two positions, we can argue that neoliberalism is based on a two-pronged theologizing ideological formulation that generates a notion of freedom in order to render the victims of the neoliberal order guilty. The first prong is realized in an almost absolute tendency to confuse choice with freedom. By (mis)taking choice for freedom, the second prong of the neoliberal theology/ideology, the punitive prong, is rationalized. The punitive feature of neoliberal ideology depends on assigning guilt to those who suffer under the conditions created by neoliberalism, a guilt that is internalized, rendering any political action beyond question, ceding authority and legitimacy to the "winners" with competition being the agency by which good is supposed to have been produced. Put another way, freedom under neoliberalism is not freedom to act, it is freedom to choose, and these choices always render the "loser" guilty (of laziness, timidity, recklessness, ignorance, overconfidence, etc.). In sum, the neoliberal ethic asserts that competition is the agency of all good in the world and the resultant division of people into "winners" and "losers" is the result not of systemic inequalities but of freedom (understood as choice).

The opening scenes of both *The Wolf of Wall Street* and *Nightcrawler* reveal how both films operate from within this neoliberal framework. Less than two minutes into *The Wolf of Wall Street* the protagonist, Jordan Belfort[3] (Leonardo DiCaprio), introduces himself as a "former member of the middle class, raised by two accountants in a tiny apartment in Bayside, Queens" who when he turned twenty-six, as the head of his own brokerage firm, made forty-nine million dollars. What follows is a display of the luxurious life he lived involving a mansion, a yacht, three horses, "two perfect kids," along with prostitutes and drugs. He claims that money not only allows you to live a more luxurious life, it "makes you a better person" because of all the donations to charity you can make.

By contrast, the introduction of the protagonist of *Nightcrawler*, Louis Bloom (Jake Gyllenhaal), follows a scene in which he has murdered a security guard and stolen some chain-link fence to sell as salvaged metal. Louis's self-introduction comes not by way of voice-over narration (which is not used in *Nightcrawler*) but as part of his interactions with the owner of a salvage yard where he intends to sell his stolen merchandise. This introduction doesn't have any of the biographical details at the heart of Jordan Belfort's. On the contrary, it seems like just a string of clichés drawn from any of a number of MBA commencement speeches and self-help seminars. He describes himself has a "hard worker" who "sets high goals." Though he has been raised within the "self-esteem movement so popular in schools" to expect his "needs to be considered," he now knows that he lives in a culture that "no longer caters to the job loyalty that could be promised to earlier generations," so his current mindset is that "good things come to those who work their asses off" and that "people . . . who reach the top of the mountain didn't just fall there." Though we already know he is a thief and a murderer, we see him situate himself as the perfect neoliberal subject, committed to becoming a "winner" in a world defined by competition rather than cooperation.

Throughout both films, the protagonists continually voice this neoliberal ethic, but with decisively different affects that engage the desire of the viewer in opposite ways. To put it another way, both Jordan Belfort and Louis Bloom identify with the neoliberal ethic. However, there is something paradoxical about the way each character voices this ethic. Jordan Belfort (DiCaprio) voices this ethic through the authoritative device of voice-over narration but in a way that is light, crude, and almost always joking, while still seeming to be giving us the truth about things. By contrast, Louis Bloom (Gyllenhaal) voices this ethic in a flat, almost affectless tone that seems committed to the seriousness of these ideas while, at the same time, making them seem absurd.

But in *The Wolf of Wall Street*, Belfort is not so much joking as selling. In telling us his story he is selling us on the neoliberal doctrine of winners and losers. In fact, for a biopic there is an awful lot of discussion of sales. The film contains two explicit television advertisements for Belfort's enterprises, one for the firm he started, Stratton-Oakmont, that opens the film, and the other an infomercial for "Jordan Belfort's Straight Line Persuasion Seminar" (what seems to be a sales pitch on how to pitch and get rich). Toward the very end of the film, when he goes to prison, he admits to us that he was initially "terrified" until he realized he was rich, and prison is a place where "everything is for sale." He then asks *us*, "wouldn't you like to know how to sell it?" Presumably, the "it" is everything. In the final scene of the film Belfort, now out of prison, is being introduced as "the world's greatest sales trainer" to a group of pathetic-looking aspiring millionaires whom, we assume, he will teach to sell and grow rich. But he is not selling any specific product. He is selling us on the idea that, in the words of his infomercial, "there is nobody holding you back from financial freedom"—a slogan for the neoliberal ethic if there ever was one.

This aligns with the general effect of the film's narrative. While Jordan Belfort is selling penny-stocks to anyone dumb enough to buy them, the movie is selling us on the idea that poverty is not a structural feature of the economy, but an obstacle that can be overcome by anyone who simply *chooses* to become rich. For example, in a scene in which Belfort is trying to summon his "troops" (he actually uses a military analogy—phones are like M-16s, his cold-callers like Marines—and they must not hang up the phone until the client "buys or fuckin' dies"), he tells them, "there is no nobility in poverty." He claims that having money can make you a good person and that when you are rich and you have to face your problems, you can, like him, "show up in the back of a fucking limo, wearing a $2000 suit, and a $40,000 gold fucking watch." He then tells them that if they think this sounds "superficial" or "materialistic" then they should be working in McDonald's "because that's where you fucking belong." (The Manichaean dichotomy of Wall Street/McDonald's is a recurring theme.) But then he says that before the losers go, they should look around at the winners in the room who one day will pull up next to them in a Porsche, with their beautiful wife, and so on, while the losers will be sitting next to "some wildebeest with three days of razor stubble and a sleeveless muumuu" in a beat-up old Pinto crammed full of groceries from the "Price Club." Of course, no one leaves the room for a job at McDonald's. It's all a sales pitch designed to sell the sellers on selling. But it also sells us. The fantasy life described by Belfort—one that he actually embodies throughout the film—is sold to us along with the message that failing to attain this lifestyle, and even failing to desire it, mark one as a loser worthy only of ridicule. The notion of competition is implicit, but the ethic of neoliberalism is explicit.

Similarly, in the infomercial he asks us if we "dream of being financially independent but struggle every month to pay our bills." Most of us would say, "yes." He then uses his own story of someone who made a *decision* as a twenty-four-year-old not simply "to survive, but to thrive." This is followed by a testimonial from an apparently middle-class couple who have just made a $33,000 profit with the husband telling us that if we "don't have the guts" to attend Belfort's seminar then "how do [we] expect to make any money?" A second testimonial, this time from a young Black man, tells us that Belfort's system worked for him because "he worked hard for it," and "if it doesn't work for you it's because you're lazy and you should get a job at McDonald's."

Thus, though the film frequently depicts Belfort and his financial warriors as not particularly smart, prone to excess, and crude at every level, it nevertheless links their success to a matter of personal choice and responsibility. This is underscored in one of the final scenes in the film when we see FBI agent Patrick Denham (Kyle Chandler) riding home on the subway. He is surrounded by tired, demoralized, working people, presumably living "unsuccessful" lives. As he quietly scans the subway car, a look of quiet despair sweeps across his face. The scene shows that the choice the agent made to go into law enforcement instead of into a career on Wall Street doomed him to this "loser" life. Earlier in the film, Belfort invited Denham to his yacht with the intention of bribing him into dropping a criminal investigation into his firm's wrongdoing. In the course of the conversation Belfort tells Denham that he has learned that at one time the FBI agent had tried to get his broker's license, and then asks him if he ever wonders what would have happened if he had continued to pursue a life on Wall Street. Denham says that sometimes when he's "riding home on the subway, and [his] balls are sweating, wearing the same suit three days in a row," yes, he has thought about it. "Who wouldn't?" The point the scene is making is that Denham's *choices* have led him to a ride on the subway instead of on an expensive yacht.

This same message is central to *Nightcrawler*. As noted earlier, right from the very beginning Louis Bloom reads his situation from within the neoliberal point of view, rejecting any notion that an economic and political system should consider individual needs. Competition, rather than cooperation, is the source of all good. Louis tacitly accepts this narrative and acts upon it. But unlike Belfort, Louis isn't selling us; he's showing us. In *Nightcrawler* we see a violent petty thief applying for an internship in a salvage yard. The very absurdity of it has the effect of denaturalizing the ideology of neoliberalism. Like the voice of his mother falling on Norman Bates in drag, when this neoliberal voice falls on Louis, we can suddenly see it divorced from its typically authoritative and reinforcing contexts. Such a voice would not seem out of place coming from the mouth of a recent college graduate interviewing for an internship at a large corporation, but in this context the words seem absurd, both because salvage yards don't have interns (but why not?) and because Louis is a thief.

Similarly, his attempt at negotiation in the salvage yard mimes typical market processes, but the scene makes clear that this kind of free-market exchange is not really free at all. Instead, it is all based on competition. Louis cannot hold out for a better offer for his wares because of the illegal way he acquired the metal. The "legal" party in this exchange, well aware of the criminal origins of Louis's product, is able to leverage this fact to his advantage. The owner doesn't mind buying stolen goods; in fact, he prefers this because it will increase his profits. In such situations, there is no free exchange, though there is choice, and the point is that competition manages to keep prices down for the consumer and profits high for the owner: Louis competes with the owner, but also with those selling legitimately acquired metal, and the owner is competing with other salvage yard owners, and so on. This sort of competition is supposed to be a mechanism for creating the greatest common good (Harvey 2005, 2).[4] But *Nightcrawler* subverts this narrative. Throughout most of the film we see Louis locked in a competition with a more established rival, Joe Loder (Bill Paxton), who dies in a mysterious car crash attributed to brake failure. The film suggests that Louis tampered with Loder's brakes so as to literally "murder the competition."

The same dynamic can be seen in Louis's relationship with his employee. In an early scene Louis has established his business as a "nightcrawler," working as a freelance photographer who gathers video footage of fires, crime, and accidents for the local television news (a sign, itself, of neoliberal policies as the night film crews from local stations have lost their jobs to this more "flexible"—i.e., cheaper—workforce). He has learned that it is very difficult for him to drive the car, find directions, park, and so on, all by himself, so he needs to hire some help. From a certain point of view, this scene is laughable, as Louis is presenting himself as if he is the owner of a large successful business interviewing an aspiring recent college graduate with a business degree. But the scene is actually much darker. The applicant is Rick (Riz Ahmed), a young man with a sad employment history that began after high school with a "mow, blow, and go" landscaping job he had to quit when he discovered he had hay fever. He's only been able to get sporadic employment since. Then, we have this exchange:

Louis: What's your address, Richard?
Rick: I don't have one. Right? Not a permanent one, I mean, right now.
Louis: You're homeless.
Rick: I was for a while.
Louis: You trick.
Rick: Work the street? No.
Louis: Wasn't a question.
Rick: I'm straight.
Louis: Plenty of straight guys trick.

The confidence with which Louis asserts this position, coupled with his generally impoverished situation, suggests that he, too, has been forced into prostitution at times in order to eat. This is a far cry from Jordan Belfort's simple "survive" vs. "thrive" set of options. Louis offers Rick the job, initially trying to get him to work as an unpaid intern (a common practice in the corporate world), but when Rick explains he needs to have some money, Louis offers him only $30 a day. Rick immediately accepts. Later, when Rick has become aware of some of the darker aspects of Louis's business model, he tries to use that information to get a higher wage. Louis responds by causing his death, deliberately putting him in harm's way as they are covering a shoot-out. As Rick lies dying, Louis explains that he could not allow Rick to "jeopardize [his] company's success." So, *Nightcrawler* shows us that winners not only murder the competition; they murder their own employees.

We also see this dynamic in Louis's interactions with Nina Romina (Rene Russo), the producer of a local TV news morning show. Nina has a job. Nina makes more money than Louis. Nevertheless, this is a prime example of choice being confused with freedom. In a crucial scene, Louis chides Nina into going out to dinner with him where he announces he wants to be in a relationship with her. She makes it clear that she does not want this, but Louis reminds her that his videos have boosted the ratings on her show and that she needs his clips in order to keep her job and her health insurance (most health insurance in the United States is tied to employment). The ensuing exchange is revealing:

> **Nina:** Where did you get the balls to suggest something like this?
> **Louis:** We're still talking.
> **Nina:** No, there is nothing more to say.
> **Louis:** You can leave.

But Nina doesn't leave. Instead, she again tries to explain that she does not want that kind of relationship with him, that the station pays him well, and she can work on getting him a retainer, and so on. But he is not interested in these financial accommodations because he knows he can sell his videos elsewhere; he wants a relationship with her:

> **Louis:** You're not listening, Nina. I happen to know that you haven't stayed at one station for longer than two years at a time and you're coming up on two years soon. I can imagine that your contract is for two years at a time and that next month's ratings directly affect that.
> **Nina:** So, you're threatening that if I don't . . .
> **Louis:** I'm *negotiating*.
> **Nina:** You're *threatening* to stop selling to me.
> **Louis:** That's your *choice*. The true price of any item is what somebody's willing to pay for it. You want something, and I want you.
> **Nina:** To fuck you.
> **Louis:** And as a friend.
> **Nina:** Jesus Christ, friends don't pressure friends to fucking sleep with them.
> **Louis:** Actually, that's not true, Nina. Because as I'm sure you know, a friend is a gift you give yourself.

The scene illustrates the cynical orientation of capitalism under which everything (and everyone) has a price (or, as Jordan Belfort would put it, "everything is for sale"). Foucault saw this as a feature particular to neoliberalism in the United States—the tendency to extend the rationality of the market into non-economic domains—that demonstrated the diffuse ways in which both liberalism and capitalism take on multiple forms specific to various historical configurations (but this phenomenon is much more widespread today as that historical configuration has spread) (2008, 323). But this scene also displays the neoliberal confusion of choice with freedom. Yes, she has the *choice* to refuse Louis's advances, but she does not have the freedom to leave; yes, she will *choose* to have sex with Louis, but she was not free to reject it. This obviously mimics the dynamic in many a "me-too" story and demonstrates the way the primacy given to *freedom to choose* under neoliberalism gets in the way of *freedom to act* when systemic factors do not allow a person a living wage, healthcare, security, and so on. Put another way, it shows that *freedom to compete* has not given us *the freedom we need* to control our own lives and bodies.

Even Nina's commitment to the kind of news show she produces is not really an act of freedom. In that same conversation at dinner, Louis explained to Nina (and the audience) that most Americans watch local news to be informed, yet the average local half hour of news devotes only twenty-two seconds to local "government coverage, including law enforcement, budget, transportation, education, and immigration" while local crime stories not only lead most news broadcasts, but fill fourteen times as much of those same broadcasts. But each station is competing with the others for ratings. Nina, like Louis, has no job security; therefore, she must pursue a competitive strategy regardless of its impact on the public good. The film shows us that the dynamic of competition does not lead to a more informative media or a wiser citizenry. Meanwhile, Louis ignores all such public interests and operates according to the dictates of neoliberalism, choosing courses of action that always favor profit and business expansion, always emphasizing competition as the central dynamic. He does not value people. He values nothing but what will make him successful. Like the commercial media he represents, he does not care about informing the citizens, preserving democratic institutions, or educating the public; he only cares about one thing: profit.

Screening the Crisis: Lacan's *écran*

Lacan understood "screen" in both its senses (*écran* implying the same ambiguity in French as screen does in English). A screen refers to both the object that impairs vision and the object on which images are projected. A television screen both prevents me from seeing what is behind it and at the same time is the object that displays images for me to see. As he explained (in a lecture attended by Foucault), "the screen is not only that which hides the real—it certainly is that—but at the same time it indicates it" (2006, 225; my translation). What is at stake in Lacan's screen is the "real." We can think of the real as the holes, gaps, inconsistencies, and so on in the symbolic order. Cast in ideological terms, ideology works by concealing the real by way of reality. The screen is the place where (the always ideological) reality is projected, thus hiding the real. It indicates the real by virtue of the fact that there is always something missing, incomplete, inconsistent, and so on in our reality. The cinematic image (with all that entails) "screens" our reality. It can do nothing else, or a film would be incomprehensible. But this does not mean every encounter with a film only strengthens our attachment to the prevailing ideology.

This is where a Lacanian understanding of the gaze is most productive. For Lacan, the subject is not founded on the (ideological) reality projected onto the screen but on the absence or lack of meaning that is the real. The subject is produced by this absence. What counts for the subject is not what is seen but what is not seen. If the absence (lack) behind the image is staged cinematically, the encounter will be traumatic for the subject and subversive to the reality projected onto the screen. Within this dialectic, the Lacanian gaze functions as the point where this reality is disrupted. As Joan Copjec puts it, the Lacanian gaze is a "blind eye." Most films do not stage an encounter with it. Instead, they screen the reality of the ideological world of the subject in a way that confirms the subject's identity, values, and pursuits. But the gaze disrupts this affirming encounter with reality by indicating the real. Copjec has summarized this dynamic well (2015, 36):

> if you are looking for confirmation of the truth of your being or the clarity of your vision, you are on your own; the gaze . . . is not confirming; it will not validate you.

> Now, the subject instituted by the Lacanian gaze does not come into being as the realization of a possibility opened up by the law of the Other. It is rather an impossibility that is crucial to the constitution of the subject—the impossibility, precisely, of any ultimate confirmation from the Other. The subject emerges, as a result, as a desiring being . . . Desire fills no possibility but seeks after an impossibility; this makes desire always, constitutionally, contentless.

Thus, if we are to ask how cinema screens the crisis, a Lacanian approach would look for the way in which a film either confirms us in our (ideological) reality by giving us the impression that the emptiness that constitutes us as desiring subjects can find plentitude within the reality screened by the film, or whether it stages for us an encounter with the gaze that indicates the real beyond this (ideological) reality, thus subverting it.

For the most part, *The Wolf of Wall Street* avoids this confrontation with the gaze. We certainly see a lot of things—nude women, drug use, outrageous behavior, yachts, and so on—that point to the excesses of Wall Street, but our desire is not really implicated because the absence (or "lack") behind these images of excess is never encountered. While the extreme behavior we see in this film might suggest the film is taking a critical view of Wall Street, this critique is undermined by the way the opulent displays that accompany such behavior offer an image of plenitude available to those who pursue enjoyment along these lines. Rather than show the absence behind these images, Wall Street is figured as an exceptional site of enjoyment that must be looked at with either resentment or envy but not as fundamentally empty (thus confirming the validity of this path).

The film itself interprets this dynamic in the exact same way. Soon after Belfort creates Stratton-Oakmont, *Forbes* does a profile of the firm, castigating them for pushing "dicey stocks" and suggesting that Belfort thinks of himself as a "kind of twisted Robin Hood" who takes from the rich and gives to himself and his "merry little band of brokers." After the article is published, he his flooded with "money-crazed kids" who want to join his firm. Belfort's shady behavior doesn't serve as a cautionary tale; it incites desire. The fact that he finds enjoyment outside the constraints of the normal social order provokes desire because we imagine he has access to something not available to the rest of us. Rather than showing us a film about young people who come to Belfort only to be disappointed because there is no enjoyment there, we see the opposite: sex with prostitutes in the office during business hours, strippers at company events, gold watches, and even a kind of community (although Jordan's wife will remind him that he always said, "there are no friends on Wall Street), and so on, which all serve as "screens" for the absence lurking behind these images.

Both films screen this dynamic through different forms of screen media. In *The Wolf of Wall Street* the screen media is advertising. The film's two formal advertisements work, like all advertising, by provoking our desire without confronting us with the gaze. The aim of advertising is to engage the subject's desire (by indicating lack) while offering a vision of plenitude that provides a path toward fulfillment. In the advertisement the seller is pointing to an object as *the one* that will bring ultimate satisfaction. The surplus, the excess, the just-out-of-reach objects all promise to be the end of desire. A good advertisement never allows us to see the role of our desire in transforming ordinary commodities into sublime objects; it leaves us believing we have discovered the sublime in our encounter with them.

Similarly, the form of screen media deployed in *Nightcrawler* is that of the crime-/accident-scene video prominent in local news broadcasts. This, too, must engage us in our desire, but its appeal to the desiring subject is less obvious. What *Nightcrawler* does is undermine the symbolic order by revealing the complicity of our desire in the construction of television news. It shows us that television news rather than showing us "what's real" is creating a "reality" in response to our own desire. The film explicitly references the ways in which the local news constructs a narrative that emphasizes the spread of "urban" crime into the suburbs. (In this case, urban is coded as Black and Brown people and suburban is coded as white.) Nina, the news director, is clear that her viewers are not interested in stories where non-white people are the victims. When the home invasion in a sprawling (white-owned) mansion turns out to be drug-related, the local news is no longer interested. They are only interested in stories that support the narrative of dangerous poor Black and Brown people invading the security of white suburbs. This narrative—the notion that the safety and privilege of suburban dwellers are under threat—validates the overall narrative of neoliberal capitalism. Suburban life—sometimes linked with the American Dream—is linked by Ta-Nahisi Coates to what he simply calls "the Dream":

> The Dream seemed to be the pinnacle, then—to grow rich and live in one of those disconnected houses out in the country, in one of those small communities, one of those cul-de-sacs with its gently curving ways, where they staged teen movies and children built treehouses, and in the last lost year before college, teenagers made love in cars parked at the lake. The Dream seemed to be the end of the world for me, the height of American ambition. What more could possibly exist beyond the dispatches, beyond the suburbs? (2015, 116)

Nightcrawler demonstrates how this aspect of local television news supports "the Dream" described by Coates. The film shows us that such news footage (as well as the movies alluded to by Coates) are deliberately staged to capture the desire of the white, suburban viewer. By showing us the role our desire plays in this reality, *Nightcrawler* confronts us with the gaze. The desire of the (mostly white) middle-class viewers to believe that their own position of privilege is the result of personal choices and hard work is exposed by the way they are invested in the narrative of the dangerous poor whose very vices threaten their well-deserved success. Coates argues that the "adherents [of the Dream] must not just believe in it but believe that it is just, believe that their possession of the Dream is the natural result of grit, honor, and good works" (2015, 98). This is the neoliberal ethic. In the United States this ethic is racialized in such a way that the object of racism always functions both as a potential threat to the so-called American way of life and as unworthy of participating in that life. Thus, a system built on privileges constructed through injustices comes to appear just in the narratives of local television news. The very division of the population into a group of worthy, suburban, winners who made all the right choices and a group of unworthy, urban, losers who chose poorly supports the neoliberal idea that competition rules the political economy in such a way as to produce a true aristocracy (rule by "the best"). But as Copjec explains, "at the moment the gaze is discerned, the image, the entire visual field, takes on a terrifying alterity. It loses its 'belong-to-me aspect' and suddenly assumes the function of a screen" (2015, 35). Television news may shock us, but it rarely robs us of this "belong-to-me aspect" of daily life. Thus, *Nightcrawler* shows us that it is all a dream of sorts, that this narrative of urban crime creeping into the city is not real, but simply a reflection of our own desire.

In the final scene of *The Wolf of Wall Street* we are given a vision of plenitude and possibility that awaits those who will commit to the journey of becoming wealthy. In the final scene of *Nightcrawler* we witness Louis's success as he now owns two news vans staffed by eager, young "interns." But rather than feeling elation at Louis's success, we are disturbed by the confrontation with the gaze. Rather than a rags-to-riches success story that affirms our sense of belonging within the neoliberal reality, *Nightcrawler* confronts us with the gaze in the vacant eyes, flat affect, and disinterested drive of Louis Bloom. Dan Gilroy's description of his film matches this analysis (in Rocchi 2014):

> I feel like the world . . . has been reduced to transactions, and that Lou thrives in that world because that's the only thing that has any relevance to him. And we approach it as a success story of a guy who is looking for work at the beginning and is the owner of a successful business at the end, and the reason I approach it that way is because I didn't want at the end for the audience to go, "oh, the problem is this psychopath!" I wanted the audience to go "maybe the problem is the world that created and rewards this character." Maybe it's a larger question.

Nightcrawler's critique suggests that what we need is not a level playing field upon which competition can continue to sort us all into winners and losers. After all, Louis started "at the bottom." Instead, it suggests that the solutions to our problems lie in cooperation, rather than in competition.

Conclusion

Neoliberalism is the crisis of our era. Its emphasis on competition as the means of achieving the common good is perverse. Equally destructive has been the neoliberal theodicy that depends on a degrading conception of freedom that blurs it with choice in order to render guilty those who suffer under neoliberal policies. In a world where there is a screen on every wall and another in every hand, thinking through how the crisis of neoliberalism is screened has become crucial to any emancipatory political project. Identifying how neoliberalism's theodicy has become the reality of our era through these screenings will involve a careful consideration of not only what is seen, but also what is left unseen, and of developing a suspicion toward all screenings that merely confirm us in our (neoliberal) reality by allowing us to avoid the traumatic encounter with the gaze.

Notes

1. On this point, see also Thomas Biebricher's *The Political Theory of Neoliberalism* (2019).
2. On "guilt" under neoliberalism see also William Davies (2016, 129–30).
3. All references to "Jordan Belfort" refer to the character in the film with no attempt to compare him to the actual Jordan Belfort.
4. See David Harvey (2005) for a definition of neoliberalism.

References

Biebricher, T. (2019), *The Political Theory of Neoliberalism*, Stanford: Stanford University Press.
Coates, T-N. (2015), *Between the World and Me*, New York: Spiegel and Grau.
Copjec, J. (2015), *Read My Desire: Lacan against the Historicists*, London and New York: Verso. First published in 1994.
Davies, W. (2016), "The New Neoliberalism," *The New Left Review* 101, pp. 121-34.
Foucault, M. (2008), *The Birth of Biopolitics: Lectures at the Collége de France 1978-1979,* trans. G. Burchell, New York: Palgrave Macmillan.
Harvey, D. (2005), *A Brief History of Neoliberalism*, Oxford: Oxford University Press.
Kotsko, A. (2018), *Neoliberalism's Demons: On the Political Theology of Late Capital*, Stanford: Stanford University Press.
Lacan, J. (2006), *Le séminaire de Jacques Lacan [séminaire XIII]. L'objet de la psychanalyse: 1965-1966*, Paris: M. Roussan.
Rocchi, J. (2014), "Interview: 'Nightcrawler' Director Dan Gilroy Talks Jake Gyllenhaal, Robert Elswit & Sociopaths," *IndieWire*, 29 October. Available online: https://www.indiewire.com/2014/10/interview-nightcrawler-director-dan-gilroy-talks-jake-gyllenhaal-robert-elswit-sociopaths-270834/.
Thunberg, G. (2019), "Transcript: Greta Thunberg's Speech At the U.N. Climate Action Summit," *National Public Radio*, 23 September. Available online: https://www.npr.org/2019/09/23/763452863/transcript-greta-thunbergs-speech-at-the-u-n-climate-action-summit.

PART III

Technology and the State of Surveillance

6

The Shock Doctrines of *The Social Network*

Zuckerberg, Trump, and Surveillance Capitalism in Big-tech Cinema

Ian Scott

Introduction

On May 28, 2020, Donald Trump took to Twitter to offer his thoughts on the latest crisis engulfing his presidency. Just three days earlier, in Minneapolis, George Floyd had been arrested by police for offering a counterfeit twenty-dollar bill at a market. The arresting officer, Derek Chauvin, together with three colleagues, reprimanded Floyd, who dropped to the floor to stop himself from being put in a police car, at which point Chauvin proceeded to apply his knee to the man's neck and kept it there, for nearly nine minutes. Despite pleas from Floyd that he could not breathe, heard on a smartphone capturing the incident, he then became unresponsive and died at the scene. All four officers were fired the next day and Chauvin was quickly charged with third-—later elevated to second-—degree murder, when two autopsies concluded that homicide had been the cause of death.

Over the next three days peaceful protest in Minneapolis turned to outrage that finally led to violence as the facts of the case emerged. At that point, on the evening of the 28th, Trump wrote the following on Twitter: "Any difficulty and we will assume control but, when the looting starts, the shooting starts." As *The New York Times* reported, the provocative phrase had been used before, notably by the Miami police chief Walter Headley at the height of disturbances in the late 1960s and was a totemic symbol of police intimidation and tactics toward people of color in particular (Wines 2020).

Having posted his tweet, Twitter invoked a clause in its rules serving due warning to messages that incite violence. The tweet thus acquired a cautionary sign over it, and Trump went into apoplexy making dire warnings of retribution against social media companies. But on Facebook, where the tweet had gravitated to, the post received no warnings from that company. The CEO Mark Zuckerberg was forced to defend his company's action, arguing that Facebook's policy was to allow state actors to warn of the use of force. Zuckerberg did criticize Trump's comments but argued that accountability came from scrutiny of leaders via their comments, not the blocking of them (Wong 2020). The backlash to Zuckerberg's position was almost as vituperative as the comments that had precipitated it. Civil rights leaders as well as many of Facebook's own staff publicly condemned Zuckerberg, arguing that he was "weapon[izing] hatred" and "facilitating Trump's call for violence" (Hern and Waterson 2020).

In the course of a decade and a half, Zuckerberg had progressed from being a Harvard undergraduate trying to set up an online dating site, to becoming a business titan on the global stage, with the power of persuasion and proclamation over what the president of the United States, let alone anyone else, might say or do. As the 2020 election lurched into view amid the coronavirus pandemic and rioting in the streets, John Naughton proclaimed that if Facebook were to close off its famed microtargeting algorithms to presidential candidates Trump and Joe Biden, the former's administration would most likely be over and "the nightmare ended on 20 January 2021" (2020, 21). Despite some criticism by the Democrats of dubious campaign ads that continued to appear, when the tallies were eventually counted—and recounted in some cases as Trump persisted with falsities about electoral fraud—Facebook ended up avoiding some of the criticism of four years before when outside interference, whether in cahoots with the Trump campaign or not, had seemingly inveigled the social media site to his cause. Biden had won, and the two elections together had shown that Zuckerberg, in fifteen short years, had seemingly acquired a majority stake in who should capture the White House.

A decade earlier, Facebook was barely five years old. At its moment of rapid maturation, director David Fincher and writer Aaron Sorkin joined forces to describe the birth and bedding in of this new online social media phenomenon in their movie *The Social Network* (2010). Long-standing forces in the industry, Fincher was emerging from the acclaim of thirteen

Oscar nominations for his adaptation of F. Scott Fitzgerald's short story *The Curious Case of Benjamin Button* (2008). Sorkin, who was responsible for the runaway success of political drama *The West Wing* (1999–2006) on TV, was already dabbling in a script about the media with a plot treatment called *More as This Story Develops*, which would later evolve into the acclaimed HBO series *The Newsroom* (2012–14). On screen, he had recently completed the script for Mike Nichols's movie *Charlie Wilson's War* (2007), for which he earned a Best Screenplay nomination at the Golden Globes.

Sorkin acquired an unpublished draft of Ben Mezrich's *The Accidental Billionaires* detailing Zuckerberg's rise, before reportedly saying yes immediately to Columbia Pictures' call for him to adapt the book into a screenplay. In Mezrich's tale of friendship, loyalty, betrayal, and revenge lay the age-old characteristics that Sorkin usually looked for in a narrative. The book and the script developed somewhat in tandem, with conversations between the two writers about structure and events taking place intermittently, a weaving of character and motivation that had little to do with the technological invention of Facebook itself much of the time.

Originally starting as FaceMash, a program Zuckerberg had written in his second year of study at Harvard, the online site appropriated pictures from the different university houses' face book, a collection of photos and information about the whole student body gathered on servers, and a rifling of data off an institutional source that came close to getting Zuckerberg expelled. Through 2004 and 2005 *The* Facebook as it was still known expanded its program across several US university campuses, and around the world. Incorporated in the summer of 2004 and moving its base of operations to California, the definite article got dropped and Facebook went on to acquire over six million users by the end of 2005.

By rights, *The Social Network*, largely following the pattern of these events and the ruptures that trailed Zuckerberg and his acolytes who set Facebook up and then disbanded amid acrimony, should have quickly become an historical curio. Such was its presentation of the fledgling social media environment in the early 2000s as one of innocent exploration and progressive online social engineering. But a small-time operation designed to offer little more than personal profiles that could be shown and shared was, in 2010 as the movie arrived in theaters, already on its way to becoming arguably the most important filter for social commentary and political culture anywhere on the planet.

Deeply aware of how much its influence had grown within a few short years, Fincher and Sorkin build the future philosophic reasoning and stratospheric rise into the very first scene of the film. Not only does Zuckerberg (Jesse Eisenberg) utter his first words asking how many geniuses there are in China—the emerging chief rival to the United States economically through the decade, and technologically as online communications became ever more a commodity of social thought and surveillance capital—but he does so against the backdrop of conversational noise—a metaphoric nod to the mass of online traffic already in existence—filling in the diegetic space as he and girlfriend Erica (Rooney Mara) discuss what he'd been up to that day. Then she breaks up with him.

What follows is an accelerated lesson in coding and social interaction framed as the twenty-first century's destiny. We learn how brilliant Zuckerberg is at dissecting what people want to reveal of their lives online, and how terrible he is in person at divulging what he wants from his friends or for himself. The end game of his binary coding genius and social inadequacy when Facebook has finally made its mark is a series of depositions that the narrative periodically returns to—results of claim, counterclaim, and accusation over who invented, contributed to, and worked on Facebook. While the story unfolds via these legal questioning flashbacks, the real consequences of socially structured engineering become clear. Ultimately what should and shouldn't be public property, how Facebook connects the past with the online future, *The Social Network* argues, comes down to age-old fault lines about public perception, and the ability to make lots of money.

As a storyteller Sorkin spots that these traditional granular occurrences—what people think of one another and how much wealth one has—are recurrent narrative arcs that even populate up-to-the-minute stories about a virtual self-promotion page; the rivalries and resolutions are the same that resonate in any tale about greed and influence. This prompted several critics, nearly a decade later, to point out that *The Social Network*'s fledgling status as first social media movie hadn't actually dimmed its message at all, only reinforced it. "Like many great works of fiction, Fincher and Sorkin's movie hasn't aged poorly. It might seem a little naive now, but the lessons, the takeaways, are the same," wrote Angela Watercutter in 2019. Perhaps surprisingly then to all but the filmmakers, *The Social Network* had matured presciently in line with not only Facebook's rise to behemothic status, but via the growth in global surveillance culture, and the transformative shape of a US domestic political culture that shook up the status quo. This chapter suggests not only how, but also why, the movie was so suggestive of these developments to come.

The Movie Is the Message

The film's prophetic nature was highlighted by Zuckerberg's own philosophic ambitions for his fledgling company within a wider geopolitical nexus of increased data gathering and surveillance culture during the 2010s. His rationale was that people increasingly wanted to know what everyone was thinking and what others thought of them. The film's ongoing relevance to a world that is today a million miles away from the one Facebook was born into in 2004 continues to resonate precisely because that mantra makes it a movie about yesterday, today, and tomorrow. Zuckerberg's strive for interconnection prompted his construction of a medium that could control the form of human association, to use theorist Marshall McLuhan's words (1964, 9), which might easily have been referring to Facebook. As Zuckerberg's original partner, Eduardo Saverin (Andrew Garfield), puts it at one point: "In a world where social structure is everything, that [acceptance and appreciation] was *the* thing." Facebook's hipness as the next "big thing" may have faded in time, but only at the expense of it becoming the world's largest interactive force. If anything, Facebook's belief in connectivity in an increasingly rudderless world became an even larger, more sought-after commodity than ever before.

Fincher and Sorkin were the perfect filmmakers for extoling this prognostication. The director's cinematically classic pretensions and interest in the fantastical and metaphysical happening right before his characters' eyes are aided by a screenwriter whose 100-mile-an-hour dialogue is consciously deployed in the movie to look and sound like code, a series of cryptic clues to a language and world none of us thought we wanted, yet all learned to mimic parrot-fashion within only a few short years. *The Social Network*, like *Steve Jobs* (2015), which Sorkin went on to write for British director Danny Boyle, has pretensions to be a *Citizen Kane* for the internet age of course, because Sorkin understands the fluidity, flaws, and fatalism of such grandiose characters. Tellingly, Fincher went further and coined *The Social Network*, "the *Citizen Kane* of John Hughes movies," a conjoining of Generation X pop sensibility and cerebral Hollywood classicism that he felt suited the vibe of the picture (Knapp 2014, xviii).

Even while the lesson of the film is that Zuckerberg is a somewhat "small" person, happy to jettison those not useful to him, and anything but a business guru that within a few short years will have stock markets around the world and governments alike holding him to account, *The Social Network* is still less a story about its central protagonist than it is about the human condition more particularly that has allowed social media to govern our world and dictate our fortunes.

As the film develops, Zuckerberg's assuredness in the company of roommates Eduardo, Dustin Moskovitz (Joseph Mazello), and Chris Hughes (Patrick Mapel) gives way to a fawning trips-over-himself adulation of Napster founder Sean Parker (Justin Timberlake) who wants to buy in to Facebook's rapid expanse—a confirmation, the film asserts, of Zuckerberg's poor judgment of character and temperament, especially when Parker is involved in a drug bust that threatens the wholesome appeal of the company.

But as well as these themes of social status and the need to be validated, now, in the wake of coronavirus, it's much easier to see how *The Social Network*'s sometimes wide-eyed leanings toward super-connectivity also acted as a warning from history. It parades a perennial story of human existence transferred into a virtual world we have all become conditioned to. We worry about selling our privacy to corporations and governments yet cannot help but reveal so much of ourselves online in a self-serving social setting.

For critics like Naomi Klein, in the era of Covid-19, such conditioning allied to the power of big-tech has precipitated a "pandemic shock doctrine" whereby Google, Facebook, et al. mean to have the "new normal" as, well, normal. Our "no touch" lives are being designed for us right before our eyes, thinks Klein, and it's all in the name of big-tech control and profitability. As she points out, surveillance incarceration in the community was already a move happening well before the pandemic and now it's on an accelerated course that seems hard to stop (Klein 2020). We'll entertain, work, exercise, and "jail" ourselves within our own personal living spaces as the real world outside gets more remote and the virtual one inside ever more interlocking.

Surveillance is one consequence of such a post-pandemic environment, but capitalism's durability is another. Alternative realities and unconventional politics have led to what Shoshana Zuboff calls the age of surveillance capitalism (2019). Military and intelligence capabilities for protecting the homeland have been joined by a revolution in our normative lives that involves giving away our preferences, data, and modes of living for profit. As Zuboff explains, this has been done with the acquiescence of government and the approval of state intelligence agencies with a mutually shared interest in the same information that social media platforms took to be our new mode of individual expression (2019, 19).

We are social animals then, with an urge to expand our universe of influence and ambition. But we have also been enlisted in what is now termed "computational propaganda," an exponential rise in programmed misinformation campaigns rampaging across the whole internet. As the Oxford Internet Institute reported, there were eighty-one countries in 2020 where social media manipulation campaigns were in full swing (Bailey 2021). We don't socialize online to stay connected; we promote ourselves online to stay relevant, and state-sponsored apparatuses have taken advantage of the Facebook-inspired need for exposure.

But arguably Facebook, Instagram, and the rest are also all we have to cling to in the perilous 2020s, our memories stored of a reasonably benign and protective past, and of our belief in individual states of being and thinking. The irony is that Facebook has somewhat protected individual identity—what we represent and think and say—but at the same time has conditioned us to daily norms that are increasingly universal, contingent, and facile. This change, these themes, that future society are all the things Fincher's filmmaking and Sorkin's writing have been about for over a quarter of a century.

In the aftermath of his early experiences as a filmmaker, and certainly from around the time he made *Fight Club* (1999), Fincher became more garrulous in his reaction against consumption and consumerist culture.

The Starbucks, Apple, American Express world was "the ontological legacy of postmodernism" as Lawrence Knapp calls it in his collection of the director's interviews; an ecosphere worn down by late-stage capitalism and its dehumanizing philosophy that has featured several times and with increasing fervor in Fincher's films (Knapp 2014, xi).

As Knapp recalls, having early on rejected the notion of being a metteur-for-hire director—something he had seen other filmmakers fall into the trap of—Fincher has long argued that cinema shouldn't simply be comforting all the time. "I'm fascinated by movies that scar," he said. "I've always been more interested in noir, in seventies movies like *The Parallax View*," parading his affinity for Hitchcock and Scorsese in films such as *The Game* (1997) and *The Girl with the Dragon Tattoo* (2011). The attitude has kept at bay criticism of a fawning reverence for past greats. Neither has it made his filmmaking seem reductive in the way other filmmakers with similar pretensions have been criticized for (Knapp 2014, xi).

A Common Set of Facts

If the cinematic referents are apparent in *The Social Network*, the cultural ones are equally pervasive. The film is about everyone wanting to be their own cover story, an online fantasy about adorning the front of *Rolling Stone*. A cool but not too cool publication; pop culture, but of the establishment rather than the avant-garde; a bastion of convention, but also with things still to say.

In fact, the comparison is well made not least for the singularly driven vision that *Rolling Stone* founder and editor Jann Wenner had over that magazine. A Facebook for the counterculture age that became a mainstay of liberal establishment thought, as Joe Hagan has remarked, *Rolling Stone*, like Facebook, was always a business. But the way it acted and felt in the hands of Wenner, just as Facebook's profile was so heavily conditioned, as *The Social Network* explains, by Zuckerberg's personality, made it *his* vision of the world, and his only (Hagan 2018, 502).

Wenner interviewed Barack Obama on several occasions for *Rolling Stone*, reacting to Obama's belief that until everybody had agreed on a common set of facts about the world—a view Obama re-promoted to historian David Olusoga in a November 2020 BBC TV interview—that diverted us away from conspiracy theories and fake news, then we were facing a crisis of legitimacy in what was accepted norms of behavior and values (Wenner 2016). Wenner opined that if that was to remain the establishment's principled position, then the government might need to bail out the "real" news corporations in the face of online competition that seemed to care little for "common facts."

Wenner was like Zuckerberg in that respect. A Janus figure who spoke, on the one hand, for the traditions of truths, in-depth reporting, and legitimacy, and yet, on the other, understood the power of celebrity—celebrity that was immune to political niceties, that generated money, that in turn generated yet more fame and wealth, and enough in time to buy the White House. Zuckerberg was arguably the disciple of Wenner in that regard; they'd concocted a vision that had bought power and influence while reformulating a social and cultural landscape that the establishment didn't like, and which threatened their very existence. It is no coincidence that *Rolling Stone* was one of the few publications in 2015, as he embarked on his presidential bid, to take Trump seriously and give him a hearing. They/Wenner got it. As Hagan says, "[t]he message and the medium had merged" with Trump, and lo and behold anyone who failed to take that seriously (Hagan 2018, 502–3).

Zuckerberg had been an equally fascinating character to *Rolling Stone* as far back as 2008. The magazine's interest then was piqued by former friends and associates who claimed they had been "royally screwed" by a "brilliant but ostracized nerd" who they hired to code and who then stole the whole kit and caboodle. Claire Hoffman's profile invoked the renegade programmer as a new kind of social animal back then, only comfortable behind the protection of a screen, suddenly able to fashion biting commentary where once awkward silence stood.

But the most persuasive aspect of Hoffman's characterization of Zuckerberg came toward the end of the piece. The slacker dork personality hides someone, she said, more akin to Donald Trump than a hacker seeking a personal life. Zuckerberg was always moving forward, ruthless to the point of obsession, and not afraid to break the terms of a contract—personal, professional, social—if it suits his purposes (Hoffman 2008). In other words, there was a grudging admiration for Zuckerberg's cold-blooded instinct, paraded as libertarian conceit.

A decade later, the terms of reference had changed and by 2018 Matt Taibbi was arguing in the same magazine: "We shouldn't be asking Facebook to fix the problem. We should be fixing Facebook. It's our collective misfortune that this perhaps silliest-in-history supercorporation—a tossed-off hookup site turned international cat-video vault turned Orwellian surveillance megavillain—has dragged us all to the very cliff edge of modern technological capitalism" (2018).

That word, surveillance, which by now had become almost ubiquitous with Facebook, had Machiavellian intent about it but was now also being adopted as a consequence of the sheer size and scale of the corporation. By the beginning of a new decade, ten years after *The Social Network* was released, Adrienne LaFrance was moved to describe Facebook as a "Doomsday Machine." LaFrance's insinuation arises from the description of what a self-controlling, computerized megadeath device would look like and do, as theorized in Herman Khan's influential 1960 book *On Thermonuclear War* (LaFrance 2020). But the example might as well come from where it gained real notoriety as a concept: the cinema, and in particular Stanley Kubrick's *Dr. Strangelove or: How I Stopped Worrying and Learned to Love the Bomb* (1964). LaFrance's allegory is that rather as we had to learn to live—ironically and satirically as Kubrick would have it—with the "bomb," so we now must learn to "survive" with Facebook (LaFrance 2020). While the corporation has made wrong turns, and engaged in PR disasters like the Trump acquiescence, LaFrance suggests, the crux of the rumor, as Facebook entered its next decade, was that now no one, least of all Zuckerberg himself, could control what the invention had become. Not despite but because of itself, "Facebook is an agent of government propaganda, targeted harassment, terrorist recruitment, emotional manipulation, and genocide—a world-historic weapon that lives not underground, but in a Disneyland-inspired campus in Menlo Park, California," said LaFrance (2020).

The natural conclusion is to presume that this is all a long, long way from where Fincher and Sorkin directed their story about Facebook's inception and early infighting. But the truth to power of the film is that Facebook's villainous intent, its Jekyll and Hyde transformation, sits right there in the story, lurking about its fringes, bleeding out from the acrimony and repercussions that infuse the narrative. It encircles that very first scene between Mark and Erica in the bar.

Erica takes the empowering initiative to end a relationship that is at best awkward and at worst manipulative and self-serving. If the boot were on the other foot, and Zuckerberg had terminated their relationship, there would almost be no reason for Facebook to exist. But he is not the one ending it; Erica is. And her reward is to be trolled—arguably the first in human history?—in the most publicly humiliating and vindictive manner, all for an experiment in human behavior. Bad news, hyped-up slander, attracts any number of callers, and invites any number of "joiners" to march in and observe if not participate in the public stoning. But of course, that's not quite what Facebook's modus operandi was ever meant to be or has been. By and large it operates as an invite-only, rosy-colored, rainbow-endowed, unicorn-frolicking approximation of what the world is really like. It has been at the edges where the Doomsday Machine started thinking for itself, offering antidotes to the pleasantness that abounded, and disinformation to the masses generally who were becoming ever more unsure of the twenty-first-century world in which they lived.

As LaFrance recognizes, all of this check-and-balance could be self-contained until the moment Facebook hit escape velocity and its size and scale meant it was representing, and in part regulating, the better portion of the mass of humanity all on one site. Then, its sheer presence alone became a threat, whatever it allowed to be said and done. Indeed, Fincher talks of *The Social Network* bringing to light a hyper-masculine-not-being-appreciated-enough complex that devours Zuckerberg, drives his initial revenge plot against Erica, and is a mode of behavior that affects many of the film's other protagonists like Sean as well (Levy 2014, 164).

Fincher warms to his theme in realizing on screen the way innovation and technology were changing the workforce leading to what Zuckerberg creates from nothing in a dorm room (Levy 2014, 163). Sorkin's script presents the montage sequence of Zuckerberg building Facebook's online platform as if mystically offering a dose of this and pinch of that to a magical potion. In fact, with hindsight, the film is suggesting how the next decade would see the power of the press if not political institutions diminished by computers and coding inventing a social world where the elite had no power over the message unless they reinvented themselves. That required a celebrity force to galvanize a coalition of willing believers happy to hear how their pleasant world was being undermined by globalization, identity politics, and political correctness. Step forward Donald Trump.

Fincher and Sorkin spoke frequently about how one person is no one thing. The film's structure conveys those multiple perspectives, an arrogance but vulnerability in Zuckerberg and in the surrounding lives about him, a worth but weakness too. Sorkin acknowledged that "a dramatist's job is to be reductive," to distil everything down into a basic two-step program; Zuckerberg wants revenge on a girl who's slighted him, and at the same time sees a way to conquer the world (Levy 2014, 174). The first is the stepping-off point. What remains after that is how we are all driven by a social media "death instinct" that Facebook has unleashed, and which more often than not results in the unhinging of our rational—and for some irrational—persona. Donald Trump knows this feeling all too well.

Conclusion: Success and Its Discontents

Two months after the 2020 election, on January 6, the day that the US Congress met to formally ratify electoral college votes in favor of Joe Biden's victory, the president held a "Save America" rally on The Mall in Washington. Helping to galvanize the more extreme elements of Trump's base to go and march on the Capitol, hundreds of demonstrators proceeded to enter the congressional halls and ransack the House of Representatives, the Senate, and the offices of United States Representatives. Trump offered up a video soon after that, called on the violence to stop but nevertheless repeated his baseless claims of election fraud while thanking the "patriots" who took part in the rally, claiming, "we love you." On Twitter and Facebook where the video initially appeared, Trump's accounts were suspended, but the pressure on both to close him down permanently and stifle the oxygen of publicity that had been given to Trump while in office mounted considerably.

Facebook's former head of information security, Alex Stamos, claimed that Trump had to be "cut off." "There are no legitimate equities left," he said. "The last reason for keeping Trump's account up was the possibility that he would try to put the genie back in the bottle, but that is impossible for him" (Hern 2021). Twitter and Facebook had made Donald Trump, but he had come to preside over them like a colossus, a force too large to tame it seemed. Until, that is, misinformation, misrepresentation, and plain simple lies gave way to violence directed at the central pillars of democracy. Then the planks of Trump's social media framework came crashing down. Redemption seemed the only way out, just as it does for Zuckerberg in *The Social Network*. The movie's final scene that has Mark sitting in the meeting room of the lawyers' offices might be read as a sad indictment of loneliness and rejection. He repeatedly taps refresh on his Facebook screen in the hope that Erica might "befriend" him once more, and he can return to how it was before invention, discovery, fame, and power overtook his life.

Yet in the age of Trump, that gesture now prophesizes a larger-than-life character emerging center stage in the 2010s but who, in defeat and finally stung by the power of rejection, seeks affirmation in an act of hubris so misconstrued as to be senseless. Trump's final two months in office, but especially that day on January 6 when he all but led his "troops" in an assault on the democratic institutions of the United States, was his failsafe point, the moment of no return, the second at which there was no rowing back from the overinflated rhetoric, the false claims, the life lived in an alternate reality. A day later, Trump promised a legitimate handover of power even while he continued to believe that he had not just won the November presidential election, but won in a landslide, and that now, in retreat, "the greatest presidency in American history" was, for the moment, coming to a close.

The clampdown of Trump vocally demanded in the wake of the events of January 6 made perfect sense on one level. However, Facebook, Twitter, and Instagram saw the dilemma, and the irony. They had the power to cut off at the knees a figure who had gone from comic entity, to unlikely inheritor of the greatest office, to dangerous demagogue, most of it at warp speed thanks to the enabling power of big-tech. But what would happen to every public representative in Trump's wake on their platforms? Once set, where would the precedent end? Why not silence those of more moderate disposition but who some just didn't want to hear from or give publicity to? Why shouldn't some corporations with authority and money be emboldened while others without the resources frozen out of the conversation?

Facebook had made Trump, but now its greatest creation had planted the seeds of disaffection into its core being in a way that Fincher and Sorkin realize in Zuckerberg's motivations and revenge theory—revenge against Erica, Eduardo, the Winklevoss brothers (Armie Hammer), and Divya Narendra (Max Minghella) who brought the lawsuit against him, and against Sean Parker whose behavior almost cost Zuckerberg the company and his future. Everything built upon revenge sooner or later gets consumed by its own vanity, however. Exactly one year before the siege on the Capitol, reports circulated that at a dinner meeting Zuckerberg had congratulated Trump for being "No. 1" on Facebook, even though Trump's followers and likes—if that were a measure of being "first"—didn't even come close to the numbers of other celebrities on the site (Wood 2020).

What Zuckerberg was doing, as so many had in the ascent of Donald Trump, was providing an enabling strategy for the man's vanity superseding any reality that might challenge his picture of himself. But what Zuckerberg represented in such an act was Facebook's own strategy for all individuals, not just Trump. Being the maker and member of one's own Porcellian—the exclusive invite-only Harvard club Mark originally wants to gain membership to—is the metaphor that runs through *The Social Network* and captures the defect in Facebook's wiring; the need not just to be accepted, but to have to parade oneself as the most, the best, the only. To feel the need to establish oneself as a success.

In Julie Levinson's account of the "success myth" in American cinema, she identifies those movies where, to borrow William Whyte's phrase, the "organization man" theory of cautious career progression is usurped by a maverick individual intent on tearing up the rulebook and bringing a swagger to the boardroom. "In *The Social Network*," she observes, "David Fincher's portrait . . . is of the giddy ascendance of an outsider . . . vanquishing all who would stand in his way. He solves his problems with the corporate establishment by bypassing it to create his own business model and set of rules" (Levinson 2012, 107).

For Levinson, Zuckerberg is in the end undone by his own hubris as that final scene seeking to redeem himself with Erica demonstrates for her. There's a duality at work, she believes, that is partially about letting loose the reigns of individual ambition in order to succeed all the while acknowledging that corporate America is a somewhat malfunctioning model (Levinson 2012, 108). While Levinson is undoubtedly right about the business message, for Facebook's dress-down, low-strung model of corporate imagery succumbed to its own form of convention in time, in a way success under the Facebook/Trump universe became less about corporations or maverick individuals, and much more about the laxness of probity throughout public life. Mere opinion as received truths, abhorrent behavior as locker room banter, being No. 1 when the term is meaningless except in one's own head; these were the conventions America got used to in the 2010s and which *The Social Network* predictively drew attention to at the start of the decade.

Facebook had become not only a business then, but arguably *the* twenty-first-century business by the 2020s. As Mark informs Eduardo in one scene when the pair are talking about Facebook's early commercial possibilities, there is nothing final about the company's profile because,

"It will never be finished, the way fashion is never finished." There is no end product in the commercial online world just as there is no end game in public life any longer either. After the 2016 presidential election, Donald Trump never began the process of governing; for him politics was forever about campaigning, and campaigning to prove that he was the best ever, a reaffirming accomplishment that in Trump's eyes, if not his supporters, never ends.

For Zuckerberg, a similar sort of affirmatory circular logic manifests in his voter share power on Facebook's board, which he consolidated during the 2010s in just the way we see him dilute Eduardo's original slice of shares in the film, and which became the reason for at least one lawsuit against him. His success is also upheld by purchasing other "behavioural surplus" sites like Oculus and WhatsApp which, as Shoshana Zuboff states, "ensur[ed] Facebook's ownership of the gargantuan flows of human behaviour that would pour through these pipes" (Zuboff 2019, 103). Just as Trump was reputedly shocked by victory on election night 2016, an against-the-odds triumph that even he had not dared believe would actually come true, so Zuckerberg seemed genuinely taken aback by Facebook's reach and power as a result of these acquisitions. He was even more astonished after the election to have to explain his company's actions before Congress, as though the dorm room hacker had been found to be building a doomsday machine after all. *The Social Network*, a movie that might have been no more than a glimpse of a moment in time, the beginning and end of a socially interactive concept that could have burnt brightly and then faded, foretold it all. Fincher and Sorkin give us less a picture of fledgling social media in amber, more the unfolding creation of a new universe on our smart devices that was not just about change in us; it was about changing our whole world and all we thought we knew and believed in.

References

Bailey, H. (2021), "Trump's Twitter Ban Obscures the Real Problem: State-Backed Manipulation Is Rampant on Social Media," *The Conversation*, 13 January. Available online: https://theconversation.com/trumps-twitter-ban-obscures-the-real- problem-state-backed-manipulation-is-rampant-on-social-media-153136.

Hagan, J. (2018), *Sticky Fingers: The Life and Times of Jann Wenner and Rolling Stone Magazine*, Edinburgh: Canongate.

Hern, A. (2021), "Donald Trump Twitter Ban Comes to an End Amid Calls for Tougher Action," *The Guardian*, 7 January. Available online: https://www.theguardian.com/us-news/2021/jan/07/donald-trump-twitter-ban- comes-to-end-amid-calls-for-tougher-action.

Hern, A. and J. Waterson (2020), "Mark Zuckerberg Criticised by Civil Rights Leaders over Donald Trump Facebook Post," *The Guardian*, 2 June. Available online: https://www.theguardian.com/technology/2020/jun/02/mark-zuckerberg-criticised-by-civil-rights-leaders-over-donald-trump-facebook-post.

Hoffman, C. (2008), "The Battle for Facebook," *Rolling Stone*, 26 June. Available online: https://www.rollingstone.com/culture/culture-news/the-battle-for-facebook-242989/.

Klein, N. (2020), "How Big Tech Plans to Profit from the Pandemic," *The Guardian*, 13 May. Available online: https://www.theguardian.com/news/2020/may/13/naomi-klein-how-big-tech-plans-to-profit-from-coronavirus-pandemic.

Knapp, L. F. (2014), "Introduction," in L. Knapp (ed.), *David Fincher: Interviews*, Jackson: University of Mississippi Press.

LaFrance, A. (2020), "Facebook Is a Doomsday Machine," *The Atlantic*, 15 December. Available online: https://www.theatlantic.com/technology/archive/2020/12/facebook-doomsday-machine/617384/.

Levinson, J. (2012), *The American Success Myth on Film*, Basingstoke: Palgrave.

Levy, E. (2014), "Social Network: Interview with Director David Fincher," in L. F. Knapp (ed.), *David Fincher Interviews*, Jackson: University of Mississippi Press, pp. 159–75. First published in 2010 on https://emanuellevy.com.

Marshall McLuhan, M. (1964), *Understanding Media: The Extensions of Man*, New York: McGraw-Hill.

Naughton, J. (2020), "Whoever Controls Facebook Holds the Reins in the American Presidential Race," *The Observer*, The New Review, 7 June, p. 21.

Taibbi, M. (2018), "Can We Be Saved from Facebook?," *Rolling Stone*, 3 April. Available online: https://www.rollingstone.com/politics/politics-features/can-we-be-saved-from-facebook-629567/.

Watercutter, A. (2019), "*The Social Network* Was More Right than Anyone Realized," *Wired*, 5 February. Available online: https://www.wired.com/story/social-network-right-all-along/.

Wenner, J. S. (2016), "The Day After: Obama on His Legacy, Trump's Win and the Path Forward," *Rolling Stone*, 29 November. Available online: https://www.rollingstone.com/politics/politics-features/the-day-after-obama-on-his-legacy-trumps-win-and-the-path-forward-113422/.

Wines, M. (2020), "'Looting' Comment From Trump Dates Back to Racial Unrest of the 1960s," *The New York Times*, 29 May. Available online: https://www.nytimes.com/2020/05/29/us/looting-starts-shooting-starts.html.

Wong, J. C. (2020), "Facebook Declines to Take Action Against Trump Statements," *The Guardian*, 30 May. Available online: https://www.theguardian.com/technology/2020/may/29/facebook-trump-twitter-social-media-us.

Wood, C. (2020), "Facebook CEO Mark Zuckerberg Congratulated Trump for Being 'No. 1 on Facebook,' According to Trump," *Business Insider*, 7 January. Available online: https://www.businessinsider.com/trump-mark-zuckerberg-dinner-number-one-facebook-2020-1?r=US&IR=T.

Zuboff, S. (2019), *The Age of Surveillance Capitalism: The Fight for a Human Future at the New Frontier of Power*, London: Profile Books.

7

"I Figured You Were Probably Watching Us"

Performing Gender and Citizen Surveillance in *Ex Machina*

Kayla Meyers

In the film *Ex Machina* (Alex Garland 2014), Caleb (Domhnall Gleeson), a mid-level coder for Blue Book, a proxy for Google, wins the chance to spend a week with the fictional tech company's CEO Nathan (Oscar Isaac). What was marketed as a week of luxury and leisure is quickly revealed to be a more unique opportunity: Caleb will administer a Turing test to Ava (Alicia Vikander), a possible AI. Ava is constructed as a life-sized woman, confined to a room in Nathan's bungalow. Though she has a human appearing face, her body is a distinctly robotic mix of metal, plastics, and carbon fiber. Throughout the test sessions, Ava seduces Caleb and convinces him to help her escape. While fleeing, she abandons Caleb in a sealed room, and Kyoko (Sonoya Mizuno), another cyborg, kills Nathan.

Surveillance plays a central role in the film: Nathan watches Caleb watch Ava, who is aware of her role as test subject, the setting encased in a web of cameras and screens. While surveillance typically assumes a unilateral flow of power from the "surveillant" to the "subject of surveillance," the film creates a complicated matrix where characters constantly shift between roles.[1] In the film's moment of production and distribution, surveillance was and continues to be ubiquitous and a source of omnipresent global anxiety. Though a British production, the characters, their accents, and their backgrounds position the film within the US cultural context, where such anxiety was heightened by the 2013 Snowden leaks at mid-production. As such, the film's focus on surveillance and its fluidity is prescient and incisive.

Surveillance intends to build knowledge and certainty through seeing, hearing, and mining people's data. In the proliferation of the globalized economy and Global War on Terror, surveillance has become central to managing and demarcating fluid populations and permeable borders. Surveillance in airports, on borderlines, and in the media has been deployed and encouraged by the state in the name of defending US citizens from foreign threats. The Global War on Terror itself has been facilitated by surveillance through the Uniting and Strengthening America by Providing Appropriate Tools Required to Intercept and Obstruct Terrorism Act of 2001 (better known as the US Patriot Act) and the adoption of Information Operations (IO), which encompass "the surveillance, control, and destruction of communications networks, psychological warfare and propaganda, and more routine methods of public affairs and media relations" (Winseck 2009, 151). Citizens, too, are instructed to remain on the lookout for perceived global threats. Though the Global War on Terror deploys the surveillance-state apparatus in the name of citizen safety, this same apparatus inevitably turns its eye on the citizen. The state has authorized public, participatory surveillance where "they consolidate the gaze of the state and subject a growing number of routine daily activities to intrusive monitoring," eroding distinctions between civilian and military threat, public and private (Larson and Piché 2009, 187). Citizens accept such intrusion as long as mass-surveillance practices are framed as anti-terrorist, executed in the name of rooting out the other rather than monitoring the citizen (Gao 2015).

As state surveillance manifests at intimate levels of the body politic, it has also been applied to questions of gender, institutionalizing the queer body's historic surveillance. Toby Beauchamp's definition of surveillance claims it as "built into the production of the very category of transgender" (2014, 208–10). Thus surveillance continually attempts to delimit gender by *knowing* the body, always concerned with discovering "fraudulent," non-gender-conforming individuals. Post-9/11 surveillance assumes gender surveillance in practice: US airport security scanners determine anomalies based on which gender the official enters (Waldron and Medina 2019). Such impulses to reify gender norms have only intensified following the 2008 economic crisis, which ushered intense backlash to contemporary understandings of feminism and leveraged population control toward propping up neoliberal hegemony in the wake of its collapse. Public, participatory surveillance deployed for domestic security and issues of control is central to legislation like 2016 House Bill 2 in North Carolina. Though repealed in 2017, the bill criminalized entering a bathroom for a gender different from the sex on one's birth certificate. Thus, systems of surveillance and social anxieties around gender norms have been imbricated and intensified.

To analyze the role of surveillance in *Ex Machina*, I use Judith Butler's theory of gender performativity to unravel the complexities particular to lateral surveillance, or the ways citizens spy on and police one another such that the boundaries between surveillant and the subject of surveillance collapse. Butler theorizes that gender performance is not a conscious gendering of the self, but the repeated performance of gender based on norms that have accumulated historical power and social primacy. But the subject can never perfectly reproduce the norms they are compelled to replicate: the performance is always doomed to fail (2013, 22–3). In the film, Caleb and Nathan continually deploy systems of surveillance to reassert their heteropatriarchal control over Ava and Kyoko. But both cyborg subjects elude patriarchal control through heightened gender performance and sexuality. Not only does surveillance's failure to secure masculine control highlight the performativity of gender, but it also reveals the performativity of surveillance itself. As Butler argues, the performative possesses "resources from which resistance, subversion, displacement are to be forged," presupposing the tools of its own undoing (2013, 23). *Ex Machina* registers how surveillance of others easily slips into self-surveillance, how surveillance fails as a system of knowledge aggregation, and ultimately how the subject of surveillance can resist their own subjugation through the performativity inherent to surveillance culture.

Can We Just Be Two Guys?

To understand surveillance's performativity in *Ex Machina*, it is essential to grasp how surveillance becomes a system through which the film constructs gender, and particularly masculinity. While concentration on the Turing test positions the film in a genealogy of cinema that investigates AI's imagined possibilities and threats, the plot's tension derives mostly from the relationships and hierarchies that humans impose, particularly Nathan and Caleb's homosocial relationship. Caleb, a timid employee, arrives at Nathan's secluded bungalow expecting a week of male bonding before he is aware of Ava. Nathan, too, desires such a relationship with Caleb; when Caleb is star-struck upon meeting him, Nathan laments, "I get the moment you're having. But—dude—can we just get past that? Can we just be two guys?" In their quest to "just be two guys," Nathan and Caleb continually reassert and cling to contemporary notions of white, heteropatriarchal masculinity as afforded by the office and fraternity film genres. However, such masculinity proves performative as the two men continually fail to embody gender ideals. In these moments, Caleb and Nathan deploy hyper-masculinity through surveillance, allowing them to dominate technology, women, and whole populations.

Ex Machina draws from the office film and fraternity film genres, which focus on male homosociality, to construct Nathan and Caleb's masculinity and the gendered hierarchies in the film. The 1990s office film emerged in a moment of masculine anxieties "about the shifting fortunes of the white-middle-class male" and depicted the focal point of this anxiety: the office. Office movies privilege the relationship between father and son, manifested in a mentor–mentee relationship, where the transfer of knowledge between men leads to the reassertion of their patriarchal power (Hunter 2011, 77). The fraternity film, instead, imagines antics as a rite of passage that ensures ascendance to patriarchal power in the form of a stable, office job. The workspace plays oppositional roles in either genre, the adversary in the office film but the aim in the fraternity film, underscoring the contradictory nature of heteropatriarchal masculinity. But what is clear is that heteropatriarchal masculinity depends on a cocktail of knowledge transfer, aggression, and male kinship framed by the workspace. Though the film takes place in Nathan's secluded bungalow, couching their relationship in the natural world, the film presents both Caleb and Nathan as part of Silicon Valley, a male-dominated space where fraternity culture proliferates (Wajcman 2004, 12). Director Alex Garland explicitly states, "[Nathan] uses the word 'dude' and 'bro' a lot. And I felt like this was sometimes how tech companies present themselves to us" (2015). Not only are these companies male-dominated, but they also serve representationally as sites where college fraternity behavior can continue.[2] In Silicon Valley, the masculinities of the fraternity film and office film manifest.

Inhabiting both genres, Caleb and Nathan secure their masculinity through mentor–mentee knowledge transfer of Ava's behavior and creation. This construction, two men connecting through shared information about a woman, also mirrors Eve Sedgwick's conception of the homoerotic triangle. Using René Girard's calculus of power in the rivalry between two men over a woman, Sedgwick reconfigures this triangle to observe homosocial relationships between men. She asserts, "it is the use of women as exchangeable, perhaps symbolic, property for the primary purpose of cementing bonds of men with men" (Sedgwick 1985, 25–6). Caleb and Nathan's homosociality is built particularly around the surveillance of Ava. Early on, the film establishes Caleb and Nathan's double surveillance of Ava: Caleb records Ava's responses during the test sessions, Nathan monitors Caleb and Ava, and Caleb watches Ava outside of the test sessions through the television in his room. While these forms of surveillance are intended to build knowledge and certainty about who, or what, Ava is, Ava crucially is a site through which Nathan and Caleb negotiate their relationship. Thus, being "just two guys" will always include Ava.

Discussion about Ava between both men permeates the film, but is most concentrated in a scene following the second test session where Nathan details her construction. As the two men enter a sterile room of stainless-steel tables and tools, Nathan says, "This is where Ava was created." Though the statement's syntax centers Ava, the logic of the homosocial triangle promises to bond Nathan and Caleb. Throughout this scene, Nathan and Caleb leverage surveillance's promise of patriarchal control to assert their masculinity. First, Nathan explains how he programmed Ava's voice and facial reactions using limitless cell phone data collected through Blue Book without user consent. Nathan reveals this ethically questionable move to Caleb like a fraternity brother might admit a drunken misdeed, revealing his intention to bond with Caleb over this mastery of technology. After Nathan explains how he created Ava's software, Caleb responds, "You hacked the world's cell phones?" Nathan scoffs, "Yeah, and all the manufacturers knew I was doing it too, but they couldn't accuse me without admitting they were doing it themselves." This assertion implicates the audience in Ava's construction, while reminding the audience of their own subordination to a larger matrix of state and corporate surveillance. This matrix imbricated with Nathan's surveillance underscores the dominance that these male agents hold over processes of surveillance, and thus implies their power over the audience.

Then, Nathan reasserts his power and centrality in Ava's construction. Moving to a stainless-steel table, he picks up a blue orb, sliding it out of a metal enclosure, and states, "Here we have her mind." The camera is low, gazing up at Nathan as he holds Ava's "brain" in one hand. Nathan looms over the viewer like a god; human consciousness literally sits in his hand. He then explains the materiality of Ava's mind: "structured gel—I had to get away from circuitry. I needed something that could arrange and rearrange at a molecular level." Contrasting his previous passive statement that centered Ava, Nathan positions himself as the subject: "I need." It is not Ava who needs this technology to achieve consciousness and selfhood, but Nathan who needs to claim himself as creator.

Nathan's claim of domination is also a means through which he and Caleb develop a masculine bond that equalizes their relationship, which is emphasized both rhetorically and physically as the scene progresses. When they first enter the workshop, Nathan is positioned as Caleb's patriarch: Nathan instructs Caleb to look around, which he does nervously. Nathan looms behind him with his hands casually in his pockets. As Nathan shares information with Caleb, this hierarchy begins to collapse. By the end of the scene, their relationship equalizes. As Nathan explains Ava's software, he passes the blue orb to Caleb, signifying a transfer of knowledge and suggesting Caleb has finally attained equal footing with him as the patriarch. While Nathan explains how he monitored the public vis-à-vis Blue Book to develop Ava's software, the camera closes in on the blue orb in Caleb's hands. His hands dwarf her mind, underscoring the physical power they have over her. This emphasizes the patriarchal nature of Ava's construction while positioning both Nathan and Caleb as gods, echoing Caleb's assertion from early in the film: "If you've created a conscious machine, it's not the history of man. It's the history of gods." In imagining themselves as all-powerful gods, Caleb and Nathan come together over Ava's mind. Ultimately, through the exchange of knowledge revolving around surveillance and their mutual ability to monitor and thus dominate Ava, Nathan and Caleb develop a homosocial bond founded on notions of masculinity privileged in fraternity and office films.

You Can See That I Am a Machine

While Nathan and Caleb imagine themselves as the sole proprietors of surveillance, Ava and Kyoko appropriate systems of surveillance to achieve their own autonomy. Ava is the locus of all of Nathan and Caleb's surveillance efforts, but negotiates these systems of surveillance by manipulating how she is seen and understood by both men. Kyoko, though her capacity for human consciousness remains unclear, similarly comports herself to gendered and racialized feminine norms. Both cyborgs mold themselves into desirable, sexualized beings, reinscribing themselves with the features of passive femininity under surveillance's gaze. Because, in the logic of the film, surveillance is perceived as a force of patriarchal domination, Ava and Kyoko's manipulation of surveillance depends on their performance of hyper-sexual, but unthreatening, femininity.

The film continually insists upon the visualization of Ava as an essential part of the Turing test. Caleb administers the test and carefully observes Ava's responses, while Nathan monitors their sessions. When Caleb administers the test, is enclosed entirely in a glass box within her room. He can see Ava, but they can never physically interact. The first shot of Ava shows her backlit from a small window to the outside, framed like a picture. Both are enclosed as if exhibits to be viewed, studied, and ultimately classified. While Ava and Caleb's glass enclosures would suggest a mutual economy of looking, the interspersed clips of Nathan watching their interaction and the cinematic framework undercut this seeming equality. Laura Mulvey's theory of the male gaze asserts that through the cinematic screen, looking at a woman character simultaneously means the woman is passively displayed to the gaze (Mulvey 1989, 47). Thus distinctions between viewing and monitoring blur when framed by the film camera, as the audience's gaze maintains a unidirectional flow of power onto the female form, collapsing into the patriarchal surveillance of Ava.

Ava is acutely aware of the gaze on her body. In the first session, she states, "you already know my name and you can see that I am a machine," recognizing that she is being watched closely and that her ontology is determined by what both Caleb and Nathan observe. She also understands the imbalance of power associated with this surveillance. In the sixth session, Ava asks Caleb yes or no questions, and then analyzes whether his answers are truthful or not. As Caleb grows uncomfortable under her critical eye and suggests they end this game, she demands, "What will happen to me if I fail your test?" Even as she tests Caleb, she understands that her test is insignificant: if Caleb fails her test, nothing happens to him. But her failure to pass the Turing test could be dire; she could be destroyed. Surveillance determines her future viability, so she must negotiate these systems carefully to achieve agency.

Ava and Kyoko are both inscribed with patriarchal understandings of cis-womanhood. Though Ava is the first creation with human consciousness, the viewer is shown other female robots Nathan has created. These clips imply that Kyoko was likely an early iteration, now subjugated to the role of Nathan's house servant and mistress. Racialized as Japanese and completely mute, Kyoko reads on the surface as a geisha stereotype, present to appease Nathan's whims with utter compliance. The montage firmly roots Ava's formation to the sexual gaze. In fact, Nathan admits at the end of the film that he constructed Ava's facial features based on Caleb's internet porn preferences. Ava and Kyoko's construction and physical appearance are imbued with white, heteropatriarchal conceptions of desirability. If the logics of their mental processes spring from Nathan's patriarchal surveillance, their mental formations take on the same patriarchal structure. They have both learned how to behave like a human through mass surveillance, suggesting their own capacity for surveillance, but simultaneously internalized naturalized gender relations mirrored in public behaviors. Their mutual understanding of how they can monitor or appropriate the power promised by surveillance is also imbued with notions of feminine gender norms.

Ava ultimately gains agency by manipulating how she is observed, both in and out of the test sessions. But how she manipulates such systems depends on her performance of feminine passivity and sensuality. During the third session, Ava surprises Caleb by wearing a dress and wig, covering her robotic parts. She asks, "Do you think I'm attractive?" His ogling of her suggests that he does. She asks Caleb, "Do you think of me when we aren't together? Sometimes at night, I wonder if you are watching me through the cameras and I hope you are." As Ava dares him to watch her, Caleb appears to be uncomfortable, but he continues to watch her when he leaves the session. After this scene, the camera cuts immediately to Ava undressing. She turns her head, appearing to look directly into the surveillance camera. The camera cuts to Caleb's eyes, illuminated by blue light, back to Ava, and then again back to Caleb's throat swallowing hard. In this scene, we see not only Caleb watching Ava, but also Ava acknowledging his gaze and seizing control over it. Caleb observes her and feels aroused by his own surveillance, which she knows and invites because she understands that Caleb will help her escape if she can make him desire her sexually. By literally fashioning her body to look categorically feminine, she makes herself desirable to Caleb, manipulating how he observes her.

Part of Ava's plan includes breaking down the relationship between Caleb and Nathan, which Ava executes by physically manipulating the surveillance systems in the house. Throughout the film, Ava uses her robotic body to shut down the power system of the house, thereby turning off the surveillance cameras and removing the gaze from her body. The first time this happens during a test session, Ava asks Caleb if he trusts Nathan and if they are friends; she first insinuates and then outright states that Caleb should not trust Nathan. This plants the seeds of doubt in Caleb's mind, prompting him to lie to Nathan about what happens when the cameras turn off during the sessions. Through electronically manipulating the surveillance systems, Ava influences Caleb's behavior and begins to break down the exchange of knowledge and the knowability that Caleb and Nathan's surveillance originally promised. During the fifth session, Ava reveals that she is the one causing the power cuts, reasoning, "so we can see how we behave when we're unobserved." Her justification suggests that she and Caleb can be free from surveillance during the cuts because they are not subject to Nathan's patriarchal surveillance. In doing so, she falsely reassures Caleb that she is passive, incapable of surveillance. But Ava is using these cuts to monitor Caleb's sexuality and desire, slowly convincing him of her entrapment and his responsibility in freeing her.

The process of surveillance ultimately becomes embedded in Caleb's desire for Ava. After the fifth session, Caleb dreams of escaping with Ava and kissing her on a mountaintop, again insisting on his ability to conquer Ava and the natural world as essential to his masculinity. In the first shot of Caleb's dream, the viewer sees Ava through Caleb's point of view, gazing back at him. But she is viewed from above as if through a surveillance camera. Caleb's power to monitor her foregrounds their imagined sexual encounter and suggests surveillance as essential to the heterosexual interaction and part of heterosexual desire itself. The camera angle also underscores how Ava has manipulated Caleb's surveillance of her so that his interactions with her are no longer purely scientific, but also imbued with sexual and romantic feelings.

Though Kyoko remains peripheral to the Turing test, she also deploys hyper-femininity to wrest power from the systems of surveillance around her. Throughout the film, the camera registers Kyoko's capacity for surveillance, closing in on her face as she listens to Caleb and Nathan's conversations and Ava's test sessions. Internalizing the geisha stereotype embedded in her creation, she exploits hyper-sexuality to gain control over both Nathan and Caleb and secure access to systems of surveillance. When Caleb discovers the clips of previous cyborgs on Nathan's computer, the camera cuts to Kyoko lounging behind him naked. Passive and available, Caleb remains unthreatened, but she monitors his gaze. With her own gaze, she directs

Caleb to look around Nathan's room to discover other prototypes. She then peels her synthetic skin to reveal her cybernetic construction. Through her sexuality, she controls Caleb's gaze and knowledge. Following this scene, Kyoko is seen sitting behind Nathan's computer, watching the various surveillance feeds from across the bungalow, her gaze in the seat of control.

Both Ava and Kyoko's appropriation of surveillance in turn relies on their performativity of feminine gender roles. As Nathan and Caleb use surveillance to reassert their white, heteropatriarchal masculinity, and as Ava and Kyoko comport to the gaze of the surveillant, one can see how surveillance is gendered. All characters enact surveillance based on their understanding of socially naturalized gender. Thus the performative nature of gender is also amplified by surveillance. But central to Butler's theory of performativity is the potential for animating gender norms to unravel themselves. Surveillance, too, proves to be an unstable and unreliable process for shoring up gender norms and, ultimately, controlling and delimiting bodies.

Over time, Ava's careful disruption of the surveillance system fractures the homosocial bond between the two men. After Ava reveals she is the one creating the power cuts, Caleb and Nathan hike a pristine mountain surrounding Nathan's bungalow. At the top, Caleb demands, "Can we talk about the lies you've been spinning me?" Nathan first feigns ignorance, but Caleb pushes back, insisting that he knows the competition he won was a cover. Nathan relents that the competition was a ruse, but insists Caleb's selection resulted from his talent as a coder. While this is ultimately revealed as a lie, Nathan can only patch over their homosocial crisis through insisting upon their shared genius, the same shared genius that paired them in the workshop.

But the relationship remains on unstable ground, so both men seek to reassert their heterosexuality through sexual encounters with Ava and Kyoko that incorporate acts of surveillance. Nathan, after aggressively beating a punching bag, turns around to Kyoko, watching him. Before Nathan kisses her, he brings her hand up to his neck and his hand to hers. But they maintain two very different grasps. Kyoko's hand rests on Nathan's neck as she looks at him. Nathan instead grabs her neck, placing his thumb under her chin and turning it upward, physically removing her gaze from him. He then inspects her face. What he is looking for is unclear, but this act asserts his refusal to be watched by her and insists on his role as surveillant. Meanwhile, Caleb dreams of him and Ava escaping together. The camera cuts back and forth between these two scenes, mixing the sexual encounters together and drawing them into conversation with one another. This camera work echoes Sedgwick's conception of the homoerotic triangle, implying that these sexual encounters are simultaneously attempts to reestablish their homosocial bond in the face of its instability.

Their bond ultimately deteriorates as Ava successfully influences and breaks down the control that the men achieve through systems of surveillance. Ava convinces Caleb to help her escape, and when Caleb begins to execute the escape plan, he is caught by Nathan, who had installed a secret camera during the final session when Caleb explains his plan to Ava. By installing a battery-powered camera, Nathan again asserts himself as the dominant surveillant. He then reveals to Caleb the real goal of the test: "Ava was a rat in a maze. And I gave her one way out. To escape she'd have to use: self-awareness, imagination, manipulation, sexuality, empathy, and she did. Now if that isn't true AI, what the fuck is?" Nathan hoped Ava would use Caleb to escape. But Nathan underestimates Ava, and the seeds of doubt she planted take bloom. Caleb admits, "I figured you were probably watching us during the power cuts," so he had already set escape plan in motion. Caleb's own manipulation of the surveillance in the last test session tricks Nathan, subverting his surveillance and ultimately breaking down his control over his home, Caleb, and Ava. With the electricity out now, Caleb and Nathan are literally powerless in the bungalow.

As the systems of surveillance crumble, so do the characters' understanding of their gender. Without surveillance, Caleb and Nathan can no longer stabilize their heterosexuality or relationship through the mutual surveillance of Ava. In learning that his role was to be manipulated by Ava, Caleb becomes acutely aware of the surveillance directed toward him and that he was never Nathan's equal. Moreover, Caleb learns that Nathan selected him not for his coding skills but based on surveillance of his online search history, suddenly degrading him to Ava's status. Caleb is not only personally violated by this surveillance but also emasculated by the technological apparatus of surveillance. Nathan, trying to console Caleb, says that the search inputs revealed a "good kid," but Caleb interjects, "with no family . . . and no girlfriend." His interruptions show that this shift from surveillant to surveilled is a blow to his heterosexuality, his masculinity now unstable and mutable.

Even Nathan's power through surveillance, and thus masculinity, deteriorates in the end. While Nathan and Caleb argue, Kyoko slips into Ava's room and stands in the glass box, appropriating Caleb's role. When Nathan learns that Caleb has already changed the lockdown procedures, Nathan walks out into the hallway to find Ava whispering into Kyoko's ear. The homoerotic triangle reconfigures for the first time in the film. Sedgwick notes that the power structure of erotic triangles depends on the gender of those at all points. When the triangle is configured woman-woman-man, the women's homoerotic relationship is developed in relation to the patriarchy, in this case Nathan (Sedgwick 1985, 25). Kyoko and Ava's desire for freedom from surveillance's patriarchal control defines their homosocial relationship. Since Nathan, their literal father, prevents such autonomy, their homosocial relationship is founded on mutual hatred for him. Now he is the symbolic site through which Kyoko and Ava will negotiate their relationship.

In this negotiation, the film betrays internalized racial bias over who can subvert surveillance and who is permanently under its gaze. Kyoko kills

Nathan and perishes, Ava escapes, and Caleb is left trapped in the bungalow. Though Kyoko, like Ava, uses gender performance to grasp control of surveillance in the bungalow, ultimately killing the patriarch, her agency is limited as she never leaves the bungalow to become a true citizen. Ava, however, covers her limbs and torso in synthetic skin until she presents as a white cis-woman, exits the home, and boards a helicopter that will take her back to civilization. The logics of US surveillance define threats to national security as non-white, but white subjects can pass undetected as threats in the public. While Kyoko's race is not an explicit threat, the film fails to imagine the possibility of a racialized subject moving unnoticed into the public, but takes for granted Ava's capacity to slip into the body of the nation-state. In this moment, the film unconsciously suggests that true subversion of surveillance is limited in terms of race.

Ultimately, the performative nature of gender is magnified through the lens of surveillance because surveillance is the means through which normative gender roles are conceived and assured. Particularly, surveillance is posited as a tool for exacting heteropatriarchal power. However, through appropriating surveillance, Ava disrupts surveillance's promise to control and to know, finally escaping Nathan and Caleb's concentrated power in the frontier bungalow. Not only does this further highlight the performativity of gender, as gendered roles collapse and distort in this final scene, but also the performativity of surveillance. Surveillance, too, fails because it is a performance between characters and also presumes the tools of its own undoing. This failure is ultimately productive, allowing Ava to escape, gain autonomy, and move undetected into the body politic.

I Figured You Were Probably Watching Us

While the film isolates the action to the bungalow, it continually registers the public's engagement with, complicity in, and production of surveillance through the layered cameras and gazes in the film. Laura Mulvey theorized that the goal of film is to erase the audience's awareness of their gaze and of the camera lens (Mulvey 1989, 53). However, the overt surveillance in *Ex Machina* disturbs this process, making the looks of the camera and audience apparent. The surveillance cameras along with the cinematic camera create a double gaze, where viewers watch Nathan and Caleb watching Ava. Viewers are simultaneously aware and complicit in monitoring Ava. But the audience does not simply take on the role of surveillant. The audience's simultaneous vulnerability to surveillance is reinforced throughout the movie, such as when Nathan references hacking the world's cell phones to build Ava, and with it the need for populations to self-monitor and regulate through lateral, citizen surveillance.

Lateral surveillance as the end goal is encoded in the final scene. The scene begins with the camera angled toward what appears to be a tile hallway, capturing people's indistinguishable shadows as they walk past. But one shadow emerges in the center recognizable as Ava. The camera cuts to just outside of a window, which Ava approaches and gazes out of. Her eyes dart around quickly, and then she disappears. She is the only distinguishable person, which asserts her primacy while the ambiguity of the crowd suggests her need to view and identify the public. Ava first revealed her desire to visit a street intersection on her and Caleb's hypothetical first date. The bulletin board in her room is littered with images of busy streets, taken from above as if from a surveillance camera. Her positioning, looking down from a tall building, suggests that she internalized this impulse to monitor the public as if a surveillance camera. Here, instead of shrugging off surveillance outside of the bungalow, Ava assumes Nathan's place as surveillant. However, Ava engages a very different type of surveillance; instead of using the technologically advanced, mass-surveillance systems that Nathan deployed, she participates in lateral surveillance, or "the ways in which citizens carry out surveillance on one another" (Reeves 2017, 14). This scene directly identifies the audience's everyday impulses to monitor and their vulnerability to surveillance.

The logics of state surveillance have embedded themselves into our everyday behaviors as we attempt to identify foreign and queer bodies in the name of state security. From airports to bathrooms, the public is in a constant state of awareness, trained by "see something, say something" public announcements. The citizen is both an object and tool of state surveillance (Reeves 2017, 11). Thus, the boundary between who is the surveillant and the subject of surveillance necessarily collapses for lateral surveillance to continue. With the two concepts merged, the public can imagine themselves as perpetual watchdogs, as opposed to the feminized, racialized, queer objects of state surveillance.

Yet, the watchdog impulse derives from a perpetual sense of insecurity under the gaze of state surveillance, becoming a method for proving oneself a good citizen and thus displacing the gaze of state surveillance. But as Joshua Reeves argues, "citizens are not just asked to see anything and say anything—rather, they are urged to see the right things and say the right things" (2017, 14). Following 9/11, US state and media apparatuses coached US citizens in the semiotics of terror, encouraging them to report objects and people who fit into the category of terrorist. Reeves continues that this "economy of soft, omnipresent anxiety has proven effective at recruiting citizens to take an active, seeing/saying role in security apparatuses," so monitoring becomes a means for asserting good citizenship (2017, 141). But only certain surveillance will do. While the state has encouraged citizens to monitor through Department of Defense programs like Threat and Local Observation Notice, whistle-blowing surveillance, like that enacted by

Snowden and Chelsea Manning, is not tolerated and instead strips subjects of their citizenship or autonomy (Reeves 2017, 151, 163). Seeing and saying is only permissible when it helps maintain neoliberal hegemony, which has become even more critical in the wake of the 2008 financial crisis that revealed the vulnerability of contemporary capitalist systems. So subjects must perform correct surveillance to maintain their citizen status.

Under the ubiquitous threat of terror, and thus ubiquitous surveillance, citizens unconsciously perform to the gaze. This practice is underscored in *Ex Machina*'s plot twist when Caleb reveals he has already enacted the escape plan. Nathan performs his role as dominant, state-imbricated surveillant by placing a battery-powered camera into the test session space. But an essential part of this re-intrusion is that it remains undetected. In order to authentically know Caleb and Ava's interactions, they must believe they are not being watched. However, this is never the case. Ava, as argued before, is keenly aware of the gazes on her body at all times. Caleb, too, reveals that he "figured [Nathan was] probably watching," and thus performs to Nathan's gaze. He verbally pronounces a false plan to mislead Nathan. In these heightened performances for surveillance's gaze, the characters not only reveal surveillance as an imperfect system for knowledge aggregation but also reveal surveillance as performative.

In uncovering the performative nature of surveillance, *Ex Machina* highlights the mutability of surveillance. The characters, performing for the gaze, intentionally lie, mislead, trap, and harm one another until the surveillance apparatus of the bungalow is completely unreliable. Just as Butler imagines gender performativity to presume the tools for its own subversion, surveillance too maintains the power to undo itself in *Ex Machina*. While the movie stops short of offering a revolutionary escape from lateral surveillance, acknowledgment that citizens simultaneously perform for and manipulate surveillance reveals surveillance's subjectivity. The film underscores how surveillance demands subjects perform socially and politically dictated roles, not only as keen domestic surveillants, but also as the subjects of surveillance, disciplined to the gaze. Ultimately, in understanding surveillance as performative, we can begin to imagine the productive slips it affords us.

As I write this, the Covid-19 pandemic has ushered in a new crisis. In March of 2020, the US economy along with the rest of the world crashed as businesses closed to stop the spread of the virus. Urgent attention was placed not on eliminating the virus, but on revitalizing the US economy and maintaining business as usual, echoing sentiments following the 2008 crisis. Preserving the neoliberal status quo now imbricated economic and literal survival. State leaders assured reopening businesses presented low risk, so long as citizens took individual responsibility and stayed vigilant, invoking the rhetoric of lateral surveillance. Additionally, surveillance through contact tracing promised to allow the economy to move forward while still eliminating the virus as a threat. As always, surveillance, both lateral and state-sanctioned, functions to maintain systems of power by delimiting intrusions. But lateral surveillance has proved unstable, if not impossible, as the virus oozes undetected across populations and borders.

Notes

1 Throughout, I use combined terminology found in David Lyon's *Surveillance Studies: An Overview* (2007) and Sean P. Hier and Josh Greenberg's essay (2009). In both pieces, "surveillance" refers to the general act of or invisible apparatuses of surveillance. "Surveillant" refers to the individual or system exercising surveillance, and "subject of surveillance" refers to the individual or population being monitored. "Surveilled" serves as the adjective form indicating that the modified noun is the subject of surveillance.

2 During the film's production, *Bustle*'s Emma Cueto (2014) reported that companies like Dropbox called conference rooms "The Bromance Chamber" and actively sought employees who fit into the frat-club atmosphere, exemplified by the Titstare App presented at TechCrunch's hack-a-thon a year prior.

References

Beauchamp, T. (2014), "Surveillance," *TSQ: Transgender Studies Quarterly* 1 (1–2), pp. 208–10.

Butler, J. (2013), "Critically Queer," in D. E. Hall, A. Jagose, A. Bebell, and S. Potter (eds.), *The Routledge Queer Studies Reader*, New York: Routledge, pp. 18–31.

Cueto, E. (2014), "Why You May Not Want to Work in Tech," *Bustle*, 19 February. Available online: https://www.bustle.com/articles/16011-how-tech-company-frat-culture-is-keeping-the-industry-from-attracting-women.

Gao, G. (2015), "What Americans Think about NSA Surveillance, National Security and Privacy," *Pew Research Center*, 29 May. Available online: http://www.pewresearch.org/fact-tank/2015/05/29/what-americans-think-about-nsa-surveillance-national-security-and-privacy/.

Garland, A. (2015), "More Fear of Human Intelligence than Artificial Intelligence in 'Ex Machina'," interview, *All Things Considered*, National Public Radio, 14 April.

Hier, S. P. and J. Greenberg (2009), "The Politics of Surveillance: Power, Paradigms, and the Field of Visibility," in S. P. Hier and J. Greenberg (eds.), *Surveillance: Power, Problems, and Politics*, Vancouver: University of British Columbia Press, pp. 14–32.

Hunter, L. (2011), "Fathers, Sons, and Business in the Hollywood 'Office Movie'," in E. Watson and M. E. Shaw (eds.), *Performing American Masculinities: The*

21st-Century Man in Popular Culture, Bloomington: Indiana University Press, pp. 76–102.

Larson, M. and J. Piché (2009), "Public Vigilance Campaigns and Participatory Surveillance after 11 September 2001," in S. P. Hier and J. Greenberg (eds.), *Surveillance: Power, Problems, and Politics*, Vancouver: University of British Columbia Press, pp. 187–202.

Lyon, D. (2007), "Surveillance, Visibility and Popular Culture," in D. Lyon (ed.), *Surveillance Studies: An Overview*, Cambridge: Polity Press, pp. 139–58.

Mulvey, L. (1989), *Visual and Other Pleasures*, Bloomington: Indiana University Press.

Reeves, J. (2017), *Citizen Spy: The Long Rise of America's Surveillance Society*, New York: New York University Press.

Sedgwick, E. K. (1985), *Between Men: English Literature and Male Homosocial Desire*, New York: Columbia University.

Waldron, L. and B. Medina (2019), "When Transgender Travelers Walk into Scanners, Invasive Searches Sometimes Wait on the Other Side," *ProPublica*, 26 August. Available online: https://www.propublica.org/article/tsa-transgender-travelers- scanners-invasive-searches-often-wait-on-the-other-side.

Wajcman, J. (2004), *TechnoFeminsim*, Cambridge: Polity Press.

Winseck, D. (2009), "Communication and the Sorrows of Empire: Surveillance and Information Operations 'Blowback' in the Global War on Terrorism," in S. P. Hier and J. Greenberg (eds.), *Surveillance: Power, Problems, and Politics*, Vancouver: University of British Columbia Press, pp. 151–68.

PART IV

The Housing Crisis and the Home Question

8

Stand Your Ground

Neoliberal Horrors, *The Purge* Franchise, and the Allegorical Moment of US Trauma

Tony Grajeda

> *The tradition of the oppressed teaches us that the "state of emergency" in which we live is not the exception but the rule. We must attain to a conception of history that is in keeping with this insight. Then we shall clearly realize that it is our task to bring about a real state of emergency, and this will improve our position in the struggle against Fascism.*
> WALTER BENJAMIN, "THESES ON THE PHILOSOPHY OF HISTORY" (1968, 257)

Although the single presidential term of Donald Trump was marked by the breaking of political "norms" with outrageous rhetoric, extremist conspiracies, and seemingly endless chaos, the many material horrors that so-called Trumpism embodied, from neoliberal economic inequality to systemic racism to flirting with fascism, are not new. Indeed, while such problems run very deep in US history, a certain entrenchment and *normalization* of these developments can be traced to a post-9/11 political culture in the United

States, such that the 2013 Boston marathon bombing, to take just one example, reminded the country at the time that the so-called War on Terror, some twelve years running, was still very much alive.

While the Boston bombing was a clearly unmistakable sign of the war brought home, the War on Terror had already made itself at home in the United States, a nation that had become over the course of the Bush–Cheney years a willing semi-police state. Such a state did not just appear overnight, of course, but the establishment of the Department of Homeland Security in the immediate aftermath of 9/11 provided some institutional building blocks for a US-style police state, along with a number of other alarming developments, including: an acceleration in the trend toward "warrior" cops and heavily militarized police forces with the swelling presence of SWAT teams in cities large and small; the increasing use of domestic drones patrolling the borders and elsewhere; and a creeping expansion of what has been dubbed the surveillance-industrial complex—the visible and invisible signs of a steady militarization of the home front. This perpetual state of insecurity has also been rattled by evermore frequent mass shootings and everyday gun violence, further exacerbating a widespread culture of fear and paranoia.

This ongoing social and political crisis in the United States, as I aim to explore here, corresponds to a far-reaching cultural struggle over civil society, one that has found cultural expression in perhaps the most unlikely of sources: the US media franchise of *The Purge*. Beginning with the original 2013 film, *The Purge* (James DeMonaco), followed by two sequels, a prequel, and a two-season television series, the *Purge* franchise provides something of a popular barometer of the fraught sociopolitical landscape of US society in the twenty-first century. As a mixed genre text—part political thriller, part horror film, part critical dystopia—the 2013 film relied on the home invasion trope that resonated at the time with the 2008 implosion of the housing market, along with the ever-present War on Terror. With its narrative set in 2022, the film's premise is that the nation has been preserved by state-sanctioned violence through an annual event known as the Purge when, for one night, "all crime is legal, including murder." The film cast a very wide net over the post-9/11 national crisis: class warfare, structural racism, mass shootings, militarization of the home front, the surveillance society—all of it draped in evangelical rhetoric. As one of the opening intertitles intones: "Blessed be America, a nation reborn."

Subsequent films in the series have only sharpened and extended its commentary on the continuing trauma of life in the United States, even as it problematically aestheticizes the very violence it purports to critique. The sequel, *The Purge: Anarchy* (James DeMonaco 2014), foregrounded the initial premise by revealing how the Purge was intentionally designed by political and economic elites to effectively eliminate the poor, with the upper class using its means and money to bid on murdering the already marginalized of society for sport. The third installment, *The Purge: Election Year* (James DeMonaco 2016), with its timely tagline "Keep America Great," was released before the election of Donald Trump that year but clearly had its finger on the pulse of the United States as a deeply troubled land; it added to the franchise's repertoire such topical issues as references to the Black Lives Matter movement and police brutality, while fingering the National Rifle Association by name as profiting from the annual killing spree. With the last film in the series, *The First Purge* (Gerard McMurray 2018), allusions to the 2017 white nationalist mob in Charlottesville, Virginia, and the Charleston, South Carolina, African American church massacre in 2015 are added to its explicit depiction of the nation as an authoritarian dystopia, where racist class warfare is waged by armed white supremacists (cloaked in Ku Klux Klan robes and sporting Confederate and neo-Nazi regalia) determined to exterminate the "undesirables." At this point in the series, the victims-turned-heroes are almost entirely people of color.

In keeping with a cultural studies theoretical framework, my analysis of the films will be informed, in particular, by the work of both Walter Benjamin on allegory and the struggle against fascism (as my epigraph suggests) and Frantz Fanon on decolonization and his call for armed struggle against racist colonial rule. Accordingly, by examining the narrative arc of *The Purge* franchise, from a projected dystopian future at the beginning of the series to an allegorical account of the dystopian present by its end, this chapter will consider the ways in which the four films together offer a critical, if somewhat fractured, mirror to the neoliberal horror show of contemporary life in the United States. Despite its low genre conventions, *The Purge*, as I argue, confronts this historical moment as a national allegory, one shot through with savage inequality, perpetual insecurity, genocidal white supremacy, and collective trauma.

Sociopolitical Context for *The Purge c.* 2013

It bears recalling that, along with the preexisting War on Terror, the more immediate context within which to situate *The Purge* entails the economic crisis of the Great Recession of 2007–9. More specifically, economic instability rooted in the 2008 collapse of the housing market and Wall Street's free fall—the sudden evaporation of over 50 percent in value of stocks—had only magnified an already precarious sense of insecurity. In short, the housing crisis of countrywide foreclosures, underwater mortgages, and forced evictions served to inhibit many from finding home as at least a symbolic shelter from the storm, since the home itself had become by this time a palpable source of anxiety.

In light of this national turmoil throughout the Obama years, so-called home invasion movies acquired a more urgent political valence. Although many such films fall within the horror genre, other home invasion films, as with *Mother's Day* (Darren Lynn Bousman 2010), *Trespass* (Joel Schumacher 2011), or *Foreclosed* (Nick Lyon 2013), as well as the 2011 remake of *Straw Dogs* (Rod Lurie) and Michael Haneke's 2007 remake of his own 1997 film *Funny Games*, trade on the thriller/suspense formula, often playing on the fear of vulnerability from within one's own home. Among this spate of home invasion films, the 2013 film *The Purge* arrived as an unusual entry, exceeding the typical confines of its kind by mounting a more ambitious, if problematic, statement about US society than the trope commonly affords. In its narrative staging of domestic insecurity within both a gated community and a high-tech home security system, *The Purge*, I will suggest, negotiated the dual anxieties of post-9/11 threats from outside and socioeconomic instability from within, thereby offering an allegory of vulnerability where neither home nor home front stands immune from invasion.

My interest here resides in treating the home invasion narrative less in terms of its somewhat accustomed relation to horror and more in terms of the thriller/suspense genre. Beyond considerations of genre, moreover, I am primarily concerned with reading such texts in relation to allegory or the allegorical moment, for which questions of history overrule those of genre or style. To take a relevant example of such a reading, consider *Panic Room* (David Fincher), a home invasion film *par excellence*, which was made before 9/11 but released in 2002; an allegorical reading would end up positioning the film within its historical moment unavoidably defined by the overriding crisis of 9/11, regardless of its own narrative specificity, genre conventions, or other possible framings. What I am proposing here in reading *The Purge* franchise allegorically is not unlike Adam Lowenstein's treatment of a range of horror films that "communicate historical trauma" in different national contexts. "The allegorical moment exists as a mode of confrontation," writes Lowenstein, "where representation's location between past and present, as well as between film, spectator, and history, demands to be recalibrated" (Lowenstein 2005, 12).

While some of these aforementioned home invasion films could be seen as little more than symptomatic of their historical moment, *The Purge*, by comparison, exceeds the generic trappings of the home invasion trope not only by incorporating elements of other genre conventions, such as the political thriller and dystopian fiction, but also by tapping into quite specific reservoirs of social, cultural, and political anxieties festering away at the body politic for generations. As such, *The Purge* can be treated allegorically in terms that are both spatial (as a bounded nation-state) and temporal (this historical moment), capturing a well-placed sense of dread during this conjunctural crisis even as it acknowledges more deep-seated problems in the country, problems that threaten to irremediably fracture the US's already fragile sense of nationhood.

To speak of the allegorical moment invokes at least brief consideration of that key twentieth-century theorist of allegory, Walter Benjamin, who, in a typically enigmatic statement, wrote: "Allegories are, in the realm of thought, what ruins are in the realm of things" (1985, 178). In his 1928 study of the seventieth-century German tradition of the *Trauerspiel* or "mourning play," according to Susan Buck-Morss (1991, 178), "Benjamin had argued in the *Trauerspiel* study that Baroque allegory was the mode of perception peculiar to a time of social disruption and protracted war, when human suffering and material ruin were the stuff and substance of historical experience—hence the return of allegory in his own era as a response to the horrifying destructiveness of World War I." For Benjamin, then, the allegorical mode itself was not ahistorical or transhistorical so much as it was a way of perceiving history at specific moments that themselves were marked by nothing less than catastrophe.

Benjamin's early theory of allegory aligns with his later Marxist approach to historical materialism in his well-known essay "Theses on the Philosophy of History," with the two approaches intersecting, for instance, in the ninth thesis that finds Benjamin reflecting on the Paul Klee drawing "Angelus Novus" (1920). As opposed to the traditional historian who remains beholden to the Enlightenment belief in inevitable progress, leading to the narration of history as "a chain of events," the historical materialist, writes Benjamin, "sees one single catastrophe which keeps piling wreckage upon wreckage" of human suffering and violence, the accumulation of which forms a "pile of debris" that "grows skyward." As Benjamin adds bitterly, "This storm is what we call progress" (Benjamin 1968, 257–8).

Benjamin's allegorical and materialist rendering of history in the 1920s and 1930s speaks to our own time, I would suggest, a time of historical impasse between those who see the "pile of debris" as a sign of "progress" and those who, perhaps, see that "wreckage" for what it is. The difference between these two perspectives on the state of the nation may also correspond to what Benjamin called the "state of emergency," another dividing line demarcating whether or not one recognizes that "the 'state of emergency' in which we live is not the exception but the rule." While that "rule" is not always apparent, at least not without the benefit of critical distance, it does appear, to both the allegorist and the historical materialist, strewn across the littered landscape of US popular culture, a landscape that includes, among many other forms of debris, *The Purge*.

Reading *The Purge* against the Grain of History

The internal, fictional historicity of *The Purge*, if its narrative time is to be believed, is 2022, a near-enough future (from its 2013 release) that its mise-en-scène of home décor, SUVs, and, crucially, surveillance cameras and video monitors resembles nothing so much as the present. But in the United States of 2022, as the opening intertitle states: "Unemployment is at 1%. Crime is at an all-time low. Violence barely exists. With one exception." This bit of backstory is immediately followed by a second, more ominous, text, one that is presented as an unattributed quotation in italics: "*Blessed be the New Founding Fathers for letting us Purge and cleanse our souls. Blessed be America, a nation reborn.*" The evangelical Christian diction here is only the first of several blatant signs that something more than a standard-issue, home invasion film is afoot.

The conflation of class, nation, and religion in text form immediately dissolves into the initial set of images accompanying the opening credit sequence that likewise perform a conflation, this time of bodily violence, the surveillance society, and a certain filmic *tone* by way of soundtrack. Identified as "Purge feed," a montage of shots unspools like video footage—ironically scored to Debussy's delicate *Clair de Lune*—that resembles the grainy, stationary camera, middle-distance footage signifying city surveillance cameras. What is caught on camera here, from "feeds" across the country (time-coded and tagged as Jacksonville, Florida; Cheyenne, Wyoming; Houston, Texas; and so on), is one scene of mayhem after another—beatings, stabbings, shootings, arson—in what we presume to be video documentation of the Purge, but which could just as easily be mistaken for surveillance footage of actual US mayhem and its visual record of everyday violence. The credit sequence prepares us for the narrative proper, which begins shortly before the Purge is to commence, as we are introduced to James Sandin (Ethan Hawke), a top salesman of high-end, high-tech home security systems. His neighbors in this exclusive, gated community are the kind who show up with homemade cookies, only to note that the Sandins have gotten rich by selling home security systems to everyone on the block. Behind a clenched smile, one neighbor impolitely points out that "some people are actually saying this neighborhood paid for that new addition on your house." Although a seemingly minor moment, it is worth noting that the film, by foregrounding from the start this object lesson in *intra*-class resentment, is already signaling a more nuanced take on class warfare than the customary class struggle of the rich vs. the poor that appears, if it ever does at all, in US popular culture (to which I return shortly).

The Sandin nuclear family—father James, mother Mary, teenage daughter, and son—settle into their suburban mansion which, thanks to James, is equipped with what is billed as a fortress-like security system. When the Emergency Broadcast System announces the start of the Purge (which airs on one of the many television sets populating the house), Sandin arms the home system, bringing metal shutters down over all the windows and doors—one massive panic room—complete with a bank of video monitors displaying surveillance feeds from across their property and down the street. Thus begins the annual Purge, the twelve-hour event that has been institutionalized as a kind of national holiday, one that commences with the following public service announcement:

> This is not a test. This is your emergency broadcast system announcing the commencement of the Annual Purge sanctioned by the U.S. Government. Weapons of class 4 and lower have been authorized for use during the Purge. All other weapons are restricted. Government officials of ranking 10 have been granted immunity from the Purge and shall not be harmed. Commencing at the siren, any and all crime, including murder, will be legal for 12 continuous hours. Police, fire, and emergency medical services will be unavailable until tomorrow morning until 7 a.m., when The Purge concludes. Blessed be our New Founding Fathers and America, a nation reborn. May God be with you all.

As the family disperses itself throughout the sprawling house, a television program on the Purge plays in the background, with various shots of "ordinary" life in the Sandin home intercut with fleeting shots of the ensuing violence in the streets that has erupted across the country.

What is heard, however, is something that would not be out of place in the actual world of contemporary cable news commentary, a mise en abyme moment with a news personality addressing an apparent controversy over the purpose of the Purge:

> Now, is the Purge really about releasing aggression and containing violence, or is it something else? Purge detractors often postulate this evening is actually about the elimination of the poor, the needy, the sick. Those unable to defend themselves. The eradication of the so called "non-contributing members" of society, ultimately unburdening the economy. Is the Purge really about money? Either way, crime is down. The economy is flourishing.

One could not hear "non-contributing members of society" in 2013 without recalling the 2012 US presidential campaign season, with its talk radio harangues of "takers" and "makers," or the right-wing valorization of "job-creators."

The film's blunt critique of class in America becomes overdetermined, in quick fashion, by that of race; it almost goes without saying that this gated community and the denizens of prosperous suburbia are for the most part uniformly white. Into this bastion of whiteness, however, will appear a figure whose racial otherness will constitute only one of several factors to disrupt the false tranquility that at least the Sandin parents are counting on, as inferred by James when he casually mentions that "we should watch a movie later with the kids." No sooner does the Purge get underway than the Sandin teenaged son Charlie (Max Burkholder), stationed in front of several video monitors, spots a man running down the street. Badly injured, the man is desperately calling out for help. A second and then third shot from the perspective of a surveillance camera reveals that the man, who will go nameless in the film (but is listed in the credits as the "Bloody Stranger"), is African American. Charlie disarms the security system, allowing the Bloody Stranger (Edwin Hodge) to slip into their house. He is tracked down to the Sandin residence by a group of purgers who, besides wielding machetes, guns, and all manner of weaponry, are also donning Halloween-type masks, the type molded into that exaggerated frozen grin that only adds to the sense of malevolence.

The putative leader of the pack, who also goes nameless (and is similarly listed in the credits as the "Polite Stranger" [Rhys Wakefield]), strolls up to the front door and, shot in extreme wide angle to approximate a door's peephole view, delivers the following warning:

> Your home tells me you're good folk, just like us. One of the "haves," and ... that you support the Purge ... Let me introduce us. We are some fine, young, very educated guys and gals. We have gotten gussied up in our most terrifying guises, as we do every year, ready to violate, annihilate, and cleanse our souls. But things took a turn. Our target escaped us, and ... several of your dear neighbors informed us that you, the Sandins, have inexplicably given him sanctuary. Mr. and Mrs., the man you're sheltering is nothing but a dirty, homeless pig. A grotesque menace to our just society, who had the audacity to fight back, killing one of us when we attempted to execute him tonight. The pig doesn't know his place, and now he needs to be taught a lesson. You need to return him to us. Alive. So that we may Purge as we are entitled.

As was the case with one of the opening scenes in which class resentment was found to have infected a certain stratum of society, as the film would have it, to suggest a Hobbesian world of "war of all against all," so, too, the "haves" here fail in maintaining their class solidarity as forged against the "have-nots." "Don't force us to hurt you," snarls the Polite Stranger, before adding, "we don't want to kill our own."

Just as significant in the world of *The Purge* as these class dynamics is the Polite Stranger's coded accusation that the Sandin family has "inexplicably given him sanctuary." By invoking the term "sanctuary" in relation to a Black man on the run from a gang of marauding white people in the United States, the film is undoubtedly reaching, at least allegorically, for an allusion to a very dark chapter in US history—one that conservative white Americans would just as soon forget—that of a runaway slave. But a much more recent past, one perhaps more difficult to avoid, is caught in the glint of the Bloody Stranger's necklace. During one scene where he is shown cowering in fear, hiding out somewhere in the giant Sandin house, the light from a mobile camera device deflects off metallic plates dangling from his neck—a different kind of chain clasping what can only be dog tags. Not unlike the housing crisis at the time, the "war on terror" forms an uneasy context within which to read such signs as army dog tags, themselves used as means to identify the remains of those killed in action, but here compounded not only by the figuration of race as worn by a young African American veteran but also by his further identity as, in the words of the Polite Stranger, a "homeless pig."

The film doesn't do much more with these transient fragments of US wars in the twenty-first century and the War on Terror generation of veterans chewed up in the global machinery of US militarism. From all this richly suggestive material, *The Purge* reverts to genre conventions, in particular, the horror home invasion ones. Predictably enough, the Sandin house has its power cut (or at least the lights) by the gang of purgers, who have stormed their way into the premises, at which point the film resorts to assaulting its audience with one genre jolt after another: rapid-fire jump cuts, shaky handheld camerawork, low-rumble dread on the soundtrack, plenty of special-effects splatter, and blood-soaked violence to fulfill, rather than breach, expectations.

Perhaps just as predictably, the Sandins fight back, and for the most part fend off the purgers, but less predictably, the film attempts to summon its social commentary one last time. Most of the Sandin family are unexpectedly saved by their neighbors, who suddenly appear at the end to purge the purgers in yet another orgy of bloodshed and onscreen violence. But then the neighbors, those resentful fellow members of the affluent class sharing their lot within a gated community, in turn, turn on the Sandins. One more speech, this one from the same neighbor who at the beginning delivered cookies, brings home, so to speak, a final flourish of god and country and, more crucially, the need for sacrifice. "You will sacrifice yourselves to make the world a better place," she tells the remaining Sandins, "now let us do our duty as Americans."

Indeed, who among us must be sacrificed in order to "preserve" the nation? Who has yet to give of themselves? Who has given too much already? While the film appears ill-prepared to answer its own unwieldy question about the relation between sacrifice and nationalism, the narrative itself seems better prepared to implicate its audience in whatever desire for violence its genre conventions have elicited. Accordingly, just as Mary Sandin and her two children are about to be put to slaughter, the Bloody Stranger abruptly reappears to save what is left of the Sandin family from the ritual sacrifice. He then offers the Sandins an opportunity to purge themselves of the purgers. But Mary Sandin declines to pursue any retribution, deciding instead that, as she states, "We are gonna play the rest of this night out in motherfucking peace," adding, "Does anyone have a problem with that?" Thus, the end of *The Purge* tries to forestall the logic of the Purge by having a survivor, one who has been saved from it, refuse to participate, and fulfill her patriotic "duty as Americans" by exacting vengeance and purging her fellow citizens.

Yet, for the audience, narrative pleasure had already arrived in the figure of the Bloody Stranger killing one of the neighbors to stop the purging of the Sandins, along with Mary's bloody beatdown of another neighbor intent on going through with the ritual. It is both rather horrifying to delight in the neighbor's comeuppance, beaten and bloody but *still alive*, Purge be damned, and quite horrifying to realize that the audience has been *invited* to feel delighted by all the brutal violence. Although such manipulation goes with the genre territory, it is still worth asking to what extent we have become complicit with the film's premise of US society's putative need to vent violent tendencies. I will here forestall my own attempt at addressing this question until the conclusion, since to reach that point, we must first consider how the franchise deals with its own conceit about human nature.

From Freud to Marx and Fanon: *The Purge* franchise's trajectory of political violence

Marking some distance from the housing crisis at the time, the 2014 sequel, *The Purge: Anarchy*, largely abandons the home invasion narrative structure for a different kind of survival trope, in which a small band of diverse people are thrown together to survive the night of the annual Purge in something more like an urban action spectacle. To be sure, home invasion elements remain at the margins of the narrative, acting as a partial framing device near the beginning and at the very end of the first sequel, while playing an even less significant role in the second sequel, *The Purge: Election Year*, which also unfolds as an urban survival film. What is intriguing in terms of genre conventions, however, is the way in which the home invasion trope *returns* in the final film of the franchise, *The First Purge*, rewritten by this point as less a home that must be defended against invasion and more like an entire community that must fend off an invasion. What is crucial here is that a mostly minority community, a mix of economically disadvantaged Brown and Black people, bands together to fight off a militia of mercenaries distinctly marked as white marauders, a narrative development that clearly begs for a critical reading of the text informed by Frantz Fanon's work on postcolonial subjectivity and the imperative to overthrow colonial rule—by any means necessary.

But before getting to the prequel, which establishes the ostensible origins of the Purge and thus the entire narrative arc of the franchise, it bears emphasizing that much as the 2014 sequel abandoned the home invasion trope, so, too, did it reveal the trumped-up premise of the Purge itself as a pseudo-Freudian take on human nature, thus trading Freud for Marx as the film proceeds to sharpen its class analysis of what's really wrong with the United States. Recall that in *The Purge* much is made of how the Purge was intended to "release the beast," as it is put repeatedly throughout the narrative, where citizens are granted immunity once a year to act on their supposed id-like savage impulses and primal desires, thereby purging themselves of the otherwise necessary quotient of repression that even Freud had prescribed (short of excess repression), the sublimation of which allowed civilized society to function. In one of several instances of diegetic radio or television commentary heard in the background as the Sandins are shown preparing for the Purge, one such commentator remarks:

> History has proven this over and over again. We are inherently a violent species. Wars, genocide, murder. The denial of our true selves is the problem. The Purge not only contains societal violence to a single evening, but the country-wide catharsis creates psychological stability by letting us release the aggression we all have inside of us.

This background noise is moved to the foreground at another point when father James tells his son Charlie why they support the Purge:

> Look, I know this is difficult to understand at your age, but tonight allows people a release for all the hatred and violence and aggression that they keep up inside them. Okay? And yes, if your mother and I were so inclined, uh, we would participate. Because it works. You don't remember how bad it was, Charlie. The poverty, all the crime. This night saved our country.

While the first film in the franchise perhaps flirted with the idea that there may be something to this thesis of nationwide catharsis, the second film begins to disclose how such a rationale of why the Purge is said to "work" has been manipulated all along, a realization that by the end of the series becomes explicit: the Purge was entirely manufactured, deliberately designed as a form of population control and even genocide against people of color and the poor, a fabricated racist war waged by ruling white elites against the subaltern, all-too reminiscent of the long, sordid history of Western colonialism, which includes, lest we forget, the US's own bloody history of genocidal colonization of indigenous American Indians.

That the Purge has been "sold" to the American people forms part of a critique mounted by an underground revolutionary named Carmelo Johns (Michael Kenneth Williams), a Malcolm X-type figure who first appears in *The Purge: Anarchy*. Echoing how the initial film in the series laced its narrative with diegetic commentary from radio and television programming running in the background of several scenes, the sequel similarly places renegade podcasts and pirated broadcasts by the militant Johns throughout the film as a kind of counter-narrative, issuing communiqués aiming to expose the actual intent behind the Purge:

> The Purge is not about containing crime to one night and cleansing our souls by releasing aggression. It's about one thing: money. Who dies tonight? The poor. We can't afford to protect ourselves. Whatever happened to, "Give me your needy, your tired, your huddled masses yearning to breathe free"? The redistribution of wealth upward through killing has to stop. We must pick up arms. This year, we will fight back!

In a straight-up Marxist depiction of naked class conflict, the rich are shown buying up the poor to purge: an elderly and ailing Black man sells himself to a wealthy family to be butchered in the safety of their own home, staged as a *tableau vivant* shot of four white people armed with long knives surrounding their purchase, themselves surrounded by living room furnishings tastefully draped in plastic sheathing. Another set piece features well-healed patrons of a private club bidding on rights to go "hunting," the prey being a representative flock of "huddled masses" rounded up by mercenaries on Purge night and lined up on a stage to be auctioned off for sport. "Ladies and gentlemen," announces the little old dowager host, "since this is the last Purge of the evening, the entry price will be $200,000." With that the bidding commences.

But perhaps the most telling revelation in *The Purge: Anarchy*, as regards the overall narrative arc of the series, is that the political party behind the Purge, the New Founding Fathers of America (NFFA), has devised its own plot to "supplement" the Purge, since apparently the common people have been failing to muster sufficient enthusiasm for killing off one another. As the ringleader of a heavily armed paramilitary force working on behalf of the NFFA declares at the end of the film:

> The unwritten Purge rule: don't save lives. Tonight, we take lives. We make things manageable. Unfortunately, the citizens aren't killing enough. So we supplement it all to keep things balanced. It's important work the NFFA does and we can't have any interference . . . Blessed be America, a nation reborn.

Such a revelation will indeed become the basis of the fourth and final film in the franchise, which I will turn to momentarily.

Before turning my attention to *The First Purge*, however, it is worth noting that the third film in the series, *The Purge: Election Year*, released the summer before the 2016 presidential election, is in many ways the most obviously "topical" of the films, with its main plotline of a white female liberal senator (read Hillary Clinton) running for president against the NFFA candidate and pledging to put a stop to the Purge. As such, it is the least allegorical of the films, as it clearly aims to offer a political solution to its own dystopian premise of a nation so racked with intractable problems that it is nearly beyond redemption. For example, the mostly multicultural militants of *The Purge: Anarchy*, here found to be plotting to assassinate the NFFA presidential candidate, are told to stand down by the good senator, who gives a number of Lincoln-esque speeches on the order of appealing to our "better angels." Ultimately, *The Purge: Election Year* reverts to a liberal vision of America, reconceived as a nation suddenly capable of coming to its collective senses and electing a reformist. Meanwhile, as the film preached keeping faith in the system, outside the movie theater multiplex enough of the country lurched toward the demagoguery of Donald Trump to elect him president.

Which brings us, lastly, to *The First Purge*, released two years into the Trump presidency but which goes back in narrative time to explain how the country, teetering on the brink of total calamity, elects a new political party, the NFFA, which proposes a daring social experiment described as a "societal catharsis" to cure the nation of rampant crime, chronic poverty, high unemployment, and a raging opioid epidemic, among other entrenched problems. The first test run of what will become known as the Purge, set on the "controlled" environment of Staten Island, is based on the work of a behavioral scientist, who postulates that the "benefit of acting violently without worry of consequence" will be a "freeing violence." The scientist predicts a high level of "considerable participation," especially among low-income citizens. The experiment is met by resistance from community activists, led by a young Black woman named Nya (Lex Scott Davis), who claims that the NFFA has "monetized and incentivized murder," since "participants" are being paid to stay on the island. As Nya exclaims, "This is another way to keep Brown and Black people down!" Taking a page from Spike Lee's *Do the Right Thing* (1989), *The First Purge* places three "witnesses" to the proceedings near the frontlines early on, a mixed-race trio of elderly men, one of whom offers the following observation: "This is the greatest shit show on Earth. They turning our island into ancient Rome, our hood into the Colosseum. Now, the question is: Are we gonna be the Christians or the lions? Gladiators or the slaves, right?"

The problem for the NFFA proponents of the Purge is that the mostly minority communities left on Staten Island spend their Purge night holding street parties rather than engaging in any "freeing violence." Puzzled, the scientist ponders such "variables" as "human nature": "Data suggests that this socioeconomic group is not reacting the way I predicted." Seizing upon what was only insinuated earlier in the series, that there is in fact no "beast" to release, *The First Purge* points instead to the political violence of the state, with the NFFA unleashing secretly held militia forces and roving gangs (cleverly wearing masks to disguise their "whiteness" as outsiders) to fabricate "waves of violence all across the borough," as one news anchor puts it. The scientist discovers only too late that the NFFA has rigged the experiment, accusing them of "sending soldiers into the island disguised as gangs, as citizens, hunting people down," then adding, "You're making it look like people are participating because there wasn't enough purging." As one NFFA apparatchik confides: "This country is overpopulated, Doctor. There's too much crime, too much unemployment . . . People don't want us to raise taxes? Our debt has tripled. We can't pay for anything." To which the scientist contends: "You're trying to depopulate the lower classes just so the NFFA doesn't have to support them." "Come on," he responds, "We both know there's no easy answer where somebody . . . some group doesn't suffer."

In what we have come to expect from the franchise's genre conventions, however, the community fights back against the NFFA legion of mercenaries (identified at one point as "Blackwater" and other "badasses for hire") and white gangs on motorcycles festooned with Confederate, "White Power," and neo-Nazi outfits, emblems, and tattoos. The chief armed opposition group this time is a drug gang led by the conflicted kingpin Dmitri (Y'lan Noel), who becomes "conscious" after realizing that the NFFA was "hoping that we'd off each other," adding, "Our neighborhood is under siege, from a government who doesn't give a shit about any of us." Dmitri rallies his gang members to the cause before the final bloody conflagration by saying, "Let's show these white-haired motherfuckers never to fuck with our island again." And so the last film in the series solicits one last catharsis for its audience, delivering a most righteous display of people of color surviving the Purge by taking up arms and defending their community against fascist white supremacists.

As hinted at earlier, my claim here is that *The Purge* franchise ends up endorsing a position of militant self-defense that roughly aligns with the work of Frantz Fanon, especially his argument "Concerning Violence" in the classic statement on decolonization, his 1961 book, *The Wretched of the Earth*. For Fanon colonialism was never a "civilizing" mission but rather a state-sponsored form of capitalist exploitation in which "violence forged the relationship between the native and the settler" (Fanon 1968, 36). In French colonial Algeria, for example, where Fanon worked as a practicing psychiatrist and joined the National Liberation Front in 1954 in their struggle for independence, "colonialism is not a thinking machine, nor a body endowed with reasoning faculties," writes Fanon. "It is violence in its natural state, and it will only yield when confronted with greater violence" (61). The hypocrisy of the colonizer, in particular, is called out by Fanon, who here first speaks of the colonized:

> He of whom *they* have never stopped saying that the only language he understands is that of force, decides to give utterance by force. In fact, as always, the settler has shown him the way he should take if he is to

become free. The argument the native chooses has been furnished by the settler, and by an ironic turning of the tables it is the native who now affirms that the colonialist understands nothing but force. (84)

As the militant anti-purger Carmelo Johns in *The Purge: Anarchy* declares, "Change only comes when their blood spills."[1]

In Fanon's more psychoanalytically oriented approach to colonialism in his 1952 book *Black Skin, White Masks*, where he explores the psychic damage of the colonial experience on the subjectivity of the colonized, Fanon proposed a "therapeutic" theory of violence with what he called "collective catharsis," an idea which, by the time of *The Wretched of the Earth*, is tied to revolutionary struggle: "The colonized man finds his freedom in and through violence" (86). And in one of the more provocative passages in the 1961 book, following his analysis of the degree to which the colonized subject internalizes the racist dehumanizing effects of colonialism, Fanon writes:

> At the level of individuals, violence is a cleansing force. It frees the native from his inferiority complex and from his despair and inaction; it makes him fearless and restores his self-respect. Even if the armed struggle has been symbolic . . . the people have the time to see that the liberation has been the business of each and all and that the leader has no special merit . . . When the people have taken violent part in the national liberation they will allow no one to set themselves up as "liberators." (94)

All of which is to say, freedom is not a condition that can be granted to the colonized by the goodwill of the colonizer; it must instead be won through the struggle to achieve it.

What is perhaps unexpectedly propitious about reading *The Purge* franchise through Fanon's work on the "cleansing force" of violence is that the films end up reinforcing both his diagnosis of colonialism and his prescription for decolonization. As becomes increasingly clear across the length of the series, the reason given for the Purge all along, that "we are inherently a violent species," as we heard in *The Purge*, turns out to be a ruse: the penchant for violence in the United States has little to do with some supposed innate human nature and instead has everything to do with the concrete and structural mechanisms of an unjust and unequal society. In other words, *The Purge* franchise unmasks the United States itself as a nation of systemic, targeted violence, just as Fanon argued that the violence of the colonial situation was fundamentally historical, social, and political. Rather than "blaming the victim" for the violence that was constitutive to colonialism from the outset, Fanon insisted that the colonized had no choice but to overthrow colonial rule *by any means necessary*, in the memorable words of Malcolm X. In short, the "cleansing force" of violence was meant to expel that which was implanted by the invaders themselves. This form of violence, not for its own sake but rather purposefully directed toward revolutionary ends, is akin to the fictionalized violent uprising that takes place by the subaltern in *The Purge* films which, in dramatizing Fanon's call for armed struggle, is depicted as a form of self-defense against a ruthlessly violent society. "Wake up, people!" implores Carmelo Johns: "It's time to take a stand. Tonight, we write our message in blood—their blood!"

Indeed, by drawing upon what Benjamin called a "tradition of the oppressed," and by heeding Fanon's call to arms for liberation from that oppression, *The Purge* franchise, for all its low genre trappings, reaches for decidedly pointed, rather than pointless, violence. As such, *The Purge* films don't so much offer a mere reflection of life in America these days as much as they provoke a critical allegory of how it might be lived by those for whom the "state of emergency" is all too real. *The Purge*'s allegorical fiction projected into a near-future, one clearly about the nation's present moment, signifies a present seemingly incapable of defining the nation, which itself then stands as a national allegory of the United States—a land at a time of one disaster piled upon another.

Note

1 Taking issue with critics of Fanon's insistence on the necessity for armed struggle, Robert Stam emphasizes the wholly uneven use of violence by the colonizers in the context of the Algerian war for independence: "It is this disproportionate and asymmetrical violence that is forgotten when critics speak as if Fanon were the partisan of violence for its own sake. By focusing only on the reactive terrorism of the colonized, the violence of other forms of terrorism—colonialist terrorism, state terrorism, the vigilante terrorism of the *ratonnades*—is rendered innocent and invisible" (Stam 2003, 22).

References

Benjamin, W. (1968), "Theses on the Philosophy of History," in H. Arendt (ed.), *Illuminations*, trans. H. Zohn, New York: Schocken Books, pp. 253-64.
Benjamin, W. (1985), *The Origin of German Tragic Drama*, trans. J. Osborne, London: Verso.
Bucks-Morss, S. (1991), *The Dialectics of Seeing: Walter Benjamin and the Arcades Project*, Cambridge, MA: The MIT Press.
Fanon, F. (1968), *The Wretched of the Earth*, trans. C. Farrington, New York: Grove Press. Originally published in 1961.

Lowenstein, A. (2005), *Shocking Representation: Historical Trauma, National Cinema, and the Modern Horror Film*, New York: Columbia University Press.

Stam, R. (2003), "Fanon, Algeria, and the Cinema: The Politics of Identification," in E. Shohat and R. Stam (eds.), *Multiculturalism, Postcoloniality, and Transnational Media*. New Brunswick, NJ and London: Rutgers University Press, pp. 18–43.

9

Horror, Race, and the Economics of Interiority

Homeownership in the Blumhouse Universe

Leah Pérez and William J. Simmons

Introduction

Horror as a genre has long been considered a part of culture of the masses, though the definition of that term remains tacitly white. Horror films, often screened alongside or sometimes indistinguishable from B-movies and pornography, were not considered avant-garde and were often shown in parts of town deemed dangerous or poor. As a result, horror movies have rarely received critical acclaim and instead thrive on cult fame or word-of-mouth fame driven by sensational advertising strategies. In 1974, William Friedkin's *The Exorcist* famously became the first horror film to make a notable sweep of awards at the Oscars, a feat that would not be replicated until *The Silence of the Lambs* (Jonathan Demme 1991). When Jordan Peele's *Get Out* (2017) was released to an explosive reaction from audiences and critics, there was talk of whether or not the film would be worthy of any Oscar nominations, since the horror genre (and indeed films by Black directors) were and remain so underrepresented. While *Get Out* did win one of its four Oscar nominations, in the same year *Hereditary* (Ari Aster 2018), another well-received horror film by an independent studio, did not receive a single nomination. It is clear then that while the horror genre often emphasizes the social and economic issues of its era, there is still a cultural perception that horror is not worthy of serious analysis or cultural appraisal. Such occlusions in terms of genre, as Peele's film made clear, are inextricably bound to race.

A central component of horror films is the command or plea to get out, alongside its necessary opposite, the erotic desire to get in. Horror therefore becomes a drama of representation and exclusion, of boundaries pleasurable and terrifying. In his 1983 stand-up special *Delirious*, Eddie Murphy makes a joke prompted by watching *Poltergeist* (Tobe Hooper 1982) about how if Black people were to be in a haunted house they would immediately leave. The bit ends with Murphy saying, "Get out!" in a ghostly voice as he and his partner split the scene. Jordan Peele is himself a Black comedian and has most likely seen Murphy's stand-up. Murphy's joke and Peele's film play with the idea of Black people having a better awareness of danger than their white counterparts and a necessary, lifesaving understanding of boundaries of interior and exterior that are, in some sense, invisible to white people, or perhaps ignored as a result of white spatial privilege. From the migration of European settlers to the Americas to white flight prompted by the abolition of slavery, white Americans have historically been allotted the privilege to flee situations they find dangerous or inopportune. As a result of financial security, fleeing one's home—getting out—does not narratively result in homelessness for white people. Homeownership in the United States is a privilege that white people benefit from to which Black and Brown people do not have the same access. As historically Black and Brown neighborhoods become prey to gentrification, often the same neighborhoods that housed theaters that would screen horror films, Black and Brown Americans increasingly exist in a liminal space of never truly having a place in the United States that is safe for them or their own creative outlets. Perhaps the freedom of movement in horror films, and indeed the freedom of economic and social mobility, for white folks is a filmic trope epitomized by horror. Moving away from the metaphorical haunted house results in white people finding peace and safety in a world that prioritizes their lives, while Black and Brown people face limited options upon getting out, or even getting in at all, especially in the wake of the global crisis we currently face, or in other moments of racialized catastrophe, like the 2007–8 financial crisis or Hurricane Katrina.[1] In a sense, the haunted house gives one a reason other than eviction to leave their home in a hurry, and the privilege and agency inherent in leaving or staying have everything to do with race.

Get Out: The Spatial Politics of Horror

In 2017, after finally finding financial backing from the studio Blumhouse Productions, Peele made his directorial debut with *Get Out*. The film was produced on the small budget of $4.5 million and accumulated a worldwide gross of $255.4 million—an astonishing profit. From the film's trailer, it was clear that it would confront issues of race relations in the present-day United States, but its widespread cultural impact could not have been predicted. Coming out one year after the election of Donald Trump, the film was actually written during the Obama administration. In an interview, Peele explained that the project had been ready long before 2017, but he had not been able to successfully pitch the film to any studio, suggesting that studios were unwilling to take a financial risk (Connley 2018). The premise of the film is that a Black man is going to meet the parents of his white girlfriend. In the beginning, Chris (Daniel Kaluuya) and Rose (Allison Williams) seem to be a happy couple. Visual and narrative cues, as well as whispers about the film's plot, cause the audience to feel nervous about Chris meeting his girlfriend's white parents. However, they seem just as sweet and welcoming as Rose, though her dad does make the microaggressive comment that he would have voted for Barack Obama a third time if he could. That microaggression quickly turns violent, even within the placidness of Rose's beautiful childhood home that also boasts a Black maid. As the plot progresses, Chris finds himself the target of a group known as the Coagula, who for decades have been capturing Black people and using their bodies as the vessels for their white minds. It is revealed that Rose is the honey trap for her family's human trafficking operation, bringing in Black men and women for possession and auctioning off for white geriatrics to purchase. This engenders a racial flip on the classic zombie horror plot. There is no stereotypical Black voodoo priest at play, but an evil plot by white folks to use Black bodies. *Get Out* defiantly subverts the tropes of the genre, in the tradition of horror films like *Night of the Living Dead* (George A. Romero 1968), *The Thing* (John Carpenter 1982), and *Candyman* (Bernard Rose 1992). *Get Out* was made with the intention of not making race a background character but the main motivator of the narrative structure.

Get Out is moreover a racialized metaphor for the economics of the interior. Not only is Black subjectivity frequently erased in horror and in films generally, but the frequent prosperity symbolized by homeownership, so central to many horror plots, becomes an unspoken racialized barrier, which illustrates that the narrative of the home and the interior is largely reserved for white people. *Get Out* was so positively received because of the fact that it focuses on a Black male lead, who generates unwavering sympathy, and who is ultimately a cathartic figure for the Black men in America who have lost their lives at the hands of white supremacy. We want to state at the outset that *Get Out* does not require academic validation in order to resonate sociohistorically. It is enough that it brought liberal racism to the forefront of a national conversation on race. Our metaphorical reading is meant to be both supplementary and a pedagogical intervention that adds to the cultural relevance of the film quite outside the critique and deconstruction of academic writing.

Get Out resonated so widely and so deeply because of the paucity of agency and narrative centrality for Black people in horror films since their inception. In the canonical book *Horror Noire: Blacks in American Horror Films from the 1890s to Present* (2011), Robyn R. Means Coleman traces the history of Black representation in the horror genre from the invention of cinema into the early 2000s. With Coleman's history in mind, we can see that *Get Out* emerged from a lengthy history of violence and an erasure of Black interiority/subjectivity in horror films. Returning to Eddie Murphy's stand-up, there has been a cultural understanding that Black men seem to always die first in horror films, hence their foresight to get out as soon as possible. Even in family horror films like *Gremlins* (Joe Dante 1984) and *Jurassic Park* (Steven Spielberg 1993) Black men die first in order to portray the power of the monsters. Black men are thus sacrificial to the plot, their death becoming the impetus of the "more important" story of the white characters. Stanley Kubrick's *The Shining* (1980) is notorious and shockingly obvious in this regard. The only Black character, Dick Hallorann (Scatman Crothers), is the first to be axed by the deranged Jack Torrance. Dick's narrative transgression in addition to being Black is penetrating the interior from the exterior, as an outsider, coming to rescue the Torrance family from the horrors inside the hotel and inside Jack's mind. Indeed, the two are inextricable, hence the violent need to eliminate Blackness as a (spatial/subjective) threat.

In Coleman's overview of some 100 years of cinema, she speaks to issues of representation, stereotype, and racial histories to contextualize Black bodies within the horror genre. She begins her archival history of horror with D. W. Griffith's *The Birth of a Nation* (1915). In the 1840s and 1850s, the first camera prototypes were invented, and ten years later the United States would abolish slavery. In 1888, Eastman invented the Kodak moving camera. These technological advances of the moving image, and indeed changes in the forced migration of bodies, modified the course of visual culture, to be sure, but more important for our purposes is the continued relegation of Black bodies to a space outside mainstream histories of the image. This displacement continues, despite the pioneering work of scholars like Deborah Willis, who argues in her essential volume *Reflections in Black: A History of Black Photographers, 1840 to the Present* (2000) that Black people were centrally involved in photography in the nineteenth century as artists and entrepreneurs. It is not coincidental that Chris in *Get Out* is an aspiring photographer. Likewise, as art historian Katherine Manthorne (2019) and Willis have pointed out, there was a Black presence in photography and the moving image in the nineteenth and early twentieth centuries despite many acts of violence and erasure. In a sense, the histories of photography and film actively negate the space occupied by artists of color in favor of a seamless, hegemonic art history, indeed a white history as epitomized by *The Birth of a Nation*.

Coleman's reading of *The Birth of a Nation* as a horror film is crucial to the history leading up to *Get Out*'s important cinematic intervention. The audience is presented with a melodramatic and nostalgic story of a white Southern family after the Reconstruction period in the United States. As the family struggles financially amid the abolishment of slavery, the Black characters of the film, all portrayed by white actors in blackface, deal with a multitude of feelings amid their newfound freedom. We might say that the horror of the film begins with white fragility as a result of racialized financial anxiety about losing property and the safety of the interior of the home. In its purposefully grotesque depictions of Blackness, the film accurately depicts, according to Coleman, the fears of white America in the early twentieth century. The film relies on a variety of stereotypes in order to stoke an American nightmare—the nightmare of Blackness and its mobility, as well as the possibility of financial ruin for white people should Black people rise up and take the slave owner's house and the slave owner's land, indeed for the forced laborers placed definitively outside to come inside and become the slave owners/landlords. *The Birth of a Nation* was so profoundly felt by white audiences that it was a factor that prompted a rebirth of the Ku Klux Klan.

In one of the most notable scenes of the film, Flora, the daughter of the Cameron family, is being chased by a man named Gus, who is sexually interested in her and is played by a white man in blackface. Flora, when chased toward a cliff, decides to throw herself off it, choosing death over miscegenation. The melodramatic pity that Griffith hopes to create for a dead white woman is meant to be both tragic and horrific. A fear of and lust for mixture, of allegedly different bodies and temporalities coming together—self and other, interior and exterior, miscegenation—is enough to provoke white self-destruction through abjection—the expulsion of the self from the filmic scene by jumping off a cliff. Both this scene and the film as a whole have become exemplary of the fears white men possess that white women will be taken and defiled by Black men. As Coleman puts it, *The Birth of a Nation* is a horror film for white folks that depicts the threat of miscegenation—one of their worst nightmares. Nearly 100 years after *The Birth of a Nation*, we have Jordan Peele's *Get Out*, a horror movie that also traces the simultaneous desire and repulsion caused by miscegenation within the space of the white upper-middle-class home. While *Get Out*'s plot is similar to *The Birth of a Nation*, Chris is not the perpetrator of violence but the victim. A hundred years later, the fear of white American men remains the same—a Black man with a white woman and a violation of white space with Black bodies, even as the Armitages lust for the interior of Black bodies in order to host their own failing ones.

Yet *Get Out* also suggests the impossibility of rectifying a Black history of forced migration and the erasure of history—history itself being a necessary manifestation of interiority. The film opens with a song in Swahili called "Sikiliza Kwa Wahenga." The lyrics in English loosely translate to "listen to your ancestors," a warning that is stymied by the legacy of colonialism and forced migration. The song functions as a warning that cannot be heard, as so many Black people were brought to the United States in bondage and there is thus a linguistic disconnect from the ancestral home. The sense of theft as a result of the transatlantic slave trade and other colonial abuses places Black bodies within a timeless and placeless space that is nevertheless restricted and outlined by racism—a haunted house, even. *Get Out* presents this duality in the mental limbo that Chris refers to as "The Sunken Place"—a place between history and its obliteration, between interior and exterior, indeed the dissolution of those binaries altogether. Relatedly, James Baldwin writes in his essential extended essay *The Devil Finds Work* that "the black performer has been sealed off into a vacuum" and explicates that segregation of creativity alongside the racial and class politics of the horror film, informed in so small part by his experience in Hollywood writing the screenplay for an ultimately shelved adaptation of *The Autobiography of Malcolm X* (Baldwin 2011, 99). "The Sunken Place" is constricting, crushing for the mind, for creativity, and for non-white spatiality altogether. The impetus of "The Sunken Place" is in fact an invasion of space and subjectivity, forcibly entering the home of the mind. As soon as Chris senses that something is off with the Armitages, he attempts to leave the house for a smoke break. Quite unexpectedly, he is stopped and hypnotized mid-exit, mid-getting-out, by Missy (Katherine Keener), Rose's mother. We, as viewers (though necessarily the film requires that we acknowledge that viewership is not monolithic), begin to beg Chris to get out. This kind of narrative anticipation, a movement toward the edge of one's seat or burying one's face in their hands, has everything to do with the transgression of interior and exterior boundaries, hence Linda Williams's inclusion of horror along the "body genres" of melodramas and pornography (1991). We know from the start of *Get Out* that Chris should not go to meet Rose's parents, since a Black man meeting his white girlfriend's parents is only going to lead to some kind of horror. So we sit up straight and clench our jaws as Chris, conversely, sinks into an ersatz interior that is dark and barren, quite unlike the Armitage estate.

The Blumhouse Model and Gentrification

In 2009, Paramount Pictures distributed *Paranormal Activity* (Oren Peli 2007), a film that certainly did not earn any Oscar nominations but nevertheless galvanized a national conversation. It was financed by

Blumhouse Productions, the same independent studio that would go on to back *Get Out*. *Paranormal Activity* was originally filmed in 2006, but was not commercially released until 2009, after the 2007–8 housing crisis, and, in a sense, the film bookended the economic collapse. *Paranormal Activity* nevertheless posted huge profits, in large part because of its lean budget. With a production budget of only $15,000, the film grossed $193.4 million, making it the most profitable film ever made. Executive producer Jason Blum greenlit the film after passing on *The Blair Witch Project* (Daniel Myrick and Eduardo Sánchez 1999) when working at Harvey Weinstein's production company Miramax. In an attempt to rectify his mistake, Blum took a chance on the first-person perspective low-budget film, which resulted in a major shift in his career and ending up being the catalyst for the creation of his production company Blumhouse Productions. Since the success of *Paranormal Activity*, Blumhouse has pioneered a business model of low-budget horror films with high profit returns. This method continued with enormously successful films like *Insidious* (James Wan 2010) and *Sinister* (Scott Derrickson 2012). Though the studio has produced some of the most successful modern horror franchises, like *Paranormal Activity*, *The Purge* (James DeMonaco 2013), and *Insidious*, the success of *Get Out* thrust the studio into an unprecedented notoriety within the horror genre and the film industry generally. *Paranormal Activity* focuses on a young couple in their early twenties who are dealing with an infestation of demonic forces in their home in Oceanside, California. Katie (Katie Featherstone), the main victim of these demonic attacks, finds that she is being followed by the same evil force that occupied her childhood home, which burned down. When a photo that was understood to be lost in the fire appears in her home as an adult, Katie becomes afraid of malevolent forces occupying her home, which they do in full force. In order to get at the root of the problem, she invites a medium over to communicate with the spirit. In their conversation with the medium, Katie and her boyfriend Micah (Micah Sloat) explain that she is a college student and he is a day trader, and that the two plan on getting married after she finishes college. It is quite unimaginable now for two twenty-somethings to be able to own a home together and have marriage on their horizon, regardless of their occupation.

There is a stark contrast between the lives led by Chris and Rose in *Get Out* and Micah and Katie in *Paranormal Activity*. Factors of race, time, space, and lifestyle clearly play a role in their strikingly different situations. The owning of space and a home, indeed interiority altogether, is an overlooked privilege allotted to white people. According to USAFacts (2020), Black people are the least likely group in the United States to own homes while white people are the most likely. A history of enslavement, racism, and prejudice have all played a factor in the exclusion of Black families from real estate ownership. Even though Chris is a successful artist, he lives in a seemingly modest apartment that he likely rents. Conversely, the fact that Katie is able to own a home as an adult and also references her family's ownership of her childhood home is a privileged experience that many people of color are unable to have. What is interesting here in terms of the goals of this volume is the impetus of the Blumhouse model occurring around the 2007–8 financial crash. Although *Paranormal Activity* was cheaply made, it implies that a couple in their twenties could afford buying a house, creating thereby a historical-financial disjoint in terms of form and content. As with many horror films, the focus is on the terror of the interior, the house as a metaphor for the mind, and in the midst of the financial crash it becomes clear that horror trope is class-driven and, therefore, racialized as well.

That violence is epitomized perhaps not by the conventions of horror films, but by a briefer scene—Mr. Armitage selling of Chris's body to a largely white audience who hope to use it as the host for their withering bodies. Instead of relying on gore to portray the horror of the film, Peele deliberately conjured up the spirit of the auction block. Peele does not need to emphasize the violence experienced by Black Americans as it is readily available in every other facet of media. Thus the violence against Chris is both racialized and monetized and emerges from the financial privilege implied by *Paranormal Activity*. Without making too literal a connection, while nevertheless acknowledging the marked intentionality of *Get Out*, we should consider the advertising campaign for the film, itself a kind of auction for movies that *Get Out*'s creative team deliberately racialized. In one series of billboards, the text "Do you belong in this neighborhood? Get out" hovers over cookie-cutter, manicured homes (Figure 9.1). The question works in a multifarious fashion; it is a foreboding question that inspires fear differently depending on who you are and what part of town you live in. The sign emphasizes a feeling of unsafety for folks of color who happen to be passing through white affluent neighborhoods and reiterates the role in gentrification white people have in communities of color. One cannot help but recall Barbara Kruger here, with her jarring and discomfiting combinations of text and image, especially in the context of financial, racial, and gendered disparities. Kruger's *Untitled "Who Is housed when money talks?"* (2020) is an exemplary comparison (Figure 9.2). Created pro bono for the advocacy group Housing is a Human Right, the housing advocacy division of AIDS Healthcare Foundation, the mural asks an urgent question to drivers on Sunset Boulevard in Los Angeles. Both *Get Out* and Kruger directly address the viewer. The inside/outside binary is made literal in their questions about homelessness and gentrification, which are of course deeply racialized and gendered.

The address of these public art projects is aimed at the bystander/spectator in addition to the buyers. Likewise, Peele explores the dangers of "good" white people, those whose racism for the most part is concealed/interiorized in the inviting and expensive walls of a country home, those white people

FIGURE 9.1 *Photo taken by an unnamed photographer on February 13, 2017, and uploaded to dailybillboardblog.com.*

who would have voted for Obama a third time if they could. At no point in the film are racial slurs spoken, nor do Rose's liberal parents ever do anything that could be perceived as racist. They are not backwoods hicks with missing teeth á la *The Texas Chainsaw Massacre* (Tobe Hooper 1974), but rather J. Crew donning, upper-middle-class, well-educated, landowning East Coast liberals. But they are also running a human trafficking ring that specifically targets Black people. *Get Out*, in this way, is akin to Stanley Kramer's *Guess Who's Coming to Dinner?* (1967) in their focus on affluent, home-owning, and seemingly harmless white people (not irrelevant is the fact that the mother in *Guess Who's Coming to Dinner* is an art gallery owner involved in the buying and selling of visual culture and, in a sense, bodies). Even Jim Hudson, a blind photographer who hopes to regain his sight by occupying Chris's body, ironically comments that for him it is not about race but that he just wants Chris's eye—his artistic eye as a photographer and his physical eye. It is impossible to separate the eye from racism, violence, and pain; it is an eye developed by a Black experience, an eye at the boundary of public and private that forms a kind of scaffolding or frame for the architecture of subjectivity. While Hudson does not consider himself a racist, he is an active participant in the Armitages' racism and epitomizes the white liberal

FIGURE 9.2 *Barbara Kruger,* Untitled (Who Is Housed When Money Talks?) *2020. Courtesy of the artist and Sprüth Magers, Los Angeles.*

motto of "I don't see color." The literal use of Black bodies functions as a larger metaphor for how whiteness uses and consumes every element of Black culture and Black bodies, with no regard for Black life or interiority, while upholding the spatial privileges of whiteness like gentrification, safety in public spaces, and visuality.

Horror and the Fear of Homelessness

A film frequently cited as a precedent to *Get Out*, *Guess Who's Coming to Dinner* focuses on the Draytons, whose young daughter Joanna (Katharine Houghton) has become engaged to a Black doctor. Although the Draytons consider themselves to be card-carrying liberals, the pair are confronted by their own prejudices when they are not enthusiastically supportive of their daughter's engagement. The film concludes not with bloodshed, but with a happy ending in which both couples enjoy a dinner together and they solve the complexities of interracial marriages in a matter of 120 minutes. Thanks to the close relationship of Sydney Poitier and prominent Black painter Charles White, *Guess Who's Coming to Dinner* features a painting of White's in the office of Matt Drayton, Joanna's father (Jones 2017). Though the Draytons are up-to-date on modern art and even own Black art, they, like Hudson, do not value Black life. They are willing to buy into the diverse trends of the art world and are open to welcoming Black art (as white audiences did with *Get Out*) into their home but cringe at the idea of their daughter being romantically involved with a Black man.

In an interview with Criterion, Peele cites *Rosemary's Baby* (Roman Polanski 1968), a timeless domestic horror story, as one of his inspirations for making *Get Out*. The author of the novel *Rosemary's Baby*, Ira Levin, was a Jewish atheist who wrote a number of thriller novels all pertaining to issues of class, politics, and prejudice (Chan 2017). The plots of novels such as *Rosemary's Baby*, *The Stepford Wives*, and *The Boys from Brazil* are now all well-known and widely referenced elements of pop culture in the United States. Being of Jewish ancestry, Levin perfectly understood otherness and the frailty of American culture of the 1960s. In *Rosemary's Baby*, he was able to put himself in the shoes of a woman in a misogynist and capitalist culture. The film adaptation by Roman Polanski, himself Jewish, expanded the story into a visual entity that, not unlike *Get Out*, creates a sort of Satanic drawing room play or an urban Gothic narrative of the interior, driven by the financial concerns of a struggling actor (who lives in a beautiful apartment building made to look working class). Additionally, *Rosemary's Baby*, in the tradition of the drawing room play or Gothic literature, is foundationally interested in the interior. Indeed, much of the book and film take place inside, leading historian of literature Sharon Marcus to call Rosemary "a heroine who almost never leaves her apartment" (1993, 127). Marcus goes on: "As the novel's plot gets underway, the city, defined as the public, exterior spaces that include streets, stores, skyscrapers, parks, and night-spots, disappears from the scene, leaving the reader alone with the interior spectacle of the painful pregnancy that confines Rosemary to her apartment" (132). It is additionally important to note that Rosemary and Guy's apartment, in the film and the novel, is connected to the Castevets' apartment through a linen closet, thus connecting evil literally to the interior. The cult's conspiracy against Chris in *Get Out* likens itself to *Rosemary's Baby*, but this time the issue is not of gender but of race. While Rosemary urges her husband to be wary of the Castevets, he dismisses her fears as hysteria, until the very last minute when it is revealed that he offered up his wife's womb to the devil in exchange for fame and fortune as an actor. The womb, a locus of interiority and the impetus of exteriority, becomes an investment, an asset, a stock to be traded. Rosemary's own body is in fact owned by two men, her husband and Satan, to do business upon and through. *Get Out* expands this buying and selling of bodies from reproductive rights to modern slavery.

Much of the horror within *Rosemary's Baby* results from the fact that Rosemary (Mia Farrow) is given a fair number of warning signs leading up to the big revelation at the end of the film, as is the case with Chris in

Get Out and the almost instant microaggressions from the Armitage family. *Rosemary's Baby* begins with an opening shot of the New York skyline, and then cuts to Rosemary and her husband Guy (John Cassavetes), shopping for an apartment as newlyweds. Rosemary instantly falls in love with the apartment they see at the Bramford building. This was hardly a working-class location. It was shot at the iconic Dakota Apartments in New York. Guy is hesitant about the apartment as it is out of their budget, but he relents. Notably the person showing the apartment to the couple lets them know that the previous owner died in the apartment. After the pair moves in and Rosemary overhears an argument between the Castevets next door, Terry (Victoria Vetri), their live-in guest, is seen splattered across the New York sidewalk after successfully committing suicide. From nightmares about the devil to an old book gifted to her by her late friend Hutch, Rosemary is given a number of red flags about her future and the future of her child if they stay in the Bramford building, though nothing could prepare Rosemary for the reality that she has been impregnated by the devil. Similarly to Chris in *Get Out*, Rosemary senses that something is terribly wrong but has no idea what that thing is. *Rosemary's Baby* moves the horror genre from the haunted houses of suburbia and vampire mansions to the metropolitan New York landscape. Her sense of sanctuary in both her own home and body are overtaken by a Satanic cult. While Rosemary is unemployed and Guy is a struggling actor, the pair seemingly live a rather lavish life. A large motivator in Guy eventually selling Rosemary's body to the coven is their promises of wealth and fame for him and Rosemary. The horror of *Rosemary's Baby* occupies the domestic space of Rosemary's world as a homemaker, a space of confinement that is nevertheless also a product of white privilege.

Not long after, the taste for horror stories of the interior would emerge spectacularly again. In 1975, the Lutz family moved into a home in Amityville, Long Island. Their story would go on to be the plot of the 1979 film *The Amityville Horror* (Stuart Rosenberg). The real-life case of the Lutzes would begin in 1974, prior to the Lutzes moving in. The previous owners, the DeFeo family, were mysteriously murdered by the eldest son, Ronald DeFeo Jr. Though DeFeo shot each family member, no signs of any of them being awoken by the gun shots could be found in forensic reports and no neighbors recall hearing gunshots in the middle of the night. Though the Lutzes were aware of the murders prior to their moving in, they did so anyway, unable to resist the price of the home, which had been significantly discounted in light of the murders. Soon they reported to news outlets that they were being haunted and had paranormal encounters in the home. After allegedly being terrorized in the house, the Lutzes fled one night and never returned, only having lived in the home for twenty-eight days. Since the family had originally purchased the house, tabloids and news outlets suggested that their experiences had been fabricated in order to get out of a mortgage they knew they could not afford in the first place, not unlike the predatory lending that caused the 2007–8 financial crisis. Since the Lutz family went on to profit from their experiences in the initial 1977 book adaptation entitled *The Amityville Horror*, tabloids questioned the validity of their story after the subsequent homeowners did not share the same paranormal experiences (Kernan 1979). The film became a classic and a very profitable film, with $86.4 million at the box office on a $4.7 million budget, recalling the massive profits produced by the Blumhouse model. Though the Lutzes may have experienced mysterious events in their Amityville home, their story epitomizes the freedom and sympathy allotted to white individuals that Means Coleman directly points at in *Horror Noire* (2011). While in horror films like *Candyman*, the violence experienced by Black Chicagoans in the Cabrini Green housing projects is questioned and passed off as the typical urban violence experienced by Black and Brown individuals in "the hood." The Lutzes, however, were able to leave their own and go on to live a seemingly normal life.

Conclusion

Given these examples, we might consider how to build a theory of the kind of racialized-horrifying-economic landscape of *Get Out*. Here we turn to Baldwin, who importantly expands the possibilities of academic writing and allows these films to signify in multiple ways. He writes, again in *The Devil Finds Work*: "*The Exorcist* is not concerned in the least with damnation, an abysm far beyond the confines of its imagination, but with property, with safety, tax shelters, stocks and bonds, rising and falling markets, the continued invulnerability of a certain class of people, and the continued sanctification of a certain history" (2011, 116). Few things frighten Baldwin, he writes (120):

> For, I have seen the devil, by day and by night, and have seen him in you and in me: in the eyes of the cop and the sheriff and the deputy, the landlord, the housewife, the football player: in the eyes of some junkies, the eyes of some preachers, the eyes of some governors, presidents, wardens . . . He does not levitate beds or fool around with little girls: *we* do.

Certainly, the essay, given its title, is a reflection on horror, or at least what the devil represents in terms of a hated and feared other. At the same time, Baldwin also points poetically to the business of fear, the business of housing and socioeconomic disparity, the business of racialized/racist visual culture, the business of narrativity altogether, not in the sense of an economic survey of art auctions or film sets, so fashionable in art and film history, but rather as an economics of visual responsibility.

In this vein, we conclude that *Get Out* marks both a cultural and a financial confrontation of the horrors of reality—poverty, racism, houselessness. Yet the bet on a racial horror formula has not succeeded again. While *Get Out* successfully addressed both issues of racism and diversity, the Blumhouse projects that would follow with the same intention did not fare so well. *Ma* (Tate Taylor 2019), for instance, portrays Octavia Spencer's titular character as an incel-type, basement-dwelling villain with no self-awareness about being the only Black character in the film. Perhaps audiences noticed, since the film boasts a whopping 55 percent on Rotten Tomatoes. Hulu then released Blumhouse's *Culture Shock* (Gigi Saul Guerrero 2019), which also received its fair share of criticism, despite hoping, in the spirit of diversity, to showcase the journey of Mexican migrants north to the United States. The film cast actress Martha Higareda, a white Mexican who was accused of attempting to prevent Yalitza Aparicio from receiving an Ariel Award nomination. While *Get Out* marks an unprecedented moment in the horror genre, it is not the marker of a post-racial world. As white liberals continue to misread it as a film for the Trump era, the film is relevant to the entire history of the United States (Arkin 2021). For socially concerned horror movies to work there must be a confrontation of why *Get Out* was so successful and thought as to when and how diversity is necessary, something Blumhouse has failed to do without Peele. We might say then that it was not the Blumhouse financial model that succeeded; rather, it was Peele. We might also consider the Blumhouse model to be a post-recession gentrification of the horror genre. As Baldwin states, the fears of communities of color need no embellishment. They are not living in fear of monsters or ghosts but the violence that white people enact upon others via an all-encompassing control of interiority.

Note

1 For an important discussion of images of Black tragedy, especially folks trying to survive on their roofs, during Hurricane Katrina, see "A Litany for New Orleans, 2005" in Courtney R. Baker's *Humane Insight: Looking at Images of African American Suffering and Death* (2017).

References

Arkin, D. (2021), "Movies That Defined the Trump Era," *Nbcnews.com*, 9 January. Available online: https://www.nbcnews.com/pop-culture/movies/movies-defined-trump-era- n1252888.

Baker, C. R. (2017), *Humane Insight: Looking at Images of African American Suffering and Death*, Champagne: University of Illinois Press.

Baldwin, J. (2011), *The Devil Finds Work*, New York: Vintage.

Chan, A. (2017), "Waking Nightmares: A Conversation with Jordan Peele," *Criterion*, 23 February. Available online: https://www.criterion.com/current/posts/4439-waking- nightmares-a-conversation-with-jordan-peele.

Connley, C. (2018), "Oscar-Winner Jordan Peele Explains Why He Didn't Think 'Get Out' Would Ever Get Made," *CNBC*, 5 March. Available online: https://www.cnbc.com/2018/03/05/oscar-winner-jordan-peele-didnt-think-get-out-would-ever-get-made.html.

Jones, K. (2017), *South of Pico: African American Artists in Los Angeles in the 1960s and 1970s*. Durham, NC: Duke University Press.

Kernan, M. (1979), "The Calamityville Horror," *The Washington Post*, 16 September. Available online: https://www.washingtonpost.com/archive/lifestyle/1979/09/16/the-calamityville- horror/3daedbf6-10e5-46cd-945c-faf52dc4db17/.

Manthorne, C. (2019), *Film and Modern American Art: The Dialogue between Cinema and Painting*, New York: Routledge.

Marcus, S. (1993), "Placing 'Rosemary's Baby'," *Differences: A Journal of Feminist Cultural Studies* 5 (3), pp. 121–54.

Means Coleman, R. R. (2011), *Horror Noire: Blacks in American Horror Films from the 1890s to Present*, New York and London: Routledge.

USAFacts (2020), "Homeownership Rates Show That Black Americans Are Currently the Least Likely Group to Own Homes," *USAFacts*, 28 July, Available online: https://usafacts.org/articles/homeownership-rates-by-race/.

Williams, L. (1991), "Film Bodies: Gender, Genre, and Excess," *Film Quarterly* 44 (4), pp. 2–13.

Willis, D. (2000), *Reflections in Black: A History of Black Photographers, 1840 to the Present*, New York: W.W. Norton.

10

Resignifying the National Home

Gendered Domopolitics and Neoliberal Geographies of Exclusion in Debra Granik's Cinema

Hilaria Loyo

Introduction

Two working-class Irish brothers in Pittsburg, Pennsylvania, are the warriors defending home in Gavin O'Connor's *Warrior* (2011). Through the two protagonists characterizing the title's singular combatant, this film clearly registers the connection of the two threats menacing US citizens after the housing crisis: foreclosure and another terrorist attack after 9/11. This connection also juxtaposes two meanings of home: on the one hand, home as house and embodiment of family values, and on the other, home as nation/homeland. The film also identifies the banks and their ruthless tactics as well as the War on Terror and its fatal chaos at the battlefront as the real causes of their life-threatening situation, but the film's narrative channels the protagonists' anger away from them and directs it toward the capitalization of their suffering in the show business of martial arts, and against an alcoholic, neglecting father. The film clearly reveals the capitalist mechanisms that transform working-class anger into family dramas as profitable spectacles of emotional and physical pain, in this case, in an explosive display of testosterone. Debra Granik's films, however, offer a very different perspective about the real warriors and the struggle in the defense of homes against the threats generated by the War on Terror and the housing crisis as key factors in the current context of crisis.

Granik's three feature films to date, *Down to the Bone* (2004), *Winter's Bone* (2010), and *Leave No Trace* (2018), are inscribed within a new cinematic trend found in the work of many independent women filmmakers (Kelly Reichardt, Courtney Hunt, Megan Griffiths, and Ava DuVernay, among others) that *The New York Times* film critic A. O. Scott called "neo-neorealism" (in Badley 2016, 123). Sharing the thematic and stylistic interests that characterize the neo-neorealism of women's indies, Granik's films exhibit a key concern about "the threat of dispossession and, specially, homelessness," and the socioeconomic violence against women and children (Badley 2016, 124). Stylistically, they are characterized by "its 'slowness' and nuanced minimalism," a documentary style, the casting of non-professionals or little-known actors in protagonist roles, and the depiction of female-centered social worlds (122–4). In particular, the choice of slow-paced cinema that characterizes this new realistic mode prompts a different viewing experience. Extended time frame allows the spectator to pay greater attention to small details and to meditate upon them (de Luca 2016).

Most significantly, drawing upon French philosopher Jacques Rancière's thought on the politics of aesthetics, film scholars of slow cinema have called their attention to the possibilities this type of cinema may offer to create alternative "modes of experience" questioning a "consensual" social order (de Luca and Barradas Jorge 2016, 13). The work of Rancière has attracted a special attention in recent debates on the depoliticization of politics, in particular his claim that "politics is about contesting the prevailing logics through which individuals are assigned a (non)political place" (Darling 2014, 75). As Rancière argues, "[p]olitical struggle is not a conflict between well defined interest groups; it is an opposition of logics that count the parties and parts of the community in different ways" (2001, 19), which he sees most notably in the specific confrontation between the rich and the poor.

Rancière, Jonathan Darling observes, "foregrounds the disruptive nature of politics as a means of intervening within, or interrupting, an established order of perception which places individuals and groups in a hierarchical form" (2014, 75). This chapter argues that, in their invitation to meditate on the contemporary realities of poverty in areas of exclusion of white people, Granik's female-centered films constitute an act of political intervention in the sense given by Rancière. By offering the perception of the poor, the meditations inspired by her films constitute political acts insofar as they disrupt the dominant narrative about the main factors contributing to the life-threatening precarization of women under neoliberalism in the last few decades, in which the housing crisis, the current housing politics, and domopolitics play a central role.

Gendered Domopolitics and Neoliberal Geographies of Exclusion

Some of the political implications of the housing crisis can be uncovered by inscribing it within the larger context of "domopolitics," a term that derives from the emergence of so-called neoliberal security states, particularly after the 9/11 terrorist attacks and the beginning of the War on Terror. But the contemporary securitarian regime in the United States has a long history that stretches back to the 1970s. In the context of the Cold War, the moral panics caused by the urban insurrections of the 1960s, which threw into sharp relief "the material conditions of the poor, working class, and people of color" (Camp 2016, 1), led to the almost simultaneous declarations of the War on Crime and the War on Drugs as counterinsurgence measures (Chomsky 1998; Camp 2016). Since then, and long before the 9/11 terrorist attacks, the fear of crime and violence has been, as Jonathan Simon has argued, "a key strategy of American governance" that has made the country "less democratic and more racially polarized" (2007, 6). The declaration of the War on Terror just aggravated the pervasive sense of insecurity and reinforced the contemporary securitarian regimes in the United States and elsewhere. The introduction of a law and order approach and a culture of fear and control, however, has not made people more secure, but rather it has placed a "greater and greater burden on ordinary Americans" (Simon 2007, 6).

Domopolitics refers "to the government of the state (but, crucially, other political spaces as well) as a *home*" (Walters 2004, 241). In the United States, this form of government was clearly encapsulated by the establishment of the Department of Homeland Security in 2001. Domopolitics, William Walters writes, "rationalizes a series of security measures in the name of a particular conception of the home" (241). As he remarks, the home is commonly associated with positive images of shelter and haven, but also with the idea of "*domo* as conquest, taming, subduing; a will to domesticate the forces which threaten the sanctity of the home" (242). In this sense, security measures are established not only to protect the "nation home" from external threats (e.g., traffickers, illegal immigrants) but, most significantly, from the hidden ones within; as he succinctly puts it, "the homeland becomes the home front, one amongst many sites in a multifaceted struggle" (242). If the notion of home has traditionally been at the heart of contemporary constructions of nation-states and, hence, modern notions of citizenship and national identity—to be at home, in a literal and metaphorical sense, confers a sense of belonging, of being a citizen—the modern notion of nation-states entails the creation of an ideal citizen that, as Judith Butler has noted (Butler and Spivak 2007, 4–5), "'binds' as much as 'unbinds' members in the national territory," an ideal of membership that, in the words of Kathleen Arnold, "cannot be realized" (2004, 48), and that changes over time.

Based on an ideal model of citizenship, domopolitics constitutes "a perceptual regime" that creates specific ways of depoliticization through the establishing of a selective logic behind the governmental measures of inclusion and exclusion at the border in the name of national security (Darling 2014, 73). In the United States, according to Walters, domopolitics has constituted "a master identity and narrative" defining the state and citizenship (2004, 243) in a way that establishes a moral selective criteria to distinguish, for example, between "desirable" and "undesirable" immigrants or asylum seekers, but that it has also retrieved an old classification that divides the poor between "deserving" and "underserving" (or "underclass") categories. The resurrection of this moral categorization has gone hand in hand with long-running economic and social neoliberal policies that led to further economic dispossession and dislocation. Most notably, the dismantling of the welfare regime, particularly as a result of Bill Clinton's welfare reform of 1996, supplanted traditional forms of social welfare with "the idea of 'asset-based welfare'" that encouraged "minority home ownership as a long-term, structural response to the widening social inequalities of neoliberal America" (Cooper 2017, 140). This shift of focus from public housing to private home ownership required easy access to private credit, presented as a lasting way to "wealth democratization," which the subprime crisis of 2007 proved not only "impossible," as Melinda Cooper (157) argues, but has rather resulted in disastrous opposite effects: foreclosures, loss of savings, and exorbitant housing prices. These policies have transformed housing as "lived, social space" into "an instrument for profit making," thus creating "a conflict between *home* and *real state*" (Madden and Marcuse 2016, Introduction) that has contributed to intensifying class polarization and to increasing figures of poverty and homelessness in the United States, particularly noticeable after the financial crash of 2008. Meanwhile, the legitimate demands for dignity and freedom of the dispossessed have been construed, since the Cold War to the War on Terror, as internal threats to the country's security and, hence, in need to be checked through fear, surveillance, and punishment, leading to a "war against the poor" and the criminalization of poverty itself (Wacquant 2009, 3) in a political trajectory that has transformed US's welfare state into a carceral state.

The morally based discriminatory categories in domopolitical policies and discourse rest on the neoliberal citizen as the current ideal citizen model: "autonomous, self-managing, entrepreneurial and financially productive" (Lonergan 2018, 5). As feminist scholars have demonstrated, this apparently gender-neutral notion of neoliberal citizenship and belonging is, however, heavily gendered and assigns "an unmarked form of masculinity" (Salzinger 2020, 197). Feminist scholars have also unveiled an invisible social dependency underlying the false autonomy of the neoliberal citizen, assumed in the idea of being the "entrepreneur of himself" (198). The presumed autonomy of the neoliberal citizen, Leslie Salzinger argues, "requires not only an underlying social scaffolding, but an affective one as well"; it requires, she further explains, "another kind of self nearby, shouldering the labor of caring for children, aging parents, and other forms of 'inevitable dependency'" (198). On this regard, Gwyneth Lonergan has also recalled that the liberal discourses of citizenship "have relied upon a gendered conceptualization of the 'private home' in order to give meaning to the political 'public sphere'" (2018, 2). Designated as "private" and hence apolitical, women were made responsible for the reproduction and maintenance of the home and the "correct" nation-state, in line with "dominant discourses of belonging and citizenship" (3). But with the curtailment of welfare and privatization of state-sponsored caring support, women are made responsible for those caring services, "free of charge, in 'private'" (Lonergan 2018, 8), or "forced to care," in Evelyn N. Glenn's words (2010). Significantly, this private obligation, Lonergan cautions, has led to the "securitized intervention into, and disciplining of, the activities of those responsible for reproducing this home, and raising the next generation of citizens" (2018, 9). This regulating intervention has inflected the meaning of house as "technology for the organization and distribution of life, health, illness, and death" (Willse 2015, 2), and hence those of home as embodiment of family values and homeland.

These thoughts on the recent domopolitical inflections of the correlated notions of house, home, and homeland caused by the ascendency of economic neoliberalism and the establishment of securitarian regimes necessary to sustain it will guide the following analysis of Granik's films. I shall be arguing that these films challenge the rationale behind current domopolitics in the United States by exposing the life-threatening neoliberal securitarian mechanisms regulating the poor in certain geographical areas of exclusion located in deindustrialized, rural regions. In their struggle for survival, the female protagonists in these films also hint at alternative, lifesaving notions of the nation-home. Although each film depicts different geographical areas of exclusion during different crises of the twenty-first century—marked, respectively, by the 9/11 terrorist attacks and the War on Terror, the financial meltdown of 2008 and the ensuing Great Recession, and the electoral victory of Donald Trump and the ascendancy of xenophobic nationalism—the three films also deploy common elements that transversally define the dominant factors plaguing poor whites, especially women and children, under contemporary domopolitics: the inescapable presence of the War on Terror, the spoils of drug use, surveillance and criminalization as disciplinary and punishing measures, the difficulty to make ends meet, and strained racial relationships. In Granik's films these recurrent contextual factors are associated to failed homes, characterized by the unfitting masculinity of household heads in traditionally ignored areas, which place a crushing burden on poor women in as much as they bear the responsibility for the maintenance of their homes and the survival of future citizens.

On the Brink of Homelessness: Failed Homes in Neoliberal Geographies of Exclusion

Shot on location, the three geographical areas of exclusion in these films play an important role in sketching the conditions that threaten the female protagonists' homes. *Down to the Bone* is set in a decaying small town in Upstate New York, an area hit hard by deindustrialization. Based on Daniel Woodrell's eponymous novel, *Winter's Bone* is set in the Ozark Mountains in Missouri, a depleted mining area whose population, along with those residing in the Appalachians in West Virginia, have traditionally incarnated the stereotypical image of the rural underclass: intergenerational poverty, drug use, domestic violence, and dependency (Young 2017). Based on a true story, *Leave No Trace*, a film adaptation of Peter Rock's novel *My Abandonment*, is set in Forest Park, Portland, Oregon, and the mountains in Washington State. In an area particularly stricken by the general economic collapse, local tax policies, and unaffordable housing (Neel 2018, 41–2), these federal lands have become "home" for what Granik calls "economic fugitives" (in Gilbey 2018, 48): "veterans, drug addicts, and workers." In these geographies of exclusion, the three films start by introducing a form of failed home in need of being reconfigured.

The opening shots of *Down to the Bone* already establish the connection between the economic decline in the area and the War on Terror as the contextual frame of the protagonist's failed home. A montage sequence takes us from an extremely long shot of the exterior of a grocery store with a deserted parking lot to close-up shots of goods at the checkout. From the initial shots of desolation, the sequence concludes with some images of patriotic propaganda urging customer to participate in the war effort. Throughout the film, the camera pauses on the area's urban landscape inviting the viewer to reflect on the spoils of war on the home front. Still images, juxtaposing the omnipresence of the Stars and Stripes with derelict buildings and other signs of economic decay, render the patriotic invitation to support the war a cruel economic demand. These images are also intercut with shots of engineering achievements that bring memories of a prosperous, not too distanced industrial past.

The opening sequence also introduces the female protagonist, Irene (Vera Farmiga), working as a checkout cashier at the grocery store. She is the mother of two kids, struggling with drug addiction and an unsatisfying marriage. The economic precariousness of the family (and the home) is revealed by the poor conditions of the house they live in. Irene is always presented as a good housewife and a caring mother, who only loses her temper when under the effects of drugs. Not only does she keep the house clean and tidy—in a complete departure from the traditional representation of the underclass home—but she also prepares a laborious Thanksgiving dinner for her family and friends. Together with economic precarity and the protagonist's drug habit, the damaged masculinity of her husband seems the third element distinguishing this failed home.

The family-values rhetoric characteristic of neoliberal economic and social policies entails a highly heteronormative vision of the familial. Accordingly, the demands for women to be full-time wives and mothers are based on the understated assumption that "proper" care labor occurs, as Glenn has noted, "within a self-sufficient male-headed household" (2010, 162), in which "economic support and caring are divided along gender lines" (166). Irene's husband, Steve (Clint Jordan), fails as a breadwinner, and seems an insensitive father and husband. A drug user himself, Steve departs from the ideal neoliberal citizen as family provider, but somehow he clings to neoliberal rationality by exploiting his manhood and virility as the only expression of self-worth when presenting himself as human capital—an asset that will help him find a new sentimental partner after the couple's eventual split.

A similar pattern can be found in the presentation of unsuccessful homes in the other two films, in which males fail to live up to the neoliberal doctrine of family economic self-sufficiency. In *Winter's Bone*, the female protagonist, Ree Dolly (Jennifer Lawrence), a teenager from the Ozarks, is also introduced in the middle of a domestic crisis. The family's survival depends on the young protagonist's performance of a double parenting role: that of the male economic provider and that of the female caregiver. In addition to economic precarity derived from the lack of income, the burden of Ree's responsibility is increased by the mental illness of her mother (Valery Richards) and a missing father, Jessup, involved in the illegal production and distribution of methamphetamine. Her father has used the family house as bail collateral and finding him before the trial is Ree's only chance to keep their home.

The home is presented as a core narrative trope from the very onset of the film. The lyrics of the lullaby "The Missouri Waltz" highlight the moments of domestic life that open the film by invoking the important roles of the mother and father, now absent. The early scenes suggest the need to "spell house," to redefine it, as she instructs her siblings when walking them to school. The terms reconfiguring this home will be given in the film's subsequent narrative unfolding that combines slow-paced domestic scenes of Ree instructing her siblings on survival and caring skills with those, equally prolonged, of her quest to find her father to legally keep their house/home and their land.

In *Leave No Trace*, Tom (Thomasin McKenzie), a teenage girl, lives with her father Will (Ben Foster), a veteran suffering from PTSD, in Forest Park. As in the other films, the camera lingers on the preserved wilderness of the park and a makeshift camp/home with specific, compartmentalized areas for domestic life and routines. Will has taught his daughter the skills and knowledge necessary to survive in the woods, and we see him training her how to hide from the authorities through routine drills. But we also see them walking out of the forest to Portland, where they visit a Veterans Hospital to get prescribed drugs that Will sells to other veterans, also camping in the park, to afford some groceries at the supermarket. If this area is home of "economic fugitives," as Granik describes it, the film initially presents it as an area of voluntary exclusion, of self-exile, driven by a desire for a life off the grid, closer to nature, in a gesture that reclaims public space for the poor. The distinction made at the supermarket between "need or want" when choosing a chocolate bar also reinforces the idea that their alternative home rests on the rejection of consumerism and other material trappings of neoliberal society.

When Will and Tom are finally spotted by a runner and the authorities remove them from the forest to be sent to the local social services, the film brings in the legal measures that exclude these veterans from the area. The film also taps into the figure of the veteran as refugee that emerged after the Vietnam War to incarnate the estrangement and mistreatment of white vets and white working-class men suffering at the economic decline of postwar decades, and that since the 2016, during Donald Trump's electoral campaign and presidency, has gained a new salience. The image establishes equivalence between white vets and other non-white refugees, a "being like" that, as Joseph Darda has noted (2019, 85), "is freighted with racial and national meaning." As Darda further observes, "[i]f the refugee analogy situates white vets as wounded embodiments of the nation, it casts Americans of color outside it" (2019, 86). This analogy constitutes a significant element in the film's final racial configuration of the nation-home.

The problematic masculinity of the father, Will, and the absent mother also trouble the alternative home in the Edenic wilderness of the park. Will is presented as a good father, but he is psychologically damaged by a war-related trauma that drives his obsessive efforts to escape from the constraining measures of neoliberal poverty governance. He incarnates a form of staunch individualism and freedom more closely associated with the American frontier tradition and road movies that with the autonomy of the neoliberal subject.

The loss of the mother becomes a central element to the three films' narrative development. In this film, their removal from the forest will initiate a journey of maturity in which Tom will learn the terms that will redefine home in an effort to regain her maternal attachment. This bond is symbolized through the yellow color, a hue component of a warmer chromatic palette that will characterize her new home. Absent mothers and fathers, economic precarity, the War on Terror, and the omnipresence of drugs in theses rundown areas place unduly demands on the three young heroines in their struggles to save homes and families.

Female Struggles: Unveiling Neoliberal Regulations of the Poor

The three films devote extensive narrative time to the female protagonists' struggle to preserve their homes. In the elaborate depiction of their struggle, each film offers details that help uncover important neoliberal domopolitical regulatory mechanisms designed to discipline the poor and their households, in a way that dismantles the moral values that sustain them. These contextual references contribute to the films' departure from representations based on the prevalent assumption of personal disabilities for women's precarious conditions, thus disrupting stereotypical representations of marginal women.

Down to the Bone assigns ample screen time to the life and circumstances of drugs and addiction, which diverges from the conventional vilification of drug-using wives and mothers—"the welfare queen"—that has so centrally contributed to their construction as undeserving poor of welfare programs (Singer and Page 2014, 19). Irene is seen desperately craving for cocaine: we see her efforts to quit it in an unsupportive environment of general drug use, her attendance to rehab sessions, her relapse, and her struggle to stay clean again.

Slow-paced images also invite the viewer to reflect upon the context of this social problem, the criminalization of poverty through drug control and punishment, as well as the scant attention the government offers to drug addiction. The film, for instance, depicts the surveillance of workers at the store, and the monitoring of their working rate, in one of those poorly paid jobs that low-income families are forced to take in order to receive public assistance. The scene recalls the consequences of the legal measures designed "to reduce dependence of low-income families on government aid, promote employment and self-sufficiency, promote marriage, and reduce births outside marriage" (Glenn 2010, 167). The link between the exploitative working conditions of the poor and drug abuse is established when we learn that Irene was high on cocaine when she met the performance demands at work, but paradoxically she loses her job when she is clean. Surveillance of poor neighborhoods is also executed through routine police control on drugs. When Irene and Bob (Hugh Dillon), a former drug addict and her lover, go to New York City, they are arrested in a routine drug control for the possession of half an ounce of heroine, for which the charge is a big felony that involves, if convicted, a prison sentence and, consequently, the loss of her children. In a scene that brings in the draconian laws enacted in the last two decades to severely punish those arrested for drug-related offenses, the lawyer and the prosecutor offer her a chance to escape prison on condition that she attends a number of counseling sessions and meetings within a year.

Slow-paced cinema conventions are also used in the scenes at the rehab center to reveal, and reflect upon, the limited government assistance available for drug treatment in a depiction that renders the institution more devoted to the control of drug addicts than to their rehabilitation through proper medical care. Contrary to the promise stated in a poster that reads, "New Hope, New Strength. A Bridge Back to Life," the center seems to lack specialized medical staff and be run by former drug addicts, now in charge of following control procedure and dispensing medication. On her first day at the center, Irene is questioned by a former addict about her use, her role as a mother, and, more importantly, her job situation ("unemployment doesn't seem to be a problem," he approvingly remarks), this being a requirement for admittance at the center. The camera also lingers on other more questionable therapies consisting in practicing physical exercises, acupuncture, and confessional meetings, sometimes in local churches once released from the rehab center. The controlling function of the institution is also stressed in the mandatory urine tests Irene has to pass while on parole. In one of the sessions, Hector (Hector Vasquez), a Latino inpatient, questions the effectiveness of one of the therapies to stop drug consumption and exposes the common dehumanization of drug addicts performed through language (Singer and Page 2014, 18) when the instructor reassures him that the technique will help him calm his "monkey mind," to which he replies, "Am I a monkey?"

Ree's struggle to save her family home in *Winter's Bone* also occupies ample narrative time while long takes and static shots offer details of the social factors responsible for her straining, at-risk-of-homelessness situation in the area. In the opening shots, the area is presented as "a post-industrial wasteland," in the words of Frame, which he associates with "the misery of the aftermath of recession" (2020, 353), but also as "a shatter zone," a term used by political geographers to designate borderlands serving as "places of resistance to and refuge from some of the most destructive of state-making and state-rule" (Moon and Talley 2010). The lifestyle of the communities in this region, an enclave of the US American underclass now devastated by crystal meth addiction and endemic subsistence poverty, has traditionally constituted, as Granik also reminds us, "a form of defiance, a form of individuality that goes beyond the American fantasy of individualism," and where "people's self-worth is not defined like the rest of the country's, through material gain" (in Bell 2010). The film, however, depicts the regulating and exploitative mechanisms that have transformed the communities in this area into difficult sites of resistance.

The very first scenes of the film suggest that the central narrative goal to "spell house" is pursued in the context of the scant opportunities offered to young people in the area. At the school where she takes her siblings, Ree's gaze guides us to another classroom where male and female adolescents are receiving parenting lessons, a pressing instruction in a region characterized by premature parenthood. As she walks the school corridors, her eyes also direct us to a group of young men and women receiving military instruction. The scene clearly suggests the connection of these two options: the exploitation of the poor population's reproductive capacity to feed the army corps in times of war. Both options seem dismal prospects for Ree's future. The unhappiness of her friend Gail (Lauren Sweester), a teenage mother, alerts her to the miseries generated by the untimely responsibilities in a teenage marriage. When at a moment of despair Ree tries to join the army as the only option to get the enlisting money and save the family home, the recruitment officer turns her down and reminds her that her most imminent duty is to take care of her family. The verbal exchange between the two characters reveals such different mindsets. They seem to speak, as Pasquale Cicchetti has noted, "two completely different languages" (86), in which the recruiter's insistence on women's caring obligations as primary patriotic value underlies his ignorance about the community's pressing reality.

In her quest to find her father, Ree's central confrontation, however, involves the members of her own community. Apparently away from the social control of the modern nation-state, this secluded community functions as a criminal organization with its own strict rules of blood, loyalty, a code of silence, violence, and overbearing masculinity. Women's lack of worth in this stern patriarchal world is soon displayed in the film. In her search for the truth about her father, Ree is threatened, intimidated, and beaten up, not just because she is breaking the code of silence, but also because she is stepping out of her role as a woman. When she insistently tries to reach "the Big Man," Thump Milton (Ron "Stray Dog" Hall), the matriarch of the Milton family, Merab (Dale Dickey) scolds her by saying, "Don't you got no men to do this?" In a society segregated by sex, the women of the Milton family are in charge of punishing Ree for her unacceptable inquiries, but they are also the ones who will eventually help her find the truth about her father and the way to save her home, which would prevent her and her family from being "turned out in the fields like dogs." Other women in the film also offer some help to Ree: her neighbor Sonya (Shelley Waggener), her friend Gail, and her father's former lover, April (Sheryl Lee). This form of female solidarity seems the answer to Ree's desperate request addressed to her mentally ill mother, "Mom, look at me. Can you please help me this one time?"

The men in this community, however, fare no better. We learn that Jessup, an extraordinary meth cook, was killed because of his collaboration with the police to escape a ten-year sentence. Fierce loyalty to the rule of silence in the criminal network involves, however, the betrayal of a much older rule of blood in the Ozarks. Ree grounds her request for help on kinship obligations, but Merab replies that "blood don't mean shit to the big man." Ree's uncle, Teardrop (John Hawkes), a drug user like everybody else in the community except Ree ("Not yet"), is caught up between these two contradictory rules: the loyalty to the criminal rule of silence or to the traditional rule of blood. After some hesitation, Teardrop decides to help Ree as he realizes that the only prospect for a man in this land of no economic opportunities other than the illegal drug trade is a premature death. Interestingly, in her search for Thump Milton, Ree follows him to a Livestock Marketing Center, in a scene that suggests how the Milton patriarch laundries the drug money and, hence, who are the real beneficiaries of drug-related trade and crimes. Not coincidentally, it is after this moment of discovery that Ree receives the most violent physical punishment by Merab and the women of the Milton clan. Thus, the Orzak community may have traditionally been construed as the antithesis of capitalist credo, but the drug-dominated economy in the area certainly places them within the machinery of neoliberal economy in its extraction of value out of the worthless. The family as the foundation of alternative community formation in the Orzaks loses its old signification and gains a new one as a form of kinship obligation at the service of a neoliberal economy that profits from the illegal drug business. In the depiction of this struggle, the film uncovers the obscure domopolitical mechanisms deployed to regulate the underserving poor, whose survival seems to depend on their embrace of ruthless neoliberal market rules in their illegal drug business.

In *Leave No Trace*, Tom's central struggle for the redefinition of home exposes the neoliberal management mechanisms that transform homelessness into "a productive deprivation" (Willse 2015, 2)—another domopolitical strategy to discipline the poor. When Will and Tom are taken to the social center, they are separated and interrogated in different rooms. The time frame devoted to the interrogation procedure discloses the underlying assumption about the pathological and criminal personality of the homeless. Then, Tom is taken to a female section of the shelter that she shares with two other girls, a Black and a white, abandoned by their parents. In their conversation, they immediately cast Tom as "homeless" when she explains her living in the woods, despite her defensive remark that "they simply don't understand that it was my home." The film then establishes a distinction between house and home, between homelessness and houselessness—as Tom later asserts, "home is where my father is," reasserting home as lived, social space.

The social agent (Dana Millican) informs Tom that they believe her father has taken good care of her physical and intellectual growth, but, as she observes, "school is about getting social skills, not only intellectual ones." The social agent also alludes to the father's masculine responsibility to provide Tom with "shelter and a place to live." Disregarding their living in the woods as home, and conflating the notions of home and house, she insists that "it's not a crime not to have a home, but it's illegal to live in public lands." Will and Tom are relocated away from the city and given a house to live. Soon we learn that "[t]o be housed is to be disciplined into ways of living and being that allow for forms of security and protection afforded within a neoliberal economy," as Craig Willse (2015, 11) has argued. Will is forced to take a job at a Christmas tree farm, while Tom is sent to school where the other students consider her a stranger. Will rejects the technological devices commonly used to discipline populations: a TV set he hides in a closet and a cellphone he declines. They are also forced to attend church ceremonies and eat different food. These elements characterize the way of living they have to adapt to, paradoxically, "so that you guys can be independent," as the social agent instructs.

In this new home, Tom explores the surroundings on her own and makes a new acquaintance, a young boy (Isaiah Stone) who shows her a mobile house that he is building with his own hands and that he plans to take somewhere else. This independent move is an important step in Tom's maturity and self-awareness that will help her determine the terms of the type of home she desires: one closer to nature allowing a greater control on one's work and greater freedom of movement. Feeling trapped, like the horse he tends at the stable, Will eventually asks Tom to pack the essentials and leave the place.

On the road, up to the north of Oregon and into Washington State, Will and Tom will have to use unconventional means to travel in order to avoid routine police control of homeless youth on public transport. Typically, they hop into a freight railway wagon and then cross the state frontier in a truck, whose driver gives them a ride in exchange for their company. In his chatter, the driver comments on how marihuana has become legal in the area, but it is pain medication that is ruining people's lives, families, and marriages, in a clear reference to the opioid epidemic plaguing poor whites in the United States. On the journey, Will shows his obsession for escaping from the tracking mechanisms of the neoliberal securitarian regime as the necessary way to carrying out his defection from the suffocating nation-home under US domopolitics. His imperative need "to be on the move" suggests a sense of mobility that Ghassan Hage had dubbed "existential," a form of imaginary mobility assumed in "a viable life" (2009, 98), which Will, like some others, can only find by disappearing in a solitary life into the woods. Tom, however, articulates a different option in her explicit desire to have a home for both of them, "a cabin in a tree," a type of home that she will finally find in a trailer park run by Dale (Dale Dickey) along with other socioeconomic (white) fugitives.

Resignifying the Nation-home: From Glass Case to Beehive

Granik's three films disrupt the logics of the dominant perception of home established by US neoliberal domopolitics by offering the perspective of those that this system excludes. The three of them expose the constraints of domopolitics on poor (white) families and the difficulties to conform to the male-headed, self-sufficient home assumed under neoliberalism, which exacts an excruciating burden on women. In this sense, by dealing with wounded white male figures affected by dispossession, which was aggravated during the economic recession, the three films share the cinematic interest in representing its uneven impact on the genders, but depart from the cursory cinematic approaches that present the crisis as an opportunity for reinvention. The unveiling of neoliberal domopolitical disciplinary measures to regulate the poor is presented, instead, as the narrative motivation for pursuing an alternative to the logic of dominant discourses that have morally condemned the poor in the different contexts of the twenty-first century.

In *Down to the Bone*, Irene will attempt to create a new home with Bob, in line with the neoliberal heteronormative model of marriage and the familial. Characterized as a sensitive and caring person, and an important affective support for Irene, Bob fails as male partner in the new home. His relapse indicates that he is unable to perform his role as breadwinner and sexual partner, and more significantly, incapable of protecting Irene's children. Bob's almost suicidal drug use—a desperate and lethal way to a life off the grid—seems an obstacle to her kids' and her own survival. As in the other two films, Irene receives vital help from a neighbor and particularly from Lucy (Caridad de la Luz), the Latino mother and drug user who seems to provide her with the practical and affective support she needs. Seen as a threat, Bob is locked out from Irene's home in a scene that renders visually the thin wall separating survival from self-destruction, in which individual responsibility and self-control, as well as the help of others, appear crucial. Through framing, the glass pane separating Irene from Bob in the final scene suggests both the fragility and entrapment of the reconstructed home—one that the film symbolically links to the snake she buys as a birthday present for one her sons, kept in a glass case. Irene's heroic struggle for her home's survival resonates with the dominant discourse on the "security mom" in the wake of the War on Terror (May 2017, Epilogue), but the new role as domestic protector entraps her within the fragile confines of her home.

A slightly different sense of entrapment, or "stuckedness," in Hage's terminology (2009), is conveyed in the final scene of *Winter's Bone*. Once Jessup's death is proven and the threat of homelessness is over, the film's closing scenes depict moments of restoration of Jessup as a father figure through family pictures, wooden toys he made, and his banjo; elements that evoke a happier family life in the past, but also a recognition of Jessup's legacy for the future. Ree and her siblings burn the family pictures, in a gesture demarcating the rupture from his desire to escape from the community—Jessup's desperate and futile move toward integration into the mainstream, a life "on the grid"—that is reaffirmed by Ree's statement, "I ain't going anywhere," when sitting on the porch of the house with her siblings. The closing scene also reinforces the importance of blood ties, to be a Dolly "bread'n' buttered," that includes Teardrop. Ree offers him her father's banjo signaling him as the proper heir of Jessup's legacy, which Teardrop declines. A distinctive element of cultural identity in this regional community, the banjo ends up in Ashley's hands, the youngest sister (Ashlee Thompson), as if Jessup's legacy and desire for mobility will have to wait for a more distant future. Unlike the framing of Irene trapped within the new single-parent home, Ree and her siblings are framed in a long shot that portrays them outside at the threshold of the domestic space, and captures her pensive gaze aimlessly looking into the desolate landscape. The shot composition and her expression seem to suggest Ree's defiant resilience as the way to stand up against the uncertainties of the current violent and precarious world outside, controlled by the Milton patriarch, an important cog in the all-encompassing economy, who anonymously places the money to liberate the Dolly's home and land from the bond. Through the Ree character, the film emphasizes the importance of resilience or "waiting out the crisis," an ambivalent term coined by Hage (2009, 102) that connotes existential immobility but also endurance. If freedom is associated with agency and mobility, endurance asserts some kind of agency—one that contravenes the dehumanization assumed by a situation of "stuckedness" (101)—through the acquisition of skills necessary to confront the crisis and adapt to changing conditions. In this sense, it is possible to inscribe these films into a current narrative trend that celebrates survival—a "heroism of the stuck," in Hage's words, a "mode of confronting the crisis by a celebration of one's capacity to stick it out rather than calling for a change" (98). Agency in resilience opposes the idea of agency seeking structural change, which drives activist movements. Resilience linked to endurance, however, has become, as Hage has noted, "a governmental tool that encourages a mode of restraint, self-control and self-government in times of crisis" (102), which these films seem to assume lies on the shoulders of poor (white) women.

The home reconfigured in *Leave No Trace*, however, departs from this idea of home as a site of resilience and endurance. In the new, sunnier home found in Dale's trailer park, Tom takes part of a larger family of white "economic fugitives" bound together by a common sense of abandonment, vulnerability, and rejection of the constraining neoliberal securitarian nation. This is a community governed by an unwritten rule of mutual support and collective solidarity, rather than the rule of blood, as key governing tools that go beyond survival. These alternative tools constitute the basis for a reconfiguration of home that offers a glimpse of hope for structural change. From the warmth of the beehive Tom discovers in this new family, she learns that "it is a question of trust" rather than fear how the sense of community is wrought as the basis for the new nation-home, in opposition to the atomization, competition, and fear characterizing the nation-home under neoliberal securitarian states. Without totally rejecting capitalist social forms such as money, the alternative community in *Leave No Trace* rejects the assigned position of citizen-consumers under neoliberal modes of governance and their emphasis on market forces and self-regulation. Although Tom's choice of home may resonate with some current libertarian and far-right tribal movements in the United States, it differs from the glorification of the virile, self-reliant masculinity in contemporary far-right movements (Neel 2018, 24–6). The alternative trailer park community, assuming the vulnerability of human beings and the need of mutual support to survive, bears closer similarities to the recent nomadic lifestyle movement reported by Jessica Bruder in her book *Nomadland* (2017), adapted by Chloé Zhao in recent eponymous film (2021). The nurturing mother figures running the trailer park community seem to reclaim the need to reestablish, at the margins, the sense of social cohesion that neoliberal forms of governance have destroyed (Brown 2019) as the foundation that may help restore the state's role of protecting its people's well-being.

Conclusion

The political intervention in Granik's films, rendered through a neo-neorealist aesthetic approach, allows the disclosure of domopolitical mechanisms and the discourses that sanction neoliberal citizenship as a model that excludes the poor. By offering the perspective of the poor, the films question domopolitics' moral perception of homes and reveal the dehumanizing realities plaguing the underprivileged, whose survival creates exorbitant demands on women. The acclaimed agency and heroism of these female protagonists have awarded Granik's films the label of "feminist work" (Denby 2010, 79). Her work has been also celebrated for making class more visible (Ortner 2013, 191). Indeed, the three films bring to light the unrecognized economic and political contribution of what Silvia Federici (2012) has called "reproductive labor" and the need to politicize home and housework and hence the need to politicize housing and reclaim its role in strengthening social cohesion in the United States as a nation-home. Ree Dolly's heroism in *Winter's Bone* as a self-reliant protector of her rural home has also been perceived as "a Red State version of an American archetype" (Enelow 2016, 56), which inevitably prompts the question on the racial configuration of these new homes: whether they "will enable a new cross-racial, cross-gendered alliance among America's poor," as Cooper

(2017, 157) proposes as a desirable way out of the current crisis. Granik's films to date, in the context of current racial strife in the United States, do not even picture this desirable solution, but they expose the realities toppling the country's myths of white privilege.

References

Arnold, K. R. (2004), *Homelessness, Citizenship, and Identity: The Uncanniness of Late Modernity*, Albany: State University of New York Press.
Badley, L. (2016), "Down to the Bone: Neo-Neorealism and Genre in Contemporary Women's Indies," in L. Badley, C. Perkins, and M. Schreiber (eds.), *Indie Reframed: Women's Filmmaking and Contemporary American Independent Cinema*, Edinburgh: Edinburgh University Press, pp. 121–37.
Bell, J. (2010), "Meth and the Maiden," *Sight and Sound* 20 (10), pp. 28–9.
Brown, W. (2019), *In the Ruins of Neoliberalism: The Rise of Antidemocratic Politics in the West*, New York: Columbia University Press.
Bruder, J. (2017), *Nomadland: Surviving American in the Twenty-First Century*, New York and London: W.W. Norton and Company.
Butler, J. and G. C. Spivak (2007), *Who Sings the Nation-State? Language, Politics, Belonging*, London, New York and Calcutta: Seagull Books.
Camp, J. T. (2016), *Incarcerating the Crisis: Freedom Struggles and the Rise of Neoliberal State*, Oakland: University of California Press.
Chomsky, N. (1998), "The Drug War Industrial Complex: Noam Chomsky Interviewed by John Veit," *High Times*, April. Available online: http://www.chomsky.info.
Cicchetti, P. (2013), "'I Ain't Going Anywhere': The House, the Mobile Hero and the Frontier in *Winter's Bone*," in R. Hamilton, A. MacLeod, and J. Monroe (eds.), *Spaces of (Dis)location*, Newcastle upon Tyne: Cambridge Scholars Publishing, pp. 73–89.
Cooper, M. (2017), *Family Values: Between Neoliberalism and the New Social Conservatism*, New York: Zone Books.
Darda, J. (2019), "Like a Refugee: Veterans, Vietnam, and the Making of a False Equivalence," *American Quarterly* 71 (1), pp. 83–104.
Darling, J. (2014), "Asylum and the Post-Political: Domopolitics, Depoliticisation and Acts of Citizenship," *Antipode* 46 (1), pp. 72–91.
De Luca, T. (2016), "Slow Time, Visible Cinema: Duration, Experience, and Spectatorship," *Cinema Journal* 56 (1), pp. 23–42.
De Luca, T. and N. Barradas Jorge (eds.) (2016), *Slow Cinema*, Edinburgh: Edinburgh University Press.
Denby, D. (2010), "Thrills and Chills: 'Knight and Day' and 'Winter's Bone'," *The New Yorker*, 5 July, pp. 78–9.
Enelow, S. (2016), "The Great Recession," *Film Comment* 52 (5), pp. 56–61.
Federici, S. (2012), *Revolution at Point Zero: Housework, Reproduction, and Feminist Struggle*, Brooklyn, NY: PM Press.
Frame, G. (2020), "The Cultural Politics of Jennifer Lawrence as Star, Actor, Celebrity," *New Review of Film and Television Studies* 18 (3), pp. 345–68.

Gilbey, R. (2018), "Vanishing Point," *Sight & Sound* 28 (7), pp. 46–8.
Glenn, E. N. (2010), *Forced to Care: Coercion and Caregiving in America*, Cambridge, MA and London: Harvard University Press.
Hage, G. (2009), "Waiting Out the Crisis: On Stuckedness and Governmentality," in G. Hage (ed.), *Waiting*, Melbourne: Melbourne University Press, pp. 97–107.
Lonergan, G. (2018), "Reproducing the 'National Home': Gendering Domopolitics," *Citizenship Studies* 22 (1), pp. 1–18.
Madden, D. and P. Marcuse (2016), *In Defense of Housing: The Politics of Crisis*, eBook, London and New York: Verso.
May, E. T. (2017), *Fortress America: How We Embrace Fear and Abandoned Democracy*, eBook, New York: Basic Books.
Moon, M. and C. Talley (2010), "Life in a Shatter Zone: Debra Granik's Film *Winter's Bone*," *Southern Spaces*, 6 December. Available online: https://southernspaces.org/node/42625.
Neel, P. A. (2018), *Hinterland: America's New Landscape of Class and Conflict*, London: Reaktion Books.
Ortner, S. B. (2013), *Not Hollywood: Independent Film at the Twilight of the American Dream*, Durham, NC and London: Duke University Press.
Rancière, J. (2001), "Ten Theses on Politics," *Theory & Event* 5 (3). Available online: http://muse.jhu.edu/journals/theory_and_event/v005/5.3raciere.html.
Salzinger, L. (2020), "Sexing Homo Oeconomicus: Finding Masculinity at Work," in W. Callison and Z. Manfredy (eds.), *Mutant Neoliberalism: Market Rule and Political Rupture*, New York: Fordham University Press, pp. 196–214.
Simon, J. (2007), *Governing through Crime: How the War on Crime Transformed American Democracy and Created a Culture of Fear*, New York: Oxford University Press.
Singer, M. and J. B. Page (2014), *The Social Values of Drug Addicts: Uses of the Useless*, Walnut Creek, CA: Left Coast Press, Inc.
Wacquant, L. (2009), *Punishing the Poor: The Neoliberal Government of Social Insecurity*, Durham and London: Duke University Press.
Walters, W. (2004), "Secure Borders, Safe Haven, Domopolitics," *Citizenship Studies* 8 (3), pp. 237–60.
Willse, C. (2015), *The Value of Homelessness: Managing Surplus Life in the United States*, London and Minneapolis: University of Minnesota Press.
Young, S. T. (2017), "Wild, Wonderful, White Criminality: Images of 'White Trash' Appalachia," *Critical Criminology* 25, pp. 103–17.

PART V

Politics, Affect, and the Crisis of Public Values

11

White Identity, Great Replacement Politics, and Auteurism

The Cinema of S. Craig Zahler

Carlos Gallego

Donald Trump's rise to presidential power was largely determined by a political narrative focused on the increased marginalization of white Americans, an ethno-nationalist ideology exemplified in the slogan "Make America Great Again."[1] This idea of white Americans being under threat originates with "the great replacement," one of many conspiracies originating in the alt-right's world of alternative facts.[2] Trump harnessed the desire underlying such fantasies by promoting an idealized vision of the 1950s as more authentically American than today's multicultural society, going as far as stoking great replacement anxieties with false stories about violent crimes against white people. Trump's exacerbation of white anxieties, aligned with Latino threat discourse (Chavez 2013), is evinced in his description of Mexican immigrants as "rapists" and "bad hombres," which encouraged militia-style organizing around the country (Ross 2016).[3] The convergence of Trump's ethnopopulist rhetoric with militia organizing resulted in an attempted siege of Congress on January 6, 2021, a forewarning of US democracy's potential future.

The sociopolitical crises inspired by Trump also influenced popular cultural production, with film playing a significant role in representing the effects of ethnopopulism. One film many feared would inspire violence around white disenfranchisement was Todd Phillips's *Joker* (2019). Although the film did not produce the social unrest some anticipated, *Joker* nevertheless remained the subject of critical debates concerning white identity and violence, with Joaquin Phoenix walking out of an interview after being asked about the film inspiring "white terrorism," a thought he later claimed had never crossed his mind (Ransome 2019; Schwartz 2019). *Joker*, even with its white male protagonist and dramatized violence, is difficult to view as grounded in ideologies like the great replacement, especially considering that the film avoids themes like white nationalism despite the crucial role sociopolitical tensions play in the film. More importantly, the white terroristic violence many expected did eventually erupt but as a reaction to Trump's rhetoric about election results, Black Lives Matter demonstrations, and his "dominate the streets" philosophy (Saja 2019; Yakin 2021; Alper, et al 2020).

Keeping in mind the rise of white identity politics and ethnonationalism under Trump, this chapter examines how S. Craig Zahler's filmmaking foregrounds core ideological tropes central to conspiratorial narratives like the great replacement, particularly the victimized white family man who sutures collective wounds inflicted by a threatening, racialized other through heroic sacrifice, thus rectifying cultural displacement, socioeconomic disenfranchisement, and existential alienation. Although current US cinema can lay claim to various auteurs, the notion of auteurism in relation to contemporary white identity politics is less discernible. Zahler's filmmaking, however, is potentially indicative of such auteurism with its unique and consistent use of specific stylistic and thematic traits, such as: establishing a white male protagonist who is unjustly disenfranchised; incorporating humor to both develop characterization and channel racist tropes; and Zahler's signature trait of using graphic violence as a catharsis for white victimization. Reframed in terms of Andrew Sarris' theory of auteurism (Sarris 2009), Zahler's consistent choice of protagonists speaks to his "interior meaning" as an auteur—something I redefine for the purposes of this argument as sociopolitical vision—while reliance on humor and violence characterizes his style. My general thesis is that Zahler's filmmaking, which is still early in its development, is tending toward the type of white identity politics that coincides with great replacement narratives. Analyzing the central traits that define Zahler's unique style could potentially confirm him as an auteur of such politics. To accomplish this aim, I focus specifically on *Brawl in Cell Block 99* (2017), with brief comments on *Bone Tomahawk* (2015) and *Dragged Across Concrete* (2018).

Zahler's debut film, *Bone Tomahawk*, provides a general introduction to his style and his propensity for sociopolitical commentary through the use of racial tropes. Though the storyline is less complicated compared to his later films, *Bone Tomahawk* circumvents a somewhat formulaic plot through a unique combination of comedy, violence, and horror within the Western genre. Showcasing Zahler's predilection for a white male protagonist protecting his family from the threat posed by racialized others, the film focuses on Arthur O'Dwyer (Patrick Wilson), Sheriff Hunt (Kurt Russell), and a small posse assembled to rescue Mrs. O'Dwyer (Lili Simmons) from cannibalistic "Indian" savages (Troglodytes). The film introduces viewers to Zahler's distinctive use of humor and graphic violence to either accentuate or distract from the film's sociopolitical ideology. In *Bone Tomahawk*, the ideology endorses an ethnopolitics that posits racialized others as savage and white society as civilized. Despite the film opening with graphic white-on-white violence, its two main protagonists are nevertheless ethical white men willing to sacrifice themselves to protect civilized society from savagery. Critical praise notwithstanding, the problematic racial politics underlying *Bone Tomahawk* would prove to be more subtly developed in both *Brawl in Cell Block 99* and *Dragged Across Concrete*, demonstrating some aesthetic maturation while also highlighting Zahler's stylistic limits and sociopolitical leanings.

The main protagonist in *Brawl* is Bradley Thomas (Vince Vaughn), a former boxer and drug runner who is introduced as being laid off from his auto-repair job only to go home and discover that his wife, Lauren (Jennifer Carpenter), has been having an affair. Displaying his brute strength, Bradley dismantles Lauren's car with his hands and then calmly walks into their home to discuss their marital troubles. After philosophizing on his bad luck, he forgives Lauren, and they decide to start a family despite Bradley's newfound unemployment. In response to his financial situation, Bradley returns to work as a drug runner for his friend Gil (Marc Blucas) while the couple restart their lives. The film then cuts to a year and a half later, as Bradley and a pregnant Lauren are seen enjoying a more spacious home, their financial and relational situation having improved with Bradley's return to the drug trade.

This brief, but significant, opening frames Bradley's character for the rest of the film, depicting him as an unjust victim of both infidelity and an economic system that preys on working class people. It also shows his capacity for extreme violence, as well as reasonableness, forgiveness, and familial love. Thus, despite his criminality, Bradley is represented as a good—albeit dangerous—man, his trade being a by-product of his circumstances and his refusal to accept a life of victimization. He embodies the quintessential working-class-hero-turned criminal in an unjust world populated by bad people impeding a good man's efforts at achieving a better life for his family. This heroic framing is supported by the racialized others Bradley is compelled to interact with due to his friendship with Gil.

Gil is introduced as a prejudicial character who enjoys the non-politically correct freedoms of a white man with financial power and influence in the criminal underworld. This is evident when he welcomes Bradley to his lavish home, making a derogatory comment about "faggoty mineral water," to which Bradley quips, "I didn't know H2O's got a sexual orientation." After Bradley reports that the transaction he just finished went smoothly, Gil replies, "Yeah, I like that nigger. Or is it—is it 'nigga' with an *a* at the end, when you're saying it nice?" Mindful of Gil's racism, Bradley answers, "Don't think someone like you can say that word any way polite," demonstrating a pragmatic understanding of racial politics. Their interaction is significant in that, despite being friends, Gil's rhetoric and position as "boss" represent a continuation of the same system that disenfranchised Bradley in the first place, his language signaling a disconnect from people lacking his socioeconomic or racial privilege. Moreover, Bradley's disinterest in using racist or homophobic slurs further underscores his role as an ethical family man who maintains his integrity regardless of the situation.

This characterization is solidified in Bradley's dealing with Eleazar (Dion Mucciacito), Gil's "new source" who "has lines to Mexico and a steady stream to good, cheap crystal." When Bradley notes that Eleazar "brought amigos," Gil states, "Mexicans ain't comfortable being by themselves. You know how they grow up. Five to a bed. Ten beds per adobe." Gil's racist attitude toward African Americans and Mexicans is typical of Zahler's aesthetic in that it is too casually dismissed as comical. Zahler even states in an interview that "the movie is not a politically-driven agenda movie, but a fun badass guy movie with some surprising humor" (Douglas 2017). However, formally speaking, such humor introduces a subtle shift regarding what is politically acceptable and what is not, best represented via the juxtaposition of Bradley's character and actions with that of others, such as Gil and Eleazar. Gil, having privilege and power, communicates his prejudice without restraint or self-awareness, while Bradley maintains his integrity in a world defined by economic, racialized, and gendered inequities, demonstrating that his ethics is above society's sociocultural biases, with the worst of those prejudices represented in the film through racialized characters like Eleazar. This dynamic overdetermines the film's racial others as villains, while Gil—who is openly racist, homophobic, and sexist—is depicted positively, being humorous and offering assistance to Bradley and his family.

When discussing plans for a "pickup," Bradley promptly and assertively states that he will not do business with Roman (Geno Segers), who he suspects of "using." Eleazar vouches for Roman's reliability, stating that he has "been clean for two years" and is an asset in "adverse situations." Bradley apologizes, stating "Words from a stranger don't drop instinct," again displaying his unwavering character. Gil notices the impasse and requests a private conversation with his "best runner." Recognizing that he needs Bradley to "protect [his] interests," Gil proposes a deal: "You help me set up this partnership, I'll give you two months off when your little baby's born." Having his existential weakness exposed, Bradley capitulates after negotiating three months off and the stipulation that he is in command. After

Eleazar assures him that his men "shall mind" him, Bradley asks Roman, "If I say 'dump the package' what do you do?" Roman replies, "dump" as ominous music plays in the background, foreshadowing the betrayal of this agreement. Bradley's unease in going against his "instinct" is accentuated by the brief domestic scene that precedes the "pickup," in which Bradley touches Lauren's pregnant body until he feels the baby, an experience that heightens his fatherly expectations.

The film cuts to the fateful "pickup" scene that introduces the first of many ethical challenges Bradley will face. As he and Eleazar's runners walk toward Gil's boat, tensions escalate when Bradley disarms Roman after he shoots at a tarp, foreshadowing Roman's violent impulsiveness. Moreover, Roman and Pedro (Victor Almanzar) refer to Bradley as "Blanco," meaning "white" in Spanish, further highlighting the existential differences that define their respective racialization (impulsivity versus composure). After they retrieve a trunk containing bags of drugs, the film uses the tropes of foreigners and patriots in order to highlight Bradley's ethical heroism. This ideological difference is subtly hinted at when Roman throws the empty trunk overboard and says to Pedro, "Help make America beautiful, right?" referring to a well-known anti-littering public service announcement. The film cuts to Bradley's irked expression at Roman's sarcastic comment, highlighting the patriotism that will motivate his actions later in the scene. Tensions between the two hit a high point upon returning to the pier, when Bradley notices Pedro handing a gun to Roman, the latter stating that the "pickup's done, Blanco" and that if Bradley attempts to disarm him again, Roman will "break [his] jaw."

As they walk to their vehicles, Bradley suddenly stops, his "instinct" compelling him to throw the bag of drugs into the bay. He orders the other two to do the same, but Roman refuses. When Bradley reaches for the bag, Pedro puts a gun to his head and orders him to "release it" while Roman temporarily incapacitates Bradley with a couple of blows. The police show up almost immediately afterward, directing Pedro and Roman to "drop their weapons and put their hands up." The two begin shooting at the police, giving Bradley an ideal opportunity to escape. However, he hesitates when he realizes that the police are outgunned, facing the moral dilemma of returning to his family or risking arrest in order to save police lives. Upon hearing retreating police officers plead for help, Bradley turns around, saying, "stupid assholes" as he walks toward Roman and Pedro.

A key moment in this scene occurs when Roman takes a grenade and yells, "Get ready for 9/11: Part Two," thereby associating the two Mexicans with Islamic terrorists, a xenophobic joke that reinforces the film's racial politics and exemplifies Zahler's disquietingly humorous approach to violence initially displayed in *Bone Tomahawk*. Conversely, Bradley is portrayed as rescuing vulnerable officers from excessively violent and ignorant Mexicans (i.e., savages), at risk to his own life and liberty. Bradley is nevertheless arrested, as the camera centers on him placing his hands behind his head, covering his highly visible crucifix tattoo—a symbolic representation of the state punishing an ethical man who is prepared to sacrifice himself for a greater good—as an officer is heard saying, "Don't move, asshole."

The ingratitude shown by the arresting officers that Bradley rescued is representative of a sociopolitical system that has moved away from the values he embodies, seemingly corrupted by the same powers that undermine balance in the world, preventing "things even[ing] out fair" as Bradley notes early in the film. Bradley's martyrdom is apparent in the interrogation scene with Detective Watkins (Clark Johnson). Watkins, an African American, points to the US flag hanging prominently in front of Bradley and asks him if he wants to "burn it," "wipe [his] ass with it," or "cut it up into little pieces and send to Putin." After Bradley calmly replies that he has "one over [his] front door," Watkins acknowledges that he knows Bradley is "a patriot" because he "saw that video," implying that he recognizes Bradley as an ethical man in comparison to "the people who profited from all [his] hard work while they wiped their dirty asses with that," again pointing to the flag.

Although Watkins's assessment resonates as an accurate description of the disenfranchisement Bradley has suffered, he refrains from acknowledging the shortcomings of a political-economic system that forces ethical people into criminality as a way of rising above impoverished conditions of existence. Watkins instead turns the system, represented by the flag, into a victim by suggesting that the Mexican "assholes" who forced Bradley into making a difficult ethical decision are also guilty of wiping their "dirty asses" with the US flag. Watkins expects Bradley to get a minimum sentence of "four years, maybe five" since "no police were killed in that event" due to his "selfless actions," proving that he has "a moral compass" and is "a man principled, who had a run of bad luck and just went the wrong way." This valuation proves accurate, as Bradley sits uncomfortably through Watkins's existential synopsis. After a brief argument over the fairness of a justice system that sentences drug traffickers more harshly than men who commit violence against women and children, Bradley ends the conversation by stating that he accepts the consequences of his actions. As Watkins leaves the room, he reminds Bradley that he will be absent for the birth of his daughter, underscoring the most painful loss his incarceration will entail.

Bradley is sentenced by an African American judge (Charles Dumas) who is unimpressed by his heroism, condemning him to a seven-year prison term with the ironic proclamation, "This hearing has come to its lawful conclusion." The camera focuses on the judge as he makes this statement, but it also features Bradley's crucifix-tattooed head blurred dominantly in the foreground, formally underscoring his being a victim of racial revenge. The harsh prison sentence is simply another injustice Bradley must endure as part of his burden; and there is little doubt that Bradley's situation is framed as a white man's burden, especially when an African American judge administers systemic injustice to a white "man principled, who had a run of bad luck and just went the wrong way." What is noteworthy is that the judge's racialization in this scene adds a sociopolitical dimension to the film that seems unnecessary to the plot yet significant in its recurrence, thus complicating Zahler's claims of "not" making "a politically-driven agenda movie." Such claims ring hollow when the racial tensions that formally underlie the content of the film reinforce actual ideological conspiracies that emphasize the vulnerability of the specifically white, Western, familial tradition, one that defines Bradley's character and is represented as heroic and threatened by racialized otherness.

Zahler's signature style of incorporating racial tensions in his films by framing them around scenes of violence and humor is conspicuously present in the second half of *Brawl*, beginning with the relationships that Bradley establishes at the Franklin R. James Detention Center. The first is with his prison orientation guide, Lefty (Willie C. Carpenter). Being an older, African American inmate, Lefty offers Bradley some advice about prison politics while they walk casually around the prison, undisturbed by guards, which sets up a contrast with the Redleaf Detention Center, a maximum security prison Bradley is transferred to later in the film. Moreover, Lefty's character establishes a contrast with Andre (Mustafa Shakir), an African American guard who reminds Bradley of their hierarchical relationship by telling him, "Before you go in your coffin, there are some rules to apprise you of." After quickly summarizing the protocols for both "headcounts" and inspections, Andre suddenly digresses to ask Bradley if he boxes, to which the latter replies, "no." Andre attempts to recruit Bradley into the prison's boxing program, to which Bradley quickly replies, "Not interested." As Andre persists, Lefty interrupts by saying, "Pester him some other time." The antagonistic impression Andre makes, which continues when Bradley fails to respond to the evening headcount, is accentuated by Lefty's paternalistic care (he gives Bradley a candy bar, anticipating his hunger later that evening) and will prove important when Bradley initiates the violence that results in his prison transfer.

The need for this transfer is established in the scene following the evening headcount, as the film cuts from Bradley sitting in his cell to Lauren sleeping in their home. Startled by intruders, she grabs a handgun but is quickly rendered unconscious after being shot with tranquilizers. The film then cuts back to Bradley, as he awakes and says, "Eighty days," referring to Lauren's due date, thereby establishing the primary storyline—Lauren's pregnancy and kidnapping—that defines the narrative thread for the rest of the film. This is quickly developed when Bradley is informed that there are complications around Lauren's pregnancy that her obstetrician needs to discuss with him in person. Though we initially see a white guard take the morning headcount, the officer who escorts an anxious Bradley to the visitation booths is Andre, who continues to pester Bradley, teasing him about being a "boxing legend."

Bradley immediately notices that the man waiting for him is not Lauren's doctor. Placid Man (Udo Kier), who speaks with a foreign accent, instructs Bradley to sit down and proceeds to inform him that Eleazar has kidnapped Lauren and is holding her hostage, showing Bradley a picture of her bound and blindfolded. He then explains that Bradley owes a debt to Eleazar as a result of his actions: "There is an abortionist from Korea. He works for my employer. He claims that he can clip the limbs of a fetus yet leave the child in such a condition that it will live to be born. This little operation will only happen if you don't pay your debt to my employer."

To settle this debt, Bradley must kill Christopher Bridge, an inmate serving a life sentence at Redleaf Detention Center, specifically cell block ninety-nine. Bradley will have to be transferred by showing the staff that he requires maximum, not medium, security. Bradley immediately sets upon this task when returning to his cell, after Andre attempts to alleviate the tension between them, asking Bradley if there is anything he would "like to talk about," even going as far as apologizing. Being unrestrained, Bradley sees an opportunity and attacks Andre, catching him by surprise and graphically breaking his arm as the other guards arrive. The scene ends with Bradley initiating a fight with the three guards escorting him, who knock him unconscious and do "some justice" onto him by stepping on the back of his head, leaving a scuff mark over his crucifix tattoo, a visible reminder of how Bradley's character is stained due to Eleazar's savage threat.

The extreme violence Eleazar introduces exemplifies Zahler's reliance on racialized tropes as a means of centering a white heroic narrative. Although Zahler avoids addressing the depth and complexity of systemic racism in the United States, he nevertheless utilizes race as a plot device to frame his white protagonists as ethically superior, especially when compared to more severe forms of dehumanization, like medieval-styled prisons and torture. This is the extremism that Redleaf symbolizes, in addition to the racialized, foreign threats represented by Placid Man and the Korean abortionist (Tobee Paik). The latter, much like Roman, is depicted as an extreme danger to the world that Bradley represents, with Mexicans and Koreans personifying the "lowlifes" and "dirty assholes" who disrespect the flag and thus endanger the very world that Bradley is defending. In fact, both Roman's reference to "9/11: Part Two" and the Korean abortionist's horrific specialization (fetal dismemberment) underscore their terroristic nature, reminiscent of the Troglodytes in *Bone Tomahawk*. Roman and the Korean abortionist are extreme versions of what the judge and Andre embody institutionally— racialized depictions of an immoral system that has displaced US patriots from their rightful place as leaders who maintain order and ethical balance in the world.

The remainder of the "fun badass guy" film does little to alter Zahler's crude portrayal of racial politics, but it does reinforce his emerging auteurism. The subtle, but effective, repositioning of the Overton window regarding what is considered extreme dehumanizing behavior, a common tactic among right-wing extremists, is foregrounded in the prison transfer scene. As Bradley is taken to Redleaf, the guards discuss its controversial history, specifically a scandal in the 1950s regarding "humane treatment." The allusions to Redleaf's dehumanization of inmates create a new extreme that repositions Gil's racist jokes as mild in comparison. This is visually reinforced by the highly militarized look and weaponry of the all-white guard that greets Bradley at Redleaf (reminiscent of a Third Reich aesthetic[4] in clothing and intimidation tactics), which is heightened by the calm, yet unapologetically domineering, rhetoric of Warden Tuggs (Don Johnson), who explains—after being informed that Bradley "took out three" guards—that "the men here aren't like those faggots over there at The Fridge." Tuggs redefines maximum security as "minimum freedom," inviting Bradley to "test" his veiled threats, and then orders Bradley to publicly undress outside and change into "his neons." This dehumanization is compounded when Tuggs reassigns Bradley to a feces-riddled cell, another example of the film continually escalating what constitutes *real* violence in comparison to racist humor.

In the prison yard, Bradley learns that all inmates in cell block ninety-nine are isolated from the rest of the prisoners, as it specifically houses "child molesters, rapists, guys with death sentences, [and] psychotics," which establishes a new standard for extreme criminality. Having framed Redleaf as a "minimum freedom" facility with a reputation for inhumane treatment, the film again uses racialized tropes to further the plot, as Bradley instigates a fight with a group of Latino inmates, claiming he is "psychotic." In typical Zahler fashion, the violent confrontation is accompanied by racist jokes, including yet another reference to the US flag: "Last time I checked, the colors of the flag weren't red, white, and burrito." Bradley then proceeds to assault all four Latino inmates, at times displaying extraordinary strength, whereas the Latino inmates are depicted as incompetent, with one inmate accidentally knocking another unconscious. Bradley then injures two of the guards trying to restrain him, breaking one's arm in a manner recalling Andre's compound fracture. He is finally subdued when Tuggs places a cocked revolver to the back of his head and informs Bradley that he has "just lost [his] minimum freedom," adding the ominous, but welcomed, clarification, "You're going to ninety-nine."

Cell block ninety-nine is a hidden "prison within a prison," the darkest depths of an already established barbarous institution. The first room Bradley encounters speaks to the continually shifting extremism within the film, a sentiment affirmed by Tuggs when he switches on the dungeon lights, revealing torture instruments and stating, "I suspect that Amnesty International would frown upon the contents of this room." One of the instruments is a remotely activated electrocution belt that releases a crippling amount of voltage, which is used against Bradley to discipline his transgressions. Additionally, his new cell floor is covered in shards of glass instead of feces, accentuating the newfound extremism at Redleaf while representing both the lowest point in Bradley's "run of bad luck" but also the peak of his martyrdom, as it confirms his unyielding and heroic commitment to family. Consistent with this motif is the revelation that Eleazar manipulated Bradley's prison transfer, thus shifting accountability for the extreme violence and dehumanization he experiences from Warden Tuggs to Eleazar, since Tuggs's involvement in Eleazar's elaborate trap is never addressed. The film thus returns to the narrative of the threatening and racialized others—the "dirty assholes"—that continually undermine Bradley's ability to lead a simple and patriotic family life.

Zahler's reliance of racist tropes is evident as the scene cuts from Bradley's newfound torture to Lauren helplessly bound to an examination chair, with Placid Man and the Korean abortionist arriving to take pictures and "perform a preliminary examination." The film switches from a terrified Lauren back to Bradley who, after making inquiries, is informed by the other inmates that there is no Christopher Bridge in cell block ninety-nine. He is subsequently escorted to Eleazar's cell, confirming the villainous racial other as the ultimate cause of Bradley's suffering. This is further underscored by the fact that Eleazar's bodyguards include Roman, M.P.V. (Gabriel Sloyer)—one of the Latino inmates he assaults—and an Asian prisoner, Johnny Mu (Jonathan Lee). Bradley attempts to attack Eleazar, but the latter uses the electrocution belt as a means of neutralizing him. The scene ends with Roman telling Bradley, "It's a long, slow payback, Blanco," as they proceed to beat him unconscious, exemplifying the racial revenge fantasy.

Once Eleazar is revealed to be the ultimate threat, the film cuts to Bradley's cell, as he regains consciousness and begins plotting his retaliation. He counteracts the electrocution belt by using the inner soles of his shoes as buffers, which permit him to surprise the guards who return to escort him back to Eleazar. Bradley attacks them, forcing them into his cell but not before accidentally killing one in the process, chastising him for being another "stupid asshole." He then undoes his restraints, walks to Eleazar's cell, and proceeds to kill Johnny Mu, graphically scraping his face across the concrete floor before stomping on it. Bradley then breaks M.P.V.'s spine and violently crushes Roman's face, as Eleazar calls Placid Man, ordering him to commence the abortion and "flush [Lauren] down the toilet," again framing Bradley's extreme violence as righteously justifiable in comparison to the depravity posed by racialized others. Consequently, Bradley's response—graphically breaking Eleazar's leg, gaining access to his phone, and calling Placid Man to tell him that he is prepared to leave Eleazar in cell block ninety-nine where the inmates "will fuck him bloody"—is upheld as heroically virtuous. Fearing more torture, Eleazar agrees to release Lauren and have her safely delivered to Gil.

The ending is consistent with Zahler's aesthetic, as Bradley orchestrates Lauren's escape and his revenge (she shoots the Korean abortionist after

Gil shoots Placid Man), while Tuggs and his men wait outside cell block ninety-nine, respecting Bradley's threats of killing Eleazar, whom he has taken hostage. The final conversation Bradley has with Lauren ends with him tearfully speaking to his unborn daughter, who seems to acknowledge his words, as Lauren says, "I just felt her move." While uncharacteristically sentimental for a "badass guy" film, this moment solidifies Bradley's martyrdom as a family man. Satisfied with Lauren's safety, Bradley exacts his final revenge by graphically killing Eleazar, stomping on his head until he decapitates it, with the head falling into the cell toilet. Upon entering, Tuggs orders Bradley to place his hands over his head and turn around, the latter quietly saying, "seventy-eight days," again referring to Lauren's pregnancy. The final camera shots emphasize Bradley's family ethos and sacrifice, showing his hands covering his crucifix tattoo and turning to face Tuggs, who shoots Bradley three times, with his body collapsing off-screen.

Even if *Brawl* does not foreground white nationalism as a politics, Zahler's depiction of Bradley as a noble hero who exemplifies an unyielding commitment to family and country distinguishes his white US identity from the racialized, villainous "assholes" threatening to replace his world. Thus, Zahler's claim that *Brawl* is "not a politically-driven agenda movie" is undermined by the white identity politics formally established via distinctive ideological investments that actually render the film's political message formulaic: globalization leads to increased immigration and a declining domestic economy, which negatively impacts white citizens who are suffering a demographic (great) displacement that they need to resist through the reestablishment of traditional Western values centered on family and patriotism. Not surprisingly, and consistent with his emerging auteurism, such political messaging is equally visible in Zahler's latest film.

Dragged Across Concrete develops the narrative of the victimized white male in a manner that speaks more directly to great replacement ideologies, particularly the conspiratorial claim that policies instituted to benefit historically racialized communities are in actuality political tools used to disenfranchise white citizens. This mindset is represented by the film's main protagonists, Brett Ridgeman (Mel Gibson) and Anthony Lurasetti (Vince Vaughn). What differentiates *Dragged* from Zahler's previous films is the inclusion of a third main protagonist, Henry Johns (Tory Kittles). The inclusion of Johns permits Zahler to foreground racial politics more prominently in the plot, using the presence of an African American protagonist to counterbalance some of the film's overt racism. This is evident in the stereotypically racialized tropes used to introduce Johns; upon his release from prison, he has sex with a prostitute and is then driven home by his childhood friend Biscuit (Michael Jai White) to discover that his mother is prostituting herself due to economic difficulties. The fact that Johns's storyline is one of three narrative threads (the other two pertaining to detectives and violent bank thieves) makes *Dragged* Zahler's most complicated film to date. However, even with a more elaborate plot and diversified cast, Zahler's signature use of racist tropes persists, again serving to underscore the heroic sacrifice of the actual main protagonist, Detective Ridgeman.

The plot centers mainly on Ridgeman's problems after he and his partner, Anthony, are suspended without pay due to the use of excessive force against a Latinx couple at the start of the film. The storyline focuses on how they respond to their increasing sense of disenfranchisement, offering ongoing commentary on contemporary US culture and the damage political correctness has done to traditional values. Ridgeman is depicted as contemptuous throughout, disdainfully referring to criminals as "imbeciles," recalling Bradley's use of "assholes" in *Brawl*. He personifies a tired and futile resistance to a contemporary world that has forgotten people like him. Ridgeman's old partner, Lt. Calvert (Don Johnson), reprimands both detectives for their unprofessionalism, adding that their "Mexican-American inspector"—an indicator of the great replacement—is "unlikely to be lenient." Ridgeman complains, "Politics, like always," to which Calvert replies, "politics are everywhere."

Ridgeman is compelled into criminality due to what he perceives to be his unjust marginalization. Zahler depicts this overtly, again relying on the tropes of victimized white families and threatening, racialized environments. This is apparent in the scene introducing Ridgeman's wife Melanie (Laurie Holden) and daughter Sara (Jordyn Ashley Olson). The scene begins with a young African American male riding a bike down a sidewalk in an inner-city neighborhood. As Sara walks home from the bus stop, the young man—without provocation—dumps a cup of soda on Sara, celebrating with his friends afterward. The scene switches to Sara demonstrating her "cop DNA" as she enters the family apartment saying, "I won't," implying that she refuses to cry. While Sara endures unjustified persecution, Melanie suffers from a debilitating illness (multiple sclerosis) that compels her to stay home. A key sociological detail the film foregrounds but fails to explain is *why* the Ridgeman household suffers economic limitations equivalent to inner-city African American families, the implication being that they have simply been abandoned by a system that no longer values them.

Melanie explains her fears regarding their disenfranchisement, essentially articulating the political unconscious underlying Zahler's filmmaking:

> Four blacks, one on a bike . . . *This fucking neighborhood, it just keeps getting worse and worse* . . . she's getting older, more womanly. And these boys are gonna start having different kinds of ideas about her pretty soon, if they don't already.
>
> *You know, I never thought I was a racist before living in this area. I'm about as liberal as any ex-cop could ever be. But now* . . . We really need

to move . . . Or someday, someday you and me, we are in a hospital room with our daughter talking to a rape counselor. (emphasis added)

Melanie's commentary goes beyond the concerns of a mother and ventures into racist speculations about the inevitability of Sara being raped by "Blacks" in "this fucking neighborhood." Her plea and warning inspire Ridgeman to devise a criminal plan to "acquire proper compensation," which establishes the main plot that connects the three major narrative threads in the film. Ridgeman's centrality to the film's storyline renders the inclusion of Johns perfunctory, as his protagonism only reinforces Zahler's signature approach to race as either a plot device or a reservoir of tropes that, when filtered through humor and violence, formally distract from the obvious foregrounding of white marginalization and sacrificial heroism. Despite the film's conclusion suggesting some form of racial reparations, it fails in offsetting Zahler's highly problematic representation of violence and race relations.

When viewed in conjunction with his first two films, *Dragged* confirms Zahler's propensity for promoting a white identity politics through the strategic framing of racial others. Whether this threat is presented through Manichean tensions like savagery versus civilization, patriots versus foreigners, or "proper compensation" versus violent criminality, protecting the sanctity of the white family as the last vestige of traditional—and thus civilized—society is an ideological constant in Zahler's filmmaking. What is disconcerting is that the white identity politics underlying his style and sociopolitical vision supports the far-right's ideological rhetoric regarding "shithole countries," the patriotism of militia vigilantism, and the xenophobic need to maintain "law and order," all of which support a grand replacement narrative. These films could mark the beginning stages in Zahler's career as a white identity auteur or simply the initial phase in a complicated filmmaker's continual aesthetic maturation. If it is to be the latter, Zahler must rethink how he incorporates racial tensions in his films or cease circumventing the political complexities around them; otherwise, he will continue contributing to the very problem he seems intent on avoiding.

Notes

1 The author would like to thank Hilaria Loyo, Robert Kendrick, and Chloe Sparrow.
2 The "Great Replacement" theory was first coined by Renaud Camus in his book *Le Grand Remplacement* (2011), in which he argued that the presence of Muslim peoples throughout France posed a direct threat to French culture and civilization. This view of immigrant populations took root in the United States shortly thereafter, exemplified by the Unite the Right rally in Charlottesville,

Virginia, in August of 2017, during which white men marched with torches, chanting, "Jews will not replace us." For a firsthand account, see Vegas Tenold's "Author's Note" in *Everything You Love Will Burn: Inside the Rebirth of White Nationalism in America* (2018).

3 The logic underlying contemporary white identity politics and its connection to Trump is examined by David Neiwert in *Alt-America: The Rise of the Radical Right in the Age of Trump* (2017).

4 It is worth noting that Zahler wrote the screenplay for *Puppet Master: The Littlest Reich* (Sonny Laguna and Tommy Wiklund 2018).

References

Alper, A., et al. (2020), "Trump Suggests Governors Call In National Guard to 'Dominate the Streets'," *World News*, Reuters, 6 June. Available online: https://www.reuters.com/article/instant-article/idINKBN23D08M.

Camus, R. (2011), *Le grand Remplacement, Introduction au Remplacisme Global*, ed. D. Reinharc, Paris: David Reinharc Editions.

Chavez, L. R. (2013), *The Latino Threat: Constructing Immigrants, Citizens and the Nation*, Stanford: Stanford University Press.

Douglas, E. (2017), "'Brawl in Cell Block 99' Director S. Craig Zahler on Taking Vince Vaughn to a Different Place as an Actor," *The Tracking Board*, 5 October. Available online: https://www.tracking-board.com/brawl-in-cell-block-99-director-s-craig-zahler-on-taking- vince-vaughn-to-a-different-place-as-an-actor/.

Neiwert, D. (2017), *Alt-America: The Rise of the Radical Right in the Age of Trump*, London: Verso Books.

Ransome, N. (2019), "'Joker' Is a Terrifyingly Realistic Window into White Terrorism," *Vice*, 16 September. Available online: https://www.vice.com/en/article/ne877m/joker-is-a- terrifyingly-realistic-window-into-white-terrorism.

Ross, J. (2016), "From Mexican Rapists to Bad Hombres, the Trump Campaign in Two Moments," *The Washington Post*, 10 October. Available online: https://www.washingtonpost.com/news/the-fix/wp/2016/10/20/from-mexican-rapists-to-bad- hombres-the-trump-campaign-in-two-moments/.

Saja, H. (2019), "Families of Aurora Theater Shooting Victims Ask Warner Bros. to Support Gun Reform on Eve of 'Joker' Movie Release," *The Denver Post*, 24 September. Available online: https://www.denverpost.com/2019/09/24/joker-movie-aurora-theater-shooting/.

Sarris, A. (2009), "Notes on the Auteur Theory in 1962," in L. Braudy and M. Cohen (eds.), *Film Theory and Criticism*, New York: Oxford University Press, pp. 451–4.

Schwarz, D. (2019), "Joaquin Phoenix Won't Talk About the Ties Between 'Joker' and White Terrorism," *Vice*, 23 September. Available online: https://www.vice.com/en/article/7x54n9/joaquin-phoenix-walked-out-of-an-interview-over-a-question-about-causing-real-life-violence.

Tenold, V. (2018), *Everything You Love Will Burn: Inside the Rebirth of White Nationalism in America*, New York: Nation Books.

Yakin, H. (2021), "Extremist Groups Getting Attention and the Significance of April 19," *Times Herald Record*, 18 April. Available online: https://www.recordonline.com/in-depth/news/2021/04/18/extremist-groups-attention-april-19-rallies-protests-over-the-past-year/7224042002/.

12

A Crisis of Confidence

Fracture and Malaise in the US Polity in *Dragged Across Concrete*

Fabián Orán Llarena

> *Life, they say, is only tolerable if one can see some purpose in it, if it has a goal and one that is worth pursuing.*
> EMILE DURKHEIM, ON SUICIDE (1897)

Introduction

On July 16, 2015, Donald J. Trump announced his bid to become the forty-fifth president of the United States.[1] In what was an unusually somber speech for a presidential candidate, Trump conjured up images of a nation in profound decay, deprived of purpose, and defenseless against a dismal future. He topped off the speech saying that "the American Dream is dead." We know for a fact that the message resonated with a sizable share of the US electorate. Since then, we have learned that most Trump voters—80 percent—feel their lives have deteriorated in the past five decades and 65 percent expect life for the next generation to get even worse (Abramowitz 2018, 169). For a political culture that so cherishes the tropes of renewal and optimism, it is shocking that such a gloomy politics mobilized formidable popular support—a politics which openly hanged on to the past for orientation, as its famous campaign motto suggests, and which entertained the notion that the future is a menacing, ominous thing. The underlying causes for the rise of Trumpism are heterogeneous and multifaceted, many of which exceed the scope of this chapter—among others, his unapologetic fueling of racial fears and resentment among the white population; a backlash, both economically and ethnically motivated, against free trade; an unfiltered populist rhetoric, at odds with Republican orthodoxy, that spoke of infrastructure spending and ending costly wars overseas; and his success with two-time Obama voters who flipped the Rust Belt.[2] This chapter concerns the feeling of gloom and despair that informs the politics of Trumpism.

In his third feature film, *Dragged Across Concrete* (2018), writer-director S. Craig Zahler delivers a crime film that, in its utter bitterness and fatalism, seems to have been calibrated to explore the feelings of stagnation, purposelessness, and frustration Trumpism has tapped into. I argue that *Dragged Across Concrete* addresses key grievances in this regard. The film explores the loss of faith in the future as well as the fracture of the US polity owing to inequality and social fragmentation. In fact, the film addresses whether the US polity is still sustainable as a supposedly egalitarian community based on shared beliefs, peaceful coexistence, and the maintenance of social bonds among its citizens. In developing these themes, the film lays out a profoundly pessimistic vision of contemporary US society. In this sense, the film is ideologically intricate. It appears as though it legitimizes some claims pertaining to the US far right. But, on the whole, such claims are examined from a rather ambivalent and nuanced perspective. Far from being an ideologically monolithic text, the film can be more productively seen as an expression of contrasting ideological narratives that negotiate the film's subtexts and messages. The film also centers on the affects that have been harnessed by Trumpism as it engages with themes and mobilizes visual and narrative resources—static shots, long dialogues, leisurely rhythm, low-key lighting—that articulate an all-pervasive tonality of hopelessness.

Theoretical Approach: Cultural Studies and Affect Theory

In order to analyze *Dragged Across Concrete*, I propose a historically grounded and textually engaged cultural studies approach. I intend to look at the film as a site for the interplay of different discursive layers. Following Terry Eagleton (1991, 101) and Stuart Hall (1996, 40), I view popular culture texts as a domain of ideological contestation and negotiation, where competing meanings and values intersect, struggle, and inform each other. Therefore, I avoid tracing some alleged ideological uniformity in the film and, instead, focus on identifying ideological disclosures and how they relate with and/or refute each other within the broader ensemble of the film and its cultural and political context. In so doing, I adhere to Jackie Byars's position as regards ideological representation in film: "Film texts are not reflections of American society, in the sense that they present a homologous picture from which we can unproblematically 'read off' the society that produced and consumed them. They are themselves conflicted in many ways" (2005, 44). Much like Robin Wood's reading of a variety of US films from the 1970s as "incoherent texts"—contested terrains of accumulated contradictions and social confusion (2003, 41–62)—I aim to analyze the film by delineating the contrasting values and narratives that make up its overall subtexts.

This approach includes the question of affect to try to account for the ways the film zeroes in on feeling and emotion. I am mindful of the fact that affect theory can oftentimes be hard to operationalize for the reading of texts since it seems as though the notion of affect lumps together all things non-semantic or non-representational (Grossberg 2010, 316). As regards affect theory, I stick to some concepts as authored by Lawrence Grossberg and Laurent Berlant so as to incorporate affect in a way that widens the analytical framework while remaining theoretically unambiguous and operational in the reading the film. In *Under the Cover of Chaos*, Grossberg talks about how "affect defines the various organizations of intensity and feeling that give texture and a sense of lived reality to our lives" (2018, 91). He goes on to map what he calls the "affective landscape" of current US politics and writes that one of its traits is a form of anomie he defines as "temporal alienation," a feeling of dislocation that, among other things, makes the individual see the future as beyond rescue, no longer the promise of amelioration, while s/he remains stuck in an unpromising present (104–9). The film very explicitly engages with this mood of anxiety and disquiet toward the future. In a similar vein, Berlant explores the concept of "cruel optimism" in her homonymous book. For Berlant, relations of cruel optimism occur when subjects become invested in practices that simultaneously ground their selfhood and wear them out, help them establish life goals, and set them on a path toward self-destruction. Individuals who "have x in their lives might not well endure the loss of their object/scene of desire, even though its presence threatens their well-being, because whatever the content of the attachment is," writes Berlant, "the continuity of its form provides something of the continuity of the subject's sense of what it means to keep on living on and to look forward to being in the world" (2011, 24). This notion can offer valuable insights into the violent and ultimately self-destructive behaviors of some of the characters in Zahler's film.

Untying the Ideological Knots: Strangers in Their Own Land

Dragged Across Concrete is the latest film by S. Craig Zahler after the horror Western *Bone Tomahawk* (2015) and the prison thriller *Brawl in Cell Block 99* (2017). His films tend to garner praise in independent circuits (Sims 2019) but receive very limited theatrical release.[3] This should not come as a surprise. Zahler delivers a product that can be considerably hard to market: slow-tempo narrations, old-fashioned characters, lengthy dialogues, seemingly unquestioned stereotypes concerning race and gender, and bursts of extremely explicit violence and gore. *Dragged Across Concrete* is but a confirmation of his stylistic and thematic hallmarks. The film runs over two and a half hours; it is a leisurely exposed story which consistently sidelines crime and action to prioritize the protagonists' anxieties, discontents, banal conversations, and life minutiae. Although violence is only occasional, it is depicted in the most graphic and uncomfortable of ways—with the villains, the three bank robbers, acting with astonishing cruelty. The film centers, on the one hand, on detectives Brett Ridgeman (Mel Gibson) and Anthony Lurasetti (Vince Vaughn), and, on the other, on African American parolee Henry Johns (Tory Kittles). Separated at the beginning, their paths grow increasingly intertwined as the narration moves forward. Ridgeman and Anthony get suspended after getting caught on video being unnecessarily rough with a suspected drug dealer. The suspension comes as they struggle to maintain what appears to be a nominally middle-class status—particularly Ridgeman, who lives in a crime-ridden neighborhood and whose wife suffers from multiple sclerosis. He decides to go rogue and convinces Anthony to do likewise. They will try to thwart a bank robbery and get the stolen gold. Involved in the robbery is Henry as henchman to the ruthless bank robbers. The film opens with Henry recently out of prison, only to find his mother prostituting herself to make ends meet and provide for Henry's disabled brother. Henry's reengaging in crime comes as the only way out of economic destitution.

Ideological representation in this film is knotty enough to require a detailed parsing out that may go beyond mere pigeonholing. The film may seem to legitimize very reprehensible conducts and worldviews—all of them tied up to the idea that the prevailing cultural and political system unjustly undercuts the white middle class in favor of minorities. I argue, though, that the narration questions and undermines these conducts and worldviews. Although the film is fundamentally a crime story, the narration is patently more interested in character introspection. Static shots dominate almost the entire film while non-diegetic music is nonexistent, creating an atmosphere of intimacy and quietness. The film features a slew of dialogues where crime itself becomes peripheral and attention is clearly placed on the characters' longings and concerns. This often plays out in shadowy or ill-lit spaces, mostly at nighttime, supplying certain sequences with a confession-like tinge. Such visual grammar allows for a focus on feeling and emotion that can help us make out the more multifaceted and conflicted ideological subtexts offered in the film

One way to start making sense of the film's ideological contours is to bear in mind Carl Plantinga's study of moral judgment in fiction films. Plantinga differentiates between allegiances, requiring conscious moral evaluation, sympathies, less dependent on morals and generally aroused by injustices or harm done to the characters, and likings, which may be elicited by a whole set of factors—wit, charisma, viewer-character affiliation, and so forth (2010, 41–2). As I will later indicate, allegiance is clearly bestowed upon Henry, and it is hard not to sympathize, to some extent, with Ridgeman and Anthony, deeply flawed human beings as they are. However, the film includes objectively heinous characters—the three bank robbers Henry teams up with—whom we see maim, gut, torture, and slaughter minor characters. In an admittedly odd and fleeting narrative digression, we see one bank teller (Jennifer Carpenter) on the verge of breakdown as her maternal leave is expired and must resume her duties at the bank—the very same bank which will be robbed. In a matter of a few minutes, we go from seeing her crying for leaving her baby home to witnessing her brutal murder in a gruesome close-up. The film restricts the realm of possible viewer-character identification to a specific set of characters—Henry, Ridgeman, and Anthony—in grotesquely clear fashion.

One sustained criticism levied against Zahler is that his oeuvre smuggles reactionary worldviews.[4] Zahler's films have been produced by Cinestate, a small production house said to cater to "red-state viewers" (Sims 2019). Similarly, it is hard to miss the parallels between Ridgeman—a racist, old-fashioned cop suspended for being caught on video using excessive force—and Mel Gibson himself, whose stardom has faded away amid controversies surrounding racist and xenophobic comments, one of which was famously recorded (Collin 2019). Beyond these extratextual matters, there are elements in the film that can be interpreted as entertaining some grievances and longings associated with conservative political imagination. A good deal of the film's tonality of pessimism and fatalism stems from a sense of loss and victimhood that grips Anthony but especially Ridgeman.[5] Political scientist Corey Robin has identified loss and victimhood as fundamental tropes for conservative ideology:

> The conservative, to be sure, speaks for a special type of victim: one who has lost something of value, as opposed to the wretched of the earth, whose chief complaint is that they never had anything to lose . . . victimhood endows the conservative complaint with a more universal significance . . . People who aren't conservative often fail to realize this, but conservatism

really does speak to and for people who have lost something. It may be a landed estate or the privileges of white skin, the unquestioned authority of a husband or the untrammeled rights of a factory owner. The loss may be as material as money or as ethereal as a sense of standing. It may be a loss of something that was never legitimately owned in the first place; it may, when compared with what the conservative retains, be small. Even so, it is a loss, and nothing is ever so cherished as that which we no longer possess. (2018, 55–6)

Throughout the film's setup, the narration seems patterned so as to cast Anthony and Ridgeman as victims undercut and oppressed by an unjust and hypocritical system.[6] The film does not shy away from portraying their prejudice and harshness—Ridgeman abuses the suspected drug dealer and, in a particularly uncomfortable scene, he and Anthony heartlessly mistreat the former's girlfriend. However, the narration places greater emphasis on the dire consequences of such actions than on the actions themselves. We learn Ridgeman's status as middle-class is fundamentally nominal and the six-week suspension posits a substantial economic problem for him. In an exchange with his lieutenant—Calvert, played by Don Johnson—to discuss the terms of the suspension, it is mentioned that their superior in the chain of command—a Mexican-American inspector, who happens to share ethnicity with the arrested drug dealer—"is unlikely to be lenient" as regards his case. Calvert, however, calls the incident "bullshit," implying he somewhat condones Ridgeman's and Anthony's actions and that the punishment may be excessive. We are then informed that Calvert and Ridgeman used to be partners and, as the exchange unfolds, it is suggested that Calvert has climbed up the ladder because he has managed to adjust to a different cultural and social time—that is, to the ubiquity of digital devices and social media; to a less violent police culture. Mise-en-scène pinpoints their difference in hierarchy and status, showing Ridgeman up closer than Calvert, the latter framed more distantly sitting at a large desk in a spacious office. Ridgeman has remained loyal to his identity and principles while his former partner has hypocritically adapted to new norms. Ridgeman's get-things-done methods continue to be useful to catch criminals, yet they are no longer socially sanctioned.

Editing works to strengthen this narrative of victimhood and loss. Immediately after the exchange with Calvert, the film cuts to a dialogue-free scene where a menacing African American youngster assaults Ridgeman's daughter. As it is later disclosed, Ridgeman and his ailing wife Melanie (Laurie Holden) have been planning on leaving what is now a crime-infested neighborhood. The link between crime and African Americans, expressed visually in the scene where their daughter gets assaulted, is very plainly restated by Melanie: "I never thought I was a racist before living in this area. I'm about as liberal as any ex-cop could ever be. But now, now we really need to move." One could contend that this amounts to lending credence to quite reactionary grievances. Sociologist Arlie Russell Hochschild writes about how pockets of the white working class and middle class have come to feel economically, culturally, demographically, and politically strangers in their own land, blaming institutional powers for having deprived them of labor stability and safety in favor of ethnic minorities, thus paving the way for the politics of the Tea Party and Trumpism to gain traction (2016, 222–30). Ridgeman does seem to have been dispossessed of economic stability and moorings to manage and execute his job. In the film, this predicament is linked to minority groups—his Mexican-American superior; African Americans in his neighborhood—and culture and society becoming less permissive of violence—as embodied by his former partner and now current boss Calvert. Both factors are undeniably represented as undercutting his life and status. Similarly, him being portrayed as a father worried for what may happen to her daughter and sick wife warrants a modicum of sympathy toward him. Notwithstanding these disclosures and their saliency, they coexist with additional layers that widen and add nuance to the film's overall ideological portrait.

Broader Perspectives: Cruel Optimism and Its Fatal Attachments

The adding of perspective and ambivalence to the grievances examined earlier is accomplished through deliberately leisurely pacing—the average shot length in the film is six and a half seconds, twice what we find in most contemporary Hollywood films—along with the use of "anamorphic widescreen, to let the camera still and watch action unfolding" (Bordwell 2018). This makes it so that subjectivity and introspection take center stage. A closer look at some key sequences suggests Ridgeman's situation can be linked much more significantly to factors other than minorities' gains and shifts in culture and society. When discussing the terms of the suspension, Calvert calls him out for having grown increasingly cruel and violence-prone over the years. Visibly uncomfortable, Ridgeman claims his character and way of doing things have not changed since their days together. At one point during this rebuke, and motivated by Ridgeman's gaze, the camera cuts to a newspaper clipping, hanging on the wall, of a major case solved by two young-looking officers: Ridgeman and Calvert. The scene heightens the friction between both men's diverging career paths. But most importantly, it hints at some form of self-deception on the part of Ridgeman: someone from his past warns him that his current predicament may owe less to systemic biases against him than to his own shortcomings. These hints will get articulated in increasingly clearer fashion later in the film. In this vein, one particularly eloquent sequence is that of Ridgeman's rationalization for going rogue. The scene epitomizes many of the visual and narrative motifs of the film—a drawn-out, eight-minute-long dialogue scene inside Anthony's car, made up exclusively of static shots, in which the two characters are captured in dimly lit medium shots and medium close-ups. Crime itself—the reason behind the encounter—takes a back seat soon enough, and what is really addressed is Ridgeman's apprehension and dread. When he opens up about the frustration that informs his decision, we get the longest-running close-up in a film that deploys this resource very sparingly. Ridgeman's vulnerability and weary look become obvious and, coupled with a lighting carefully modulated to enhance shadow and darkness, the scene feels like a confession (Figure 12.1). The point he makes is worth quoting in full:

> I'm a month away from my sixtieth. I'm still the same rank I was at twenty-seven. For a lot of years, I believed that the quality of my work, what we do together, what I did with my previous partners would get me what I deserved. But I don't politic and I don't change with the times. And it turns out that that shit's more important than good honest work. So yesterday, after we stop a massive amount of drugs from getting into the school system, we get suspended because it wasn't done politely. When I go home and I find my daughter has been assaulted for the fifth time in two years because of the shit neighborhood my shit wages force me to live in.

The raw honesty of the account betrays an inability to acknowledge one's own rituals and practices as originating pain and dissatisfaction. It is obvious that his way of doing his job as a cop is part and parcel of his personality. Otherwise he would not have stuck to his guns so earnestly all those years seeing no promotions or amelioration. Granted that he may have got his

FIGURE 12.1 *Ridgeman comes clean about his motives.*

sense of identity out of that experience, delivering this "good honest work" the way he is used to is also what has eroded his middle-class status and turned him into a violent, out-of-touch man—it is also what gets him killed in the end since trying to foil the bank robbery is yet another iteration of rugged individualism and masculine might. I view this as an instance of Berlant's cruel optimism. We find a character who is deeply invested in an ethos—violent individualism; rejection of changes in society and culture—which serves as the basic foundation for his identity and selfhood. This ethos is also what undermines and holds him back as a human being, compounding his inability and unwillingness to make sense of the current social situation. It so happens that Ridgeman attaches himself to a mode of being that matches Berlant's description of cruel optimism, that is, a way of living that "wears out the subjects who nonetheless, and at the same time, find their conditions of possibility within it" (2011, 27).

By foregrounding subjectivity and personal longings the film participates in what film scholar Luis García-Mainar has called the "introspective realist crime film." García-Mainar identifies families of transnational crime films from the 2000s that have used the conventions of the crime film to shift "their focus away from the expected action or suspense and onto the characters' personal, emotional experience of the social context of crime" (2016, 38). Although in *Dragged Across Concrete* we do not find the gritty realism of desaturated images, natural light, and handheld camerawork of many of the films studied by García-Mainar, Zahler's film does share other core traits of this generic trend, for example, a swerve toward introspection, a heavy focus on subjectivity, pathos, enhancement of non-eventful passages, and minimal non-diegetic sounds (García-Mainar 2016, 22–4). Thus, some conventions of the crime film are here given a fresh dimension. For instance, Ridgeman resembles in some ways the leading characters of films such as *Bullitt* (Peter Yates 1968), *Dirty Harry* (Don Siegel 1971), or *The French Connection* (William Friedkin 1971)—cops skeptical of institutional power who end up endorsing vigilantism over an institutional system they think has failed them (Leitch 2002, 229). Nonetheless, the emphasis laid on his feelings of dread and anxiety vis-à-vis his personal and social context makes for a more nuanced and complex portrait, one that is not marked by abrupt episodes of violent trauma or epiphanies, but by the slow accumulation of small-scale, years-long defeats that have taken their toll on the character we see onscreen.

No Future: The Impossibility of the US Polity

Henry acts as an important counterbalance to Ridgeman. Although Ridgeman appears on screen considerably more than Henry—approximately thirty minutes more—he is arguably the other protagonist of the film along with the veteran cop. The plot opens and finishes with him at radically different settings and in completely different situations. The parallels and divergences between Ridgeman and Henry, which become all the more obvious when they meet at the end, are instrumental in developing the themes of the film. In the end, Ridgeman dies while Henry lives, and their grievances come from quite contrasting places socially and culturally. Henry's reengaging in crime owes to more pressing reasons than those of Ridgeman. Despite the latter's urge to protect his family being certainly understandable and worthy of sympathy, Henry's situation is presented as more desperate and his involvement in the robbery strikes us as more legitimate: escaping pervasive poverty and helping out his disabled brother and mother, who gets ahead by prostituting herself. In fact, Henry gets portrayed as a fundamentally pragmatic character, bent on working out ways to continue to be alive. In one the first sequences of the film, he finds the sorry state of his household. When his mother starts ranting about his missing father and his being in prison as causing the family's economic needs, Henry reacts in the most practical of ways: "Ma, let's fast-forward all this. Ain't no point in arguing about a bunch of yesterdays." He cannot afford the sort of ruminations about the past Ridgeman and Anthony are so prone to engage with. It is true that Henry is not depicted with the same degree of introspection and character nuance as Ridgeman—film critic David Sims (2019) rightly points this out. However, this makes Henry far more worthy of allegiance than Ridgeman. The latter's goals are driven not just by an objective economic need but by a sense of social and cultural vindictiveness that is totally absent in the former, whose sole reason for taking part in the robbery is the much more earthly wish to break a cycle of severe poverty.

Their differences are brought to the fore in dramatic fashion when the two storylines finally converge in the last quarter of the film, once the bank robbers and Anthony have been gunned down during a bloody standoff. The scenes take place in an abandoned lot at nighttime, a location that befits the film's desolate and gloomy spirit. Once the standoff finishes, Ridgeman and Henry agree to share the stolen gold. Even though both characters open up to each other about their respective problems, suspicion and distrust remain all pervasive. Couched in low-key lighting and leisurely tempo, they are shown cleaning up evidence and gathering the stolen gold in long and medium shots either in singles or in two shots that locate the characters as separately as possible within the frame, thus heightening the distance between them. Almost at no point are they shown together in medium close-ups, a far cry from the way we have seen Ridgeman and Anthony interact, or Henry and his friend Biscuit (Michael Jai White). Mise-en-scène and framing help strengthen the fact that a coming together of both characters is not possible.

Henry has recorded on his phone the standoff and is therefore in possession of evidence against Ridgeman. The former swears he will delete the video once they go separate ways. Feeling terribly suspicious about Henry's intentions though, Ridgeman tries to outmaneuver Henry and puts a gun on his neck so that he deletes the video immediately. Henry shoots Ridgeman, killing him. The unfolding of these events drives home the pessimism that runs through the film concerning the sorry state of social bonds in the United States and whether the US polity as an egalitarian community can assimilate such degree of internal fracture and tension. Both men remain distrustful, but it is mostly Ridgeman who fails to recognize that Henry's needs are as legitimate and justified as his. Through its emphasis on fracture and suspicion, the film promises no future for a white middle class embittered and alienated from their peers. The temporal alienation Grossberg sees as a defining trait of our time, where the future is a menacing thing and the present a period of stagnation, gets symbolized through Ridgeman's and Anthony's deaths at the end of the film. It could be argued that the film places hopes for renewal in Henry, who goes on to live as a wealthy man. The contrast between Henry's life at the beginning and at the end is exacerbated through composition and lighting. The narration crafts two similarly composed long shots of Henry entering a house—one at the beginning, one at the end. The first shot is shadowy and presents Henry as poverty-stricken, living in a crime-ridden neighborhood and in a house in total disarray (Figure 12.2). The second shot is filled with light, dominated by whites, and indicates Henry is now extraordinarily rich and lives in a mansion by the sea, his family's every need now met (Figure 12.3). In producing these images and outcomes for the characters, Zahler represents a society in which common ground or simply coexisting peacefully cannot be envisaged. The future as a commonly held promise of amelioration, as Grossberg's temporal alienation indicates, is beyond rescue. Henry's rag-to-riches progression and its accompanying images of extreme wealth reveal the ever-increasing levels of income inequality the US economy has been nurturing for decades, as if the only possible class positions were economic destitution or plutocratic opulence. Similarly, Ridgeman's frustrations and final demise cast doubts as to whether there is such a thing as middle-class

FIGURE 12.2 *Released from prison, Henry gets reacquainted with a world of destitution.*

FIGURE 12.3 *At the end of the film, Henry appears surrounded by a world of luxury.*

society anymore in the United States.[7] It is not surprising that a film that oozes pessimism and anxiety delivers a message so deeply bleak about the future and about social cohesion.

Conclusion: The Unrepentant Hopelessness of S. Craig Zahler

During the 2000s and 2010s a handful of US films tried to reimagine the concept of the American Dream along less materialistic and success-driven lines. Films like *Sideways* (Alexander Payne 2004), *Little Miss Sunshine* (Jonathan Dayton and Valerie Faris 2006), *The Visitor* (Tom McCarthy 2007), or *Nebraska* (Alexander Payne 2013) resituate the American Dream in stories of second chances and restitution of family and emotional links as a way out of toxic forms of solipsism and individualism (Sánchez-Escalonilla and Rodríguez-Mateos 2016, 20–4). *Dragged Across Concrete* seems painstakingly calibrated to express that such a reimagining is, at best, naïve. Thanks to its pervasive tonality of despair and its sustained focus on personal longings and uncertainties, the film manages to instill, in almost every shot and sequence, the characters' loss of hope and feeling of having been left behind socially, culturally, and economically. Still, Zahler looks at their characters from a distance. Claiming that the film validates Ridgeman's or Anthony's ideology seems to ignore the ambiguities and nuances implicit in the story. One could say that strong political affiliations do not seem to befit a film intensely pessimistic and nihilistic in its portrait of US society as a deeply eroded community. The middle class is doomed—Ridgeman and Anthony die—and Henry's success in escaping poverty and becoming extraordinarily rich suggests the US economy produces either precarity or extreme wealth. These outcomes drive home an image of the future that is as dry as it is depressing. All in all, *Dragged Across Concrete* does not really present a distinct political project. Rather, it is a film that manages to articulate a series of moods and portraits of anxieties, fragmentation, accumulated defeats, and uncertainties that have been key in paving the way for a politics like that of Trumpism to come to fruition.

Notes

1. This work is part of the research project "Narratives of Happiness and Resilience" (Subproject One: "The Premise of Happiness: The Function of Feelings in North American Narratives," ref. PID2020-113190GB-C21), funded by the Ministry of Science, Innovation, and Universities. Research contributing to this chapter was also funded by the research project "Narraciones en crisis: Respuestas del cine norteamericano a la Gran Recesión y sus consecuencias (2008-2020)," funded by the University of La Laguna (Convocatoria 2021 de Ayudas para la Incentivación de la Actividad Investigadora del Personal Docente e Investigador de la Universidad de La Laguna).
2. See Davis (2017), Anderson (2017, 58), Abramowitz (2018, 122–3), Riley (2018, 21), Kruse and Zelizer (2019, 347), Frank (2020, 218), and Blyth and Lonergan (2020, 25).
3. According to IMDb, Zahler's films have underperformed in the box office. All of his budgets outweigh box office returns.
4. David Sims (2019) and Charles Bramesco (2019) sum up these criticisms. Manohla Dargis (2019) has some harsh words for what she views as the film's uncritical treatment of racism and xenophobia.
5. It may seem that my analysis focuses too much on Ridgeman and neglects Anthony, but this is because Anthony's grievances and anxieties pretty much overlap with those of his partner.
6. This notion of loss has been instrumental in the political history of US conservatism. Richard Nixon's Silent Majority and Ronald Reagan's Southern Strategy are all but iterations of this narrative of white middle-class uneasiness—white majorities lose their economic and cultural status in favor of ethnic minorities as society grows increasingly soft-on-crime (Kazin 1995, 246–8, 260–3; Frank 2004, 119–20; Alexander 2012, 46–9; Taylor 2016, 54–5).
7. For overviews on the rise of income inequality and the shrinking of the middle class in the United States see Hacker and Pierson (2010), Formisano (2015), Saez and Zucman (2019), Case and Deaton (2020: 131–84).

References

Abramowitz, A. (2018), *The Great Alignment: Race, Party Transformation, and the Rise of Donald Trump*, New Haven: Yale University Press.

Alexander, M. (2012), *The New Jim Crow: Mass Incarceration in the Age of Colorblindness*, New York: The New Press.
Anderson, P. (2017), "Passing the Baton," *New Left Review* 103, pp. 41–64.
Berlant, L. (2011), *Cruel Optimism*, Duke: Duke University Press.
Blyth, M. and E. Lonergan (2020), *Angrynomics*, Newcastle: Agenda Publishing.
Bordwell, D. (2018), "Venice 2018: Assorted Malefactors," *Observations on Film Art*, 13 September. Available online: http://www.davidbordwell.net/blog/2018/09/13/venice-2018-assorted-malefactors/.
Bramesco, C. (2019), "Trolled Across Concrete: Why Mel Gibson's New Film Is a Curious Provocation," *The Guardian*, 22 March. Available online: https://www.theguardian.com/film/2019/mar/22/dragged-across-concrete-mel-gibson-troll-new-film-provocation.
Byars, J. (2005), *All That Hollywood Allows: Re-Reading Gender in 1950s Melodrama*, London: Routledge. First published in 1991.
Case, A. and A. Deaton (2020), *Deaths of Despair and the Future of Capitalism*, Oxford: Princeton University Press.
Collin, R. (2019), "Dragged Across Concrete Reviewed by Robbie Collin," *BBC Radio*, 19 April. Available online: https://www.youtube.com/watch?v=V1MAimyBL7Y.
Dargis, M. (2019), "Dragged Across Concrete Review: The Evil That Men Do (Repeatedly)," *The New York Times*, 20 March. Available online: https://www.nytimes.com/2019/03/20/movies/dragged-across-concrete-review.html.
Davis, M. (2017), "The Great God Trump and the White Working Class," *Catalyst* 1 (1). Available online: https://catalyst-journal.com/2017/11/great-god-trump-davis.
Durkheim, E. (2006), *On Suicide*, New York: Penguin Classics. First published in 1897.
Eagleton, T. (1991), *Ideology: An Introduction*, New York: Verso.
Formisano, R. (2015), *Plutocracy in America: How Increasing Inequality Destroys the Middle Class and Exploits the Poor*, Baltimore: Johns Hopkins University Press.
Frank, T. (2004), *What's the Matter with Kansas? How Conservatives Won the Heart of America*, New York: Metropolitan Books.
Frank, T. (2020), *People Without Power: The War on Populism and the Fight for Democracy*, London: Scribe.
García-Mainar, L. (2016), *The Introspective Realist Crime Film*, London: Palgrave Macmillan.
Grossberg, L. (2010), "Affect's Future: Rediscovering the Virtual in the Actual," in M. Gregg and G. Seigworth (eds.), *The Affect Theory Reader*, London: Duke University Press, pp. 309–38.
Grossberg, L. (2018), *Under the Cover of Chaos: Trump and the Battle for the American Right*, London: Pluto Press.
Hacker, J. and P. Pierson (2010), *Winner-Take-All-Politics: How Washington Made the Rich Richer—And Turned Its Back on the Middle Class*, New York: Simon & Schuster.
Hall, S. (1996), "The Problem of Ideology: Marxism without Guarantees," in D. Morley and K.-H. Chen (eds.), *Stuart Hall: Critical Dialogues in Cultural Studies*, London: Routledge, pp. 25–46.

Hochschild, A. R. (2016), *Strangers in Their Own Land: Anger and Mourning on the American Right*, New York: The New Press.

Kazin, M. (1995), *The Populist Persuasion: An American History*, New York: Basic Books.

Kruse, K. and J. Zelizer (2019), *Fault Lines: A History of the United States since 1970*, New York: W.W. Norton & Company.

Leitch, T. (2002), *Crime Films*, Cambridge: Cambridge University Press.

Plantinga, C. (2010), "'I Followed the Rules, and They All Loved You More': Moral Judgment and Attitudes toward Fictional Characters in Film," *Midwest Studies in Philosophy* 34, pp. 34–51.

Riley, D. (2018), "What Is Trump?" *New Left Review* 114, pp. 5–31.

Robin, C. (2018), *The Reactionary Mind: Conservatism from Edmund Burke to Donald Trump*, New York: Oxford University Press. First published in 2011.

Saez, E. and G. Zucman (2019), *The Triumph of Injustice: How the Rich Dodge Taxes and How to Make Them Pay*, New York: W.W. Norton & Company.

Sánchez-Escalonilla, A. and A. Rodríguez Mateos (2016), "*Introducción*: Indiewood y el nuevo sueño americano," in A. Sánchez-Escalonilla and A. Rodríguez Mateos (eds.), *Hollywood y el ocaso del American Dream*, Madrid: Editorial Síntesis, pp. 13–28.

Sims, D. (2019), "*Dragged Across Concrete* and the Sloppy Provocations of S. Craig Zahler," *The Atlantic*, 25 March. Available online: https://www.theatlantic.com/entertainment/archive/2019/03/s-craig-zahler-dragged-across-concrete-films/585424/.

Taylor, K.-Y. (2016), *From #BlackLivesMatter to Black Liberation*, Chicago: Haymarket Books.

Trump, D. (2015), "Presidential Announcement Speech," *Time*, 16 June. Available online: https://time.com/3923128/donald-trump-announcement-speech.

Wood, R. (2003), *Hollywood from Vietnam to Reagan ... and Beyond*, New York: Columbia University Press.

13

"I Guess It Comes from Being Poor"

Inequality, Affect, and Point of View in *The Florida Project*

Juan A. Tarancón

Only a few days before the Tax Cuts and Jobs Act was voted in the Senate, Donald Trump traveled to St. Charles, Missouri, to promote the bill. Although corporate capital and high-income households had more to gain from the GOP 2017 tax reform plan, in this quaint little town on the banks of the Missouri River, Trump painted an old familiar picture of blue-collar workers burdened by taxes that end up in the pockets of idle welfare recipients. He promised welfare reform and the audience burst into cheers with the enthusiasm of the religious fanatic. Never knowing when to stop, Trump went on with one of his familiar off-script musings. "I know people," he said, "that work three jobs and they live next to somebody who doesn't work at all. And the person who is not working at all and has no intention of working at all is making more money and doing better than the person that's working his or her ass off" (in Horsley 2018). Trump's incongruous anecdote resurrects the myth of the welfare queen and steers the conversation away from the material issues that impact workers' lives, but, more importantly, it prompts the crowd to make sense of their experiences at a time of economic and social crisis within a framework characterized by the stereotypical (and racialized) conflict between workers and freeloaders that lies at the heart of right-wing populism. Furthermore, with digressions like this, Trump locates issues like empathy and social justice at one end of the cultural and affective axis popularized in the country over the last decades. Let's be clear about one thing: if you actually manage to land three jobs, chances are you make minimum wage, work in appalling conditions, and are not given enough hours to qualify for benefits. It may sound incongruous, but, at this juncture, if you have three jobs, you are probably one of the 140 million people that, according to the "Poor People's Moral Budget," are struggling with poverty in the United States. It seems that, as the laboring classes become more and more fragile, there is an urgent need to downplay class categories in favor of establishing boundaries around a cultural project of belonging that marks off people into deserving and non-deserving citizens. By reframing his tax reform in this way, what Trump does is to bring people together around a rigid affective formation grounded on individualism, moral conservatism, and xenophobic nationalism. In brief, the context Trump mobilizes, where idle cheats live off the earnings of hard-working citizens, determines how people make sense of their experiences and the way they participate in society in a time of economic crisis. What is more, he legitimizes both the structural factors that produce inequality and the feelings that pinpoint the economically disadvantaged as cultural antagonists that are unworthy of our sympathy.

My intention is to take Trump's appeal to emotions in matters of social solidarity at such a critical time for all workers as my point of entry for an examination of the relation of forces that characterize the current conjuncture. In particular, my wish is to consider one specific historical process: the formation of a large underclass of people—employed as well as unemployed—trapped in a cycle of poverty. To do this, the chapter examines how Sean Baker's *The Florida Project* (2017) intervenes in the process by which we deal with inequality and, as I will argue, helps set up a different conversation. In a period characterized by the normalization of an atomistic conception of the individual and the decline in civic engagement, *The Florida Project* indicates a concern with issues like connectedness and compassion and taps into the challenges we face if we are to make acceptable a more empathic and social-minded view of the world. I propose to see the film as a story about how we look at and how we feel about the most vulnerable populations at a time when the social changes brought about by neoliberalism push workers more and more into perpetual poverty. The issue I want to tackle here is how the film enters into a struggle over the conception of society that governs the way we make sense of the challenges being thrown up in the United States as a consequence of the various crises affecting the country and that, ultimately, determines the social alternatives we are willing to accept and the ones we deem unacceptable. In other words, I want to speculate about the potentialities of an alternative affective landscape to the one mobilized by Donald Trump.

Hence my cue is taken from Lawrence Grossberg, who describes an "affective landscape [as] a complex social way of being in the world, a densely saturated space within which some experiences, behaviors, choices and emotions are possible, some 'feel' inevitable and obvious, and still others are impossible or unimaginable" (2018, 91). Put simply, we need to make acceptable, if not desirable, other ways of being together in the world. Such a project can be pursued in many different ways and in many different fronts, but it requires that "we enter into the struggle over affect" (Grossberg 1997, 23). Individual reasoning has never been completely divorced from emotions, and mobilizing feelings has always been a central political strategy, but emotions are riding particularly high in US politics since 2008. Furthermore, as illustrated by Hochschild (2016), new modes of affectivity have shattered well-established feeling patterns. Emotions have been elevated not only over factual evidence but also over self-interest. This paradox—that people oppose agendas that would benefit them—is the puzzle of our times, says Hochschild (2016, 10). It would be a mistake to think that yet another scientific study on the corrosive effects of the market and its impact on the lower classes would solve the situation. Facts alone will not bring people around to a different, more social-minded, way of thinking. At the time, producing a social consensus around values like conviviality, empathy, and social justice has less to do with ideology or with intellect than with creating a certain *disposition.*

From there my intention of exploring these issues through the use of two interdependent principles that underlie the project of cultural studies. On the one hand, the production of contextualized analyses of the ways social relations are created, where culture and society are seen as mutually constitutive. On the other, the refusal to accept that these relations are necessary and without alternative. From the first tenet it follows that cultural expressions like films do not simply mediate or represent social relations—that is, they do not simply show or tell spectators what they are already aware of respecting changes in society—rather, by articulating into the network of forces that form the relationality of the conjuncture, films provide spectators with a different understanding of the relation of forces that make up a given context. The second tenet entails that these relations are always contingent. "Reality is making itself and it will continue to," says Grossberg, and "therefore there is a contingency about the world that opens up possibilities" (2010, 318). This is my starting point: the contingency of any situation determines the possibilities for a different relation of forces and a different social arrangement.

What drew me to Sean Baker's *The Florida Project* was the way the story of Halley (Bria Vinaite), a poor, single mother in her twenties, unfolds unhurriedly around the point of view of Bobby (Willem Dafoe), the manager of the seedy motel where she lives with her daughter Moonee (Brooklynn Prince). Two things are worth noting: the deviation from the conventional melodramatic narrativization that stories about poverty and class issues usually get in mainstream (and in most fringe) films, and the viewing positions the film constructs for the audience. Films about the poor—even more so when they involve children—often derive their emotional power from a sappy melodramatic plot built around the experiences and the point of view of virtuous characters. *The Florida Project* is not that kind of film. To begin with, it is not oriented toward plot, at least not in the sense that contemporary mainstream films are; it is characterized by an unusually "objective"—when not dispassionate—rendition of events; it keeps spectators in the dark about the circumstances that drove the characters to their present situation and, during most of the film, we are rarely allowed into their minds; respecting virtuousness, well, let us say that Halley does not give spectators an easy ride. Put simply, *The Florida Project* does not invite us to adopt a melodramatic sensibility. Second, it is Bobby's point of view (his gaze as well as his emotional reactions) that determines the way spectators are gradually brought into the story and positioned respecting the lives and the behavior of these people living on the verge of destitution. The point will be made that, with these textual strategies, Baker challenges spectators to think through the way we make sense of poverty in contemporary society, that the film elicits feelings that relate to an affective landscape built, not around self-interest and vindictiveness, but around social responsibility and unconditional community-minded values.

If affect determines the conditions of possibility of a change in the way we think about society, the question we must ask ourselves is: How can we start challenging an affective landscape that legitimizes violence against the poor and marks off other alternatives as unacceptable? Despite the highly polarized positions on matters pertaining to inequality, forms of solidarity and unconditional commitment to the common good could well be the most plausible forces to change the discussion over poverty and establish the possibility of a new social consensus. But it all starts with a reconstruction of the context that prioritizes relations of interdependency and the common good. *The Florida Project* does not offer concrete solutions to the problems it merely exposes (which would seem as contrived as the syrupy Hollywood films it deviates from), but it mobilizes a different affective regime. My contention is therefore that—as well as proffering well-researched, evidence-based solutions—we need to address the affective formation that makes us blame the poor for their poverty. As I will be arguing, the emotional engagement *The Florida Project* demands from the spectator is conducive to questioning the inevitability of the relations that led us to the current state of affairs, forcing us to imagine other forms of sociability.

The Florida Project concerns a group of people living day to day in the Magic Castle, an extended-stay motel located on a crummy commercial strip that caters for tourists on their way to nearby Disney World. At the center of the film are Halley and her vivacious six-year-old daughter.

Left with no source of income, Halley turns to prostitution and pickpocketing to pay for her room. But when the word gets out, child protective services step in and resolve to put Moonee in foster care. In the final scene, Moonee figures out that she is being separated from her mother and escapes with her friend Jancey (Valeria Cotto). The film ends abruptly as the two kids approach the Cinderella castle that towers over the entrance to Disney World and gives the motel its ironic name. Their momentary flight to Disney's fantasy world will not make us forget the hopeless future awaiting them. If the film offers some kind of hope that the world could be a better place for these children, we should look for it somewhere else.

From here, this chapter proceeds in two parts, both aimed at examining how *The Florida Project* enters into the struggle over affect and at rethinking other relations between film and society. To begin with, my aim is to construct the historical context within which I propose to situate the film, focusing primarily on two interrelated historical processes: on the one hand, the ascendancy of neoliberal values, which have reshaped the contents of the debate over poverty and have produced a particular common sense according to which the poor are unworthy of our sympathy; on the other hand, the formation of a large underclass of poor and near-poor people whose ties to society are increasingly frail. Then I will analyze the textual strategies deployed by the film to address these issues, with particular attention to the narrative structure and the viewing positions it creates for the spectators. My contention is that films do not just orient us through the assemblage of forces that make up the context. Their narrative and aesthetic specificity also cause us to reconstruct the relation of forces at a particular moment in time and to unearth historical processes that would otherwise remain unarticulated, thus suggesting the possibility of a different social consensus.

According to Michael Harrington (2012, 205), "there was a sense of excitement, of social passion, in the capital" when Lyndon B. Johnson announced a war on poverty in 1964. But during the 1970s poverty dropped out of the political agendas and hence of people's consciousness. Thus, for the last four decades collective solutions have been gradually pushed aside, favoring instead individual ones. One could say that during the 1970s the conditions of possibility changed. As a consequence, it is hard to imagine that antipoverty programs now elicit "a sense of excitement" in Washington. After forty years of neoliberalism, the dominant affective regime revolves around an alleged conflict between makers and takers, between those who work hard and play by the rules and the moocher class. This approach has managed to shift the debate away from material hardships gearing it instead toward the moral character of the poor. The strategy to target an alleged "moocher class," say Perez and Sirota (2021), has been resurrected by GOP officials in recent years. Jeff Sessions, for example, thinks assistance for low-income people provides "lavish benefits" and creates a culture of dependency (Parrott et al. 2013). Likewise, conservative think tanks like the American Enterprise Institute are once again pushing the "success sequence" as the magic formula that would eradicate poverty (graduate high school, get a job, get married, and only then have children) at a time when full-time employment no longer guarantees you can meet your most basic needs. These reactions reveal how profoundly poverty has become intertwined within the culture wars. What transpires is an understanding of poverty both as an individual issue and as cultural deviance. Put simply, poverty is being conceptualized as a culture that is antithetical to core US values like hard work, opportunity, and freedom. This is a battle over common sense—over the interpretative practices we deploy to make sense of social change—*and* over the future conception of society.

The moral narratives that blame the poor for their circumstances and construct them as cultural antagonists determine what people take to be feasible and acceptable in the fight against inequality. If poverty is a moral failure of the individual, it is only natural that the solutions should take these directions: deregulation of the economy and regulation of morals. Nothing new under the sun, some might say. Except the context. Although this shift in the conceptualization of poverty has persisted since the 1960s, it worsened with the crisis and the campaign that led to the election of Barack Obama and the emergence of the Tea Party. As noted earlier, I contend that the construal of poverty as an individual, not as a structural, issue must be seen within a context marked by a revolution in employment relationships that is producing a large underclass of people relegated to the fringes of society.

By using—not without reservations—the term "underclass" I want to draw attention to the dynamics of social transformation associated with the ascendancy of neoliberal policies as a way of encapsulating part of the uniqueness of the current conjuncture: the social exclusion and the growing vulnerability of a large portion of the US population, the officially poor as well as middle-class dropouts who barely eke out a living working in low-paying jobs and who move in and out of poverty without any prospect of improving their lives. For example, as Jesse A. Myerson observed (2017), working class has come to mean "in and adjacent to poverty." The laboring and the middle classes are quickly dissolving into an underclass of low-paid workers who are condemned to a cycle of poverty from which it is increasingly hard to escape. Given this new context, we need, in the first place, to abandon old notions of class structure and class struggle and see class as a more general historical phenomenon, including economic as well as cultural forces, and second, to start from the premise that there is a fast-growing wealth and income gap between a privileged minority at the top and a large heterogeneous group of precarious low-waged workers at the bottom, and the interests of these groups are antagonistic.

This economic and social polarization is not so much the result of deindustrialization and the consequent shift from a manufacturing to a service-oriented economy, but of specific economic legislation that has weakened workers' power and has destroyed communal cohesion and the public spirit. Nor is this a matter of the country's overall economy performance, because, as Hedrick Smith notes, although productivity grew by 80 percent between 1973 and 2011, workers have been systematically cut out of their share of these gains and "pushed into poverty or to its precipice" (in Patton 2014). In different words, it is neoliberalism—the deregulation of the workplace, the gutting of social protection, and the pursuit of private good—that has undermined many people's ability to lead a dignified life in the United States. However, as noted earlier, the crisis is being lived primarily in affective and cultural terms that are not that different from those laid out by the culture wars. When poverty became more strikingly cross-racial—when it hit the white working class—cultural issues took precedence over economic ones. At a time when the distance between the poor and the working classes is rapidly shrinking, politicians like Trump mobilize affects that many workers appropriate to make sense of their experiences in the form of hate, hostility, and contempt for those in need and for the ideology of social justice itself. This echoes the stratagem used in the past to divide workers along racial lines and have all of them work for "near-starvation wages" denounced by Martin Luther King, Jr. in 1965. Now, pushed into a life of unstable labor and poverty wages, the thinking of the working classes is being "saturated" with nativism, nationalism, and nostalgia. Paraphrasing King, corporate capital took the world and gave poor workers the culture wars. As a matter of fact, from this perspective, it is the culture wars that keep class struggle from breaking out in the United States.

The recession has helped move poverty from the margins to the center of film narratives and, even more significantly, it has changed our perspective respecting the study of film, making the analysis of inequality much more urgent. Class-related issues, as David James observed (1996, 1), have been marginalized in academic study of cinema. It seems that film scholars have opted for the advice of Sullivan's butler and stayed away from poverty "even for purposes of study." They remained aloof to questions of social justice and did not articulate Hollywood's formulaic stories within the historical processes that impoverished workers. Between the 1970s and the 1990s, identity politics carried the day and class-related studies—too few and too far between—did not resonate in film theory. As Nystrom notes (2009, 7), at the time "there was no theoretical revolution in class-based theory in film studies to match what was happening in gender-oriented film theory." Scholars might have abandoned the aestheticism of previous decades, but they did not develop the idiom and the analytical strategies to make sense of the social breakdown caused by the neoliberal counterrevolution. Instead of mapping out the linkages with class issues, questions of identity were, for the most part, pursued around ethnic and gender concerns within the framework of what Ghassan Hage calls "white multiculturalism" (2000). During the last decade, more and more voices have been critical of the attitude of Academia toward questions of class and inequality. "Multiculturalism," writes Hedges, "rather than leading to a critique of structures and systems that consciously excluded and impoverished the poor and the marginal, became an end in itself" (2010, 124). While Academia supposedly intended to be concerned with the problems of those in need, it was actually more like a country club that was—and still is—basically about *itself*. One might even say that the cultural scenario of the 1980s and 1990s blew up in our faces and was one of the causes that led to the emergence of an affective regime built around individualism, anti-government sentiment, sexism, xenophobic nationalism, and anti-intellectualism. The economic recession only made things worse.

The crisis had an impact on the films that were produced, but it also demands that we reconsider the ways we approach class-related issues and that we adopt strategies that lead to unsettling established ideas about inequality and reveal the ways hierarchies of power are perpetuated through cinema in relation to particular circumstances. Mainstream productions like *Being Flynn* (Paul Weitz 2012), *Out of the Furnace* (2013), *Time Out of Mind* (Oren Moverman 2014), *Manchester by the Sea* (Kenneth Lonergan 2016), or *The Purge* franchise, only to mention a few, directly or indirectly have made the poor visible during these last few years. However, they tend to tie in with Hollywood's tendency to fetishize and commodify the lower classes. It was in the field of independent cinema that inequality found a more genuine and complex treatment. Even before the economic collapse of 2008, Debra Granik, Kelly Reichardt, Ramin Bahrani, and Sean Baker made films that provided an insight into the different forms inequality was taking. In recent years films like *Precious* (Lee Daniels 2009), *Entre nos* (Paola Mendoza and Gloria La Morte 2009), *Beasts of the Southern Wild* (Benh Zeitlin 2012), *Heaven Knows What* (Josh and Benny Safdie 2014), *Songs My Brothers Taught Me* (Chloé Zhao 2015), *American Honey* (Andrea Arnold 2016), *Ladybird* (Greta Gerwig 2017), and *Leave No Trace* (Debra Granik 2018) have challenged in one way or another stereotypical narratives concerning the poor. Also notable is the crude take on contemporary poverty offered by documentaries like *Rich Hill* (Andrew Droz Palermo and Tracy Droz Tragos 2014) or *The Other Side* (Roberto Minervini 2015). These films offer an insight into the effects of living in poverty and, in so doing, demand a more compassionate response from the audience. They imply that the problems the poor face should be taken into account and provide spectators with emotional materials that can lead to decisions on behalf of a society marked by social justice. I turn now to *The Florida Project* and the ways it enters into these contexts.

The Florida Project is an exploration of the possibilities of a different kind of narrative about the poor. By deviating from the melodramatic treatment of poverty and social marginalization in cinema, Baker forces us to confront our feelings toward poverty in a context where blaming the poor has become a political strategy. *The Florida Project* challenges us to mobilize a different mode of affectivity and put an egalitarian vision of society above any other consideration. As noted earlier, this is pursued by eschewing melodramatic tropes. To begin with, there is not much in the way of a plot. Baker himself has been straightforward about this (in Nakhnikian 2017). He deliberately deviated from the conventional Hollywood three-part narrative structure to the extent he believed US audiences would tolerate. Instead, the film has a repetitive episodic structure that conveys Halley's hopelessness but prevents us from identifying with her. Only toward the end of the film, as Halley realizes she might lose custody of Moonee, are the narrative terms clearly set and Baker makes a stylistic shift that brings spectators closer to mother and daughter.

Melodrama—or the melodramatic mode—is a multidimensional concept that involves complex navigation. No single theory of melodrama covers every aspect associated with it. On the other hand, its fuzziness and malleability have guaranteed its persistence as a popular narrative strategy to deal with the ethical challenges thrown up in society right from the very beginnings of cinema. For the purposes of this analysis, following Linda Williams (2001), I am focusing on one aspect of melodrama: how it determines our involvement through narrative organization and point of view. To put it briefly, by providing spectators with more information about the story than any of the characters has, they are put in a position of knowledge from which they can feel and identify with an unjustly victimized character and recognize his or (more often than not) her virtue. This is what we find in films like *Precious* or *Entre nos*. *The Florida Project*, however, does not solicit this kind of involvement, at least not until the end of the film, once we have seen Halley in all her vulgarity and grossness.

The Florida Project does not adopt a victimizing approach. The narrative keeps spectators in the dark about the ordeals Halley has been through. She is not presented as a noble and kindhearted victim of life's circumstances. Quite the opposite, Baker does not elude the aspects that tend to excite hostility against marginal groups and that fuel the victim-blaming narrative. Halley is an unapologetic social outcast; her representation ties in with the stereotypical representation of the poor as sexualized, undisciplined, and self-destructive pariahs. The excess in the representation of her body marks Halley as a moral other and as a threat to her daughter and to society. Without any information about the circumstances that brought her to this point, through her behavior and her bodily aspect, spectators will unanimously read all kind of assumptions about the poor on her body. In this sense, our limited perception of Halley is not different from that of the poor we see on the street. Her representation as vulgar, indecent, and repellent involves, as Bourdieu would have it (1986), a moral evaluation that not only gives us the legitimate right to pronounce judgment on the poor but also serves to attribute ourselves with certain (comparatively positive) features. However, it should be noted that these feelings start, not from the individual, but from an affective landscape where the poor are, as noted earlier, cultural antagonists.

In addition to restricting our omniscience, there are further questions to consider in the way the film deviates from melodrama, most notably with regard to point of view. For the most part, Baker documents the events in an objective way, forcing the spectator to assume the position of a distant witness. Such a perspective can most easily be grasped in the context of Hollywood's aggressive contemporary style. As David Bordwell illustrated (2006), contemporary filmmaking hinges, among other stylistic devices, on close-ups and tight singles. Baker, on the contrary, rarely gets close to the characters. In general, he employs long shots and eschews conventional patterns of decoupage based on eyeline matches and reverse shots. This creates a sensation both of detachment from and domination over the characters. Nonetheless, this pattern is occasionally broken as the story progresses: first, to show Halley and Moonee through the point of view of Bobby, and second, once the narrative terms are unequivocally established near the end, to capture Halley in close-ups. The remainder of this chapter analyzes these changes in the visual grammar of the film in greater detail. I shall argue that the shifts from an objective to a subjective configuration mobilizes an affective landscape built around unconditional care toward the less fortunate and challenges us to consider other possibilities.

Approximately sixteen minutes into the film the kids enter the utility room and shut off the power to the entire motel. Broadly speaking, the sequence that follows is a repetition of the opening one, in which Bobby had to intercede after the kids spit all over a car in a neighboring motel. This sequence includes two arresting long takes that epitomize the two viewing positions the film constructs for the audience. The first one is a tableau-like long shot that offers an "objective" view of nearly the entire motel. The second is a Steadicam shot that follows Bobby back to the office. The former, like other similar shots in the film, generates a distant and contemplative attitude and directs our attention to the relationships between characters and space. It keeps spectators observational and allows them to wander over the frame as the kids, the guests, and Bobby compete for our attention. Overall, it emphasizes the notion of the motel as a space of isolation and social erasure for the destitute. The close framing circumscribes the world of these people to the contents of the frame, revealing in this way their social entrapment by suggesting that for them the world does not exist beyond the confines of the motel. The shot is a form of interpellation, a way of involving spectators in the story and implicating them in the social diagnosis of the situation. This said, it does not provide them with a specific way to interpret the action.

The latter could not be more different. It denotes a shift in perspective and in attitude toward the residents of the motel. By changing from an objective to a subjective configuration, Baker creates a perspective from which to interpret the episode, forcing spectators to make a different emotional investment. Once the power supply has been restored, the film cuts to a shot of Bobby as he goes back to the office. Baker follows Bobby in a medium, low-angle shot against the Florida sky that contrasts sharply with the previous static long shot. Compared with the preceding shot, this one is charged with subjectivity. Some residents make cracks about the power cut but the camera stays fixed on Bobby, never cutting to show the object of Bobby's look. Here the framing is open and spectators are impelled to actively participate in the composition. We are directed into making sense of the situation these people find themselves in through Bobby's reactions. Our perception passes through Bobby (we hear what Bobby hears and see his affable, slightly shy reactions), which prompts identification with his good nature and easygoing attitude. If the static long shot of the motel invited us to view the composition from an impersonal position, this one directs us into adopting Bobby's perspective and amiable attitude in our appraisal of the situation.

Then, as in the opening sequence, we see Bobby recriminating Halley for not watching over the kids. Up until this point Baker had offered an external perspective, rarely directing our attention to the act of looking and seizing the action and the personality of the characters without the expressivity and emotiveness of classical decoupage. However, now we get a glimpse of Bobby's inner feelings and the role he will play in the film as the character—other than the kids—through whom we are made to channel our emotions and reactions to the events.

For the most part, the scene alternates shots of the kids at bed-level and medium close-ups of Bobby and Halley in the doorway, but Baker avoids conventional shot/reverse shot arrangements. For most of the scene, he opts for over-the-shoulder staging, at all times the camera slightly behind Halley, thus foregrounding Bobby's gestures and facial expressions and making us identify with him. The first shots of the kids do not originate from a specific gaze, but, as the conversation progresses, these seem to be motivated by Bobby's glances and thus invested with his subjectivity. Toward the end of the conversation the narrative cuts to a medium two shot of Bobby and Halley facing each other. Then Bobby reminds Halley she has not paid the weekly rent yet, and, when Halley leaves the frame to produce the money, a subtle change of mood occurs. Bobby looks off-screen in the direction of the kids and his expression changes. This marks a subtle rupture with the prevailing objective configuration of the film and draws spectators into Bobby's emotional state. It establishes Bobby as a diegetic observer through whom the spectator makes sense of the situation. These subjective shots create a spectator defined by Bobby's scopic activity and by his compassionate attitude. Then we are given a clear eyeline match to the kids with Moonee in the center of the frame. When Moonee realizes Bobby is looking at her—an indirect way of acknowledging and calling attention to Bobby's gaze—she makes a nervous gesture and smiles at him. For a brief moment we share Bobby's point of view, we see what Bobby sees *and* the way he sees. Then Baker cuts to a medium close-up of Bobby's reaction. Moonee does not trigger the response everyone—Moonee included—might expect. Instead of some sign of affection or shared complicity, Bobby's expression reveals unease and concern. Eyelids half-shut and mouth closed, Bobby exhales through the nose as the muscles around his cheekbones tighten and his shoulders drop. For a moment, we are allowed into Bobby's head. Even his attitude and his tone of voice change. Bobby's reaction suggests he is genuinely concerned about what will become of Halley and Moonee.

This scene is illustrative of the way the film organizes the emotional involvement of the audience, first by presenting events objectively however distasteful these might be, and then by establishing Bobby as a diegetic observer and inviting us to assume his position toward the events. Brief as these moments are, they break the film's apparent objectivity. Little by little, these shifts to an affectively charged configuration determine the way we access the action and circumscribe the way we position ourselves in relation to the story. Broadly speaking, this pattern is repeated when Bobby helps Halley get a room in a contiguous motel. For most of the sequence the action unfolds objectively, keeping spectators observational, but toward the end of the sequence we are made to see Halley's situation through Bobby's eyes.

The sequence starts with long takes of the characters as they vacate Halley's room. Again, we see the action unfold from a distance, without specific indications as to how the scene is to be interpreted other than what the characters do and say. Once more, Halley comes across as selfish and infantile, complaining about the motel's policy and reluctantly moving her stuff to another room. Afterward, when she is refused a room at the usual rate, Bobby literally runs to the rescue. He tries to talk the new manager into sticking to the deal they had with the previous owner but she refuses. Then Bobby turns to look at Halley and Moonee. There is a match on action to a shallow-focus extreme close-up on Bobby looking off-screen. This is not followed by an eyeline match. Instead, the camera remains fixed on Bobby's face, showing his emotionally charged reaction. The tight framing disrupts the objective configuration of the sequence, drawing us into Bobby's caring and sympathetic attitude. By putting the emphasis on Bobby's reaction once more, we are required to see the situation the way he sees it. Here, Bobby shows the same expression of concern as in the scene described above. Halley's attitude does not make things easy for the people around her, particularly Bobby. When she is refused a room a second time she empties a soda can on the floor of the motel reception and leaves. At this point Baker focuses on Bobby again. Shot in medium close-up, his mouth in a small gape, the camera stays on Bobby as he follows Halley with his stunned look. Match on action to a medium shot of Bobby, who stands baffled and speechless. Again, it is Bobby's attitude that offers an emotional route through the unsettling events in the film.

The allure and the power of *The Florida Project* resides in the kind of engagement this viewing position demands from the spectator. While never forgetting that actual spectators may deploy other ways of seeing and making sense of the events, it should be noted that there are certain responses built in a film that may be activated in a given context. By foregrounding Bobby's point of view, the film prevents us from standing on the sidelines regarding issues pertaining to inequality. *The Florida Project* requires the spectator to identify with him and see Halley the way he sees her—regardless of her insufferable behavior—and compels spectators to think about their small privileges and about their responsibilities to others. That is, by foregrounding Bobby's point of view (his gaze as well as his reactions), the film challenges us to make sense of inequality in ways other than the prevailing notion that poverty is a cultural choice or a moral failing. Near the end of the film, Baker lends us a hand with this by showing an unknown facet of Halley once she realizes that she will inevitably lose custody of Moonee.

As a way of rounding off my analysis, I wish to focus on the changes in visual grammar and mood after the social services come to evaluate Moonee's situation. In the last part of the film, changes in framing also force us to reconsider our perception of Halley. As previously stated, Baker eschews close framings and point-of-view shots. Only occasionally do the kids and Bobby get a close-up. However, the day after the social services come to the motel the film makes a stylistic shift. We see Ashley (Mela Murder) leaving for work. It is raining heavily. The film cuts to a reverse shot that reveals we are seeing the action through Halley's eyes from the balcony above. Then, cut to Ashley again as she slows down her pace and looks at Halley. This signals a change to a more traditional decoupage that requires us to enter the story world through Halley's eyes, thus encouraging identification with her. These shots also indicate a shift in the mood of the narrative, signaling a turning point in the story. The pace has been relaxed; the heavy rain desaturates the film's garish colors and gives the scene a dense texture. What is more, in two consecutive shots, the camera lingers on Halley's brooding expression. Then Halley takes Moonee to play outside. The camera follows mother and daughter as they run and hug and laugh. The scene has a spontaneous, carefree quality, capturing the energy, the excitement, and the sadness of the moment with a startling poetic sensibility. In the last shot Moonee runs out of the frame and, for a fleeting moment, the camera focuses on Halley. The laughter is indistinguishable from the tears and we can feel her trepidation at losing Moonee. Then she puts herself together and the mood changes again. Halley turns cleaning the room into a game and we are made to see the positive side of her impulsive personality, as if she wanted Moonee to always remember her like this: cheerful, affectionate, and serene. Toward the end of the scene Baker gives us a medium close-up of Halley looking at Moonee off-screen. This attests to the change in the way Halley is now portrayed. Close-ups, says Béla Balázs, "radiate a tender human attitude . . . a warm sensibility" and reveal "what is really happening under the surface of appearances" (1985, 256). And so it is here. As the film comes to an end, Baker breaks the distance between the audience and Halley. The subjective configuration creates a different kind of spectator, one who can identify with Halley through being given access to her inner world.

When Halley sneaks Moonee into the complimentary breakfast buffet of a nearby upscale hotel, Baker makes a bolder stylistic shift. The scene opens in a manner similar to previous episodes—long shots, deep focus, and documentary-style Steadicam shots—thus creating a distance between the story and the spectator, who is constructed as a detached witness. Once inside the dining room Baker uses a series of subtle jump cuts to edit together a succession of static extreme close-ups of Moonee in shallow focus. Then, he cuts to a close-up of Halley that reveals we are watching Moonee from her point of view. How we read Halley's feelings is determined by Moonee's disarmingly sweet reactions to the experience of eating at a hotel breakfast buffet. Again, we are aligned with Halley's gaze and with her feelings, which offer a different perspective from which to make sense of her situation. Here, Bria Vinaite's performance is more relaxed and her expression has a gravity that was lacking before. We are made to adopt her perspective *and* her attitude. Empathy comes from looking at Halley react to Moonee with serenity, concern, and love. Now that the film is drawing to an end, Baker challenges spectators to reconsider their assumptions about Halley. To borrow, again, Balázs's expression (1985, 257), these close-ups "[strip] the veil of our imperceptiveness and insensitivity." Focus on Halley's gaze and her reactions inflates emotional attachment toward her and thus breaks the distance the narrative had previously established between the events and the spectators.

These scenes are illustrative of the way *The Florida Project* organizes the emotional involvement of the viewers, but Baker's stylistic choices take on a much more significant meaning if placed within a historical context characterized by two processes: the reconceptualization of society from the perspective of the market, which is pushing more and more workers into poverty, and the emergence of an affective regime that allows people to feel good about their anger and their resentment toward vulnerable populations. By placing the narrative organization and the configuration of the gaze in this historically contingent context, *The Florida Project* challenges spectators to make sense of inequality in ways other than the commonsensical notion that poverty is a cultural choice or a moral failing and that, therefore, nothing justifies a compassionate attitude toward the poor. Although there are further questions to consider in regard to Bobby's look—most notably questions of gender and power hierarchies—I want to register the fact that *The Florida Project* requires that we align ourselves with the poor and understand why they behave the way they do, and this is revolutionary. I began this chapter with a story that demonstrates how Trump binds ordinary people's emotions to the political project of neoliberalism. Then I examined how *The Florida Project* mobilizes a different mode of affectivity, destabilizes the apparent inevitability of a social formation subordinated to market values, and challenges us to think collectively and to contemplate a different way of being in the world, one informed by empathy, selflessness, and unconditional commitment to social justice.

References

Balázs, B. (1985), "The Close-Up," in G. Mast and M. Cohen (eds.), *Film Theory and Criticism: Introductory Readings*, 3rd ed., Oxford: Oxford University Press, pp. 255–7. First published in 1952.
Bordwell, D. (2006), *The Way Hollywood Tells It: Story and Style in Modern Movies*, Berkeley: University of California Press.
Bourdieu, P. (1986), *Distinction: A Social Critique of the Judgement of Taste*, London: Routledge.
Grossberg, L. (1997), *Dancing in Spite of Myself: Essays on Popular Culture*, Durham and London: Duke University Press.
Grossberg, L. (2010), "Affect's Future: Rediscovering the Virtual in the Actual," in M. Gregg and G. J. Seigworth (eds.), *The Affect Theory Reader*, Durham and London: Duke University Press, pp. 309–38.
Grossberg, L. (2018), *Under the Cover of Chaos: Trump and the Battle for the American Right*, London: Pluto Press.
Hage, G. (2000), *White Nation: Fantasies of White Supremacy in a Multicultural Society*, New York and London: Routledge.
Harrington, M. (2012), *The Other America: Poverty in the United States*, 50th Anniversary ed., New York and London: Scribner. First Published in 1962.
Hedges, C. (2010), *Death of the Liberal Class*, New York: Nation Books.
Hochschild, A. R. (2016), *Strangers in Their Own Land: Anger and Mourning in the American Right*, New York and London: The New Press.
Horsley, S. (2018), "President Trump Turns Attention to Welfare Programs," *NPR*, 10 April. Available online: https://text.npr.org/601332980.
James, D. E. (1996), "Introduction: Is There Class in This Text?," in D. E. James and R. Berg (eds.), *The Hidden Foundation: Cinema and the Question of Class*, Minneapolis and London: University of Minnesota Press, pp. 1–25.
King, Jr., M. L. (1965), "Our God Is Marching On!," in *The Martin Luther King, Jr. Research and Education Institute*, Stanford. Available online: https://kinginstitute.stanford.edu/our-god-marching.

Myerson, J. A. (2017), "Trumpism: It's Coming from the Suburbs. Racism, Fascism, and Working-class Americans," *The Nation*, 8 May. Available online: https://www.thenation.com/article/archive/trumpism-its-coming-from-the-suburbs/.

Nakhnikian, E. (2017), "Interview: Sean Baker on Making *The Florida Project*," *Slant*, 25 October. Available online: https://www.slantmagazine.com/film/interview-sean-baker-on-making-the-florida-project/.

Nystrom, D. (2009), *Hard Hats, Rednecks and Macho Men: Class in 1970s American Cinema*, Oxford and New York: Oxford University Press.

Parrott, S. et al (2013), "Comparison of Benefits for Poor Families to Middle-Class Incomes Is Deeply Flawed," *Center on Budget and Policy Priorities*, 25 February Available online: https://www.cbpp.org/research/comparison-of-benefits-for-poor-families-to-middle-class-incomes-is-deeply-flawed.

Patton, D. (2014), "Poverty Is Not Inevitable: What We Can Do to Turn Things Around," *Yes!*, 21 August. Available online: https://www.yesmagazine.org/issue/poverty/2014/08/21/why-poverty-is-not-inevitable.

Perez, A. and D. Sirota (2021), "Ronald Reagan's 'Welfare Queen' Lie Has Been Resurrected," *Jacobin*, 14 May. Available online: https://jacobinmag.com/2021/05/gop-unemployment-covid-reagan-welfare-queen.

"Poor People's Moral Budget: Everybody Has the Right to Live," (2020), *Poor People's Campaign: A National Call for Moral Revival*, 15 June. Available online: https://www.poorpeoplescampaign.org/resource/poor-peoples-moral-budget/.

Williams, L. (2001), *Playing the Race Card: Melodramas of Black and White from Uncle Tom to O. J. Simpson*, Princeton and Oxford: Princeton University Press.

PART VI

Ecological Crisis and Visions of the Future

14

Who the Earth Is For

Reframing Rural Landscapes as Collective Polities in *Leave No Trace* and *Beasts of the Southern Wild*

Tim Lindemann

Introduction

In the past decade, roughly spanning from the aftermath of the 2008 financial crisis to the beginning of the Covid-19 pandemic, rural poverty and deep poverty rates in the United States have dramatically risen. The impact of the pandemic is set to considerably intensify these inequalities as the decades of neoliberal dismantling of public healthcare and other social institutions leave inhabitants of impoverished rural areas particularly vulnerable. Even before the pandemic, representations of rural landscape in US cinema have sought to spatially visualize the country's economic, ecological, and political crises under neoliberal capitalism. Disaster films and post-apocalyptic fantasies such as *The Road* (John Hillcoat 2009) and *The Book of Eli* (Albert Hughes and Allen Hughes 2010), for example, dramatize ecological catastrophes and imagine US rurality of the near future as a barren wasteland dominated by violent gangs fighting for resources. These visions are lacking in substance, however. Landscape in these films mainly serves as disembodied space, as a scenery to the protagonists' heroic journeys. Rural America here is, as Moya and Lopez summarize, a "dismal territory where negotiations about individual and social identity are reduced to a fight for power and domination" (2017).

In this chapter, I will argue that there exists an opposed trend in recent US cinema that similarly identifies rural landscape as a site of economic, ecological, and political crises, yet cultivates a more progressive, interactive understanding of landscape. I will focus on two films which, while stylistically and geographically diverse, display a common interest in landscape as place as opposed to space or, put another way, as a "milieu of involvement" (Wylie 2007, 161) as opposed to mere scenery: *Beasts of the Southern Wild* (Benh Zeitlin 2012) and *Leave No Trace* (Debra Granik 2018). Both films feature protagonists threatened by displacement in marginal rural landscapes and focus on their integration into alternative rural communities existing in close entanglement with their surroundings. Landscape emerges here as a primarily social category that carries with it the potential of countering neoliberal mechanisms of oppression, atomization, and marginalization through solidarity and cooperation.

Each film relies on what Hayden Lorimer has termed "embodied acts of landscaping" (2005, 85) in their construction of landscape that stands in opposition to an understanding of landscape as scenery. Such an understanding is inherently reactionary because it gives rise to ideologies "in which nature determines culture" (Olwig 2019, 15) and which thus tend to breed prohibitive, even fascist landscape concepts and policies. Ultimately, a scenic understanding of landscape, as Kenneth Olwig argues, negates "the socially defined place of people in the political landscape" (2002, 220). It works in concert with neoliberal capitalism's rationalization of the world which extends "economic values . . . to every dimension of human life" (Brown 2015, 30) and thus continuously privatizes and exploits formerly common places. The films discussed here, however, chime with Tim Ingold's concept of landscape which reveals that landscape arises through the process of human habitation and that "at its most intense, the boundaries between person and place, or between self and the landscape, dissolve altogether" (2000, 56). It is in these intense moments of dissolution that the films develop their claim for landscape as a fundamentally social, interactive category as opposed to the "subjectless structure of visual representation" (Olwig 2002, 220) inherent to scenic landscape.

I will show how this embodied approach to cinematic landscape is directly linked to the films' reimagining of the political landscape. They construct their rural communities to advocate a return to landscape as polity—a social, communal concept—and by extension as a contestation of, as Wendy Brown writes, "neoliberalism's hollowing out of contemporary liberal democracy and its imperiling of more radical democratic imaginaries" (2015, 18). I rely here on Kenneth Olwig's tracing of landscape to its original Germanic root (*Landschaft*), which, as he argues, historically carries meanings of polity, custom, and law. This shift "from a definition of landscape as scenery to a notion of landscape as polity and place" (Olwig 2005, 293) is, as I shall argue, what marks these films as progressive approaches to landscape in US cinema, responding to a sense of overwhelming crisis with a decisive call to rebuild local communities.

Leave No Trace—The Warmth of the Hive

Leave No Trace is based on Peter Rock's novel *My Abandonment* (2009), which in turn is influenced by a 2004 article by journalist Maxine Bernstein describing the real-life story of a father and his daughter who lived "off the grid" for four years in Oregon's Forest Park. Debra Granik's film recounts their fictionalized journey from initial removal from the park by social services to a temporary home on a Christmas tree farm and finally to an RV (recreational vehicle) park in the woods of Washington State. The plot is driven by the tension between the father Will's (Ben Foster) inability to live in social surroundings due to his war-related PTSD and his thirteen-year-old daughter Tom's (Thomasin McKenzie) growing desire to belong to a community. While Will and Tom care for each other throughout their journey, the film ends with their agreed separation: Tom remains with the solidary community of marginalized outsiders in the RV park, while the deeply traumatized Will ventures once again into the wilderness.

The film's very first images construct Forest Park as an untouched, Edenic wilderness: they deploy saturated, radiant shades of green and low-angle shots of majestic trees that dwarf the two protagonists in comparison. These aesthetically pleasing opening moments appear to gesture toward the American wilderness ideal, the foundational principle of the natural preservation movement and therefore the origin of spaces such as Forest Park. National and municipal parks like these reveal, as Olwig argues, "conflicting American attitudes towards landscape and country" (2002, 212). Nineteenth-century transcendentalists and environmentalists saw America's "wild" nature as the key to the young nation's development and consequently found the "visionary solution to . . . preserve the elixir of wildness by emparking some of it as a place where the nation could re-create its natural potentiality" (Olwig 2002, 188). The prominent use of such an ideologically charged space as the film's opening setting thus already suggests a larger political context.

The following scenes introduce Will and Tom's everyday life in the park and simultaneously signal the film's affinity to an understanding of landscape that Tim Ingold has termed the "dwelling perspective." According to this anthropological approach landscape emerges "with its properties alongside the emergence of the perceiver as person, against the backdrop of involved activity" (Ingold 2000, 168). It thus stands in contrast to a scenic idea of landscape as nature with culture "layered on top" (Olwig 2002, 225) and instead foregrounds, as geographers Cloke and Jones describe it, the "ongoing togetherness of beings and things which make up landscapes and places . . . [which] bind together nature and culture over time" (2001, 651). Ingold summarizes that "it is through being inhabited that the world becomes a meaningful environment" (2000, 173). This notion is acutely felt in the scenes depicting Will and Tom's "home" in the park: their everyday tasks shape their surroundings into a "meaningful environment" and, vice versa, their behavior is influenced by the forest surrounding them. They have, for example, installed a makeshift shower in a tree and stashed their important documents in a trapdoor hidden in the ground. It is this detailed focus on such "embodied acts of landscaping" (Lorimer 2005, 85), the interaction between bodies and environment that characterizes the film's approach throughout.

This fragile idyll is, however, abruptly ended when father and daughter are forcefully removed from the park grounds by the police and temporally placed in a care home. The displacement is not presented as entirely unjustified as the police are accompanied by a social worker (Dana Millican) who seems genuinely worried about Tom's well-being. Nevertheless, the film raises questions here that address the foundational idea of America's parks as a "natural commons for the country" (Olwig 2002, 212) as well as more general concerns regarding landscape and marginalization under capitalism. Will and Tom's removal lays bare the inherent problem that the preservation of a "natural commons" for the nation results in its strict policing and raises the question of who is excluded from it. According to this logic, as Olwig observes, "the only way of preserving the wild elixir of the American nation is to preserve the wild *from* the American people, not to empark it *for* the American people" (2002, 203).

The film illustrates that it is vulnerable people like the protagonists and the inhabitants of a nearby camp of homeless veterans who suffer from this restrictive concept of landscape which results in "the need to use force to protect nature from the common people" (Olwig 2002, 205). As a spatial, symbolic manifestation of US nationalism and the underlying wilderness ideal, the park repels the affective, bodily engagement Tom and Will have afforded to make it their home. Instead, the film renders visible the hegemonic "power to define what a landscape is, what it means, who belongs to it and who belongs in it" (Mitchell 2005, 53). In doing so, it calls to mind how spaces like Forest Park look back on a long history of exclusion and erasure of unwanted inhabitants as "the framing of the American national park as nature was used to obliterate the memory of earlier cultures and their marks on the land" (Olwig 2002, 206), particularly Native American cultures.

The film's title begins to take on a sinister implication here that expresses a nationalist tendency to purify the scenery of American wilderness from unwanted intruders by erasing the traces of their acts of landscaping. How, then, does the film contrast this prohibitive concept of landscape with the involved environment of the RV park, its final setting?

The trailer or RV park as a space has a fraught, ambiguous history in the United States that feeds into the film's central tension between individualism and community. Considering the countless dubious depictions of trailer parks in US film and television which harness negative stereotypes, one might not necessarily expect such a space to challenge a hegemonic interpretation of landscape. Yet, the RV park in *Leave No Trace* indeed chimes with Olwig's notion of an original, lost meaning of landscape "in the sense of polity and place" (2002, 214). Olwig argues that landscape or rather its Germanic origin *Landschaft* referred not, as many common definitions would have it, to an image, map, or representation of the environment but to an independent political community, or polity, in Renaissance Northern Europe.

This kind of polity "had a representative body, a body of living bodies. This body gave a common legal form to the customs of the landscape polity" (Olwig 2002, 214). These customs did not "simply represent an abstract identification of space" but were based on "individual and social practice. These practices were woven into the very fabric and texture of the land" (Olwig 2002, 215). Here, the connections to Ingold's "dwelling perspective" and Lorimer's "embodied acts of landscaping" become visible: it is through these customary, bodily acts and customary laws that the polity or *Landschaft* defined itself. Therefore, the *Landschaft* was founded on law and not on supposed bonds of blood that are based on the restrictive idea that "only 'native' people or species belong naturally to a particular area of land" (Olwig 2002, 226). Eventually, however, landscape was "emptied of its place-bound meaning and came to refer to the make-believe space of scenery" (Olwig 2002, 216) that went along with the incorporation of the independent *Landschaften* into the body politic of kingdoms and nations. The original meaning of bodily interaction, custom, and political community was gradually lost.

The film constructs the RV park as such a *Landschaft*, a "milieu of engagement and involvement" (Wylie 2007, 149) through its set design and mise-en-scène. Unlike the alienated environment of the tree farm where Tom and Will are temporarily housed by social services, the trailer park with its tree-lined paths and small clearings with chairs and fire places speaks of a nonconformist community that has indeed woven its social practices into the fabric of its surrounding. If, as Ingold argues, a place "owes its character to the experiences it affords to those who spend time there" (2000, 155), this environment appears as an economically marginalized, but undoubtedly hospitable, place to Tom and Will. In fact, the almost unreserved, radical hospitality that the RV park's owner Dale (Dale Dickey) affords to Will and

Tom after she learns of their predicament further qualifies it as a "world to live in" (Wiley 2007, 149), and to live in collectively as a polity. Not only does Dale initially refuse to take rent from them, the film's ending suggests that even though Will has left the community for the forest, she is still providing him with groceries.

This focus on collectiveness and environmental entanglement is most pointedly underlined in the film's employment of a beehive as a central visual motive. Tom's encounter with the bees occurs on her first morning in the trailer park. As she walks down one of the paths, she meets an older woman tending the hives. Noting the girl's interested gaze, the woman, identified as Susan (Susan Chernak McElroy) in the credits, invites Tom to open the hive. As she pulls the protective suit over Tom's head, she explains: "When I open this, the bees are gonna come up. But they're not coming out to hurt you." The film then cuts to a close-up of the hive and the swarming bees inside. A ray of sunlight on the right side of the frame conveys warmth and highlights the earthy brown color of the hive, thus supporting Susan's insistence on the bees' inherent peacefulness. She goes on: "It's kinda nice to have the trust of a whole box of creatures that have the power to come out and kill you if they wanted to." She then proceeds to drop some of the bees onto Tom's outstretched gloved hands, establishing a connection between her, Tom, and the bees.

This is an instance in which "boundaries between person and place, or between self and the landscape, dissolve altogether" (Ingold 2000, 56). It suggests an intense, interactive connection to the environment, a landscape denoted by custom and everyday activity as well as the promise of communal cooperation. The significance of the bees as a form of animal collective serves as an analogy to Tom's sense of belonging to the RV park's community. This is reaffirmed in a later scene in which Tom introduces her father to the beehive and attempts to convince him of the merits of the trailer park's community as she becomes aware of his desire to leave for the woods again. Tom herself, not just the film on a subtextual level, thus makes use of the bees as a metaphor for the RV park as a compromise between her wish for community and her father's impulse to leave society behind. "If you put your hand over it, you can feel the warmth of the hive," she explains to him. Again, the beehive is associated with warmth and safety and emerges as a powerful metaphor for the benefits of collectivism in the face of marginalization.

The film thus confronts the compound of scenic landscape and individualism that is arguably ingrained in US cinema since the emergence of the Western genre. Thereby, it touches upon one of the central tenets of neoliberal ideology: its "opposition to anything that smacks of collectivism or economic redistribution" (Braedley and Luxton 2010, 7–8). By reimagining landscape as the place of a polity emerging from embodied acts of landscaping and held together by a law of radical hospitality and solidarity, it offers an alternative to neoliberalism's dismantling of spaces which facilitate, as Wendy Brown argues, "deliberate constructions of existence through democratic discussion, law, policy" (2015, 221–2).

The film's vision of community has faced criticism, however, for its notable racial uniformity. For example, Karen Wells observes that

> *Leave No Trace* . . . uses the wandering of the main protagonists to show the viewer the deep poverty of the contemporary, rural working-class US. This landscape barely features any black or Latinx people, and there are no central black or Latinx characters. The affect is to create an almost ethnographic account of white rural working-class life and sociality devoid of any of the lines of connection or border crossings that one would anticipate in a country as diverse and large as the United States. (2020, 123)

This exclusive whiteness seemingly complicates the trailer park community's hospitality and raises the question why the film excludes people of color from its polity especially considering rural poverty rates remain "highest among racial/ethnic minority groups" (USDA 2018, 5).

The film is, however, far from supporting such an exclusion and, on the contrary, concedes the limited utopian potential of community in a country that has a long history of spatially segregated rural communities "rooted in a national racial geography" (Singh 2005, 7). The film instead focuses on the ways the rural poor actually cope with marginalization and, furthermore, displays a clear regional specificity that accounts for its relative racial uniformity.[1] As Daniel Lichter argues, while rural America "has been home throughout its history of racial and ethnic minorities . . . rural minorities are spatially segregated and invisible in ways not usually found in America's metropolitan areas" (2012, 2). The presence of people of color outside of the RV park—for example in the foster home and the group of prisoners early on in the film—suggests the film is very much aware of the specific racialized experience of (rural) marginalization. As such, it reflects the reality of poor rural communities existing in the United States' racialized geography. The absence of diversity in the RV park can thus be read as the community's inability—in spite of its integrative character—to overcome the hegemonic geography which separates the victims of America's neoliberal crises along racial lines; yet it also draws attention to the existence of these lines and the atomizing experience of rural poverty.

Beasts of the Southern Wild—The Prettiest Place on Earth

Beasts of the Southern Wild is set on a Louisiana peninsula dubbed the "Bathtub" by its multiracial inhabitants. It follows a six-year-old Black girl named Hushpuppy (Quvenzhané Wallis) who lives with her alcoholic and, as is revealed later, terminally ill single father Wink (Dwight Henry). The film's plot, based on the play *Juicy and Delicious* (2012) by Lucy Alibar, who also co-wrote the screenplay, revolves around the arrival of a tremendous storm that causes flooding of the peninsula. This runs in parallels with the film's main speculative element: the reawakening of a fierce pack of extinct aurochs caused by the melting of the polar ice caps. Wink and some of the other inhabitants of the tight-knit community blow up the levee that separates the Bathtub from the main land, referred to as the Dry Side, in order to drain the salt water ruining their crops. In response, they are forcefully evacuated by federal agents and brought to a hospital. Eventually, Hushpuppy, Wink, and the other residents of the Bathtub escape and return to their home. There, Hushpuppy confronts the arriving aurochs and Wink dies of his unspecified illness. In the film's final images, Hushpuppy leads the remaining inhabitants of the Bathtub in what could be understood as either a funeral or a revolutionary procession.

There are some obvious narrative parallels between *Beasts* and *Leave No Trace* such as the focus on a complicated father-daughter relationship, an absent mother, and the forced evacuation of the main characters from their secluded home by agents of the state. Both films interweave a coming-of-age narrative with more general reflections on inequality and poverty in the rural United States and are loosely based on real events.[2] More importantly, however, they display *opposed* narrative structures in terms of their (de-)construction of community: where *Leave No Trace* can be read as Tom's journey toward her integration into a caring, collective polity, *Beasts* describes the dissolution of a similar community by ecological devastation and neoliberal marginalization. In other words, Zeitlin's film in its opening minutes showcases and then goes on to disassemble a social landscape or *Landschaft* that *Leave No Trace* conversely posits as the destination of its female protagonist.

Beasts begins by portraying its setting as both economically and ecologically precarious while at the same time presenting its community as inextricably embedded within the environment. Thus, while the landscape can be described, as Maclear does, as an "anarchic place of car scrap and driftwood, feral animals and driftwood shacks" (2018, 603), it also emerges as a "milieu of involvement" (Wylie 2007, 161) in the sense of practices and customs being "woven into the very fabric and texture of the land" (Olwig 2002, 215). Undoubtedly, the film emits a sense of insecurity and instability from its very beginning. The first image, for example, shows Hushpuppy's small hut that rests precariously on stilts to protect it from flooding. There are holes in the walls, the cladding hangs partially off the roof, and the windows are provisionally covered with plastic film. The trees in the background shake violently from an approaching storm. The image immediately conveys poverty, marginality, and a sense of threat.

However, the film goes on to counter these impoverished living conditions with a strong sense of community and collectiveness that to a certain degree transcends the misery in the Bathtub. By heightening the spectacular Louisiana landscape through grainy 16-millimeter footage, intense colors, carnivalesque set design, and a melodious score, the film bestows an otherworldly quality to its setting. Many critics regard this striking mise-en-scène as an emulation of Hushpuppy's childlike perspective on her world. I suggest a more collective understanding, however. As in *Leave No Trace*'s construction of the RV park, the Bathtub is characterized here as a landscape that arises through the interaction of its human and nonhuman inhabitants with the environment. Especially the opening montage revels in moments in which the "boundaries between person and place, or between self and the landscape, dissolve altogether" (Ingold 2000, 56). Here, the film cuts with increasing frequency between partying Bathtub residents of different ages and races played by local nonprofessional actors. The camera moves shakily, or drunkenly, and often comes very close to the dancing, singing, and drinking characters while a raucous Cajun folk tune plays in the background. The viewer is thus visually and aurally immersed in the community's festivities.

In concert with the beginning of the film's dramatic main theme, the film cuts to overexposed images of Hushpuppy, Wink, and other Bathtub residents running through the night holding burning roman candles, visually blending in with their surroundings. Hushpuppy then delivers the final line of the voice-over before the display of the title card: "But me and my daddy, we stay right here. We is who the earth is for." With this defiant line, the score crescendos into its leitmotif that accompanies the images of eccentrically dressed Bathtub residents celebrating and rejoicing on a clearing lit by colorful fairy lights. The immersive quality of this opening montage demonstrates the film's "vision of ecological interconnectedness," as Sarah McFarlan argues (2019), in that it effectively conveys the bodily, emotional relation between inhabitants and the environment. One is reminded of Christopher Tilley's definition of landscape as "embodied sets of relationships between places, a structure of human feeling, emotion, dwelling, movement and practical activity" (2004, 25), all of which are on display in the communal cooking, fishing, playing, and dancing of the Bathtub's inhabitants. The joyfulness of the opening montage is as crucial as the visible hardship in understanding how the landscape "as a physical place [is] the manifestation of the polity's local custom" (Olwig 2002, 214).

Furthermore, the film's opening conveys a palpable sense of communal solidarity, specifically among "people lacking resources who are the principal casualties" (Nixon 2013, 2) of the climate crisis. Nixon has termed the effects of such ecological crises "slow violence": "a violence of delayed destruction that is dispersed across time and space, an attritional violence that is typically not viewed as violence at all" (2013, 2). As the community's home and livelihood are in constant danger of sinking into the ocean, *Beasts* emerges as an attempt to find images that visualize these delayed effects on society's most vulnerable communities as well as to highlight possible modes of subaltern resistance. Crucially, the solidarity and eco-activism portrayed here transcend racial difference. Considering the history of slavery omnipresent within the rural landscape of the US South, the film positions itself on the border of postcolonial and environmental concerns and presents its multiracial community as a symbol of a collective, intersectional environmentalism of the poor.

The landscape aesthetic that oscillates between the opposed imageries of social realism and speculative film genres such as fantasy is crucial to this intersectional approach. It contrasts heightened mise-en-scène elements such as Wink's boat build from the rear of an old truck and, most prominently, the monstrous aurochs with more somber, almost documentarian scenes such as the reoccurring aerial shots that adopt the impersonal aesthetic of TV news footage. This invasion of speculative elements into a naturalist setting, first, chimes with Greve and Zappe's argument that speculative genres since the 1960s "can be read as reflections of the creeping awareness of fundamental ecological and geological crises" (2019, 3). This applies especially to films that employ a childlike perspective. The aurochs as an extinct species and their release from melting polar ice caps underline the ecocritical connotation of the film's fantasy elements even further.

Second, the blurring of boundaries between realism and fantasy can be seen as an attempt to tap into a tradition of African American art that grants its disenfranchised Black protagonists agency in their construction of rural landscape. Rural America, as argued before, is haunted by its history of racism and slavery. There is, however, a Black literary tradition that is invested in "altering the conventional images of place that link black environments with low social status and spiritual despair" (Dixon 1987, 2), on which Melvin Dixon focuses in his study of Black perspectives on American rurality. African American art, he argues, "is replete with . . . spatial images that invert these assumptions about place and endow language with the power to reinvent geography and identity" (1987, 2). Dixon further argues that "Afro-American writers, often . . . segregated in negative environments, have used language to create alternative landscapes where black culture and identity can flourish apart from any marginal, prescribed 'place'" (1987, 2). This utopian argument calls to mind Wink's description of the Bathtub as "the prettiest place on Earth" in spite of its obvious disintegration.

Therefore, the film's fantastical disposition is essential in its aim to create an alternative landscape that radically subverts negative assumptions about Black rural poverty and its prescribed spaces. It is a way of, as Silvia Federici describes it, "re-enchanting the world" (2019, 8) and refuting a purely rational view of landscape as favored by neoliberal capitalism. At the same time, it serves to visualize and dramatize the "attritional violence" of the climate crisis and therefore functions as a stylistic binding agent between postcolonial and ecocritical landscape visions. *Beasts* thus effectively imagines how a rural community faced with poverty, displacement, and ecological threat can resist these oppressive forces through collectivism, solidarity, and close interconnectedness with their environment.

Conclusion

While both films construct their respective landscapes or *Landschaften* as products of collectivism and bodily interaction with the environment, they do so with varying effectiveness. In contrast to *Leave No Trace*, *Beasts* does not always manage to reconcile its fictional landscape with real issues surrounding rural poverty, race, and neoliberalism in the United States. For example, *Beast*'s approach has been sharply criticized by Black feminist scholars who consider the film's multiracial utopia naïve at best. Both Christina Sharpe and bell hooks do not accept the film's attempt to transcend the Bathtub's misery by creating an alternative landscape. Sharpe argues that "at least part of the disaster on view here is everyday black life lived in the wake of slavery and neither this film nor many of its viewers actually account for that life as disastrous" (2013). Therefore, she concludes, the film's ecocritical message relies on the abuse of Black bodies "because how else could . . . violence, the violence of extreme poverty, flooding . . . be inspiring and not tragic" (2013). In her essay on the film, hooks argues that the attempt to reconcile postcolonial and ecocritical notions comes at the price of the "continuous physical and emotional violation of the body and being of a small six-year-old black girl" (2012). The film's attempt to create a post-nationalist utopian polity where "landscape ceases to be a vehicle for environmental determinism and nature fanaticism identified with race" (Olwig 2002, 226) is, from this perspective, inherently flawed.

In addition, the film's interest in designing a utopian alternative to neoliberal "disciplinary forms of government" (Lieber 2019, 185) is plagued by internal contradictions. Lieber argues that "the film repeatedly attempts to envision a space both imaginary and real . . . in which forms of life, which from the perspective of . . . capitalist political economy must appear as fundamentally wrong . . . can freely develop" (2019, 185). The problem is, he continues, that this rejection of coercion opens the film to accusations of "reaffirming dominant political and cultural value systems such as neoliberalism" (2019, 185). Particularly the visual contrast between the organic "milieu of involvement" of the Bathtub and the sterile, alienated environment of the hospital on the Dry Side suggests that the film is critical about the state's intervention into the Bathtub community's well-being.

Hence, its message at times comes close to "libertarian ideology and neoliberal demands to end the state's responsibility for the wellbeing of its citizens" (Lieber 2019, 189).

Leave No Trace not only offers a more convincing vision of collectivism and polity to replace neoliberal bureaucracy; it also allows for more complexity in its depiction of governmental intervention as the positive characterization of the social workers signifies. By contrast, *Beasts*' ending leaves its community in disarray on a crumbling stretch of land and seems to acknowledge the community's self-destructive denial of government aid "as a powerful form of agency and an outright disregard of the . . . capitalistic . . . factors that precipitate climate change" (McFarlane 2019, 70). Unlike *Leave No Trace*, *Beasts* thus builds on a romanticized vision of rural poverty, yet ultimately fails to imagine *either* a bold utopian vision *or* a more practical, realistic approach to everyday life in the face of ecological threat and deep poverty.

Despite these varying degrees of effectiveness, however, both films emerge as striking, novel contributions to a growing awareness of the fundamental crises caused by neoliberal capitalism in the United States and the role landscape plays both in its mechanisms of marginalization and its potential contestation. Their adherence to what Ingold has termed the "dwelling perspective" by relying so heavily on the notion of everyday activity and custom contains the possibility to rethink "land as polity and place" (Olwig 2002, 226). In the context of neoliberal reshaping of democracy "that has dismantled public institutions and political spaces . . . [and] alters the principle of 'inclusion for all'" (Brown 2015, 72), these films offer concrete examples of the effects of such policies and ways of circumventing them. Both films can be read as demands to "rebuild the fabric of communities destroyed by years of neoliberal assault" (Federeci 2019, 1) by focusing on everyday practices of local resistance.

Bradley and Luxton argue that one of neoliberal philosophy's main weaknesses is that it is based "on macro analyses and broad . . . economic arguments" and disregards "effects on differently located people, their motivations and social relations more generally" (2010, 11). A totalizing, scenic vision of landscape that obscures histories of displacement as well as local customs and social relations thus works in favor of neoliberalism's "governing rationality" (Brown 2015, 30). The cinematic construction of an inclusive "living land of people" (Olwig 2002, 220) based on custom and history, however, undertakes a fundamental rethinking of landscape as polity, a social, communal concept. It thus serves to disrupt a disembodied understanding of landscape as scenery in the service of racism, nationalism, and neoliberalism's overarching extension of economic values. Eventually, both films seek to further alternative, more democratic ways of thinking about human interaction with the environment.

Notes

1 The film's depiction of the RV park is visibly influenced by the director's previous film *Stray Dog* (2014), a documentary following Ron Hall, a Vietnam veteran living on a trailer park in southern Missouri. In this film, there is a similar sense of community and, notably, also a focus on Hall's multiethnic family.

2 Many see the film as a fictionalized version of the impact of devastating Hurricane Katrina that hit Louisiana in August 2005 and caused over 1,800 deaths. Zeitlin himself states that "the storm in the film and the issues with the storm are much more inspired by [2008 Hurricane] Gustav and current land-loss in south Louisiana and the levee issues around the Mississippi and salt water intrusion and the oil spill" (in Butman 2012).

References

Braedley, S. and M. Luxton (2010), "Competing Philosophies: Neoliberalism and the Challenges of Everyday Life," in S. Braedley and M. Luxton (eds.), *Neoliberalism and Everyday Life*, Montreal: McGill-Queen's University Press, pp. 3–22.

Brown, W. (2015), *Undoing the Demos: Neoliberalism's Stealth Revolution*, New York: Zone Books.

Butman, J. (2012), "'Beasts of the Southern Wild' Director: Louisiana Is a Dangerous Utopia," *The Atlantic*, 27 June. Available online: https://www.theatlantic.com/entertainment/archive/2012/06/beasts-of-the-southern-sild-director-louisiana-is-a-dangerous-utopia/259009/.

Cloke, P. and O. Jones (2001), "Dwelling, Place, and Landscape: An Orchard in Somerset," *Environment and Planning A: Economy and Space* 33 (4), pp. 649–66.

Dixon, M. (1987), *Ride Out the Wilderness: Geography and Identity in Afro-American Literature*, Champaign, IL: University of Illinois Press.

Federici, S. (2019), *Re-Enchanting the World: Feminism and the Politics of the Commons*, Oakland, CA: PM Press.

Greve, J. and F. Zappe (2019), "Introduction: Ecologies and Geographies of the Weird and the Fantastic," in J. Greve and F. Zappe (eds.), *Spaces and Fictions of the Weird and the Fantastic: Ecologies, Geographies, Oddities*, London: Palgrave Macmillan, pp. 1–12.

hooks, b. (2012), "No Love in the Wild," *New Black Man (in Exile)*, 6 September. Available online: https://www.newblackmandinexile.net/2012/09/bell-hooks-no-love-in-wild.html.

Ingold, T. (2000), *The Perception of the Environment: Essays on Livelihood, Dwelling and the Skill*, London: Routledge.

Lichter, D. (2012), "Immigration and the New Racial Diversity in Rural America," *Rural Sociology* 77 (1), pp. 3–35.

Lieber, M. (2019), "Spaces of Communal Misery: The Weird Post-Capitalism of *Beasts of the Southern Wild*," in J. Greve and F. Zappe (eds.), *Spaces and*

Fictions of the Weird and the Fantastic: Ecologies, Geographies, Oddities, London: Palgrave Macmillan, pp. 183–200.

Lorimer, H. (2005), "Cultural Geography: The Busyness of Being 'More-Than-Representational'," *Progress in Human Geography* 29 (1), pp. 83–94.

Maclear, K. (2018), "Something So Broken: Black Care in the Wake of *Beasts of the Southern Wild*," *ISLE: Interdisciplinary Studies in Literature and Environment* 25 (3), pp. 603–29.

McFarlan, S. (2019), "The Universe Unraveled: Swampy Embeddedness and Ecological Apocalypse in *Beasts of the Southern Wild*," in Z. Vernon (ed.), *Ecocriticism and the Future of Southern Studies*, Baton Rouge: LSU Press, pp. 66–84.

Mitchell, D. (2005), "Landscape," in D. Atkinson (ed.), *Cultural Geography*, London: I.B. Tauris, pp. 49–57.

Moya, A. and G. Lopez (2017), "Looking Back: Versions of the Post-Apocalypse in Contemporary North-American Cinema," *Film Criticism* 41 (1). Available online: https://quod.lib.umich.edu/f/fc/13761232.0041.102/--looking-back-versions-of-the-post- apocalypse-in-contemporary?rgn=main;view=fulltext.

Nixon, R. (2013), *Slow Violence and the Environmentalism of the Poor*, New York: Harvard University Press.

Olwig, K. (2002), *Landscape, Nature, and the Body Politic*, Madison: University of Wisconsin Press.

Olwig, K. (2005), "Editorial: Law, Polity, and the Changing Meaning of Landscape," *Landscape Research* 30 (3), pp. 293–98.

Olwig, K. (2019), *The Meanings of Landscape: Essays on Place, Space, Environment and Justice*, London: Routledge.

Sharpe, C. (2013), "Beasts of the Southern Wild—The Romance of Precarity I," *Social Text*, 27 September. Available online: https://socialtextjournal.org/beasts-of-thesouthern-wild-the- romance-of-precarity-i/.

Singh, N. (2005), *Black Is a Country: Race and the Unfinished Struggle for Democracy*, Cambridge, MA: Harvard University Press.

Tilley, C. (2004), *The Materiality of Stone: Explorations in Landscape Phenomenology*, Oxford: Berg Publishers.

United States Department of Agriculture, Economic Research Service (2018), *Rural America at a Glance*. Available online: https://www.ers.usda.gov/webdocs/publications/90556/eib200_brochureformat.pdf.

Wells, K. (2020), *Visual Cultures of Childhood*, London: Rowman & Littlefield Publishers.

Wylie, J. (2007), *Landscape*, London: Routledge.

15

Turning Over a New Leaf

Exploring Human-Tree Relationships in *The Lorax* and *Avatar*

Virginia Luzón-Aguado

Introduction

Cultural theory tends to analyze the power relations in our society critically, whether in terms of race, disability, class, gender, or sexual orientation. In this chapter, however, I will be focusing on the power asymmetries that ecocultural critical theory assesses (Ivakhiv 1997). In this field, the principles of ecology are applied to the study of cultural artifacts, among them the cinema. Ecocultural theory has not traditionally featured at the forefront of cultural studies because, as Moore (2017, 9) points out, the field has generally tilted "towards anthropocentrism and defines consumption as a powerful resistive movement that can confront power structures." Clearly, (excessive) consumption is profoundly at odds with the fundamental principles of ecology. As conceptualized by Button (in Brereton 2004, 12), ecology

has been defined as a set of beliefs and a concomitant lifestyle that stress the importance of respect for the earth and all its inhabitants, using only what resources are necessary and appropriate, acknowledging the rights of all forms of life and recognising that all that exists is part of one interconnected whole.

By adopting this definition as the broad basis for this chapter, I shall be exploring the ways in which ecological principles are dealt with in the context of two films in which trees play prominent parts, namely, *The Lorax* (Chris Renaud 2012) and *Avatar* (James Cameron 2009).

More specifically, I aim to refer to a number of interrelated issues, that is, whether trees are respected or abused, whether they are considered inherently valuable or simply treated as mere economic resources at our endless disposal, and whether their rights as nonhuman forms of life are respected. Throughout this analysis, I shall also be referring to certain cultural, political, and public health implications of the aforementioned issues.

Reading Films Ecocritically

Ecocultural theory critically assesses the ways in which nature is treated and represented in the broad cultural arena. It also involves the dissection of human/nonhuman relations and the fostering of alternative, nonexploitative forms of interaction since the key idea underpinning ecocriticism is that, in order to avoid total environmental catastrophe, anthropocentrism, or the ideology that upholds the hegemony of the human being (especially of a certain type) over the environment and all forms of nonhuman life, should be dismantled. Instead, we should substitute a biocentric ethics that regards the human being as simply one more component in an interconnected and interdependent chain of being (Leopold 1970, 240). In order to achieve this major objective, the development of both personal and collective forms of environmental ethics, as well as the adoption of greener lifestyles, is paramount. These individual actions, while essential, can only constitute the stepping-stones to a radical change in our relationship to the natural world in the era of the so-called Anthropocene. This would be tantamount to a revolution, or "that moment when a new set of relations takes hold within a different system" (Cazdyn 2007, 649), leading to a future in which not just everyone's but everything's rights (crucially the environment, and, for the purposes of this chapter, trees more specifically) are upheld (Touraine 2011, 164). With this objective in mind, some film scholars have carried out work from the perspective of animal rights (Ingram 2004; Sturgeon 2009; Mills 2010; Brereton 2015), but not so much attention has been placed on plants, aside from certain incursions into the eco-horror subgenre (Keetley and Tenga 2016). This piece of criticism therefore aims to make a small contribution to this yet-to-be-researched area in film studies.

Without a doubt, advocating plant rights has to this date proven to be controversial (Hall 2011; Marder 2013a; Wohlleben 2016; Macfarlane 2019). Today, nevertheless, an environmental ethics that encompasses animal rights is well established in Western societies, which has paved the way for the moral consideration of the nonanimal living elements present in our ecosystems. As Marder (2013b, 2) points out, it is necessary to rethink the status of plants not only as passive objects to be protected but also as active subjects to be respected. However, research shows that human beings do not identify with plants as readily as they may do with animals (Wandersee and Schussler, in Hall 2011, 5). Yet, humans literally depend on the existence of plants for their survival. Plants (especially non-farmed ones), meanwhile, are not so dependent on humans. Still, because of the current unequal power structures operating in the biosphere plants are frequently at the mercy of humans. The time has therefore come for the development of an ethics of kinship with all nonhuman forms of life and to put an end to the often unnecessary harm that is caused to plants and the ecosystems they inhabit.

Trees and Forests in Western Culture

In their extensive research on the topic, Harrison (1992), Hayman (2003), and Griffin (2011) have documented the beliefs and attitudes toward woodlands and trees in the Old World. They have evolved in deeply contradictory ways from the Neolithic, when Mother Nature was worshiped as a goddess and there existed no clear opposition between the forest and human civilization, until the present time, during which the ideology of utilitarianism that emerged in the Enlightenment period has firmly established itself. The shifting attitudes toward nature demonstrate that trees and woodlands represent intensely cultural phenomena. As Hayman (2003, 128) points out, "nature cannot exist for us outside of its particular human context, and a tree is never far from being a political issue." These changing social and political meanings have persisted in contemporary Western societies. Thus, anthropocentric utilitarianism has certainly survived, although it has more recently transformed itself into the "softer" ecomodernist dogma of sustainable development. In contrast, radical environmentalism questions mainstream environmental values and calls for an overhaul of the capitalistic ethos which operates in contemporary consumer societies.

Since approximately the 1960s, environmentalism, whether radical or mainstream, has gained important ground as a system of thought and as a way of life. In broad ecological terms, woodlands are currently considered to be harmonious networks that have been interfered with by human parasites.

Within the ailing ecosystem called Earth, forests play the role of heart and lungs. Thus, the Amazonian and the Indonesian forests have recently become the paradigmatic woodlands to be protected (Ødermark 2015, 457). Yet, it is difficult to develop an attachment to such distant woodlands, however critical for our survival. In order to avert environmental disaster, it has become necessary to surmount the psychological alienation from nature that characterizes contemporary technology-based consumer societies. It is paramount to find ways to reconnect with those forests and other natural spaces that are closer to us or even create new ones that are more accessible. This form of direct engagement with natural sites will hopefully bring humans to the realization that we are not apart from nature but a part of nature.[1]

Believers in techno-fixes will certainly continue to appeal to scientific rationalism and sustainable development practices. Meanwhile, followers of contemporary "dark green religions" (Taylor 2008) will seek contact with nature in order to fulfill their spiritual needs. Others will choose to do likewise in their cultivation of a lay biocentric or ecofeminist environmental ethics. Be that as it may, the time has come to turn over a new leaf. In the next two sections I will try to assess how two particularly popular films may encourage us to do so.

How Bad Can This Possibly Be? *The Lorax* and Economic Neoliberalism

The Lorax is a 2012 animated musical comedy by Chris Renaud based on Dr. Seuss's popular 1971 tale of the same name. It deals with the story of a man called the Once-ler (voiced by Ed Helms), who in his search for fame and fortune came upon an unspoiled truffula forest whose woollike tufts he hoped to turn into a must-have product. After a few failed attempts, a purely haphazard event makes his "thneed" invention an instant success. The product then turns into an essential accessory that everyone craves after and *thneeds*. Because of the high demand, thneeds start to be produced unsustainably, which leads to deforestation, widespread pollution, and eventually the total devastation of the ecosystem the truffula trees were an essential part of. As a result, the remaining inhabitants of this destroyed habitat become displaced.[2]

Therefore, as initially illustrated in *The Lorax*, both industry (due to their unethical mass production processes) and the general public (due to their unending acquisition of disposable fashion fads) are made to bear the burden of ecological destruction. Unfortunately, the consumer-driven economic systems in which we live and work make sure that consumer satisfaction is never met because the health of the economy is directly dependent on people's constant need to consume, no matter what the consequences for the environment. For this reason, corporate greenwashing practices can barely hide the fact that our economic system is inherently corrupt and premised on the manipulation of consumers via marketing strategies.

Although Dr. Seuss's story was characteristically written in rhyming verse, most of the film's dialogue is not written thus. However, the original rhyming style subsists in certain pieces of dialogue and especially through the film's songs. While the lyrics do not exactly reproduce the original text, they clearly reference it and, in fact, I believe they provide the most interesting elements in terms of textual and cultural analysis. For this reason, I will be mainly focusing my ecocritical analysis on the film's songs, while never losing sight of the narrative and extra-narrative frameworks to which they constantly refer.

The first song is placed at the very beginning of the film, during a scene that depicts an idyllic gated community where everything is "plastic and fake" but they like it "that way." Although the town residents cannot enjoy the "luxury" of breathing fresh air, they seem to be numbly content with having to buy it in big containers. Here is a selection of the song's verses:

> In Thneedville, it's a brand new dawn, With brand new cars and houses and lawns, Here in Got-all-that-we-need-ville.
> In Thneedville we manufacture our trees,
> Each one is made in factories and uses ninety-six batteries! In Thneedville the air is not so clean,
> So we buy it fresh, it comes out this machine! In Satisfaction's-guaranteed-ville.
> In Thneedville we don't want to know Where the smog and trash and chemicals go. I just went swimming and I now I glow!
> . . .
> In Thneedville we love living this way,
> . . .
> Here in Love-the-way-we-live-ville
> . . .
> We-are-all-agreed-ville

The song nicely encapsulates several important environmental messages in the film. Thneedville is a seemingly happy consumer society (based on permanent *thneed*) with an abundance of brand-new cars that run on fuel and houses that rely on electricity with their artificial lawns and electronic trees. This is positively a high-energy consumption society in which social conflict is absent due to the apparent conformity and uniformity of all citizens. However, in "Got-all-that-we-need-ville," children glow after swimming in (polluted) ponds teeming with (fake) fish. However, residents live in utter (and apparently willing) ignorance of the harmful impact that the industrial processes upon which their wholly artificial way of life depends have on their local environment or on the distant ecosystems where the raw materials they consume are sourced. In "Love-the-way-we-live-ville," people are happy because they can carry on mindlessly consuming, oblivious to the polluting consequences of industrial processes, most of which lie hidden beyond the high walls surrounding their community. As long as they can buy everything they may wish, down to the air that they need in order to breathe, satisfaction will be permanently guaranteed and therefore any negative outcomes will be willingly ignored.

Fresh air has consequently become a precious, yet abundant, commodity in Thneedville that everyone seems to be able to afford, hence the lack of social conflict. It is in fact a lucrative business for Mr. O'Hare (voiced by Rob Riggle) who, unbeknownst to the residents, keeps the whole town under surveillance and so when he finds out that a local boy called Ted (voiced by Zac Efron) is trying to find a truffula tree seed so that he can plant it to impress the girl that he likes, Mr. O'Hare tries everything possible to stop him. On his grandmother's (voiced by Betty White) advice, Ted ventures out of town in search of the Once-ler, who, she says, can explain why the trees ceased to exist.

The Once-ler lives alone on the "Street of the Lifted Lorax," in an utterly devastated area of his own creation. Ted asks him about the trees, which surprises the old man as he thought "nobody cared about trees anymore." Unfortunately, here lies one of the most important flaws about the film (together with its refusal to tackle the environmental injustice of habitat destruction and forced displacement). Ted's interest in trees does not initially arise from any form of environmental awakening leading him to take action, but from his purely personal interest in Audrey (voiced by Taylor Swift). For her part, she seems to be interested in trees not because they are inherently valuable or essential for healthy ecosystems but because she finds them aesthetically pleasing, longs to smell them and touch their soft tufts. This is, however, in consonance with the total lack of awareness about the importance of trees among most of "We-are-all-agreed-ville's" brainwashed citizens. Ted's mother (voiced by Jenny Slate), for example, does not even know what the purpose of a real tree is and calls it a useless "dirty, messy lump of wood that sticks out of the ground." Still, the Once-ler believes that Ted might be the one that can bring back the trees and so starts telling him the story behind their extinction. It is here that Ted's environmental education starts.

The story is set in the not-so-very-distant future, but the Once-ler states that "It all started a long time ago," which the mise-en-scène emphasizes by having him ride a pioneer-style wagon during his search for fortune and glory. Visually, then, the scene references foundational entrepreneurial values in the United States (Figure 15.1), which a later song will also make explicit reference to.

FIGURE 15.1 *The Once-ler's pioneering effort starts.*

He strikes lucky when he comes across a beautiful area full of truffula trees. When the Once-ler announces that he is going to start cutting/killing the trees in order to produce his useless thneeds the local residents become furious. The killing of the first tree also summons the spirit of the Lorax (voiced by Danny DeVito), the guardian of the forest, a sort of environmental conscience figure who "speaks for the trees." The felled tree is mourned by him and the rest of the forest inhabitants, who react in defiance. The Once-ler promises them that he will never do it again and he will only harvest the tufts. However, when his invention becomes successful his unscrupulous family persuades him to start chopping the trees down again in order to speed up the mass production process and make money fast before the thneed fashion fad is superseded by the next one. Greed is good! Much like Gordon Gekko in Oliver Stone's *Wall Street* (1987), the Once-ler (dressed in dollar green, Figure 15.2) justifies his actions as being "natural" and "sound" through the song that ensues, whose lyrics provide a very harsh criticism of neoliberal business values:

> How bad can I be? I'm just doing what comes naturally. How bad can I be? I'm just following my destiny.
> . . .
> There's a principle in nature that almost every creature knows, Called survival of the fittest and check it this is how it goes.
> . . .
> There's a principle in business that everybody knows is sound.
> It says the people with the money make this ever-loving world go round.
> So I'm biggering my company and I'm biggering my factory,

FIGURE 15.2 *"Too Big to Fail." The song's critique of big business and neoliberalism is quite explicit.*

> I'm biggering my corporate sign!
> Everybody out there, you take care of yours and me, I'll take care of mine.
> . . .
> Let me hear you say, Smogulous Smoke! Schloppity Schlopp! Complain all you want it's never, ever, going to stop!
> . . .
> How bad can I be? I'm just building the economy,
> . . .
> How bad can I be? A portion of proceeds goes to charity!
> . . .
> All the customers are buying and the money is multiplying. And the PR people are lying, and the lawyers are denying. Who cares if a few trees are dying? This is all so gratifying! How bad can this possibly be?

This very explicitly critical tune is accompanied by even more explicit, almost horrific, compositions suggesting that in neoliberal societies human domination of nature and environmental destruction are often sanctioned in the name of continuous economic growth and the "gratifying" development of a free entrepreneurial spirit. In addition, the song ironically declares corporate greenwashing strategies to be mere marketing ruses.

Only when the last tree is felled (and hence natural resources become depleted) does the Once-ler's insatiable, but "natural," pursuit of riches end. By that time, the Lorax and the wild animals have become displaced. The Once-ler, meanwhile, is abandoned by his family and is left alone in the landscape whose total devastation he has enforced. This horrible sight eventually arouses an environmental conscience in him which leads him to preserve the last truffula seed, which he gives to Ted in the final stage of his environmental education. As the Once-ler tells the boy quoting the original text: "unless someone like you cares a whole awful lot, nothing is going to get better. It's not." He trusts Ted will plant the seed and educate the other residents in Thneedville so that they too will start caring about trees, change their consumption habits, and become aware of the tremendous impact that their wholly artificial lifestyles have on natural resources, ecosystems, and their own health.

At the end of the day, then, humans are asked to change their relations to nature in order to reduce their environmental impact because if they do not, "nothing is going to get better. It's not." Interestingly, the film's final song stresses the role of individual responsibility in environmental preservation and regeneration over and above *business* accountability, the conclusion being that businesses will not willingly reform *unless* consumers start favoring environmentally responsible companies. The burden is therefore placed on consumers to "speak for the trees" and exercise pressure on companies to modify their sourcing and manufacturing practices. During the narrative, industry and the broader economic system it sustains and feeds on have been subjected to continuous criticism. Therefore, the film's final message comes as no surprise: since companies will not implement (expensive) reform plans of their own accord, the future of the environment lies in the consumer's hand.

However, this is not enough. Averting the environmental crisis is going to take more than changing ordinary people's personal lifestyles and consumer choices. Compared to the environmental impact generated by industrial processes, ordinary people's is rather small. Therefore, "nothing is going to get better" unless the most harmful industrial practices are discarded, punishment for environmental crimes becomes a real deterrent, pressure on natural resources is drastically diminished, and destructive consumerism ceases to be the economy's sole driving force. "It is not."

"You Need to Wake Up": *Avatar*, Animism, and Deep Ecology[3]

As one of the most popular films in the history of Hollywood, James Cameron's *Avatar* needs practically no introduction. For ten years, *Avatar* stood tall as the top-grossing Hollywood film of all times (it currently stands in second place). This tremendous international popularity testifies to the fact that, beyond its mesmerizing display of digital innovations, this sci-fi fantasy's barely hidden environmental message struck a chord with audiences around the world.

Avatar tells the story of Jake Sully (Sam Worthington), a disabled war veteran who is assigned a scientific mission to Pandora when his scientist twin brother is killed. Because of their shared DNA, he seems to be the perfect substitute for his brother. However, he lacks significant scientific and cultural training for the mission, which involves driving genetically engineered humanoid avatars and making renewed contact with the Omaticaya, one of the Na'vi peoples inhabiting Pandora. In their never-ending economic expansion process, humans (or "sky people" as the Omaticaya refer to them) have come to this world in search of valuable mineral resources beyond Earth, which has become an unhealthy environment as a result of human destructiveness.

The sky people have sent the military to Pandora to fight against the rebellious local people, who are actively, even violently, resisting the destruction of their environment. The soldiers work as mercenaries for a "company" called the Resources Development Administration (RDA), but the invaders still hope to further and consolidate their extractive objectives through diplomacy. That is why they allowed Dr. Augustine (Sigourney Weaver) and her team to carry out scientific studies of the Pandoran ecosystem, which are in fact financed by the sale of unobtanium,[4] the valuable mineral humans are extracting in Pandora. For ten years, the scientific team was accepted by the Omaticaya. Dr. Augustine led the expedition and became a Na'vi expert. She also taught (indoctrinated?) the locals about the sky people's language and culture, including Dr. Seuss's environmental classic *The Lorax* (Figure 15.3), in the school they built for them in order to obtain their cooperation (or, as the RDA representative literally says, "win their hearts and minds") so that the mining operation

FIGURE 15.3 *Dr. Seuss's* The Lorax *lies abandoned on the school floor for the Na'vi.*

could go ahead, which inevitably entailed extensive wood clearings and further destructive practices.

Yet, corporate greed demanded fast results and a positive quarterly report, which the diplomatic efforts were failing to obtain. When the first trees were felled/killed, a few young Omaticaya rebelled and resorted to ecotage (i.e., they sabotaged the invaders' machinery) in order to protect not just the land they inhabit, but the delicate web of interconnections which sustain the world as they know it. To them, tree clearing represented just the beginning of the colonial dismantling of their homeland and way of life, which is importantly based on nonanthropocentric (or, rather, nonNa'vicentric), deep ecological principles that stress the interdependence of all elements in a natural ecosystem. In retaliation for destroying their property and disturbing their extracting activities, the sky people brutally murdered these young Omaticaya outside the school, which abruptly ended all forms of cooperation between Pandora and planet Earth. Still, extracting activities continued in the name of economic expansion and therefore relations deteriorated, with both peoples now being "at the brink of war."

Ecotage, or the premeditated destruction of property with the intention of protecting forests or other elements of the natural environment, started to be considered a form of terrorism only recently.[5] In the past, terrorism necessarily involved the threat to or loss of human life, but this understanding changed during the 1990s, as radical environmentalism gained ground, and intensified during the War on Terror that the September 11 attacks inaugurated (Buell 2009). Since the alien invaders cannot understand and refuse to accept Omaticaya culture,[6] the locals that rebel are treated like (environmental) terrorists when human economic interests become threatened. As Jake puts it bluntly: "This is how it's done. When people are sitting on shit that you want you make them your enemy. You're justified in taking it."[7] Certainly, the film's language is full of terms that have become habitual since the War on Terror was declared. The Na'vi are referred to as "the hostiles," but also pejoratively as the "aboriginal horde," "savages," or "blue monkeys." Moreover, their culture or "racial memory" is constantly mocked in order to boost the morale of the mercenaries, who are instructed to fight "terror with terror." Needless to say, the conflict depicted in the film is reminiscent of recent, and not so recent, historical invasions and colonial wars that have been waged in order to protect the economic interests and permanent access to resources of Earth's imperialistic superpowers and their allies.

Moreover, because of their looks, their means of transportation, their hunting and fighting methods, and their philosophy of life, the Na'vi are also (somewhat stereotypically) molded on the First Nations of the North American continent.[8] Hence, *Avatar* also seems to be making explicit reference to the history of settler colonialism. As in *The Lorax*, the ideology of expansionism transpires throughout the narrative, although it is also counteracted by some of the most important characters, crucially Jake and Dr. Augustine, both of whom eventually reject their own "racial memory," albeit for different reasons.

The sky people's interest in felling/killing the trees in Pandora in order to extract unobtanium is therefore entirely reminiscent of the felling frenzy that characterized the pioneering westward expansion in the United States. The Omaticaya village, unfortunately, is located under the sacred Hometree, in an area that seems to hold the largest deposits of unobtanium on the whole moon. Jake's initial secret mission involved getting the Omaticaya to leave Hometree and agree to relocate, much like Native Americans were forced to relocate to reservations in less productive land risking death if they resisted. Yet, the Omaticaya's attachment to Hometree is beyond most sky people's understanding. Humans cannot see the forest through their eyes. Their refusal to leave precipitates the genocidal attack against them, during which incendiary bombs destroy Hometree.[9]

To most sky people, Hometree is just one more tree on Pandora; there is no difference among them. The imperialistic invaders continue to value trees only in utilitarian terms. The Omaticaya, by contrast, regard trees as one more part of the interconnected natural system they inhabit, of which they are an important part, too. Trees, and especially the sacred Tree of Souls, are their direct link to Eywa, the Mother Earth deity they worship.[10] To the Omaticaya, all living organisms on their moon have inherent value and are to be equally respected. The balance of nature, which Eywa takes care of, depends on the premise of interpenetration and relatedness. This vision of organic interconnectivity is reminiscent of the natural philosophy of certain animistic First Nations that Hall (2011) has referred to in his anthropological study of the treatment of plants in different societies. As he explains, animism is also at the heart of certain Eastern philosophies that have influenced contemporary biocentric and deep ecological values in the West.[11] Some of the non-Westernized peoples studied by Hall consider plants and animals to be persons, albeit not in an anthropomorphic way. As he explains:

> Within wider discussions of environmental ethics, Indigenous . . . worldviews have been put forward as philosophical counterexamples to the . . . Western treatment of the natural world as a radically different, inferior Other . . . In animistic worldviews, it is a general principle that the plant, animal, and human realms interpenetrate . . . As persons, plants are recognized as volitional, intelligent, relational, perceptive, and communicative beings. [Animism recognizes that] the world is full of persons, only some of whom are human, and that life is always lived in relationship with others . . . As persons, plants are not naively thought to have human faculties. They are understood to be living beings with their

own perspective, and with the ability to communicate in their own way. (99, 100, 105, 106)

Hall's underlining of plants' own capacity for communication, agency, and volition is essential for this reading of *Avatar*.

Throughout his training as one of "the people" with Neytiri, the daughter of the Omaticaya leaders, Jake often demonstrates (and stands for) human skepticism:

> Jake: Every day is reading the trails . . . the tiniest scents and sounds . . . She's always going on about the flow of energy . . . I really hope this tree-hugging crap isn't on the final.[12] . . . I'm trying to understand this deep connection people have to the forest. She talks about a network of energy that flows through all living things. She says all energy is only borrowed and one day you have to give it back.

Despite his ambivalence, Jake learns the local "ways" (which is tantamount to saying that he receives a thorough environmental education), is accepted by the people (Figure 15.4), and eventually gets to become the leader of the Omaticaya clan, which garnered the film plenty of criticism (Erb 2014, 12).

Before the final battle against the invaders begins, Jake tries to communicate with Eywa through the sacred Tree of Souls ("I'm probably just talking to a tree here," he skeptically says, once again). He is fully aware that the Na'vi's

FIGURE 15.4 *Jake rejects colonial anthropocentric values and becomes one of the people in a ritual ceremony that pays homage to trees.*

pretechnological weapons are no match for the aliens', which leads him to, as a last resource, ask for help from Eywa. Neytiri, however, reminds him that their deity does not take sides because she only takes care of the balance of life. Yet, after the united Na'vi tribes suffer massive losses and everything seems to be lost, Eywa sends all the animals on Pandora to fight the invaders, which eventually means victory for the local "horde" and the permanent expulsion of the colonizers.

The film therefore imagines the possibility of nature going wild, so to speak, and taking revenge on the abusers. It chooses to bring nature alive and emphasize its dynamic power to redress the environmental imbalance that threatens life on Pandora. Eywa's destructive might annihilates the human parasites, who are made to return to their sick planet. Much more so than in *The Lorax*, nature adopts a very active role and reacts in self-defense. The ending therefore borrows from the conventions of the revolt-of-nature film but adds a twist. Nature's *permanent* victory sends the potent message that in the event of an anthropogenic environmental cataclysm our planet will have the resources to adapt to the new conditions and survive without humans, but humans will not be able to survive without nature. Thus, as Neytiri's mother says, humans need to be cured of their blindness and insanity in order to wake up to the reality of the Omaticaya (Figures 15.5 and 15.6), that is to say, to the non-supremacist, deep ecological values that will help avert environmental disaster and ensure planetary (and hopefully human) health and survival.

Jake's transformation from RDA's spy to Omaticaya leader represents the transition that humans need to effect in order to redefine our relationships with trees and nature. The Na'vi cannot and will not dedifferentiate between nature and culture. There exists no such a thing as Na'vi supremacism in their relations with the rest of the Pandoran ecosystem. All elements are mutually interdependent and share a relationship of mutual care. Following the Na'vi, humans need to cease to regard nature as an (inferior) other to enslave and utilize at their convenience. Following Sully, humans need to "go native" and wake up to the reality of our total dependence on the

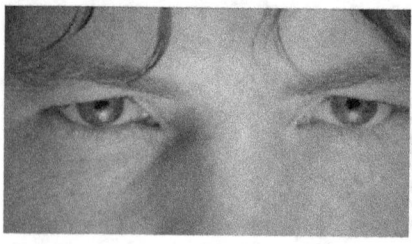 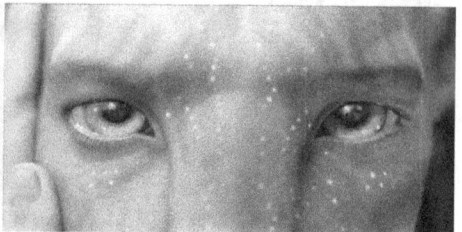

FIGURES 15.5 AND 15.6 *"You need to wake up!" Jake's transformative experience is truly eye-opening.*

preservation of natural ecosystems in order to halt our irrational drive for self-extinction. Human health is only precarious as it is totally dependent on planetary health. However, this realization will not come about unless humans become environmentally educated and start to care. It is not possible to respect something we do not know much about or care about. Hollywood films like *Avatar*, despite providing fantasy solutions to real environmental concerns, can elicit the spectator's emotional response, encourage activism, and show us to the way.

Conclusion

This chapter has attempted to provide an ecocultural analysis of two popular Hollywood films in which different forms of human-tree relations are represented. Importantly, both of the films analyzed raise the important issue that humans need to become environmentally savvier in order to redefine our relationships with plants and show them the respect they are due. Only thus will we be able to transition to a greener form of lifestyle in a less resource-hungry economy. It has become evident by now that the Earth's natural assets are finite and that our voracious economic system cannot sustain permanent growth at the current rate. Resources can simply not be (re)produced at the necessary speed. Therefore, our hope resides in "going native," so to speak, by adopting more natural ways of living that will not put the planet under so much pressure. There is a lot that we can do at the individual level, from favoring a green, circular economy to using public transport and educating children in the respectful treatment of nature. Needless to say, the youngest are currently leading the way in the redefinition of human-nature relationships, but, as they often emphasize, more needs to be done at the corporate level and especially at the institutional one. It is therefore not only a question of individuals reducing, reusing, and recycling. Intense pressure needs to be put on corporations (by boycotting those that do not implement green policies) and political parties (by voting in favor of those who take environmental issues seriously and implement tougher measures in the fight against climate change, deforestation, and the protection of biodiversity and natural ecosystems). This is not just a long-term plan for future generations to reap the benefits of.

The current pandemic, and the Ebola crisis before it, originated from the destruction of ecosystems, and particularly deforestation practices. Animals whose ecosystems are destroyed need to relocate to areas where food can be found, which increasingly means closer contact with humans, who in turn become exposed to new viruses of animal origin. For its part, poverty leads humans to eat wild animals in their proximity, with no health control of any kind. Experts predict that pandemics like the current one will become more and more common in the future (Ghebreyesus 2020).[13] Velasco (2021) cites World Health Organization epidemiologist María Neira, on this often-overlooked issue: "Our enduring attacks on ecosystems make us vulnerable. People think that this is just an issue for environmentalists, activists, for the illuminated. It is not. In the perverse relationship that we maintain with the environment, it is not the environment that has the most to lose" (my translation). Thus, we can conclude that in these dire, pandemic-ridden times there is no more escaping the fact that redefining human-nature (and therefore human-tree) relations has become the most pressing issue of our time.

Notes

1 Admittedly, myriad examples of the gothic horror genre, including *The Blair Witch Project* (Daniel Myrick and Eduardo Sánchez 1999) and *Into the Forest* (Patricia Rozema 2015), testify to the fact that the conception of the forest as a dangerous place persists (especially in the mind of alienated city dwellers).

2 The film, nonetheless, chooses not to focus on this clear case of natural habitat destruction, which betrays the plot's anthropocentric bias, which may be seen to weaken the film's environmental message.

3 This reading is based on the film's extended cut edition released in 2010.

4 The oxymoronic meaning of the made-up term seems to point at endlessly destructive human voracity.

5 Currently, the FBI (2020) defines terrorism thus: "violent, criminal acts committed by individuals and/or groups to further ideological goals stemming from domestic influences, such as those of a political, religious, social, racial, or *environmental* nature" (emphasis added).

6 As the Omaticaya see it, sky people are "ignorant like children." They "do not see" and therefore "cannot learn" that Pandora's wealth is not under the ground, but all around. As Dr. Augustine says to Parker (Giovanni Ribisi), the ruthless representative of corporate interests in the film: "You need to wake up Parker . . . If you want to share this world with them, you need to understand that!" To which he responds: "What the hell have you people been smoking out there? They're just goddam trees!"

7 This very same argument is put forward in a more elegant way by Naomi Klein in *The Shock Doctrine* (2007).

8 They are also played by non-white actors, some of whom have indigenous ancestry, including Wes Studi (who plays chief Eytukan), Zoe Saldana (who plays Neytiri), CCH Pounder (who plays Mo'at), and Laz Alonso (who plays Tsu'tey). The Pandora forest, however, was inspired by the Amazonian one in the south of the continent, where relocations continue to take place to this date.

9 While Colonel Quaritch (Stephen Lang) states that he will get rid of the Omaticaya "humanely" (i.e., he will gas them), his treatment of the sacred tree

and surrounding natural environment is unapologetically ruthless, which is consistent with his human supremacist beliefs.

10 Eywa appears to be closely connected to Gaia, the matriarchal earth goddess of the Greeks.
11 Links may also be established with James Lovelock's scientific Gaia Hypothesis (Taylor 2008, 98) and the sociological insights of Actor Network Theory (Jones and Cloke 2002; 2008).
12 This might be a direct reference to Fox's requirement that Cameron tone down the "tree-hugger crap" (Wilson 2010), which he obviously did not.
13 The World Health Organization (WHO) Director General has declared that the pandemic has "highlighted the intimate links between humans, animals and planet." He has called for a planetary or "One Health" approach in order to protect the future of human health, which is critically connected to the health of broader ecosystems.

References

Brereton, P. (2004), *Hollywood Utopia: Ecology in Contemporary American Cinema*, Bristol: Intellect Books.

Brereton, P. (2015), *Environmental Ethics and Film*, London and New York: Routledge.

Buell, L. (2009), "What Is Called Ecoterrorism," *Gramma: A Journal of Theory and Criticism* 16. Available online: http://nrs.harvard.edu/urn-3:HUL.InstRepos:4262048.

Cazdyn, E. (2007), "Disaster, Crisis, Revolution," *South Atlantic Quarterly* 106 (4), pp. 647-62.

Erb, C. (2014), "A Spiritual Blockbuster: *Avatar*, Environmentalism, and the New Religions," *Journal of Film and Video* 66 (3), pp. 3-17.

Federal Bureau of Intelligence (2020), "Terrorism," *Federal Bureau of Intelligence*. Available online: https://www.fbi.gov/investigate/terrorism.

Ghebreyesus, T. A. (2020), "International Day for Epidemic Preparedness," *World Health Organisation*, 26 December. Available online: https://www.youtube.com/watch?v=sMnhWcptYp8.

Griffin, C. J. (2011), "Space and Place: Popular Perceptions of Forests," in E. Ritter and D. Dauksta (eds.), *New Perspectives on People and Forests*, Dordrecht, Heidelberg, London, and New York: Springer, pp. 139-58.

Hall, M. (2011), *Plants as Persons: A Philosophical Botany*, Albany: State University of New York.

Harrison, R. P. (1992), *Forests: The Shadow of Civilization*, Chicago and London: University of Chicago Press.

Hayman, R. (2003), *Trees: Woodlands and Western Civilization*, London and New York: Hambledon and London Ltd.

Ingram, D. (2004), *Green Screen: Environmentalism and Hollywood Cinema*, Exeter: University of Exeter Press.

Ivakhiv, A. (1997), "Ecocultural Critical Theory and Ecocultural Studies: Contexts and Research Directions," Available online: http://www.uvm.edu/~aivakhiv/eco_cult.htm.

Jones, O. and P. Cloke (2002), *Tree Cultures: The Place of Trees and Trees in Their Place*, New York: Berg.

Jones, O. and P. Cloke (2008), "Non-Human Agencies: Trees in Place and Time," in C. Knappett and L. Malafouris (eds.), *Material Agency*, Boston, MA: Springer, pp. 79–96.

Keetley, D. and A. Tenga (2016), *Plant Horror: Approaches to the Monstrous Vegetal in Fiction and Film*, London: Palgrave Macmillan.

Klein, N. (2007), *The Shock Doctrine*, London: Penguin Books.

Leopold, A. (1970), *A Sand County Almanac: With Other Essays on Conservation from Round River*, Oxford: Oxford University Press. First published in 1949.

Macfarlane, R. (2019), "Should This Tree Have the Same Rights as You?," *The Guardian*, 2 November. Available online: https://www.theguardian.com/books/2019/nov/02/trees-have-rights-too-robert-macfarlane-on-the-new-laws-of-nature.

Marder, M. (2013a), "The Time Is Ripe for Plant Rights," *Aljazeera*, 21 January. Available online: https://www.aljazeera.com/opinions/2013/1/21/the-time-is-ripe-for-plant-rights/ 21/03/2013.

Marder, M. (2013b), "Should Plants Have Rights?," *The Philosophers' Magazine* 62, pp. 46–50.

Mills, B. (2010), "Television Wildlife Documentaries and Animals' Right to Privacy," *Continuum: Journal of Media and Cultural Studies* 24 (2), pp. 193–202.

Moore, E. E. (2017), *Landscape and the Environment in Hollywood Film*, London: Palgrave Macmillan.

Ødermark, J. (2015), "*Avatar* in the Amazon: Narratives of Cultural Conversion and Environmental Salvation between Cultural Theory and Popular Culture," *Culture Unbound* 7, pp. 455–78.

Sturgeon, N. (2009), *Environmentalism in Popular Culture*, Tucson: University of Arizona Press.

Taylor, B. (2008), "From the Ground Up: Dark Green Religion and the Environmental Future," in D. K. Swearer (ed.), *Ecology and the Environment: Perspectives from the Humanities*, Cambridge, MA: Harvard University Press, pp. 89–107.

Touraine, A. (2011), *Después de la Crisis. Por un futuro sin marginación*, Barcelona: Paidós.

Velasco, M. (2021), "La OMS alerta de futuras pandemias. ¿A qué nos enfrentamos?," *The Huffington Post*, 3 January. Available online: https://www.huffingtonpost.es/entry/la-oms-alerta-de-futuras-pandemias-a-que-nos-enfrentamos_es_5fed9726c5b6fd33110cc684.

Wilson, J. (2010), "James Cameron: I'm the Greenest Director of All Times!," *Grist*, 1 March. Available online: https://grist.org/article/2010-03-01-cameron-im-the-greenest-director-of-all-time/.

Wohlleben, P. (2016), *The Hidden Life of Trees*, Vancouver and Berkeley: Greystone Books.

PART VII

Crisis and Violence in the Borderlands

16

"No One to Call Around Here. These Boys Is on Their Own"

The Postindustrial Frontier in *Hell or High Water* and the Western as a Landscape of the Crisis

Luis Freijo

Some way into *Hell or High Water* (David Mackenzie 2016), Texas Rangers Marcus Hamilton (Jeff Bridges) and Alberto Parker (Gil Birmingham) encounter a group of ranch hands who are driving a herd of cattle away from a fire, across the West Texas plains. Hamilton and Parker, who are on their way to investigate a bank robbery, stop to offer their help to the foreman, played by the film's screenwriter, Taylor Sheridan. The foreman complains: "Twenty-first century and I'm racing a fire to the river with a herd of cattle. And I wonder why my kids won't do this shit for a living." As the Rangers drive away, unable to assist, Parker asks, "You wanna call it in?" to which Hamilton replies, "Oh, it's gonna burn out when it hits the Brazos. No one to call around here, anyway. These boys is on their own." Somewhat detached from the heist-Western narrative of the film, the scene encapsulates the main themes of *Hell or High Water*: the consequences of predatory economic organization as evidenced in the 2008 financial crisis, the lack of public protection inherent in neoliberalism, the obsolescence of certain types of US masculinity, and the rearrangement of the frontier into the coordinates of a postindustrial society. This chapter analyses these concerns in *Hell or High Water* as an example of the trend of socially aware output within the 2010s Western genre. Accordingly, an explanation of the financial crisis will be offered within the context of neoliberalism and the postindustrial society to inform and underpin an interrogation of how the crisis has reshaped the Western genre. *Hell or High Water* will be approached as a case study of the themes outlined in the scene described earlier, to demonstrate the Western's relevance and validity in the twenty-first century as a genre of the crisis, and to argue that the new US frontier is that of the economic violence posed by neoliberalism and the postindustrial society.

"That Looks like a Man Who Could Foreclose on a House": The Postindustrial Society and the 2008 Financial Crisis

The 2008 financial crisis that resonates in *Hell or High Water* must be understood within the historical context of the shift to a postindustrial society. The term "postindustrial" is understood as the transition from a society in which the industrial sector is dominant to an economic model based primarily on the service sector, which occurs within a "neoliberal model" (Hall 2011, 10) where economic activity focuses mainly on private, instead of public, ventures. Crouch summarizes the consequences of the gradual establishment of the postindustrial economy since the 1970s as "financialization and globalization, the emergence of particular high- and low-income sectors and occupations, the decline of both the economic and political weight of organized labour, and the skewed territorial distribution of some services industries" (2019, 11). This is important for the analysis of *Hell or High Water* because the emergence of these low-income sectors and the disappearance of organized labor create the conditions of economic violence that lead the Howard brothers to embark on their robberies. What is relevant, however, in explaining the 2008 crisis is that the financialization of the economy caused the elimination of regulatory laws—some of them imposed after the stock market crash of 1929—that precluded banks from taking excessive risks. The deregulation would eventually result in the new crash (Crouch 2019, 13).

Deregulation enabled low interest rates for the acquisition of debt, especially in the housing market. Since debt was cheap to acquire and the housing market was deemed too solid to crash because mortgage payment was constant, banks started taking on disproportionate amounts of debt, sometimes up to thirty-three times their real value and liquidity. With the consolidation of the neoliberal model, the system of lending in banks shifted from "originate-to-hold to . . . originate-to-distribute" (Buckley 2011, 2), that is, from a paradigm in which a bank generates a mortgage for a house and holds it until it is repaid to a model in which the main benefit is not the repayment of the debt, but its conversion into a financial product to be resold. The originate-to-distribute lending practice defines the ranch in *Hell or High Water* as a financial asset for the Texas Midlands Bank and explains the bank's interest in foreclosing on the property. The tool utilized by banks and financial institutions to trade on debt was the mortgage-backed security (MBS). A bank would acquire different mortgages and put them together in a single package, sometimes made up of thousands of mortgages, which could then be resold to other financial institutions. The level of scrutiny of the ability of debtors to pay their mortgages decreased as the benefits for the financial sector rocketed and the housing market continued to be considered solid. The disproportionate growth of secondary markets betting on MBS products fueled a bubble that ended up exploding when house prices and the repayment of debt stalled in 2007, thus causing the market crash (Buckley 2011, 2–6) and the conditions for criminal activity that are explored in *Hell or High Water*.

The consequences of the crash included the collapse of several banks and financial companies, and concerns over the spread of market fear led the US government and financial institutions to bail out other banks at an estimated cost of between $1.5 and $2 trillion (Buckley 2011, 178). The surviving banks, like the Texas Midlands of *Hell or High Water*, found a favorable business market, in which they "could gain a larger market share and earn higher fees and margins" (Buckley 2011, 260). In contrast, the US working class and its peripheral populations, which were already struggling in the face of the changes in employment brought about by deindustrialization, were left out of these bailouts. In the film, Toby (Chris Pine) and Tanner Howard (Ben Foster) represent a white working class that, albeit equipped with skills in primary activities such as rearing cattle and drilling for gas or oil, is vulnerable to the consequences of the crisis. In the aftermath of the crash, the Obama administration extended by twenty-four months the Bush tax cuts for high-income citizens, so that "in exchange for peanuts for the unemployed, the rich received $315 billion over two years" (Lazzarato 2011, 120). These political decisions are denounced in the first shot of *Hell or High Water*, in which a graffiti on the wall of the bank reads: "Three tours in Iraq, but no bailouts for people like us." These effects of the crisis on middle- and working-class US citizens can be regarded as a form of economic violence directed at their own people by the US government and financial system. This idea of economic violence is key to the reshaping of the Western genre.

"It Ain't No Army Doing It": Economic Violence and the Making of the Postindustrial Frontier

Understanding the aftermath of the financial crisis in terms of economic violence places the events of 2008, along with the neoliberal context in which they occurred, within the wider historical construction of the United States as a nation around violent encounters that revitalize the concept of the frontier. The significance of the frontier in the history of the United States was famously identified by Frederick Jackson Turner, who proclaimed in the late nineteenth century that the harsh conditions the frontier presented to immigrant homesteaders forged a unique and exclusive US character that erased the original European traits from its inhabitants (1998, 32–3). Underlying Turner's historical project was a nationalistic and ethnocentric intent, in which the formation of the United States as a modern state with these unique characteristics, embodied in the agrarian homesteader, justified the colonization of the West and the extermination of Native populations—such as the Comanche as mourned by Parker in the film—and laid the ground for future imperialistic enterprises.

Among other authors, Patricia Nelson Limerick rebukes Turner by considering the frontier not as a necessary process or an impermeable advancing line but as "a place undergoing conquest and never fully escaping its consequences" (1987, 26), a place that constituted "the point where Indian America, Latin America, Anglo-America, Afro-America, and Asia intersected" (1987, 26). The interchange between these communities enables Limerick to consider Western history "an ongoing competition for legitimacy," which involves both "the pursuit of legitimacy in property overlapped with the pursuit of legitimacy in way of life and point of view" (1987, 26). Limerick considered that this contest was still going on in a historical continuum (1987, 26). However, there is a theoretical conception of violence that underpins both Turner and Limerick's frontiers, and which neither of them has fully addressed. To expand their writings on the frontier, it is useful to conceive of the frontier as an abstract political space in which the state does not hold "the monopoly of legitimate physical violence" (Weber 2004, 33). German theorist Max Weber considered this monopoly of violence the condition for existence of the modern Western state, and this idea is applied here to argue that it is unchecked violence what impedes the formation of the state and its institutions and, hence, what leaves the frontier open. However, whereas in the nineteenth-century context that Weber discussed it was physical violence what precluded the closing of the frontier, in the twenty-first century under neoliberalism physical violence is no longer the only force that keeps it open. It is the economic violence inherent in the postindustrial society, exerted by financial institutions and companies since the 2008 crash, that recalibrates the parameters of the frontier and reopens it in the United States, no longer directing just physical violence toward Native populations but also economic violence toward the different ethnicities and groups inhabiting the West. The idea of frontier has in fact been used by different US administrations to simplify the communication of their policies, most notably in recent times by two Republican presidents: Ronald Reagan, who adopted the persona of a former cowboy star, and George W. Bush, who compared the role of the United States in the global war against terrorism with that of the Western lawman. This abstract frontier established not between European settlers and Native Americans or between civilization and savagery but between the victims and the beneficiaries of neoliberal policies and deployed to embed political discourse in the myth of the US West is where the 2010s Western now exists.

The close relation of the Western film genre with the contemporary history of the United States has become a common topic of exploration in scholarship over the last three decades. What Michael Coyne has named a "political/allegorical" approach to studying the Western, "relating the genre's narrative conflicts and thematic tensions to corresponding issues in twentieth-century US society" (1997, 12), has been taken as the dominant perspective in several works about the genre, including Stanley Corkin's *Cowboys as Cold Warriors* (2004) and Patrick McGee's *From Shane to Kill Bill* (2007). Correspondingly, some 2010s Westerns can be approached, following these authors, with neoliberalism and the financial crisis as the main historical framework. For example, *The Magnificent Seven* (Antoine Fuqua 2016) features as its villain an industrialist who preys on the middle class, *Meek's Cutoff* (Kelly Reichardt 2010) adopts strategies of slowness to evoke the politics of austerity as they relate to female concerns (Gorfinkel 2016, 123); and several segments of *The Ballad of Buster Scruggs* (Joel and Ethan Coen 2018) revolve around brutal and hopeless competitions.

However, apart from these features set in the nineteenth-century time frame of the classic Western, films that take place in contemporary times have appeared to claim the space of the Western genre to emphasize these same issues and bring them up-to-date. An uneasy consensus among scholars has named these films "post-Westerns," a term first proposed by British film critic Philip French (2005, 10) and then developed by Neil Campbell, who aligns the post-Western with a "haunting presence of the past." This presence helps the genre to "interrogate the very ideological frameworks that . . . conjured it into being in the first place" (2013, 2–3). Campbell utilizes the "post-" in post-Western as a way of highlighting the meeting point between the mythologized past of the classic Western and the "deterritorialized" present of the post-Western, wherein the present West "is unsettled by the examination of salient fragments unearthed to question its cohesion, closure, and solidity" (2013, 34, 26).

I argue, however, that the term "post-Western" as devised by these authors cannot be accurately applied to the trend of 2010s Westerns discussed in this chapter. Campbell draws a line between the Western and the post-Western as essentially different and discontinuous projects. This idea, however, does not fit with the unbroken continuity of the frontier in US history, as claimed by Patricia Nelson Limerick and as developed in this chapter in relation to the economic violence of the postindustrial frontier. The genre has mutated in the films set in contemporary times that are discussed here, but its main function remains the same, that of mapping the political and social concerns of the United States in relation to a notion of a frontier landscape. Campbell links the post-Western to the "arrival of the New West as a process of increased industrialization, commodification, and suburbanization" (2013, 67). As has been argued, however, the West is no longer industrialized; rather, it is immersed in a process of deindustrialization that can be explained not by using the term "post-Western" but by taking a theoretical step back and including such films in the Western genre, without labels, to then understand their particularities through close text analysis and not *a priori* categorizations. Once the theoretical reach of the genre is thus widened, an array of films becomes available for discussion. For example, concerns about gender and precarity have been approached through the iconography of the horse in *The Rider* (Chloé Zhao 2017), *Certain Women* (Kelly Reichardt 2016), and *Lean on Pete* (Andrew Haigh 2017). In addition, immigration and the frontier are dealt with in films about the US-Mexican border, such as *Logan* (James Mangold 2017), *Frontera* (Michael Berry 2014), and *Desierto* (Jonás Cuarón 2015), while the political and social consequences of the delocalization of industries in Kentucky are depicted in the TV series *Justified* (Graham Yost 2010–15). These films of the crisis years also mirror Hollywood films made in the aftermath of the 1929 crash, from social dramas such as *The Grapes of Wrath* (John Ford 1940) to Westerns that express distrust of bankers and industrialists, for example *Stagecoach* (John Ford 1939) and *Jesse James* (Henry King 1939). However, what distinguishes 2010s Westerns is that the social drama and the Western are combined in realist depictions of the crisis, rather than as mythologized transpositions.

Indebted Men: *Hell or High Water* and Neoliberal Rationality

Most notably among these films, *Hell or High Water* depicts brothers Toby and Tanner Howard as they engage in a series of robberies with the aim of raising enough money to pay the reverse mortgage on their family ranch before the Texas Midlands Bank forecloses on the property. Saving the property is of paramount importance for Toby's children, who live with his estranged ex-wife, since the oil recently discovered at the ranch would secure them a comfortable future. The Howards are chased by Texas Rangers Marcus Hamilton, an investigator close to retirement, and Alberto Parker, a man of Native and Mexican ancestry whom Hamilton likes to tease with racist jokes.

The Western credentials of *Hell or High Water* are found in its depiction of the economic violence of the postindustrial frontier and in its examination of the iconography of the West Texas landscape. As the pairs Toby/Tanner and Hamilton/Parker drive through the state, the landscape is shown in wide-angle shots taken from the car while Nick Cave and Warren Ellis's melancholic soundtrack plays. This is, however, a different landscape from that of classic Westerns set in Texas, such as *The Searchers* (John Ford 1956) and *Red River* (Howard Hawks 1948). In contrast to a landscape that "convey[s] an emotion, a significance, and even an odd form of hope" (McGee 2007, 169), the West Texas plains of *Hell or High Water* have been reduced to a landscape of the crisis. These shots from the car show the countryside of Texas riddled with short-term loan advertisements, punctured by pumpjacks drilling for oil, and accumulating metal waste. These shots display the signs of economic inequality, as the wealth contained in the land, especially through its oil, contrasts with the billboards that prey on Texans' poverty. Wealth, therefore, is depicted as unequally distributed through the economic violence of the postindustrial frontier, which has reached and shaped a landscape that has lost the marks of hope that McGee described and is verging on a post-apocalyptic form of hopelessness, underlined by Cave and Ellis's score.

The sense of hopelessness of the landscape translates into an emphasis on tiredness in the physicality of the performances of West Texan secondary characters. For instance, Toby's ex-wife Debby (Marin Ireland) is first shown with bags under her eyes and talking in a restrained tone, as is the waitress Jenny Ann (Katy Mixon) when she takes a break from work to speak with Toby. These waitresses, bank tellers, unemployed cowboys, and vengeful bystanders belong to the "minority of low-skilled workers—mainly but not entirely female—at the foot of hierarchies with low incomes" (Crouch 2019, 17) and damaged by the deindustralized economy and the crisis. The economic situation, however, does not translate into a form of collective organization to counter its consequences. The working class remains tied to individual solutions, which leads Camil Parvu to argue that neoliberalism is a specific form of political rationality that depoliticizes a number of issues and thus reduces political action to an individualist and "all-encompassing economic judgement" (2017, 780). The old man at the second bank that is robbed pulls out his gun and starts shooting at the Howards, a bystander in the first bank suggests a lynching, and one of the elderly cowboys at the diner contents himself with seeing "the bank robbed that has been robbing me for thirty years," but these are all individual actions incapable of solving collective problems. Only the posse formed at the climax of the film resembles some kind of civil society organization, but even this constitutes a reactive action taken to protect individual interests, with no trust being placed in public institutions or authorities.

The landscape is also haunted by the Native American genocide, which is referenced explicitly through Hamilton's racist jokes and through Tanner's invocation of the Comanche. Structurally, however, the film establishes a continuity between the expropriation and genocide of the Native tribes and the economic violence that defines the contemporary frontier. In a key scene, Hamilton and Parker are waiting next to a Texas Midlands branch for a robbery attempt by the Howards. Parker reminds Hamilton that his ancestors owned the land of West Texas until they were massacred by the colonizers, and he adds: "Now it's being taken from them. Except it ain't no army doing it. It's those sons of bitches right there." Parker concludes his monologue by pointing at the bank, which comes into focus in the shot. *Hell or High Water* acknowledges the continuity of the frontier violence and its mutation from the physical violence described by Weber to the economic violence of the postindustrial paradigm. However, Parker's speech also establishes "parallels between the dispossession of white working-class Americans and the colonization and genocide of the Comanche [which are] problematic" (Falconer 2020, 182), because the harmful austerity measures imposed on the population can never equal the genocide of a people and the confinement of its survivors in reservations where the violence continues to this day, as depicted by Sheridan in *Wind River* (2017) and *Yellowstone* (2018–).

Parker's remarks bring into focus *Hell or High Water*'s main villain: the Texas Midlands Bank, a stand-in for the postcrisis US banking system. Having already benefited from bailouts during the financial crisis, the bank is presented as an insatiable entity bent on exploiting the white US working class, through the looming foreclosure deadline on Toby's ranch. The ranch becomes an important point of analysis to map how the postindustrial frontier has changed the Western. Once a trope that epitomized the dream of retirement for the weary gunfighter, the ranch becomes a source of problems for the Howards. In previous Westerns such as *The Gunfighter* (Henry King 1950), *The Searchers*, *The Magnificent Seven* (John Sturges 1960), and *The Wild Bunch* (Sam Peckinpah 1969), the ranch is utilized to foreground the contradictory expectations of violent forms of masculinity. On the one hand, these men's professions as gunslingers cast them away from society and impede their eventual settlement. On the other hand, the ideal of the ranch endures as a symbol of a fulfilling livelihood. However, this idealism has disappeared in *Hell or High Water*, where the ranch is not a source of wealth but rather a burden that consumes time and money. The postindustrial society brought about a paradigm in which "economic activities [turn] into globally tradable financial assets" (Crouch 2019, 11–12) and, in the postcrisis frontier, a ranch property has more value as a financial product for a bank than as a source of livelihood for its owners.

The ranch also serves to articulate *Hell or High Water*'s discourse on debt, a key component of the neoliberal economy and one of the causes of the 2008 crisis. Toby's lawyer explains the bank's strategy of using debt as a tool in the confiscation of land: "They loaned the least they could. Just enough to keep your mama poor on a guaranteed return. Thought they could swipe her land for $25,000. That's just so arrogant it makes my teeth hurt." Thus, debt and credit reveal themselves not as a pathway to wealth growth, as they have been presented in the neoliberal model, but as a power control tool. The bank lends enough to keep the owner of the property poor, but also enough to be able to eventually foreclose on the property and profit from its oil production or to turn it into a financial asset. The bank's activities in *Hell or High Water* resemble Marx's primitive accumulation of capital based on "the expropriation of [the] peasant population" (2019, 87; author's translation), which, according to him, was the origin of wealthy families and companies. *Hell or High Water* denounces this process as being continuous in history, "not an historical stage, but an ever-renewed actuality" (Lazzarato 2011, 44).

The violence of debt also influences the conception of masculinity in the film. Lazzarato proposes that in a neoliberal paradigm "everyone is a 'debtor,' accountable to and guilty before capital," and that "the debtor-creditor relationship . . . intensifies mechanisms of exploitation and domination at every level of society" (2011, 7–8). The result of this pervasiveness of debt is the creation of a very specific type of citizen: "the indebted man" (Lazzarato 2011, 8). Lazzarato conceives of the indebted man and the relations of debt that he is subject to as a "power relation, one of the most important and universal of modern-day capitalism." The two pairs of men in the film suffer this condition of the neoliberal subject, "a subject that must permanently struggle to accommodate itself to the world. Not a subject that can conceive of changing the world, its structure and conditions of possibility" (Chandler and Reid 2016, 4). Parker and Hamilton, who have emerged relatively unscathed from the fallout from the crisis due to their status as civil servants, side with the state, even though they are aware of the economic violence inflicted by its institutions. Of the four characters, Parker, a family man and a devout Catholic, has adapted best to the postindustrial frontier. In their discussion of how the concept of resilience shapes the neoliberal subject, Chandler and Reid state that "the more adaptive capacity is enhanced the more resilient we are as both individuals and communities" (2016, 15). Through his faith in traditional institutions such as the family, religion, and law enforcement, Parker can adapt; he navigates the West Texas plains alongside Hamilton, without the intelligence of his colleague but also without his anxiety about retirement and irrelevance. In its conscious manipulation of Western tropes, *Hell or High Water* foregrounds the irony behind the fact that the Native American is more content than the white characters in this situation; for instance, Parker replies to one of Hamilton's racist jokes with, "Just when I was starting to feel sorry about you," to which Hamilton protests, "Indians ain't supposed to feel sorry for cowboys, it's the other way around."

Parker's opposite in the pair of outlaws is Toby's older brother, Tanner. Tanner is the result of the inability to adapt to the deindustrialized environment due to economic and social conditions, what Chandler and Reid call "vulnerabilities" (2016, 15). The poverty and violence of his family environment, including his father's repeated abuse and his subsequent killing of him with a hunting rifle, break Tanner and transform him into a man prone to violence. At several points in the film, Tanner's strategy to reaffirm his masculinity is the comparison with the Comanche that used to inhabit the land. His decision to draw the police away from Toby stems from the love he professes for his brother, but also from a radical reaffirmation of masculinity that counters its obsolescence with a suicidal sacrifice, albeit romanticizing the genocide of Native Americans through his identification with the Comanche and presenting a divergence with Toby's more adaptive and nurturing form of masculinity.

In this sense, both Hamilton and Toby are resilient neoliberal subjects whose endurance depends on their opposing the deadlines and time constraints imposed by debt on the narrative of the film. Lazzarato argues that "the debt economy is an economy of time and subjectivation in a specific sense," because the promise of future wealth through credit extends the domination of financial institutions not only to the present but also the future (2011, 46–7). The development of both characters is structured through comeuppances, those of Hamilton's retirement and Toby's deadline for paying off this reverse mortgage, but the weight of debt and the economic violence triggered by the crisis force a temporality in which future, past, and present blend and dissolve. The future is tied to the economic and blood debts of the past on the Western frontier, and is embodied by Toby's sons. Meanwhile, the present that Toby represents passes by between the menace of future debt and the indebtedness to a past conception of masculinity and politics, that of the old West epitomized by Marcus Hamilton. In his status as lawman, Hamilton anchors the film to the past by becoming the closest masculinity to that of the classic Westerner, that is, the last guarantor of a concept of justice that does not necessarily agree with that of the law. In this sense, Hamilton embodies a contradiction, because his resilience is based on his indebtedness to the past. It is significant that the oldest of the four protagonists is tasked with upholding the values of the Western, and that the film concludes with his retirement, but also his survival. Hamilton is pushed out of the Texas Rangers because his age, values, and masculinity are obsolete in the postindustrial frontier, and this is underlined by the fact that a female Ranger takes over his desk in the office. Nevertheless, Hamilton's masculinity is allowed to survive the final shoot-out, because he is the only one to conclude that Toby is responsible for the robberies and he is willing to hold him to account by way of a duel, which does not take place in the film but is promised to happen in the future, thereby transforming Toby's victory against the bank into a blood debt to Hamilton.

The present, however, belongs to Toby Howard as the brains behind the robberies. Toby repurposes the silence and self-containment associated with the male Western hero to transform them into resilience. Unlike Tanner, Toby is resilient and adaptive enough to overcome his familial history of violent abuse, the lack of employment in gas drilling after the crisis, and the threat of foreclosure on the ranch in order to survive the robbing spree and ensure a poverty-free future for his sons. However, Toby is also aware that "debt simply neutralizes time, time as the creation of new possibilities" (Lazzarato 2011, 49) and, to ensure a future for his sons, he must rid them not only of the economic debt with the Texas Midlands Bank but also of the familial debt of violence caused by his father's abuse and fueled by the conditions of the postindustrial society. In a key conversation with one of his sons, Toby gives a clear order: "Don't be like us." Toby adapts to counter obsolescence, recognizing that the pattern of familial violence can be broken only by providing Debby with the resources to lead his sons into a wealthy future. However, this adaptation also enables him to rejoin the family core from a peripheral position, from which he fixes up the ranch and performs basic parental duties. In contrast to Tanner's rigid, violent, and overtly sexual masculinity, Toby realigns the parameters of his maleness through a queering of his cowboy figure. The contrast between both brothers' approach to sexuality is foregrounded in the scene in which Tanner has sex with the receptionist of the casino hotel while Toby tries to sleep in the same room. Chris Pine's body is often displayed as pleasurable to the gaze, and its construction as aesthetically beautiful and sexually virile strays from normative depictions of masculinity in the Western. In this sense, Chris Pine's subversion of the cowboy figure through conscious beauty relates to the performances of, for example, Montgomery Clift in *Red River* and Paul Newman in *Butch Cassidy and the Sundance Kid* (George Roy Hill 1969) but, as opposed to these characters, Toby rejects the sexual attention of the females in the film, as he decides not to engage in any sexual intercourse with Jenny Ann or the solicitous hooker at the casino. Toby opts instead for self-containment and the development of sensitive and nurturing characteristics to remain in a peripheral position in the family core, which adds up to his readiness to protective violence. Rather than rendering Toby a non-sexual character, these traits queer his masculinity and expose its performative nature in the sense that it is "instituted in an exterior space through a stylized repetition of acts" (Butler 2004, 114). Through his display of masculinity, Toby redraws the coordinates of manhood in the contemporary Western "on the surface of the body" (Butler 2004, 110). It is in the body of Toby, beautifully displayed but sexually contained, where *Hell or High Water* locates a resilient new form of masculinity that is adaptive to the economic violence of the postcrisis landscape, the demands of alternative forms of family, and a Western genre struggling to find relevance.

The fact that Hamilton and Toby remain alive at the end of *Hell or High Water* means that they also remain subject to debt. By avoiding a shoot-out between them in the final scene and removing the signifier of the duel from the narrative of the film, *Hell or High Water* conveys the difficulty in removing debt from the lives of contemporary US men. The death of one or both of these two characters in a final duel would have cleared them both of their debt, but instead the promise of a future visit by Hamilton to Toby foregrounds the temporal dimension of the postindustrial frontier, forever stretching into the future due to unsettled (blood) debts. "Future is a mere forecast of current domination and exploitation," warns Lazzarato (2011, 71), and Toby and Hamilton will indeed remain dominated by it and indebted to each other indefinitely.

Conclusion

Returning to the cattle driving scene that opened this chapter, Hamilton's remark, "These boys is on their own," applies also to the Howard brothers in their fight with the bank, and even to himself once he remains the only party interested in bringing Toby to justice. Toby's success in securing the ranch property for his sons does not translate into significant changes in West Texas by the end of the film, however. Toby neither seeks nor expects help from a wider community of people damaged by bank dealings in a postcrisis context. The film ends, therefore, with the triumph of the individualistic political rationality of neoliberalism, wherein "the debate about precarity has been built around extreme forms of social isolation, such as suicides or violent acts committed by those who suffer it" (Hardt 2012, 178; author's translation). *Hell or High Water* shows what the results of that isolation are: violent bank robbery and suicidal shoot-outs with the police as the only possible response to predatory financial capitalism. There is no collective organization in *Hell or High Water*, only marginal individual retribution, and the postcrisis Western cannot imagine an alternative to financial subjugation outside of its neoliberal mold.

Nevertheless, this is precisely why *Hell or High Water* and, with it, the 2010s Western as a whole, matter as cinema of crisis. The economic violence exerted by the bank in *Hell or High Water* becomes a visceral rejection of the postindustrial policies that led to the financial crisis and its aftermath, while the film's incapability of conceiving of a strategy against these policies, one that goes beyond the very trappings of neoliberal individuality, exposes the limitations that any form of resistance faces. The urgency of the crisis transposes the frontier from the safety of the historical and mythicized past of the classic Western to the ravaged, anxiety-ridden landscape of the present and shows the consequences of the crisis in ways that are closer to naturalistic depictions of confrontation and conformity than to any symbolic repository of outlaw angst. As a Western, *Hell or High Water* might not be able to reveal a way to counter neoliberalism, but it can modify the coordinates of its own landscape so that the frontier keeps pace with a changing United States and thereby allows the Western to reclaim its space and status as a politically relevant US film genre.

References

Buckley, A. (2011), *Financial Crisis: Causes, Context, and Consequences*, Harlow: Pearson Education UK.
Butler, J. (2004), "Bodily Inscriptions, Performative Subversions," in S. Salih and J. Butler (eds.), *The Judith Butler Reader*, Malden, MA: Blackwell Publishing, pp. 90–118. First published in 1990.
Campbell, N. (2013), *Post-Westerns: Cinema, Region, West*, Nebraska: University of Nebraska Press.
Chandler, D. and J. Reid (2016), *The Neoliberal Subject: Resilience, Adaptation and Vulnerability*, London and New York: Rowman and Littlefield International.
Corkin, S. (2004), *Cowboys as Cold Warriors: The Western and U.S. History*, Philadelphia: Temple University Press.
Coyne, M. (1997), *The Crowded Prairie: American National Identity in the Hollywood Western*, London and New York: I. B. Tauris.
Crouch, C. (2019), "Inequalities in Post-Industrial Societies," *Structural Change and Economic Dynamics* 51, pp. 11–23.
Falconer, P. (2020), *The Afterlife of the Hollywood Western*, London: Palgrave Macmillan.
French, P. (2005), *Westerns and Westerns Revisited*, Manchester: Carcanet Press.
Gorfinkel, E. (2016), "Exhausted Drift: Austerity, Dispossession and the Politics of Slow in Kelly Reichardt's *Meek's Cutoff*," in T. de Luca and N. B. Jorge (eds.), *Slow Cinema*, Edinburgh: University of Edinburgh Press, pp. 123–36.
Hall, S. (2011), "The Neoliberal Revolution," *Soundings* 48, pp. 9–27.
Hardt, M. (2012), "Siempre ha habido alternativas," in G. Agamben et al. (eds.), *Pensar desde la izquierda. Mapa del pensamiento crítico para un tiempo en crisis*, trans. J. Palacio Tauste et al., Barcelona: Errata Naturae, pp. 164–80.
Lazzarato, M. (2011), *The Making of the Indebted Man: An Essay on the Neoliberal Condition*, trans. J. D. Jordan, Los Angeles: Semiotext(e).
Limerick, P. N. (1987), *The Legacy of Conquest: The Unbroken Past of the American West*, New York and London: W. W. Norton & Company.
Marx, K. (2019), *La acumulación originaria del capital*, trans. Instituto del Marximo- Leninismo, Barcelona: Dirección Única. First published in 1867.
McGee, P. (2007), *From Shane to Kill Bill: Rethinking the Western*, Malden, MA: Blackwell Publishing.
Parvu, C. A. (2017), "Contestatory Cosmopolitanism, Neoliberal Rationality and Global Protest," *Globalizations* 14 (5), pp. 776–91.

Turner, F. J. (1998), *Rereading Frederick Jackson Turner: "The Significance of the Frontier in American History" and Other Essays*, ed. J. M. Faragher, New Haven, CT: Yale University Press.

Weber, M. (2004), *The Vocation Lectures*, eds. D. S. Owen and T. B. Strong, trans. R. Livingstone, Indianapolis, IN and Cambridge, MA: Hackett Publishing. First published in 1919.

17

Bad Hombres at the Border

Masculinity and Mexico in *Rambo: Last Blood*

Gregory Frame

The US has become a dumping ground for everybody else's problems... When Mexico sends its people, they're not sending their best... They're sending people that have lots of problems, and they're bringing those problems with us [sic]. They're bringing drugs. They're bringing crime. They're rapists. And some, I assume, are good people.

DONALD TRUMP (LAUNCH OF PRESIDENTIAL CAMPAIGN, 2015)

While launching his campaign for the US presidency in June 2015, Donald Trump shocked the world with a xenophobic speech that reserved a significant amount of rhetorical bile for the United States's neighbor to the south, Mexico. Trump indulged in common stereotypes of Mexicans as dangerous criminals, and of Mexico as a lawless, chaotic, and violent place. Infamously, he promised to build a "Great Wall" between the two countries to guard against apparently uncontrolled immigration from the south. In so doing, "he consciously crafted a US-Mexico border imaginary to generate fear through a blending of national security concerns, xenophobia toward Mexicans, criminalization of immigration, and an idea of the US-Mexico border as porous" (Fleuriet and Castellano 2020, 890). Trump would continue this theme throughout his presidency. To deter people from attempting to cross the border, his administration adopted a widely condemned policy of separating migrant children from their parents. A central facet of his strategy in the 2018 midterm elections was to stoke fear of migrants moving across the Mexican border through continued reference to a "migrant caravan" making its way through South America toward the United States. It has become received wisdom that Trump rode to power on a wave of disenchantment with neoliberal globalization that had driven down wages, outsourced jobs, and hollowed out communities. Anger at the failure to make any substantive reforms to this settlement after the collapse of the economy in 2008 was apparently further fuel for his popular appeal, as he opposed international free trade agreements and promised to bring back lost manufacturing jobs. However, evidence suggests that it was his articulation of white racial fears and resentment that was the true driver of his electoral success, with his infamous slogan "Make America Great Again" signaling to voters that he "would turn back the clock to a time when white people enjoyed a dominant position in American society" (Abramowitz 2018, 124). His language on "birtherism," indulgence of white supremacists, attacks on Muslims and Mexicans, and false claims of voter fraud in African American communities "directly targeted white racial and ethnic fears" (140).

Adam Abramowitz's argument that Trump's rhetoric around economics mattered considerably less to his supporters than his incendiary language about race is further evidenced by what Trump achieved in his four years in office. He did little to change the economic status quo. His main legislative accomplishment was a sizeable tax cut that mostly benefited the very wealthy. Therefore, his rhetoric about Mexico, and South America generally, is a fairly textbook example of scapegoating, a transparent attempt to appeal to the prejudices and grievances of his supporters by blaming a racialized other for the inequities of neoliberal, globalized capitalism. As Wendy Brown argues, "almost all agree that neoliberal intensification of inequality within the Global North was a tinderbox and that mass migration from South to North was a match to the fire" (2019, 10). Throughout his presidency, Trump fanned the flames for political purposes, relying on the tendency to treat the US-Mexico border not so much as "a geopolitical location in the United States than a concept that embeds a metaphor for insecurity and lawlessness" (Fleuriet and Castellano 2020, 882). Trump's rhetoric in this area found a receptive audience, with white voters increasingly resentful at the changing demographics of the United States and the increasing social, economic, and political power of people of color since the 1960s (Abramowitz 2018, 128–9).

Trump's incendiary, cartoonish language about Mexico and Mexicans—conceptualizing them as "bad *hombres*" during the third presidential debate with Hillary Clinton in October 2016—was consistent with the characterization of the country and its people in US popular culture. Jack Beckham argues that when it comes to the US-Mexico border, "American cinema has, for years, worked its magic to manipulate popular opinion, machinating to fortify racial stereotypes, prejudice, jingoism, and hegemonic control—especially during times of political change" (2005, 130–1). Speaking of the border films of the early twenty-first century like *Brokeback Mountain* (Ang Lee 2005), *The Three Burials of Melquiades Estrada* (Tommy Lee Jones 2005), and *No Country for Old Men* (Ethan and Joel Coen 2008), Camilla Fojas (2011, 98) notes that the border film "trace[s] policy mood swings and shape[s] cultural agenda[s]," expressing US fears that economic globalization, political intervention, and transnational migration of people and goods will inevitably lead to greater cultural integration and, perhaps, degradation. Cinema also sought to "reduce the vagueness of the border region" by placing the United States and Mexico into a "binary opposition that places Anglo and American values in a hierarchical position to (stereotypical) Latino and Mexican values" (Beckham 2005, 131).

While fear of the other is no doubt a significant aspect of the border film, Mexico is often constructed as a proving ground for white masculinity too. As Janne Lahti argues (2016, 335–58), American films about the border are more often than not white, male fantasies of escape from a civilization in which they have become increasingly emasculated and marginalized as a consequence of the enormous social changes in postwar American society. As a subset of the Western genre, the border film renders "Mexico [as] a ruthless and violent dreamscape where self-made white male achievement and authority are still fathomable, but where the road to redemption is filled with dangers and corrupting temptations" (Lahti 2016, 340). It continues to offer a space for white men to "prove and recover their manliness," devoid of the restrictions on their behavior imposed by modern, urban life. The conventional border film may present Mexico as dangerous, and Mexicans as threatening, but it is also a world of adventure and excitement. A place to explore and exploit, inhabited by a people who inspire fear and fascination, "Mexico and Mexicans have always been blank slates for the projections of the U.S. psyche" (101).

However, Frank García (2018, 279) contends that American cinema of recent years has adopted an approach more critical of US policies toward the border, offering a substantive challenge to the tendency to portray Mexicans as drug dealers and gang members who pose a threat to the United States, its culture, and its citizens. For example, García argues that *Frontera* (Michael Berry 2014) critiques the vigilante militias who target migrants at the border as engaging in recreational violence akin to a videogame, using point-of-view shots to implicate the viewer in their actions (290) (however, García contends that the film ultimately reinforces the Trumpian calls to hypermilitarize the border in the name of national security). This shift is consistent with the broader generic changes in the Western. Since the 1970s, as the genre has become increasingly marginal in mainstream feature film production, it has taken a more skeptical attitude toward the concepts of American exceptionalism and Manifest Destiny. Associated with this is the genre's recent tendency to challenge the worldview of the cowboy whose "yearn[ing] for a timeless moral order" in which "strong, white men enforced a clear, unquestioned morality" is revealed to be, as in *No Country for Old Men*, impossible (101). These "revisionist" Westerns, or "post-Westerns," "become a vehicle to problematize the assumptions, explore the contradictions behind these ideals, and show the American nightmares of individualism, violence, inequality, poverty, degradation of the land, racism, or imperialistic foreign policies" (Gonzalez 2015, 56).

This chapter will demonstrate how the fifth installment in the *Rambo* series, *Last Blood* (Adrian Grunberg 2019), largely ignores the Western genre's recent revisionist approaches to the politics of race and gender, American exceptionalism, Manifest Destiny, and attitudes toward Mexico in favor of a reactionary reinforcement of Trumpian rhetoric. It achieves this by reviving the cultural imaginary of the classical Western, which tends to construct the United States as a pastoral idyll in need of staunch defense against dangerous others. In *Last Blood*, Mexico is presented as a hellish, criminal underworld, and Mexicans become the Native Americans of the Old West: bloodthirsty savages with no redeeming qualities who prey on innocent young women. The film performs the same kind of radical simplification of issues relating to the border as Trump, leaning on weatherworn stereotypes about the other that have animated American popular cinema for decades. In its mistrust of official law enforcement authorities on both sides of the border and proscription of an individualistic, vigilante approach to the Mexican criminal underworld presented in the film, *Last Blood* can be viewed as adopting the conventions of the Western as "perhaps the ultimate venue for the display of male power in conflict with both the wilderness and the bad guy" (Saxton and Cole 2012, 105). Rambo's dismissal of the possibility the police on either side of the border will do anything to rescue his niece is reminiscent of Ghassan Hage's claim that vigilantes take matters into their own hands when "they feel that their governmental national belonging is threatened or in decline" (2000, 69). This has echoes of Trumpian rhetoric, and this chapter will demonstrate the strategies *Last Blood* employs to reinforce Trump's tacit endorsement of violence against the nation's "enemies" in order to maintain white male hegemony.

By featuring an aged Sylvester Stallone as John Rambo, the film also belongs very much to the "geriaction" subgenre, which seeks to restore a violent, authoritarian model of masculinity that is increasingly marginal due to social, political, and economic change (Frame 2021). This is not a particularly new development: Mark Gallagher (2006, 45) argues that "action films provide fantasies of heroic omnipotence and escape from, or transcendence of, cultural pressures," particularly a changing social and economic landscape in which male identity is no longer defined by physicality to the same extent. As Donnar notes (2016, 247), "Stallone's films . . . represent the vanguard of the cultural counter to perceived threats to white male hegemony following post-1960s cultural shifts and 1970s economic instability." However, these changes have been intensified in the post-recession era by an ageing "baby boomer" generation of white men who have seen power and authority beginning to slip from their grasp, and have looked to reassert their centrality in an environment changing socially, politically, and technologically. Indeed, it is important to note that in the eleven years between *Rambo* and *Last Blood*, Stallone established as writer and director another successful action franchise in *The Expendables* (2010–14). This series, featuring Stallone as the leader of a group of elite mercenaries, many of whom have been resurrected from the annals of 1980s action cinema, reaffirmed the star's persona as identified with marginalized, blue-collar white masculinities, engaging with the impact of economic and cultural change on this group. As Donnar suggests, "Stallone's characters are routinely downtrodden and written-off, beaten and abandoned, and bear an insistently reiterated 'outsider' or 'underdog' status" (250). Stallone's post-recession comeback, not only featuring in *The Expendables* but also resurrecting Rocky Balboa in the *Creed* (Ryan Coogler 2015; Steven Caple, Jr. 2018) films (among other roles in action cinema), demonstrates a desire to "resist . . . redundancy, age, and expiration" (256). Therefore, not only does *Last Blood* speak Trump's language when it comes to the US-Mexico border, it also appeals to the perception on the part of many of his supporters that, as older white men, their dominant positions in society are under threat due to social reform, globalization, and deindustrialization, offering an image of resistance to this apparently inevitable obsolescence.

The *Rambo* series (1982–2019) has functioned as a barometer of US domestic and foreign policies for its nearly forty-year history. In his earlier incarnations, John Rambo was understood as "the literal embodiment of American interventionism" (Tasker 1993, 92). Rambo himself is most predominantly identified with Reaganite policies: returning from Vietnam with post-traumatic stress disorder and discarded by the society that created him in *First Blood* (Ted Kotcheff 1982), Rambo becomes an avenging angel, journeying back to Vietnam to rescue the mythical US prisoners of war in *Rambo: First Blood Part II* (George P. Cosmatos 1985) that so animated right-wing discourse during this period. Indeed, the *Rambo* series performed important cultural work for the Reagan administration throughout the 1980s, which sought to reinvigorate US militarism and masculinity perceived to have gone soft, rehabilitate the Vietnam veteran in the eyes of the public, and, concomitantly, revise the nation's first major military defeat as a noble, rather than a shameful, one. As Rambo infamously said to

Colonel Trautmann (Richard Crenna) when he is about to return to Vietnam in *Part II*, "Do we get to win this time?" (the perception that it was mostly governmental ineptitude that denied the United States victory in Vietnam plays a significant role in the *Rambo* series). The series played a vital part in establishing the United States's Vietnam veterans as "innocent victims who are finally, almost reluctantly, claiming their proper status as both giants and equals in the geopolitical world" (Muse 1993, 92). In the cultural imaginary, Rambo is often understood as "a slugglishly violent nationalistic macho," and the embodiment of the United States's willingness to ride into battle overseas to impose its will upon the world (Tasker 1993, 97). As Susan Jeffords argues (1994, 42), the *Rambo* series in its first three installments is about "the battle for democracy around the world. And the only body who can wage this battle for the beleaguered West . . . is the hardened American body."

However, as Gina Marchetti notes (2014, 221), the *Rambo* series "embod[ies] the contradictions of the times," questioning the US government in *First Blood*, offering a revisionist take on the war in Vietnam in *Part II*, fighting the Cold War in Afghanistan in *Rambo III* (Peter MacDonald 1988), before attempting to make Myanmar safe for Christianity in *Rambo* (Sylvester Stallone 2008). Marchetti argues that the series is considerably more ambivalent about US foreign policy than its reputation suggests, evincing a profound mistrust of the US authorities, critiquing the treatment of Vietnam veterans, and, in Rambo, offering us "an ambiguous figure—off the grid, a loner, a Native American, unassimilated, perpetually angry, and not easily placed within America's political party structure" (224). Like the Western hero whose violence means he cannot ever be incorporated fully into civilized society, Rambo struggles in the first four films to find a stable place for himself in the land of his birth.

Last Blood's reduction of the complexities of the US-Mexico border to a series of binary oppositions in some respects therefore represents a departure for the series, which had initially evinced some ambivalence about the United States's exercise of power overseas and had particular concerns about its treatment of veterans. Moreover, Rambo's complex heritage (he is of Native American, German, and Italian extraction, and, of course, Stallone is Italian-American) is largely effaced in favor of a straightforward construction of "us" and "them." There are "good" Mexicans in the film (the "good people" to whom Trump referred), but they are limited to Rambo's niece, Gabriela (Yvette Monreal); her grandmother, Maria (Adriana Barraza); and investigative journalist, Carmen Delgado (Paz Vega), who rescues Rambo and helps him find the cartel. These "good" Mexicans are dwarfed by the overwhelming numbers of brutish men who prey on women and perpetrate horrifying acts of violence. Indeed, Gabriela's obvious assimilation into the rituals of US adolescence going from high school to college, refusal of the sexual advances of her boyfriend, and her visible discomfort and fear upon return to Mexico suggest the film views her as a "good immigrant," whose Americanized, virginal innocence is in need of preservation and protection. This is consistent with both the contemporary vigilante film, in which recovery and demonstration of ageing masculine prowess are played out in the battle to protect or avenge young women, and right-wing discourse about immigration that constructs men of color as a sexual threat.

Having rescued the Christian missionaries from the bloodthirsty junta in Myanmar, Rambo returns to his family's ranch in rural Arizona at the conclusion of the fourth film. *Last Blood* opens with Rambo living out a pleasant existence here riding horses, living with Gabriela and Maria. Rambo remains traumatized by his experiences in Vietnam, constructing an interconnected series of tunnels beneath the ranch as a space for sleeping, forging metal, and quiet contemplation. Four decades of experience have convinced Rambo that the world is hellishly violent and savage. When Gabriela expresses a desire to travel to Mexico to confront her father who abandoned her and her mother, Rambo responds bluntly, "Why would you want to do that?" In keeping with US cinema's tendency to simplify the complex issues that underpin US-Mexico border migration, Rambo's worldview is Manichean. He warns Gabriela that "There's nothing good out there," and, of her father, that he knows "how black a man's heart can be," and that he is "not a good man." Both Rambo and her grandmother tell Gabriela that Mexico is "a dangerous place." *Last Blood* arrives at the conclusion that the US's post–Second World War interventionism, in which it has acted as guarantor of global security within the international system, has been a failure: the rest of the world is beyond redemption. The film evinces an isolationist mindset consistent with Trumpian rhetoric, particularly as it pertains to Mexico. Far from being a product of US-led globalization and neocolonial exploitation, the Mexico of *Last Blood* is simply a bad place full of bad people. Such a view is consistent with the contemporary vigilante film since the success of *Taken* (Pierre Morel 2008), in which the aging hero must protect the young, vulnerable, and innocent—particularly women and children—from forces of evil that exist beyond the borders of the United States. In so doing, he will then be able to reassert his previously unchallenged position of rescuer, protector, and defender of the nation. The US-Mexico border proves the ideal stage for *Last Blood* to enact the anxieties about masculinity, national potency, and security that were so central to Trump's political success. To borrow another Trumpian turn of phrase, *Last Blood* reinforces Trump's suggestion that vast swathes of the globe beyond US borders are "shithole" countries, and only the heroic individual male can protect the United States from the threats they pose.

The film renders visual Rambo's worldview. It begins with a wide-angle shot of Rambo's sun-kissed Arizona homestead, offering a nostalgic evocation of the frontier landscape. Medals and weapons from Rambo's experiences as a soldier adorn the walls of his underground workshop and sleeping quarters, before we cut to him demonstrating his skills on horseback, donning a white Stetson, denim jacket, and trousers. The camera revels in the spectacle of Rambo gently commanding the horse, gliding toward and around him before cutting to a top-down angle. Shortly thereafter, Rambo sits down to breakfast prepared by Maria. The kitchen has the welcoming, rustic quality of the Western homestead and, as Rambo later rides horses with Gabriela, it is clear the film intends to present a tranquil image of the US frontier, one that provides comfort and reassurance to the still-traumatized Rambo who endures vivid flashbacks to his Vietnam days while performing maintenance of his tunnel habitat. The archive footage of the carnage of war has an immediate, shocking quality, a stark contrast to the placid, rural domesticity of the opening scenes. Rambo consistently reminds us he is only able to keep "a lid" on his violent past, and it seems the warm stability of his ranch life (along with his medication) is essential to this effort. Though not abandoning Rambo's status as a victim of the nation's misdeeds in Vietnam, the film here confirms his reinstatement into US national mythology, revering his service and positioning him as the frontier hero. This is a further example of *Last Blood*'s resistance to the politics of the contemporary Western and border film, which tends to present (as in the case of *No Country for Old Men*) the Vietnam veteran as an outlaw in order to "elicit . . . public fears about the misuse and redeployment of military knowledge into criminal practice" (Fojas 2011, 101). The film invites us to admire, rather than fear, Rambo, the camera gliding over photographs of the young Rambo in military uniform, before arriving at an image of him with Gabriela and her grandmother on the occasion of Gabriela's high school graduation. While the previous films in the series appear to ask the question, "is there a place for the muscular hero in America?" here that question seems to have been answered in the affirmative (Tasker 1993, 98). Whereas previously, "as with the classic western hero, Rambo's violence [kept] him out of polite society," here he is positioned very much as father and protector, with a place to call his own and people who care for him (Marchetti 2014, 223). In so doing, *Last Blood* appears determined to reinforce the "thematic myth" of the Western: bringing civilization to the wilderness, with the strong white male "standing tall in the saddle," defending his home and his loved ones from everything outside that might pose a threat to it (Benshoff and Griffin 2009, 105).

By stark contrast, Mexico is presented as densely populated, dirty, and decrepit. Though the town in which Gabriela arrives remains unidentified, the proximity of Rambo's ranch in Bowie, Arizona, means it could be understood as the city of Juárez, a place with a reputation for violent crime and the home of Mexican *vaquero* (cowboy) culture. These perceptions are reinforced immediately. Gangs of men loiter on street corners drinking, leering at Gabriela as she arrives at her friend's dwelling, which is rundown and sparsely furnished. After her father cruelly rejects her (providing radical contrast to Rambo's caring and overprotective paternal masculinity), Gabriela goes to a nightclub, where she is drugged and ultimately sold into sex slavery. The Mexican nightclub forms a further stark contrast with Rambo's ranch: it is neon-lit and loud, with the strobe lighting and rapid cutting assaulting the senses. A further obvious contrast is drawn between Rambo and the lascivious *vaquero* who approaches Gabriela at the bar. In keeping with the simplistic mythos of the classic Western, he dons a black hat to connote his villainy and, in conjunction with his open shirt and gold chains, is constructed quite clearly as a sexual threat, shown gazing at Gabriela's body. Rapidly intercut with shots of him leering at Gabriela are brief images of intoxicated clubbers and strobe lighting, adding to the disorientating, threatening feeling of the sequence. Pills dissolve in Gabriela's drink, we cut to black, and then immediately to a long shot of Rambo's ranch at dawn. From neon to sepia, from sensory overload to calm and quiet, from urban to rural, the film makes plain the stark contrast between Mexico and the United States.

This polarization is further reinforced when Rambo travels to Mexico on his own to find Gabriela. He is obviously out of his comfort zone in urban Mexico, finding himself navigating a labyrinthine network of dark alleyways and narrow stairwells in a dingy neighborhood in search of Gabriela's captors. He is easily caught and beaten to a bloody pulp. In its rendering of Mexico as a seedy, criminal underworld, and a place where only bad things happen, *Last Blood* is consistent with the Western genre's tendency to indulge in binary oppositions between wilderness and civilization. However, in its construction of this stark contrast between the United States and Mexico, the film departs from recent developments in the Western genre that have sought to complicate the simplistic oppositions of its classical incarnations in favor of a more critical perspective on the United States. Consistent with its position within the reactionary geriaction genre, however, *Last Blood* seeks to restore, rather than critique, a violent, racist, individualistic ethos as an essential component of the United States's ability to defend itself against barbarous others. In keeping with its portrayal in earlier films set in the borderlands from *Touch of Evil* (Orson Welles 1958) to *Traffic* (Steven Soderbergh 2000), "the borderland is . . . a zone whose uniqueness lies in the economics of crime and vice" (dell'Agnese 2005, 217).

Indeed, Gabriela's capture by sex traffickers places *Last Blood* within the confines of the captivity narrative common in the Western genre. It is consistent with canonical, classical Westerns such as *The Searchers* (John Ford 1956) and also has a clear relationship with contemporary iterations of the vigilante geriaction film whereby the retired hero, often drawn from a law enforcement or military background, is pressed once more into service to rescue or avenge a loved one, usually a wife or daughter. However, Rambo fails to save Gabriela's life, and she dies of a drug overdose on the journey back to the United States. Her death is a crucial narrative development in terms of the film's view of the world, as it takes a turn toward the nihilistic thereafter. As Gabriela struggles to stay awake, Rambo tells her that she was the reason he had recovered after returning from his overseas misadventures; that in her, he saw goodness and innocence that he thought did not exist, and that he had found a family he never thought he would have. This returns us to the simplistic worldview Rambo expresses to Gabriela when she admits her desire to visit Mexico to find her father: Gabriela's goodness and innocence must be defended against the "bad" people that threaten it. Her death destroys Rambo's fragile faith in these ideological shibboleths of home, family, and childhood innocence, and justifies his previous belief that the world is hell. It also liberates him from any social obligation, meaning he can indulge his desire for revenge. Rambo gives in fully to a nihilistic perspective which echoes that of Trump's base of white male supporters who, rather than accept their gradual marginalization in a multicultural society, turn "toward apocalypse" (Brown 2019, 180). Rambo has long been identified as a representative of the dispossessed elements of US society (Tasker 1993, 101), but this takes on added resonance when we consider the confluence of the neoliberal valorization of libertarian freedom with the "wounded, angry white maleness" (itself a by-product of neoliberal economic policies) that drove Trump's electoral success. Brown argues that for constituencies in society who feel their power and influence are waning, Trump's willingness to say and do whatever he wants is reassuring, that perhaps the show is not completely over for them either. I suggest that Rambo's violence performs a similar function: far from having a goal in mind, or looking to achieve an edifying conclusion because none is possible, Rambo simply wants those who have wronged him to "feel [his] rage, [his] hate." As Brown contends of Trump and his supporters, "This is humanity without a project other than revenge, without restraint by conscience, faith, or value and without belief in either human or divine purposes" (2019, 172).

That this revenge plays out through the ritual extermination of racialized others is unsurprising, as the corrosion of the neoliberal consensus following the 2008 financial crisis resulted not in a sustained engagement with the powerful groups that caused it, but a reversion to a strategy of scapegoating racial minorities consistent with previous economic crises. *Last Blood* gives in fully to this impulse. Immediately after Gabriela dies in the front seat of Rambo's truck, the film cuts to him pulling up to the border with the United States, guarded by a tatty barbed wire fence and a couple of impotent signs warning potential migrants to "keep out." Rambo smashes through this inadequate barrier with his truck, leaving little room for interpretation as to who and what is to blame for Gabriela's death. In keeping with his rhetoric and policies toward Mexico as candidate and later president, *Last Blood* reinforces Trump's construction of a US-Mexico border imaginary "to generate fear through a blending of national security concerns, xenophobia toward Mexicans, criminalization of immigration, and an idea of the US-Mexico border as porous" (Fleuriet and Castellano 2020,

890). Rambo then transforms his once tranquil homestead into a series of elaborate traps. He lures the cartel to their deaths through an initial incursion back into Mexico to murder one of the brothers who leads the cartel, Victor (Óscar Jaenada), whom he kills by severing his head. This is a taste of things to come as the final third of the film is a catalog of bloodshed, with each member of the gang massacred in increasingly graphic and horrifying ways, before Rambo pins the other brother, Hugo (Sergio Peris-Mencheta), to the wall using a bow and arrow, and rips his heart out with his bare hands. Though fanciful in execution (Rambo appears to find it reasonably easy to slice through Hugo's ribcage in order to wrench the heart from his chest), this conclusion should be viewed rather as a reinforcement of the US myth of regeneration through violence, in which the Western hero "becomes avenger, exorcising and destroying utterly all demons," cleansing the wilderness by exterminating dark-skinned others (Slotkin 1971, 51). This spectacle, in which an ageing male hero outwits, defeats, and destroys a horde of racialized invaders, is further evidence of the film's white supremacist rhetoric.

However, while he has defeated the cartel, it is difficult to say this has revitalized or regenerated Rambo, or given him a new sense of purpose. The film concludes with Rambo, exhausted, wounded, and dejected, slumped on the rocking chair on the porch outside the homestead, facing once more a life of solitude and isolation. Rambo's voice-over narration, spoken in a gravelly drawl that bespeaks his physical decrepitude, informs us that "All the ones I've loved are now ghosts. But I will fight to keep their memory alive forever." This is unconvincing. Far from being a man regenerated by his violent actions, Rambo appears, consistent with the geriaction genre and Stallone's star persona, "used up" and largely redundant (Donnar 2016, 250). Having hinted at the possibility that he might have found a place for himself within civilized society at the beginning of the film, *Last Blood* concludes with the recognition that such inclusion within the body politic is, for someone as violent and antisocial as Rambo, impossible. He is, as he was in the first three *Rambo* films, "discarded" (Studlar and Desser 1988, 13). The comparison Studlar and Desser make between *First Blood: Part II* and *I Am a Fugitive from a Chain Gang* (Mervyn LeRoy 1932) is potentially illuminating in this regard. At the end of *Part II*, Rambo has been abandoned by society in much the same way as James Allen (Paul Muni) is in Depression-era United States, left to fend for himself as one of the nation's "forgotten men." The situation in which *Chain Gang* was released, in the nadir between Herbert Hoover's election defeat and Franklin D. Roosevelt assuming office, speaks precisely to the economic outlook that drove Trump's victory, and the context in which *Last Blood* was produced. Trump himself invoked the "forgotten man" in his victory speech in November 2016, speaking to those supporters who themselves felt discarded and abandoned by a society that had left them behind. The bloody vengeance Rambo takes finds a clear analogy in the desire of many Trump supporters to do something similar, "whether it is the rage of the economically left behinds or the rage of dethroned white masculinism" (Brown 2019, 177).

The conclusion of the film is consistent with the Western genre, where the cowboy is obligated to defend civilization, but can play no part in it due to his violent nature. *Last Blood* ends as *The Searchers* did, with no place for the hero at home despite his obvious commitment to its defense. As he surveys the destruction from his rocking chair, the wounded Rambo says in weary voiceover, "I tried to come home, but I never really arrived." He did not, because he could not. Though the previous installment had hinted at the possibility that Rambo could be welcomed back into the body politic of the United States, the conclusion of *Last Blood* is more consistent with the first three films (and the Western genre), "in which the hero's ambivalence toward civilization and the community's ambivalence toward the hero's violence precludes their reconciliation" (Studlar and Desser 1988, 14). The final shot, which pulls back from the wounded Rambo on the rocking chair to a wide-angle long shot of the Arizona landscape, recalls very much Ethan Edwards's (John Wayne) departure at the conclusion of *The Searchers* who, despite his heroism in rescuing Debbie (Natalie Wood) from the clutches of the Comanche, is left to wander the desert alone.

Not content with only this allusion to the classical Western, the montage of shots from previous installments in the series that overlay the initial end credits concludes with an image of *Last Blood*'s wounded Rambo on horseback, riding into the mountains. This is an explicit reference to *Shane* (George Stevens 1953), in which the eponymous hero, nursing a minor wound and having saved the town from the ruthless cattle baron, returns from whence he came. It aligns Rambo with the mystical, mythical power of Shane (Alan Ladd) and the frontier hero more generally, who stands in defense of civilization even if his place within it is tenuous at best. Rambo riding away into the mountains aligns his fate with Shane's—heroes with no place left for them in a changing world. Once more, Mexico has provided a proving ground for white masculinity, this time to demonstrate that the older, declining hero can still vanquish others. Indeed, Rambo's departure at the end of *Last Blood*, romanticizing the wounded warrior as he leaves on his white horse in slow motion, is reminiscent in some respects of the deification of Trump by many of his supporters: standing up for them against immigrants they perceive to be "stealing" their jobs and threatening their safety, establishment politicians that they perceive to be corrupt and self-serving, globalist economic forces and corporate multinationals that have outsourced their jobs and ransacked their communities, or liberal metropolitan elitists who sneer at their way of life (Hochschild 2016). However, rather than attempt to process the consequences of neoliberal globalization, *Last Blood* indulges in racial resentment and destructive nihilism as displacement activity, attempting to compensate for feelings of social marginalization and economic decline through an orgy of graphic violence.

References

Abramowitz, A. (2018), *The Great Alignment: Race, Party Transformation, and the Rise of Donald Trump*, Princeton: Yale University Press.

Beckham, J. M. (2005), "Border Policy/Border Cinema: Placing *Touch of Evil*, *The Border* and *Traffic* in the American Imagination," *Journal of Popular Film and Television* 33 (3), pp. 130–41.

Benshoff, H. M. and S. Griffin (2009), *America on Film: Representing Race, Class, Gender, and Sexuality at the Movies*, Chichester: Wiley-Blackwell.

Brown, W. (2019), *In the Ruins of Neoliberalism: The Rise of Antidemocratic Politics in the West*, New York: Columbia University Press.

dell'Agnese, E. (2005), "The US-Mexico Border in American Movies: A Political Geography Perspective," *Geopolitics* 10, pp. 204–21.

Donnar, G. (2016), "Narratives of Cultural and Professional Redundancy: Ageing Action Stardom in the 'Geri-action' Film," *Communication, Politics and Culture* 49 (1), pp. 1–18.

Fleuriet, K. J. and M. Castellano (2020), "Media, Place-Making, and Concept-Metaphors: The US-Mexico Border during the Rise of Donald Trump," *Media, Culture and Society* 42 (6), pp. 880–97.

Fojas, C. (2011), "Hollywood Border Cinema: Westerns with a Vengeance," *Journal of Popular Film and Television* 39 (2), pp. 93–101.

Frame, G. (2021), "Make America Hate Again: The Politics of Vigilante Geriaction," *Journal of Popular Film and Television* 49 (3), pp. 168–80.

Gallagher, M. (2006), *Action Figures: Men, Action Films, and Contemporary Adventure Narratives*, New York: Palgrave Macmillan.

García, F. (2018), "American Cinema's Return to the Borderlands: Migrant Criminalization, Critical Identity Politics, and Nativism in the Trump Era," *The Journal of American Culture* 41 (3), pp. 279–96.

Gonzalez, J. A. (2015), "New Frontiers for Post-Western Cinema: *Frozen River*, *Sin Nombre*, *Winter's Bone*," *Western American Literature* 50 (1), pp. 51–76.

Hage, G. (2000), *White Nation*, New York: Routledge.

Hochschild, A. R. (2016), *Strangers in Their Own Land: Anger and Mourning on the American Right*, New York: The New Press.

Jeffords, S. (1994), *Hard Bodies: Hollywood Masculinity in the Reagan Era*, New Brunswick: Rutgers University Press.

Lahti, J. (2016), "Borderlands in Movies: Manliness, Violence, and Anglo Crossings of the US-Mexican Border," *Journal of the Southwest* 58 (2), pp. 335–58.

Marchetti, G. (2014), "Sylvester Stallone and John Rambo's Trek Across Asia: Politics, Performance and American Empire," in C. Holmlund (ed.), *The Ultimate Stallone Reader: Sylvester Stallone as Star, Icon, Auteur*, Chichester: Wallflower Press, pp. 217–40.

Muse, E. (1993), "From Lt. Calley to John Rambo: Repatriating the Vietnam War," *Journal of American Studies* 27 (1), pp. 88–92.

Saxton, B. and T. R. Cole (2012), "No Country for Old Men: A Search for Masculinity in Later Life," *International Journal of Ageing and Later Life* 7 (2), pp. 97–116.

Slotkin, R. (1971), "Dreams and Genocide: The American Myth of Regeneration Through Violence," *The Journal of Popular Culture* 5 (1), pp. 38–59.

Studlar, G. and D. Desser (1988), "Never Having to Say You're Sorry: Rambo's Rewriting of the Vietnam War," *Film Quarterly* 42 (1), pp. 9–16.

Tasker, Y. (1993), *Spectacular Bodies: Gender, Genre and the Action Cinema*, London: Routledge.

18

We're No Longer Here

Ya no estoy aquí as an Example of Neoliberalism and Economic Crisis in the US-Mexico Borderlands

Roberto Avant-Mier

> *I think this is one of the most memorable debuts in Mexican film in the last couple of decades.*
> GUILLERMO DEL TORO[1]

Introduction

One could argue that cinema in Latin America has always been connected to colonialism.[2] For example, in Mexico and Latin America cinema came with the railway networks and trains that were making fruit and other resources more accessible and available for North America and Europe (if not making workers available as well). Of course, aside from the economic intervention(s) by the United States in Mexico and other Latin American countries, there has always been the matter of the ideological baggage that comes along with US cinema. In the early days of cinema, along with the access to new markets and trade networks came the ideology of US cultural superiority, Manifest Destiny, and the American Dream, all exhibited by simplistic tales of white-skinned heroes against violent and treacherous dark-skinned bandits, bad guys, "greasers," or revolutionaries, usually Mexicans, other Latinos, or Indians (or all of the above).[3] As Chanan argues, "North American cinema was gripped from the very start [with] an ideological servility which inevitably distorted their lensing of the Latin South" (1997, 428). As he further notes, it seems as if Hollywood has just been "incapable of not offending Latin American sensibilities" (429). For the most part (or to some extent), this pattern of representation continues into the present with the exception of the development of some independent cinema movements and nonmainstream trends.

Of course, another exception to this would be that some recent documentaries are addressing issues like the lives or status of undocumented Latino/a/x immigrants in the United States, the mobility of Mexican and other Latino/a/x immigrants back and forth, the lack of immigration policy reform, the ongoing US immigration crisis, profound economic shifts regarding employment and decreasing opportunities in their homelands, the increasing presence of gangs and/or cartels in local communities that have displaced more conventional government and politics, as well as other cultural or economic pressures to move north (Cheyroux 2018). Moreover, one could argue that here at the border, we have been in a permanent state of crisis, driven by economic neoliberalism, especially after the North American Free Trade Agreement (NAFTA) in 1994 and most recently the United States-Mexico-Canada Agreement in 2020. As scholars have noted, neoliberal economic policies and trade globalization essentially have aggravated the traditional colonial dependency between Mexico and the United States. The resulting consequences of these neoliberal economic policies often put socioeconomic pressures on the shoulders of Mexican people.[4] While examples of such pressures could include widespread job losses, movement of workers to the informal sector, the loss of agricultural jobs in Mexico, displacement and diaspora, as well as increased immigration to the United States (Saldaña-Portillo 2005, 756–7), it is also important to recognize that such effects extend beyond people in Mexico to those that are part of the Mexican diaspora in the United States, as well as to those in the borderlands and spaces in between.

Noting all of this, it makes logical sense that Mexican film directors seem to be dabbling more in addressing economic neoliberalism and recent crises, or at least making reference on the big screen to the ongoing complications in economics, politics, and/or cultural shifts. Early in his career, for example, Alfonso Cuarón began with an obscure Mexican film, *Sólo con tu pareja* (1991), that makes some references to Mexico's enduring aspirations toward modernity and to its developing urban middle class, while simultaneously making fun of worn-out tropes about Mexican national culture and supposed traditions (e.g., mariachis, tequila, and sombreros). In spite of its remarkable attempts to speak to Mexico's aspiring modernism and poking fun at its old-fashioned nationalism, overall, *Sólo con tu pareja* comes off like an uncritical, silly Hollywood-style romantic comedy for the most part.

However, after this Cuarón moved on to work in the US/Hollywood system(s), but eventually returned to Mexico to make a landmark production, *Y tu mamá también* (2001), in which the filmmaker more directly references some of the complications and challenges resulting from the ideology of "free trade" and the implementation of NAFTA in 1994. In *Y tu mamá también*, for example, two adolescent young men embark on a road trip with an older woman whom they try to seduce. In minor subplots or somewhat forgettable scenes, however, they also discover some problems along the way regarding contemporary Mexican society in which traditional occupations are no longer available and economic pressures force people to seek jobs under a new, transformed economic system. For example, in this film the omniscient voice-over narration provides details about the side character Chuy (Silverio Palacios), a working family man who becomes disenfranchised by the new laws that eventually force local fishermen to abandon their traditional trades and push them into quantified, wage-labor exchanges and working-class jobs. Meanwhile, other indigenous Mexicans are featured rather prominently through slow, long takes that seem to be inviting viewers to recognize the existence of lower- working-class people and/or indigenous people employed as domestic workers or who labor on behalf of the middle and upper classes, especially the nation's lighter-skinned population.[5] Nevertheless, as de la Garza notes, "there seemed to be consensus that [*Y tu mamá también*] had succeeded in cuing interrogation of what it means to be Mexican for a new generation, one growing up in the aftermath of NAFTA" (2009, 7). All of these elements, of course, would foreshadow what was to come in Cuarón's more critically acclaimed feature film *Roma* (2018), a film that more directly addresses the intersections of labor, social class, and race/racism in Mexico (and, by extension, politics).[6]

Meanwhile, another Mexican filmmaker, Guillermo del Toro, also made statements about NAFTA and US-Mexico relations (or Mexico-US relations) in his first feature film *Cronos* (1993), although more allegorically. In *Cronos*, del Toro uses dramatic fantasy and horror motifs, combined with Christian religious references and the plot device of a modern-day vampire and creepy vampirism (e.g., blood-sucking and a little blood-licking for good measure) as a sly allusion to NAFTA and as a metaphor for modern-day capitalism.[7] More specifically, in *Cronos*, villainous US businessmen attempt to interfere with the buying and selling of antiques in order to acquire a prized object (and the secret to "everlasting life"), which according to scholars is all analogous to late capitalism, the extension and influence of US economics into Mexico, and, perhaps, inviting viewers to contemplate US cultural hegemony in Mexico.

Not long after those films, another acclaimed Mexican director, Alejandro González Iñárritu, released *Amores perros* (2000), which also tangentially references NAFTA and cultural shifts in the aftermath of NAFTA in the early 2000s. As I argue elsewhere, some of the minor subplots, side stories, and fleeting references in the dialogue of *Amores perros* can be understood as oblique references to economic and cultural shifts in the late 1990s (Avant-Mier 2021).[8] One can even argue that the other two films in Iñárritu's "Death Trilogy," *21 Grams* (2003) and *Babel* (2006), also included some important plot points that allude obliquely to underemployment, poverty, joblessness, and other trends in the United States (*21 Grams*), or more directly to globalization and the power and privileges of US citizens in comparison to the underprivileged circumstances of global others such as Mexican domestic workers in California or other non-whites of the so-called Third World (*Babel*), or to the circumstances of other people subjected to the logic(s) of border control and border patrol (*Babel*). In fact, Iñárritu has since gone on to direct *Biutiful* (2010), which, even more directly, speaks to worldwide economic shifts, immigration, and labor exploitation through a grim and gritty story of one man's personal struggle in life and in his chosen profession as a business broker in between owners and contractors on one side and the invisible, exploited immigrants on the other.

More recently, a new film has emerged as a profound statement about Mexico-US relations. In 2019, another Mexican director, Fernando Frías de la Parra (henceforth, Fernando Frías), produced his debut feature film *Ya no estoy aquí* (*I'm No Longer Here*) with a little help from the Sundance Writers Lab and Netflix, and released it through Netflix as well, essentially making this film a coproduction with US companies. This new Frías film received a great deal of positive reviews, critical praise, and even nominations for various awards, one of these accolades being Mexico's submission for consideration for an Academy Award in late 2020 in the category of Best International Feature Film. Although this film by Fernando Frías made the short list of finalists, eventually it did not win the nomination. Yet, this recognition, along with other distinctions, has all been enough to warrant worldwide attention and even praise from various famous Mexican directors such as the aforementioned Cuarón and del Toro. For example, in an eponymous 2020 Netflix interview that is now available for streaming alongside the original Netflix film, having been so impressed by Frías's first feature, two of the "three mosqueteros"[9] speak out and publicly praise the film, calling it a memorable debut as well as an important new film. Guillermo del Toro goes as far as calling the film "impeccable" in terms of its form and "completely free" in terms of its narrative, while Cuarón says that this film is "truly original" but also important because of how it challenges expectations ("Ya no estoy aquí: A talk with Guillermo del Toro and Alfonso Cuarón").

Therefore, this chapter seeks to analyze *Ya no estoy aquí* as an important new perspective within US and international cinema. In particular, it considers

Frías's film in relation to films by the aforementioned Mexican filmmakers and how it registers and references NAFTA and current economic crises. Here I aim to demonstrate that *Ya no estoy aquí* is highly significant for its narrative structure, as del Toro suggests, but is even more significant if we attend to its context. I propose to read *Ya no estoy aquí* as a document that registers economic neoliberalism and cultural shifts in the era of free trade ideology and agreements. Thus, this chapter begins with a brief description of the film and some of its more significant features and themes and then moves forward into an analysis of the film as a critical statement on societies and cultures in crisis.

Ya no estoy aquí as a Musical Drama

Ya no estoy aquí begins and ends in the city of Monterrey in the Northeastern Mexican state of Nuevo León, but within minutes, the main character, seventeen-year-old Ulises (Juan Daniel García Treviño in his feature film debut), is shown leaving his home and on his way to the United States.

However, because of the nonlinear structure, we do not know this at the beginning. Instead, we only see that Ulises is leaving or going somewhere, and he seems to be distraught about it. Moments later, we see him as part of a construction crew in Queens, New York City. As the story develops, the film moves back and forth in a series of flashbacks and flash-forwards that depict the journey of the main character from Mexico to the United States as well as through other trials, tribulations, and further travels.

Importantly, one can argue that *Ya no estoy aquí* is a musical film since music, *cumbia* dance music in particular, is not only featured prominently throughout the film both diegetically and non-diegetically (especially the super slow-tempo *cumbia* called *cumbia rebajada*), but it is central to the lives of the main character and his group of friends in the neighborhood crew (or is it a dance crew?) and thus central to the film's premise. As we discover in the film, Ulises is totally obsessed with *cumbia* music from Colombia and the dance subculture and "Kolombia" or "Cholombiano" youth styles associated with it that were popular in Mexico in the early 2000s, although Ulises and his group of friends "Los Terkos" (the stubborn ones) like it a little slower, preferring a slowed-down effect that sometimes makes the *cumbia rebajada* music sound a little distorted.

In the director's own words, *Ya no estoy aquí* is a film about identity, roots, and belonging but also, of course, about *cumbia* and dancing, migration, and even family (or, rather, the "family" that we choose).[10] And yet, of all these aspects, music and dancing are the most critical elements for the film at first glance. For example, in the very opening scene of the film, Ulises is shocked and surprised when his girlfriend, "la Chaparra" (Coral Puente), gives him a small, portable MP3 player as a goodbye gift.

As we find out later in the film through a flashback, the device is loaded with hundreds and hundreds of songs and with their favorite *cumbias*. The MP3 player acquires increasing significance as it reappears throughout the film. For example, a minor subplot concerns how the group of friends get themselves into some trouble because of it. And, in another flashback, they decide to try and save (or get) some money so that they can buy the music player from a local vendor who assures them that it contains thousands of songs, including a ton of great *cumbia* tracks. Because they are all so obsessed with *cumbia* music and dancing, the group eventually attempt to shake down other teens for pocket change, causing territorial conflicts with other groups of teenagers who more obviously operate like street gangs, using guns and engaging in violent behavior. Yet clearly, Ulises is not in a violent street gang and not involved with the local gang's dealings, and this point is made clearer during a scene in which Ulises is the accidental witness to a drive-by shooting, making him a marked man in the neighborhood and forcing him to flee the country. So, although some groups of teens in the neighborhood are part of gangs, Ulises and his friends are basically just a group of teenagers that are obsessed with *cumbia* music and love to show off their dance moves.

Therefore, to say that music is important to this group of friends (or to the film itself) is really an understatement. Rather, music is everything to these young people and especially to the traveler-hero Ulises. Music is at the core of their very identity and at the base of their motivations for getting together and hanging out. Likewise, dancing and showing their moves to each other is common in their daily routine. To emphasize this point within the film, filmmaker Fernando Frías inserts various scenes that linger on the group of teens and in their dance performances, most notably those at public events with many people, but also in moments in which they dance only for themselves. Frías avoids edits and presents the scenes in very long takes that capture the skill and the excitement of the young people dancing with each other and/or for each other.

Because of such an emphasis on music and dancing, at times the film has the feel of a documentary or some kind of anthropological exploration and documentation of a fringe culture. Like a documentary film, the viewer is invited to watch the extended dance scenes (with few cuts or edits) as if one is watching a newly discovered tribe in the Amazon.[11] As Guillermo del Toro notes in "Ya no estoy aquí: A Talk...," the film registers "a very specific reality," documenting the uniqueness of a culture by clearly focusing on their music and dance style, but also on specific details like their neighborhood, baggy clothing style, hairstyles, and a peculiar patois that includes specific accents, code-switching, and paralanguage. In fact, within the narrative, Ulises's hair and overall style are so unique and fascinating to others that they prompt a random New Yorker to stop and ask if he can take pictures of him for a website, and in other plot point, the teenager Lin also becomes fascinated with his hair and look to the point where she befriends him so that she can show him off to others.

Furthermore, the long takes of the teenagers talking nonsense or dancing as a group serve to visually underscore the filmmaker's interest in depicting a youth subculture that is quite obviously Mexican but also influenced by US culture (e.g., they mix English words with their own Spanish, wear US football jerseys, and, more generally, mimic US hip-hop style and culture) as well as by Colombian music culture (most notably *cumbia Colombiana* and/or *cumbia rebajada*) which has long been popular throughout Latin America and even in Mexico and the United States and that is at the core of their contemporary identity. In fact, as one watches this documentation of culture, one cannot help but wonder whether this is real or constructed just for the film, and whether this culture still exists or, like the main character, Ulises, it has disappeared or gone away and changed into something else (especially since the film is set around 2011).

Returning to the analysis of the film's form, it is worth noting that *Ya no estoy aquí* jumps back and forth between Mexico and the United States in a nonlinear narrative—sometimes in a surprising way. At one moment Ulises is in Monterrey, Mexico, comfortably hanging out with his dance-crew friends, and the next moment the action shifts to Ulises navigating the streets of New York, trying to find his way, or rather trying to find somewhere to go. Surprisingly, neither the nonlinear plot nor the depictions of aimless wandering take anything away from the film. Quite the contrary, the shifting between various locales and between different worlds feels like a visual storytelling strategy that shows the viewer how Ulises is caught (or, to be more precise, *trapped*) between two worlds. Generally speaking, Ulises seems lost, and he is stuck between two vastly different domains. Basically, when he is in Monterrey, the story reveals why and how Ulises fled north to the United States, and then, when he is in the United States, we witness the travails of a young man who never wanted to be there in the first place and who is forced to migrate due to daunting sociological pressures like lack of education, a broken family, and gang or cartel violence, as well as economic pressures like poverty, underemployment, and the lack of social mobility in the age of NAFTA.

All of this, by the way, symbolically reflects or parallels the experiences of many Mexicans and other Latino/a/xs in the United States, thus making the film analogous to a statement about the similar distressing situations and the contemporary crises (resulting from significant shifts in economics, politics, and culture) faced by many Latino/a/xs in recent decades. Often, the narrative moves back and forth in time (through nonlinear editing), sometimes leaving the viewer momentarily confused and wondering where the action is taking place. It is not until the camera zooms out and you see more of the surroundings that you can understand what is going on (e.g., gray sidewalks, subway trains, or lonely walks throughout New York anchor the action in the United States while green mountainscapes and the colorful people and houses of his old neighborhood situate it in Monterrey).

At this point, though, I wish to focus on how the music advances the narrative. For example, when Ulises is wandering the streets of New York listening to his *cumbia rebajada* music, the emphasis falls on his struggles to remain true to his character and on the role that *cumbia* music plays for his identity as it begins to fade. Midway through the film, we can hear the sound of *cumbia* music playing through Ulises's earphones, although it is noticeably slow and distorted. Within the film, this is due to the lack of battery power, for Ulises has nowhere to recharge his portable MP3 player. Symbolically, though, Ulises is being sapped of all his energy since he does not fit into US culture and continually longs to be back home in Monterrey with his friends. So as Ulises becomes increasingly lonely, tired of New York, and longing for home, the *cumbias* sound increasingly odd, becoming slower and more distorted.

Therefore, *Ya no estoy aquí* can be read as an allegory of migration experiences. It is interesting that in an analysis of Cuarón's *Children of Men*, film scholar Ángel Díaz Miranda surmises that "Those . . . who are immigrants are compelled to escape through parallel movements, to find a slower speed, a disguise, a mirror; to be alert and ready; to have the will to withstand capture by the system. We are compelled to resist in destitute times" (2016, 168). Although Díaz Miranda is referring to *Children of Men* here, this assessment could not be any more apt for *Ya no estoy aquí*. As the film shows, Ulises seems to experience all of these: escape, slower speed (literally), disguise, hyperalertness, withstanding capture by the system, destitution, and also resistance. Ultimately, however, Ulises is happy when he is at home, with his friends (in his community), dancing and listening to music (which amounts to asserting his identity). Conversely, he's absolutely miserable and lonely in the United States and completely isolated from anybody or anything, eventually becoming solitary, homeless, and wandering the streets alone.

In yet another noteworthy (and poignant) scene in which Ulises is on the verge of falling apart and in real danger, he is running from somebody and walks up to a subway platform in New York City to find that there is no one except for a young man leaning against the wall and playing an acoustic guitar (presumably busking). In this scene, the young guitarist is playing an obscure pop song from the 1970s called "Superstar,"[12] and the slow, sentimental ballad (with English lyrics) is the fitting soundtrack to a sad, dire moment for Ulises. Interestingly, Frías obviously uses this song in this scene because the lyrics ("you're not really here") evoke the film's title. However, it's important to note how fitting this music is at this moment because, with its somber atmosphere, slow rhythm, and no percussion at all, it clearly matches Ulises's alienation and, in fact, feels like the complete opposite of the exciting and moving *cumbias* that he and his friends prefer for dancing.

Thus, the acoustic US pop song (sung in English) is as discomforting and alienating as everything else that he experiences in the United States.

Similarly, when Ulises becomes the center of attention for his exotic looks and style, scenes like this can be articulated to the experiences of migrants in a neoliberal economy and serve as examples of how neoliberal rationality conditions all kinds of personal relations. In this instance, the aforementioned photographer's attraction to Ulises as an exotic creature is only motivated by his professional interest (i.e., shooting his "look" for a website). In fact, the two persons who seem to be attracted to Ulises, Lin and the photographer, try to get some benefit from his eccentric looks. In other words, market values structure personal relations. As other scholars like Wendy Brown argue, neoliberalism has the potential to govern rationality and to transmogrify "every human endeavor" (Brown 2015, 9–10) and disseminates "to all domains and activities" (31).

To bring these remarks to a close, I would like to reflect on the film's form one last time. At the beginning of the film there is a brilliant transposition of images that shows Ulises strolling through his neighborhood in Monterrey, Mexico. A long tracking shot shows Ulises walking through some alleys and down a long flight of stairs when suddenly he fades away as he walks out of the frame and the caption "Ya no estoy aquí" appears on the screen, thus displaying the title of the film. This title sequence turns out to be particularly significant because the sudden fading out and eventual disappearance of Ulises is revealed to be the movie's main theme from the very beginning. For example, early in the film Ulises is in New York going out to a Latin dance club with guys from his construction crew, but the security at the door does not want to allow him entry simply because of who he is and because his weird style and appearance elicit rejection. In an awkward moment, the club bouncer allows the other guys in, but tells them that Ulises cannot enter the club. And then again, much later in the film, Ulises is rejected again when he has a door closed on his face by his new acquaintance Lin, who only wants to use him to show off with her friends. When her grandfather asks who is at the door, the young girl closes the door on him and very calmly replies, "Nobody."

After yet another denial of his very existence, Ulises drifts into a dark place. He starts strolling through city streets daily, begins to sniff paint thinner, and eventually cuts off his hair (symbolically killing his former self). In other words, he no longer wants to be there (or anywhere for that matter), and he is losing his identity as well. Toward the end of the film, Ulises seems lost and is literally wandering the streets of New York City. Obviously, he is no longer in Monterrey, Mexico, but also in New York he is practically invisible and virtually nonexistent. In *Ya no estoy aquí*, Ulises is no longer here, nor there. Significantly, scholars like Saldaña-Portillo note how cinematic images of "loneliness, isolation, and anonymity in the industrialized metropolis" can function as an allegory for NAFTA

(2005, 770). Otherwise, in this circumstance Ulises exemplifies what Wendy Brown deems "survival at the extreme" under neoliberal rationality (2015, 22). As Brown further explains, under neoliberal rationality "the very top strata acquires and retains ever more wealth," while "the very bottom is literally turned out on the streets or into the growing urban and suburban slums of the world" (28–9).

Needless to say, the significance of being neither here nor there is a manifest metaphor for Ulises and his state of mind. Although less obviously, the state of being neither here nor there also works as a metaphor for the situation of Mexican or Latino/a/x immigrants in the United States, especially with regard to their legal status. Many Mexican and Latino/a/x immigrants in the United States, whether documented or undocumented, find themselves in the uncomfortable position of feeling lost and almost not existing anymore (or anywhere). As del Toro claims, this makes *Ya no estoy aquí* essentially a story about disenfranchisement. Thus, scenes, images, and situations such as these (through form and through content) work in conjunction throughout the film to demonstrate and document the displacement and marginalization of a young Mexican in the United States.

A Conclusion of Sorts

In the previous sections of this chapter, I have tried to analyze *Ya no estoy aquí* in the context of other films by Mexican directors like Cuarón, del Toro, and Iñárritu, especially with regard to the ways that some of their films have pursued more critical explorations of global politics, labor, the economy, and various cultural shifts (and crises) in recent decades, especially those affecting the relationships between the United States and Mexico, with added emphasis on the borderlands. In particular, this chapter has considered how both the form and the content of *Ya no estoy aquí* work in conjunction to illustrate the experience of an undocumented young Mexican in the United States who is forced to flee his country (thus, a refugee), disenfranchised, and often invisible. As noted earlier, Mexican filmmaker Fernando Frías constructs this portrayal through the display of the events and actions that make up the story of Ulises and his friends Los Terkos and, even more brilliantly, through the visual style and the nonlinear narrative of the film. Their story is, by extension, that of many other migrants.

As I tried to show, *cumbia* music (used both diegetically and non-diegetically) is critical for the film, but so is its deployment through extended takes that essentially eschew edits and cuts in the action and thus avoid shifting the focus away from the music or from the dancing. In these sequences, the film adopts a documentary style. By lingering on the dances, the camera makes spectators aware of their inquisitive gaze, that they look upon these people as if they were a fascinating foreign culture or a newly discovered tribe.

Moreover, the filmmaker's deployment of other cinematic techniques like the nonlinear narrative structure (by means of recurring flashbacks and flash-forwards), the slowed-down tempo of *cumbia rebajada* to match the displacement felt by Ulises, and, then again, the transposition of the film's title on top of the image of Ulises as he fades out all correspond with the topics addressed by the film (i.e., invisibility, displacement, and disenfranchisement) and contribute to the film's significance. And it is the film's take on these issues that I want to return to here in order to put forward a conclusion.

As mentioned in the introduction, US film production has not necessarily caught on with a disruptive perspective on Latino/a/x immigration such as the one put forth in *Ya no estoy aquí*. For example, by looking at recent or contemporary Hollywood films, one would think that US-Mexico relations have not changed all that much, as filmic representations continuously depict Mexicans and/or Latino/a/xs through what Leo R. Chavez called a "threat narrative" (2008) in what we might call business as usual or, rather, "entertainment as usual."[13]

Returning to *Ya no estoy aquí*, it is important to note that this film differs from the typical take on Latino/a/xs (and from cinema's colonial history mentioned at the outset) particularly because of how it does not conform to those representations, those cinematic traditions, and that history. First and most obviously, this is a film that avoids casting Mexican youths as bad guys, violent criminals, narcos or drug dealers, or any other villainous character. Beyond that, this is a film that elicits sympathy for the main character and for the group of young friends (because they are clearly not a gang, not doing drugs or involved in drug-dealing, and not committing crimes). If anything, this is a compassionate portrayal of a young Mexican kid caught up in unfortunate and impossible circumstances, hence, a cinema of sympathy. One simply cannot help but sympathize with Ulises and his situation. Even the circumstance that forces him to leave his home and family in a rush is the result of a misunderstanding, and we already know that Ulises is not in a gang or involved in crime. As Armida de la Garza argues in an interesting analysis of Cuarón's *Y tu mamá también*, films can demonstrate "the ability to *cue* spectators" into questioning things, in her example, "questioning the status quo" of the social world within the film (2009, 6; emphasis added). Thus, the current analysis suggests that, with *Ya no estoy aquí*, Fernando Frías accomplishes a similar task. In this case he manages to *cue* spectators into sympathy for Ulises, for disenfranchised youths, for Mexican immigrants, for undocumented people, for refugees, and perhaps for other Latino/a/xs in the United States.

Allow me to return once again to how *Ya no estoy aquí* differs from US cinematic traditions. The film does not conform to Hollywood's ongoing trends and colonial tendencies, nor does it conform to the dominant US ideologies in matters of immigration. For example, there is no American Dream for these kids to pursue, and if they tried, it would have been broken or led to disillusionment. For example, even though, as Wendy Brown argues, neoliberal rationality has the tendency to "remake the human being as human capital" (2015, 34) and even though the outside world can only see him as a commodity (for his cheap labor, for an image in a magazine, or as something for people to be fascinated with), in *Ya no estoy aquí* Ulises does not succeed through hard work, he will never see his image in a magazine, and he will never get paid for the photographs they took of him. Nor will he ever really be friends with Lin, since she seems to only be interested in his friendship for some kind of symbolic exchange value (with others).

Furthermore, Ulises the traveler never wanted to move to the United States in the first place; he does not arrive in the United States in search of a job or to send money back home (as occurs in many other films), and he eventually chooses to leave the United States willingly, volunteering for deportation. More significant, perhaps, there is no comfortable sense of country or nation here, but an ongoing transfer between countries (again, both literally and symbolically) so that the sense of being in-between becomes the primary source of identification within the film. As Geoffrey Kantaris concludes in his assessment, Mexican cinema is increasingly characterized by "new rhythms and sensibilities," with "fragmented and dislocated identities." What is more, in a reference to Martín-Barbero and Rey's work on labor and political economy, he notes how it is also increasingly characterized by "time-space compression, with forms of connection which paradoxically dematerialize bodies and places" (2006, 523). Once again, this observation is applicable here and an apt assessment regarding *Ya no estoy aquí*. The time-space compression in this film works to underscore the fragmented subjectivities and dislocated identities that migrants must contend with in the new millennium.

In conclusion, how would you feel if the world kept treating you as if you didn't exist? What would you do or say if the world seemed to keep telling you that you don't really exist? How do you carry on living when your world and your reality have shifted and left you with the feeling that you're no longer here, nor there, and maybe not anywhere anymore? These are complicated questions, particularly if one goes beyond the merely personal (or the anecdotal) and attempts to articulate these to other wider, global issues related to political, economic, social, or cultural shifts (or, in other words, to structural conditions). In fact, such questions are actually related to current crises in contemporary culture throughout the world. And if anyone has managed to capture these issues in a fresh, disruptive, possibly liberating, and potentially radical film, it is the newcomer Fernando Frías with *Ya no estoy aquí*. And if any of the conclusions presented in this chapter is true, the current analysis elevates *Ya no estoy aquí* to the status of allegory regarding NAFTA, neoliberalism, neoliberal rationality, and cultures in crisis. Finally, all of the considerations addressed here make Mexican director Fernando Frías, as Alfonso Cuarón recently stated, "one of the truly important directors that the world has."[14]

Notes

1. In Mandalit del Barco's "Mexico's Oscar-Winning Directors Embrace Rise of Fernando Frías De La Parra" (2021).
2. See Michael Chanan's "Cinema in Latin America" (1997).
3. For example, see Charles Ramírez Berg (2002) and William A. Nericcio (2007).
4. In one particularly pertinent example here, Saldaña-Portillo (2005) discusses how the United States has long influenced and "shaped Mexican sovereignty" (752).
5. For more on this subject, Saldaña-Portillo (2005) provides a brilliant analysis of how the images of poor people, laborers, indigenous people, and lower-class Mexicans portray "el pueblo" (the people) and *mestizaje* in *Y tu mamá también* (767–9). Meanwhile, other scholars offer slightly different perspectives on the film's articulations to NAFTA and globalization. For example, see Armida de la Garza (2009).
6. Cuarón's *Roma* (2018) was nominated for several prestigious awards in 2018 and 2019, including the Golden Lion Award for Best Film at the Venice International Film Festival as well as several Academy Awards. For more on the film, see Dolores Tierney and Olivia Cosentino (2018), Deborah Shaw (2018), and Olivia Cosentino (2018).
7. See Deborah Shaw (2013) and Geoffrey Kantaris (2006).
8. For more on Iñárritu's *Amores perros* and globalization, see G. Kantaris (2006, 523).
9. Although some authors note how they have been referred to as "three amigos" in Anglophone countries, this chapter opts for the term "tres mosqueteros" as they are called in their home country.
10. "La identificación, el arraigo, la pertenencia ... de cumbia, de baile ... de migración ... de amistad y de la familia que escogemos" (Frías 2021).
11. It is worth noting that Fernando Frías said that to create the look for the spiked, bleached, punky hair of Ulises, he was thinking of something that resembled a pre-Hispanic Aztec warrior (in del Barco 2021).
12. The song "Superstar" (which contains the lyrics "But you're not really here") was a hit song for The Carpenters in 1971, although it was originally recorded by Rita Coolidge (with Joe Cocker) in 1970. It had been previously performed by Bette Midler and others, and it has also been recorded by many others since.
13. See also Emilie Cheyroux (2019).
14. In "Ya no estoy aquí: A Talk with Guillermo del Toro and Alfonso Cuarón."

References

Avant-Mier, R. (2021), "A Song for Rob DeChaine: Articulations of Music and Film in Cinematic Border Representations," *Communication and Critical/Cultural Studies* 18 (1), pp. 59–66.

Brown, W. (2015), *Undoing the Demos: Neoliberalism's Stealth Revolution*, New York: Zone Books.

Chanan, M. (1997), "Cinema in Latin America," in Geoffrey Nowell-Smith (ed.), *The Oxford History of World Cinema*, Oxford: Oxford University Press, pp. 427–35.

Chavez, L. R. (2008), *The Latino Threat: Constructing Immigrants, Citizens, and the Nation*, Stanford: Stanford University Press.

Cheyroux, E. (2018), "Immigrant Consumption and Cultural Visibility in Documentary Films by and about Latinos," *InMedia: The French Journal of Media Studies* 7 (1), pp. 1–23.

Cheyroux, E. (2019), "Immigrant Rights Documentaries and Engagement: Eliciting Emotion to Counter the Latino Threat Narrative," *InMedia: The French Journal of Media Studies* 7 (2), pp. 1–22.

Cosentino, O. (2018), "Feminism and Intimate/Emotional Labor," *Mediático, Special Dossier on Roma*, School of Media, Arts and Humanities, University of Sussex, 24 December. Available online: https://reframe.sussex.ac.uk/mediatico/2018/12/24/special-dossier-on- roma-feminism-and-intimate-emotional-labor/.

De la Garza, A. (2009), "Realism and National Identity in 'Y tu mamá también': An Audience Perspective," in L. Nagib and C. Mello (eds.), *Realism in the Audiovisual Media*, London and New York: Palgrave Macmillan, pp. 108–18.

Del Barco, M. (2021), "Mexico's Oscar-Winning Directors Embrace Rise of Fernando Frías De La Parra," *All Things Considered*, National Public Radio, 23 January. Available online: https://www.npr.org/2021/01/23/959458175/mexicos-oscar-winning-three-amigos- embrace-rise-of-fernando-frias-de-la-parra.

Díaz Miranda, A. (2016), "Post-apocalyptic Visions: Biopolitics, Late Capitalism, and Trauma in *Children of Men* and *Naked City Spleen*," *Transmodernity: Journal of Peripheral Cultural Production of the Luso-Hispanic World* 6 (2), pp. 156–70.

Frías, F. (2021), "Por qué Fernando Frías hizo *Ya no estoy aquí*," *YouTube*, uploaded by Netflix Latinoamérica, 13 February. Available online: https://www.youtube.com/watch?v=bptE15mTcSc.

Kantaris, G. (2006). "Cinema and *Urbanías*: Translocal Identities in Contemporary Mexican Film," *Bulletin of Latin American Research* 25 (4), pp. 517–27.

Nericcio, W. A. (2007), *Tex{t}-Mex: Seductive Hallucinations of the "Mexican" in America*, Austin, TX: The University of Texas Press.

Ramírez Berg C. (2002), *Latino Images in Film: Stereotypes, Subversion, and Resistance*, Austin, TX: The University of Texas Press.

Saldaña-Portillo, M. J. (2005). "In the Shadow of NAFTA: *Y tu mamá también* Revisits the National Allegory of Mexican Sovereignty," *American Quarterly* 57 (3), pp. 751–77.

Shaw, D. (2013), *The Three Amigos: Transnational Filmmaking of Guillermo del Toro, Alejandro González Iñárritu and Alfonso Cuarón*, Manchester: Manchester University Press.

Shaw, D. (2018), "Children of Women? Alfonso Cuarón's Love Letter to His Nana," *Mediático, Special Dossier on Roma*, School of Media, Arts Humanities, University of Sussex, 24 December. Available online: https://reframe.sussex.ac.uk/mediatico/2018/12/24/special- dossier-on-roma-alfonso-cuarons-love-letter-to-his-nana/.

Tierney, D. and O. Cosentino (2018), "Introduction to the Special Dossier on *Roma* (Alfonso Cuaron)," *Mediático, Special Dossier on Roma*, School of Media, Arts Humanities, University of Sussex, 24 December. Available online: https://reframe.sussex.ac.uk/mediatico/2018/12/24/introduction-to-the-special-dossier-on-roma-alfonso-cuaron/.

"Ya no estoy aquí: A Talk with Guillermo del Toro and Alfonso Cuarón," (2020), *YouTube*, uploaded by Netflix, 30 October. Available online: https://www.youtube.com/watch?v=1FHtkn9hamk&t=1s.

CONTRIBUTORS

Roberto Avant-Mier is Associate Professor and Research Fellow in the Department of Communication at the University of Texas at El Paso, USA, and he is also affiliated faculty in Chicano Studies at UTEP. He is the author of *Rock the Nation: Latin/o Identities and the Latin Rock Diaspora* (2010), which examines the articulation(s) of Latino/as, identity, and rock music, and co-author of *Cine-Mexicans: An Introduction to Chicano Cinema* (2018), which was based on several years of research and teaching of film theory and analysis of the image(s) of Mexicans in US/Hollywood movies and films.

Timothy Corrigan is Professor Emeritus of Cinema and Media Studies at the University of Pennsylvania, USA. His books include *New German Film: The Displaced Image*, *The Films of Werner Herzog*, *Writing about Film*, *A Cinema without Walls*, *Film and Literature*, *The Film Experience* (co-authored with Patricia White), *American Cinema of the 2000s*, *Essays on the Essay Film* (co-authored with Nora Alter), and *The Essay Film: From Montaigne, After Marker*, winner of the 2012 Katherine Singer Kovács Award for the outstanding book in film and media studies. He has published essays in *Film Quarterly*, *Discourse*, and *Cinema Journal*, among other collections. In 2014 he received the Society for Cinema and Media Studies Award for Outstanding Pedagogical Achievement and the Ira H. Abrams Memorial Award for Distinguished Teaching at the University of Pennsylvania.

Cynthia Baron is Professor in the Department of Theatre and Film at Bowling Green State University, USA. Her most recent books are *Modern Acting: The Lost Chapter of American Film and Theatre* (2016) and *Acting Indie: Industry, Aesthetics, and Performance* (2020), co-authored with Yannis Tzioumakis. She is the BGSU Research Scholar of Excellence for 2017–20.

Stephen Felder is Professor of Humanities at Irvine Valley College in Irvine, California, USA. His most recent research focuses on the intersection of theories of subjectivity and popular culture in relation to paths of resistance and emancipation in late capitalism. He has published work on Lacan,

Žižek, Nietzsche, and Merleau-Ponty and on many popular television shows and films. He holds a PhD in history from the University of California, Irvine.

Gregory Frame is Lecturer in Film Studies at Bangor University, UK. His research focuses on issues of politics and representation in American audiovisual culture. He has published in *Journal of American Studies, Journal of Popular Film and Television, Film and History*, and *New Review of Film and Television Studies*. He is author of *The American President in Film and Television: Myth, Politics and Representation* (2018), which analyzes portrayals of fictional US politicians in broader social and political contexts. His current research focuses on the manner in which American film and television have represented the nation since the 2008 financial crisis.

Luis Freijo is a doctoral researcher in the Department of Film and Creative Writing at the University of Birmingham, UK, and holds an AHRC-funded Midlands 4 Cities Doctoral Scholarship. His research expertise is in the dynamics of World Cinema as it relates to genre studies and, in particular, the global Western. He has published widely in English and Spanish on classic Hollywood cinema, European filmmakers and stars, and US television series. He has recently contributed chapters on the relation between genre filmmaking and politics to *The Routledge Companion to European Cinema* (2021) and *Sense8: Transcending Television* (2021).

Carlos Gallego is Associate Professor of English, Race and Ethnic Studies, and Film Studies at St. Olaf College, USA. His book *Chicana/o Subjectivity and the Politics of Identity: Between Recognition and Revolution* was published in 2011, and the co-edited collection *Dialectical Imaginaries: Materialist Approaches to U.S. Latino/a Literature in the Age of Neoliberalism* (co-edited with Marcial González) was published in 2018. He has published work on literature, critical theory, and film in the academic journals *Arizona Quarterly, Biography, Aztlán, Cultural Critique*, and *Western Humanities Review*.

Tony Grajeda is Associate Professor of Cultural Studies in the Department of English, University of Central Florida, USA. He is co-editor of *Lowering the Boom: Critical Studies in Film Sound* (2008) and co-editor of *Music, Sound, and Technology in America: A History in Documents of Early Radio, Cinema, and the Phonograph* (2012). His work on the culture of war has appeared in *Jump Cut, disClosure, Democratic Communique*, and *Rethinking Global Security: Media, Popular Culture, and the "War on Terror"* (2006).

Bill Grantham was Visiting Professor of Media Law and Policy at the Institute for Media and Creative Industries, Loughborough University, UK, from 2015 to 2018. He has also taught at the University of East Anglia (UK),

Southern Cross University (Australia), Griffith University (Australia), and the University of California, Los Angeles Extension (USA). He is the author of one book and many book chapters and journal articles. Now living in Ireland, he writes, produces for film and television, and practices law. His academic work is at the intersection of law, the media industries, and culture.

Tim Lindemann is a PhD researcher at Queen Mary University of London, UK. His research interests focus on cinematic landscapes, film genre, and representations of marginality on film. He has worked as a research assistant at Deutsche Kinemathek, Berlin, as a film journalist, and film festival curator.

Hilaria Loyo is Associate Professor in the Department of English and German Studies at the University of Zaragoza, Spain, where she teaches film and American studies. She is a member of the research groups "Cinema, Culture and Society" and "Film and Crisis: Social Change and Representation in the Cinema of the New Century." She has published several articles in film journals and contributed book chapters on edited volumes. Her most recent publication can be found in *The Velvet Light Trap* (spring, 2019).

Virginia Luzón-Aguado is a permanent lecturer and film scholar at the University of Zaragoza, Spain. Her most recent publications in the area of eco-criticism include "Who are the Pirates? Somali Piracy and Environmental Justice in *Alakrana, Stolen Seas* and *Captain Phillips*," in *Interdisciplinary Studies in Literature and the Environment (ISLE)*, and the book chapter "The Film Star as Eco-warrior: Harrison Ford Saves the Planet" in *Ecomasculinities: Negotiating Male Gender Identity in U.S. Fiction* (2019). She has also published in other areas, notably Star and Masculinity studies, including the book *Harrison Ford: Masculinity and Stardom in Hollywood* (2018).

Kayla Meyers is an independent scholar, writer, and educator whose work examines the intersections between visual culture, race, gender, digital media, and US politics through the twentieth and twenty-first centuries. She is the author of the book *Who Said What?: A Writer's Guide to Finding, Evaluating, Quoting, and Documenting Sources (and Avoiding Plagiarism)*, which gives writers guidance toward improving their research and source evaluation. She earned her BA and MA in American Studies from the College of William and Mary, USA.

Toby Miller is the Stuart Hall Professor of Cultural Studies, Universidad Autónoma Metropolitana—Cuajimalpa, Mexico, and Sir Walter Murdoch Distinguished Collaborator, Murdoch University, Australia. The author and editor of over fifty books, his work has been translated into Spanish, Chinese, Portuguese, Japanese, Turkish, German, Italian, Farsi, French, Urdu, and

Swedish. His most recent volumes are *A COVID Charter, a Better Future* (2021), *Violence* (2021), *The Persistence of Violence: Colombian Popular Culture* (2020), *How Green Is Your Smartphone?* (co-authored, 2020), *El trabajo cultural* (2018), *Greenwashing Culture* (2018), and *Greenwashing Sport* (2018).

Elena Oliete-Aldea is Associate Professor at the Department of English and German Studies of the University of Zaragoza, Spain. Her research centers on film genre and cultural studies. More specifically, her analysis focuses on filmic representations of gender, ethnicity, and class in the context of the current economic crisis. She is author of *Hybrid Heritage on Screen. The Raj Revival in the Thatcher Era* (2015) and co-editor of *Global Genres-Local Films. The Transnational Dimension of Spanish Cinema* (2016). She has recently contributed the chapter "Global Financial Crisis in Local Filmic Scenarios: Transnational Cinema of the Great Recession" to *Global Finance on Screen: From Wall Street to Side Street* (2018).

Fabián Orán Llarena is Lecturer in the Department of English and German Philology at the University of La Laguna, Spain. His research interests lie in the fields of American Studies and Film Studies. He has published articles in peer-reviewed journals such as *Atlantis*, *Miscelánea*, and *REN: Revista de Estudios Norteamericanos*.

Beatriz Oria is Associate Professor in Film Studies at the English Studies Department of the University of Zaragoza, Spain. Her essays have been published in *The Journal of Popular Culture*, *Journal of Popular Film and Television*, *Journal of Popular Romance Studies*, and *Journal of Film and Video*, among others. She is the author of *Talking Dirty on "Sex and the City": Romance, Intimacy, Friendship* (2014) and co-editor of *Global Genres, Local Films: The Transnational Dimension of Spanish Cinema* (2016). Her current research focuses on romantic comedy, US independent cinema, and contemporary representations of intimacy.

Leah Pérez completed her bachelor's degree in Contemporary Latino and Latin American Studies at the University of Southern California, USA, with a focus on visual art and media of both US Latinxs and Latinx Americans. She started the master's program in Curatorial Practices and the Public Sphere in the fall of 2020 at the University of Southern California. Her research interests lie at the intersection of art and ethnic culture, particularly focusing on the representation of queer Latinxs in contemporary art and popular culture.

Ian Scott is Professor of American Film and History at Manchester University, UK. He is the author of several books on Hollywood's politics and history, including, *Robert Riskin: The Life and Times of a Hollywood Screenwriter* (2021). He also works in TV and radio documentary, and his BBC Radio 4 series *The Californian Century* (2020) was nominated in 2021 for Programme of the Year by the British Broadcasting Press Guild.

William J. Simmons is a poet, curator, and historian of contemporary art and film. He is Provost Fellow in the Humanities at the University of Southern California, USA. He is the author of numerous international articles, book chapters, and monographs, and he has lectured widely. He co-edited the spring 2020 issue of *Framework: The Journal of Cinema and Media* with Ronald Gregg.

Juan A. Tarancón is Lecturer in the Department of English at the University of Zaragoza, Spain. His research centers on cinema, cultural studies, and contemporary US culture. He has written on film genre theory, on representations of immigration and Mexican American culture, and on the work of John Sayles and Carlos Saura. His work has appeared in *CineAction, Cultural Studies, The Quarterly Review of Film and Video, New Cinemas,* and varied Spanish scholarly journals. He is co-editor of *Global Genres, Local Films: The Transnational Dimension of Spanish Cinema* (2016).

INDEX

The Accidental Billionaires 101
action film 36, 201, 206, 283
   geriaction subgenre 282, 287, 289
affect 6, 9, 86, 167, 199–200, 213–17, 219, 237. *See also* emotions
   affective formation 4, 6, 214, 216
   affective landscape 200, 214–16, 222
   affective regime 9, 216–17, 220, 226
   affect theory 6, 199–200
African Americans 33, 44, 70, 138–9, 188–9, 193–4, 201, 203–4. *See also* Blacks
   art by 240
   crime and 44, 203
   exclusion of 45, 47
   violence against 133
Alice Doesn't Live Here Anymore 35
alternative facts 183. *See also* fake news; misinformation
alt right 183. *See also* far right
Always Be My Maybe 55
American Casino 5
American Dream 94, 198, 209, 294, 304
   women and 72, 78–9
American Honey 220
The Amityville Horror (film) 159
The Amityville Horror (novel) 160
Amores perros 35, 296, 305 n.8
anthropocentrism 245–6
art cinema 36
artificial intelligence (AI) 113, 115, 122
Asian-Americans 16, 27, 35
Asian century 16, 27

August Evening 32–5, 37, 39–41, 43, 46–7
August Osage County 48
austerity 2, 4, 47, 269, 272
auteur cinema, auteurism 72, 183–4, 190, 193, 195
Avatar 245–6, 253–5, 257, 259

Babel 35, 296
Baby Boom 55
baby boomers 283
Bahrani, Ramin 32, 34, 38, 40, 75, 220
bailout 6, 16, 267, 272
Baker, Sean 9, 214–16, 220–6
The Ballad of Buster Scruggs 269
bankruptcy 22, 75, 78
banks 16, 69, 163, 266–7, 272–3, 276
   bankers 16, 270
   banking collapse 5, 267
   banking system 163, 272–3, 276
Beasts of the Southern Wild 9, 220, 231–2, 237
Being Flynn 220
Biden, Joseph R. 100, 108
The Big Short 47, 80 n.1
The Birth of a Nation 23, 151–2
Biutiful 35, 296
Blacks 31, 33, 43–5, 87, 94, 138, 140, 142–3, 148–58, 160, 174, 194–5, 237, 240. *See also* racism; slavery
   black bodies 150–3, 157, 241
   black characters 151–3, 161, 240
   black culture 157–8, 240
   black families 35, 154

black history 153
black interiority 151, 153–4, 157–8, 161
black neighborhoods 149
representation of 151
Blacks Lives Matter 133, 184
The Blair Witch Project 154, 260 n.1
Bless Their Little Hearts 34
blue-collar workers 70, 213, 283
B-movies 148
Bone Tomahawk 184–5, 187, 190, 201
The Book of Eli 231
border, borderlands 9, 32, 40, 114, 126, 132, 166, 172, 279–82, 285, 287–8, 294, 302
border control 296
border crossing 237
US-Canada border 41
US-Mexico border 9, 32, 270, 279–85, 288, 293
border films 1, 9, 281, 286
The *Bourne Conspiracy* trilogy 1
The Boys from Brazil 158
Brawl in Cell Block 99 184–5, 201
Bridesmaids 54
Broadcast News 55
Brokeback Mountain 281
Brown, Wendy 58, 232, 237, 280, 301–2, 304
Bullit 206
Bush, George W. 1, 132, 267, 269
Butch Cassidy and the Sundance Kid 275

Cameron, James 246, 253, 261 n.12
Candyman 150, 160
Capitalism 2–3, 5–6, 8, 15–16, 32, 36, 69, 70, 78, 84–5, 90–1, 104–5, 234, 273, 295
financial capitalism 78, 276 (see also financialization)
global capitalism 3, 280 (see also globalization)
neoliberal capitalism 94, 231-2, 240, 242 (see also neoliberalism)
surveillance capitalism 3, 8, 99, 104

Capitalism: A Love Story 5, 75
Capitol attack 108, 110
Carol 72
Certain Women 270
Chan Is Missing 35
Charlie Wilson's War 101
chick flick (genre) 8, 53–4, 57–66
post-recessionary chick flick 53, 58–66
Children of Men 300
Chop Shop 34
cinema vérité 34
citizen, citizenship 58, 123–5, 165–7, 178, 193, 199, 242, 273, 281
deserving/non-deserving citizen 214
neoliberal citizen 166–7, 169, 178
noncitizen 38
Citizen Kane 103
class 3, 55, 66, 69, 71, 73, 75–7, 79, 136–8, 140, 153, 155, 158, 178, 208, 214, 216, 218–20, 245, 295
class barriers 19, 35
class crossing 60
class polarization 166
class solidarity 138
class struggle 136, 218–19
class warfare 2, 132–3, 136, 142
intra-class resentment 138
climate crisis 3, 84, 239, 241–2, 259
Clinton, Hillary 142, 281
Clinton, William J. "Bill" 166
Cold War 25–6, 165–6, 284
colonialism 141, 144–5, 153, 255, 293. See also postcolonialism
neocolonialism 285
commodification 79, 270
common sense 5, 9, 177, 217–18, 225–7
community. See also gated community; trailer park, trailer-park community
alternative community 174, 178, 232–3, 235, 237
community-minded values 216
dissolution of 42, 209, 235, 242, 280, 290
egalitarian community 199, 208

longing for   233, 236
neoliberal assault on   242, 276
racialized community   193, 240, 268, 280
rural community   172–4, 177, 232–3, 237, 241
sense of community   1, 178, 239
The Company Men   2, 5, 69
compassion   214, 220, 303
compassionate attitude   224–5, 227
conservatism   202, 210 n.6, 214
consumers   21, 35, 78, 88, 178, 248–9, 253
consumerism   54, 170, 253
consumerist culture   104
consumer society   247–9
Contagion   6, 35
corporations   16, 21, 24, 88, 104, 106–7, 109–10, 259
corporate capital   2, 213, 219
corporate class   1, 2, 200
corporate dramas   60, 62, 69, 80
corporate greed   32, 255
corporate greenwashing   249, 252
corporate media   4, 105
Covid-19   4, 104, 125, 231
Creed   283
crime   89, 91, 93, 132, 136–7, 141–4, 175, 185, 201, 205, 207, 210 n.6, 267
crime film   199, 201, 206
crime-ridden neighborhood   201, 203, 208
crimes against whites   183
criminality   188, 191, 194–5
criminal organization   173–4
criminal underworld   185, 282, 287
drug-related crimes   174
environmental crimes   253
hate crimes   38
urban crime   94–5
War on Crime   165
Cronos   295
Cuarón, Alfonso   294–6, 300, 302–3, 305, 305 n.6
Culture Shock   161
culture wars   2, 218–19

The Curious Case of Benjamin Button   101
Curtiz, Michael   8, 75, 80 n.4

dance   20, 39, 297–9, 301–2
cumbia   297–300, 302, 305 n.10
cumbia rebajada   297, 299–300, 303
The Dead Girl   34
debt   16, 45, 70, 144, 266–7, 273–6
Debtocracy   5
deindustrialization   167–8, 219, 267, 270, 274, 283
del Toro, Guillermo   293, 295–8, 302
democracy   2, 26, 109, 183, 242, 284
democratic ethos   7
democratic institutions   91, 109
liberal democracy   232 (*see also* liberalism)
Department of Defense   25–6, 124
Department of Homeland Security   38, 132, 165
deregulation   47, 218–19, 266
Desierto   270
The Devil Finds Work   153, 160
The Devil Wears Prada   65
diaspora   294. *See also* displacement
digital media   80 n.5. *See also* social media
Dirty Harry   206
disaster films   35, 231
disenfranchisement   48, 184, 188, 194, 302–3
Disney World   107, 216–17
displacement   115, 151, 184, 193, 232, 234, 241–2, 250, 290, 294, 302–3. *See also* diaspora
documentary films   32, 243 n.1, 298
documentary style   34, 164, 226, 298, 302
domopolitics   8, 163, 165–7, 175–6, 178. *See also* housing politics
dotcom bubble   21
Do the Right Thing   143
Down to the Bone   34, 164, 168, 171, 176

Dragged Across Concrete 2, 9, 184–5, 193, 198–9, 201, 206, 209–10
Drag Me to Hell 35
Dr. Strangelove 107
drugs 85, 94, 103, 169–72, 174, 187, 205, 279, 287, 303. *See also* opioid epidemic
　drug addiction 168–9, 171–2
　drug use 2, 92, 167–9, 171–2, 174, 176
　War on Drugs 165
dystopian films 2, 132–4, 143

ecology 35, 245–7, 253
　eco-activism 240, 259-60 (*see also* environment, environmentalism environmentalists)
　ecocriticism 9, 240–1, 246, 249
　ecocultural theory 245–6
　ecological catastrophes 231
　ecological devastation 238, 248
　ecological interconnectedness 239, 241
economic crisis 2, 4, 9, 35, 47, 54, 69–71, 76, 78, 133, 154, 168, 213–14, 220, 231–2, 288
　economic crisis of 2008 1, 5, 16, 54, 65, 68–71, 78, 80, 114, 125, 166–7, 220, 231, 265–6, 268, 273, 280, 288
economic destitution 201, 208, 216, 300. *See also* poverty
economy 33, 44, 54, 57–9, 66, 69–71, 76, 84, 87–8, 125, 137, 149, 168, 177, 185, 193, 208–9, 219, 241, 248, 252–3
　debt economy 274
　deindustrialized economy 274 (*see also* deindustrialization)
　deregulation of 44, 218
　economic fugitives 168, 170, 177
　economic precariousness 57, 59, 64, 75, 166, 169, 171, 201, 208, 238 (*see also* precarity)
　economic recession 2, 26, 32, 35, 54, 69–72, 172, 176, 219–20

　finance economy 16 (*see also* financialization)
　global economy 22, 114 (*see also* globalization)
　neoliberal economy 33, 131, 166-7, 169, 174-5, 248, 288, 294, 297, 301 (*see also* neoliberalism)
　regulation of 18, 32
elections 100, 218, 289
　2016 presidential election 111, 133, 142, 150
　2018 midterm elections 280
　2020 presidential election 100, 108–9, 184
　electorate 198
emotions 6–7, 36, 62, 64, 66, 75, 164, 200, 202, 209, 214–16, 220, 223, 227, 239, 271. *See also* affect
　emotional experiences 33, 43, 78, 206, 259
　emotionality 54, 60–2, 216
empathy 69, 122, 214–15, 226–7
employment 20, 24, 70, 89, 90, 171, 218, 267, 275 294. *See also* unemployment
　part-time employment 33
　underemployment 22, 296, 299
Entre nos 220–1
entrepreneur 65, 71, 151, 167
　entrepreneurial spirit 57, 166, 250, 252
environment (natural) 17, 36, 241, 246, 249–50, 253–5, 258–60, 260 n.2, 261 n.9
　environmental awakening 250
　environmental catastrophe 9, 246, 248, 252, 258
　environmental conscience 240, 251, 253
　environmental crisis 68, 253
　environmental education 250, 253, 257, 259
　environmental ethics 246–8, 256
environmentalism
　environmentalists 233, 240, 247, 255, 260 (*see also* eco-activism)

environmentally-friendly companies   23, 253
environmental preservation   253
environmental programs   3
environmental values   247
   neoliberalism and the   3
ethnicity   203, 269
evictions   16, 70, 75, 133, 149. *See also* foreclosures; mortgages, mortgage crisis
exceptionalism   282
The Exiles   35
Ex Machina   8, 113, 115–16, 123, 125–6
The Exorcist   148, 160
The Expendables franchise   283

fake news   4, 8, 105. *See also* alternative facts; misinformation
family values   163, 167, 169
Far from Heaven   72–3
far right   178, 199. *See also* alt right
   far-right rhetoric   195
fascism   131, 133
Fast Food Nation   35
feelings   64, 71, 95, 108, 175, 200, 202, 214–16, 221–3, 226, 239, 302, 304. *See also* affect; emotions
   feelings of anxiety   206
   feelings of despair   199
   feelings of dislocation/ disorientation   200, 287
   feelings of marginalization   290
   feelings of nostalgia   73
   feelings of stagnation   199, 209
   feelings of unsafety   155
feminism, feminists   55, 65–6, 80 n.4, 114, 166–7, 178
   black feminism   241
   ecofeminism   248
   neoliberal feminism   57–9
   postfeminism   62
Fight Club   104
film genres   35–6, 59, 115–16, 132–4, 139–40, 144, 240
financial crisis films   2, 5, 69, 71–2, 79

financial crisis of 2008   1–2, 5–6, 8, 16, 59, 68–9, 125, 149, 155, 160, 166–7, 231, 265–7, 269, 272, 276, 288. *See also* economic crisis, economic crisis of 2008
financial elites   37, 46, 69
financial institutions   2, 35, 267–8, 274
financialization   47, 266
financial sector   45, 84, 267
Fincher, David   8, 100–5, 107–11, 134
The Florida Project   9, 213–17, 220–1, 225–7
Floyd, George   99
Food Chains   40
Foreclosed   134
foreclosures   133, 163, 166, 272, 275. *See also* evictions; mortgages, mortgage crisis
4:44: The Last Day on Earth   6
The French Connection   206
Frontera (2014)   270, 281
frontier   9, 123, 170, 266, 268–72, 274, 276–7, 285–6, 290
   closing of the   268
   frontier violence   272
   postindustrial frontier   265, 268, 271–4, 276
Frozen River   32–3, 35, 40–3, 46–8
Funny Games   134

The Game   105
Garland, Alex   8, 113, 116
Gas Food Lodging   35
gated community   134, 136–7, 139, 249–50
gender. *See also* transgender people
   gender(ed) hierarchies   116, 227
   gender and crisis   8, 71
   gender and labor   58
   gender backlash   70–1, 79
   gendered domopolitics   163, 165, 167
   gendered surveillance   114, 121
   gender inequalities   59, 70, 186
   gender norms   114–15, 118–19, 121
   gender relations   119

INDEX

gender roles 71, 74–7, 79,
  121, 123
gender stereotypes 201
performativity of 115, 121,
  123, 125
Generation X 103
Generation Y. *See* Millennials
gentrification 45–6, 149, 153, 155,
  157, 161
George Washington 34
Get Out 8, 148–61
The Girl with the Dragon Tattoo 105
globalization 9, 108, 193, 266, 281,
  283, 285, 296
  migration and 193
  neoliberalism and 3 280,
  290, 294
Gone with the Wind 25
González Iñárritu, Alejandro 35, 296,
  302, 305 n.8
gore 155, 201
gothic (genre) 2, 158
Granik, Debra 8, 34, 163–4,
  167–8, 170, 172, 176, 178–9,
  220, 232–3
The Grapes of Wrath 270
Great Depression 18, 22–3, 69–72,
  74–5, 78, 289. *See also* stock
  market, crash of 1929
Great Recession 39, 42, 54, 69–70,
  74–5, 78, 80, 133, 167. *See also*
  financial crisis of 2008
Great Replacement 9, 183–4, 193–4,
  195 n.2
Green New Deal 3
Gremlins 151
Griffith, D.W. 23, 151–2
Griffiths, Megan 164
*Guess Who's Coming to
  Dinner?* 156–7
The Gunfighter 272

Haynes, Todd 8, 69, 71–2, 75–7,
  79–80, 80 n.4
Heaven Knows What 220
hecovery 70
Hell or High Water 9, 265–7,
  270–3, 275–7

Hereditary 149
heteropatriarchy 115–16, 119,
  121, 123
The High Note 55, 63
Hito Hata: Raise the Red Flag 35
Hollywood 1, 7, 15, 17–21, 24–7, 34,
  36, 61, 153, 204, 220, 253, 259,
  294, 303–4
  classical Hollywood 20, 22–3,
  25, 270
  Hollywood style 36, 103, 216,
  219, 221–2, 270, 295
  Hollywood system 19–20
home 6, 8, 15, 69, 74–5, 122–3,
  133–4, 140, 142, 150, 152–5,
  158–9, 163–78, 208, 234,
  237–8, 240, 286, 288, 290, 297,
  300, 303–4
  class and 152, 156, 169
  gendered home 167
  homeownership 148–50, 154–6,
  160, 166
  as nation/homeland 8, 163,
  165–7, 170, 175–6, 178
  as real state 166
  as site of violence 7
  trailer home 41
  as troubled space 77–9, 142, 154
home invasion 8, 94
  home invasion films 8, 132, 134,
  136, 140
homeland 104, 255, 294
homelessness 2, 8, 149, 155, 157,
  164, 166, 168, 172, 174, 176,
  234, 300
Homo oeconomicus 58
homosociality 115–18, 121–2
hope 9, 59, 172, 178, 208–9, 217,
  259, 271
  hopelessness 15, 199, 217,
  221, 271
horror (film genre) 7–8, 35, 132,
  134, 148–55, 157–61, 184,
  260 n.1, 295
  eco-horror 246
  horror conventions 8, 295
  horror Western 201
Hostel series 1

houselessness 161, 174
housing crisis 7–8, 133, 139–40, 154, 163–5. *See also* mortgages, mortgage crisis
housing market 132–3, 266–7
housing politics 8, 165, 178. *See also* domopolitics
How to Be Single 55, 65
Hughes, John 103
humor 40, 184–7, 189, 191, 195
Hunt, Courtney 32, 40, 164

I Am a Fugitive from a Chain Gang 289
identity politics 108, 184, 193, 195, 219
ideology 9, 44, 54, 92, 187, 189, 193, 199–202, 209, 215, 219, 232–3, 246–7, 260 n.5, 269, 293–4, 304
  ethno nationalist ideology 183, 185
  ideological contestation 200
  ideological subtext 202
  ideological uniformity 199–200
  neoliberal ideology 55, 59, 75, 85, 88, 236, 242, 295, 297 (*see also* neoliberalism)
  reactionary ideology 76, 195
I Feel Pretty 55, 62
immigration, immigrants 9, 23, 31–3, 37–9, 45, 47, 70, 91, 165–6, 193, 195 n.2, 268, 285, 290, 296, 304. *See also* migration; Latinos, Latino immigration
  criminalization of 280, 288, 303
  undocumented immigrants 32, 39–40, 165, 294, 302–3
In a World… 55, 65
incarceration 43–5
  prison industrial system 16, 45, 47
  prison population 44
  surveillance incarceration 104
independent cinema 7–8, 31–2, 34–5, 39, 43, 46, 216, 220, 294
Indigenous peoples 31, 34–5, 41, 47–8, 141, 256, 260 n.8, 295, 305 n.5. *See also* Native Americans
  Blackfeet Nation 48

  Comanche 268, 272, 274, 290
  Mohawk people 32, 41
  Muckleshoot 48
individualism 47, 55, 63, 65, 170, 172, 206, 209, 214, 220, 235–6, 276, 282
inequality 3, 9, 84, 133, 199, 213–14, 216, 218–20, 225–6, 238, 282
  economic inequality 131, 208, 210 n.7, 271
  gender inequality 70
  neoliberalism and inequality 280
Insidious 154
Instagram 80 n.5, 104, 109
The Intern 55
Isn't It Romantic? 55, 62
isolation 289, 301
  isolationism 285
  social isolation 37, 41–2, 276
  space of 222

Jesse James (1939) 270
jobs 19, 43, 54, 213–14, 290, 294–5. *See also* labor; employment
  loss of 6, 20, 89, 280
  low-wage jobs 37, 171, 218
  outsourced jobs 280, 290
Joker (2019) 184
Juicy and Delicious 238
Jurassic Park 151
Justified (TV series) 270

Katrina (hurricane) 149, 161 n.1, 243 n.2
Kerrigan, Lodge 35
Keynesian policies 23
Killer of Sheep 35
King Jr., Martin Luther 219
Klein, Naomi 3, 104, 260 n.7
Kruger, Barbara 155, 157
Kubrick, Stanley 107, 151
Ku Klux Klan 133, 152

labor 2, 8, 16–17, 19–20, 24, 32–3, 37, 39, 46–7, 204, 219, 295–6, 302, 304
  division of 58
  female labor 54, 78, 167, 169, 178

INDEX

laborers, laboring classes 36, 38–9, 45, 46, 64, 152, 214, 218, 305
labor exploitation 144, 173, 273, 276, 285, 296
labor market 64
labor unions, organized labor 266
manual labor 33, 37, 45–6
racialized labor 35
unskilled labor 33, 43, 46–8
Ladybird 220
landscape 9, 16, 31, 45, 177, 232–43, 252, 271
 frontier landscape 270, 277, 285
 landscape of crisis 75, 252, 265, 271
 postcrisis landscape 276
 rural landscape 9, 231–3, 240
 urban landscape 159, 168
 Western landscape 271–2, 276, 290
The Last Days of Lehman Brothers 80 n.1
Late Night 53, 55–6, 58, 61–5
Latinos 32, 172, 176, 191–2, 281, 294, 299, 303
 Latino immigration 183, 270, 279, 284, 294, 300, 302–3
 Latino threat 183, 303
Lean on Pete 270
Leave No Trace 9, 34, 164, 168, 170, 174, 177–8, 220, 231–3, 235, 237–9, 241–2
Leo, Melissa 41, 75
liberalism 23, 32, 84, 91
Like a Boss 55, 63, 65
Little Miss Sunshine 209
Logan 270
Long Shot 55, 62
Lopez, Jennifer 53, 56
The Lorax 9, 245–6, 248, 254–5, 258

Ma 161
The Magnificent Seven (1960) 272
The Magnificent Seven (2016) 269
mainstream cinema 7, 65, 216, 220, 282
mancession 8, 69–72, 74–7, 79

Manchester by the Sea 220
Manifest Destiny 282, 294
Manning, Chelsea 125
Man Push Cart 32, 34, 36–41, 43, 46–7
Margin Call 5, 47
marriage 54, 57, 73, 78, 154, 169, 171, 175
 heteronormative marriage 71, 176
 interracial marriage 157 (*see also* miscegenation)
 teenage marriage 173
Marx, Karl 2, 140, 273
 Marxism 2–3, 135, 142
masculinity 26, 115–18, 121–2, 167–8, 178, 266, 274–5, 279, 283, 285, 287. *See also* heteropatriarchy
 damaged masculinity 169–70
 hyper-masculinity 116, 173
 masculinity and the natural world 120
 masculinity crisis 71
 normative conception of 275
 performative masculinity 115
 queering of 275
 violent forms of 272–3, 275, 282
 white masculinity 281, 290
Matewan 34
Meek's Cutoff 269
Melancholia 6
melodrama 7, 35, 54, 79, 153, 221–2
 male melodrama 69, 79
 melodramatic mode 72, 75, 152, 216, 220–1
Michael Clayton 1
middle class 17, 39, 43–4, 54, 70–1, 85, 87, 201, 203–4, 206, 208–9, 218, 269, 295
 middle-class audience 17, 94
 middle-class home 152
 middle-class men 116
 urban middle-class 294
Middle of Nowhere 33, 35, 43–4, 46–7
migration 149, 151, 153, 280–1, 285, 297, 300. *See also* immigrants; Latinos, Latino immigration

migrants 161, 280–1, 288, 301–2, 304
Mildred Pierce (1941) 8, 75, 80 n.4
Mildred Pierce (2011) 8, 69, 71–2
Mildred Pierce (novel) 71, 74
military 25–6, 254
  militarism 114, 283
  militarization 132
Millennials 62, 64
minorities 70–1, 201, 204, 210 n.6, 237, 288
miscegenation 152. *See also* interracial marriage
misinformation 104, 109. *See also* fake news
mobility 152, 175, 177, 294. *See also* social mobility
  immobility, stuckedness 176–7
Morning Glory 55, 63
mortgages 133, 159, 266–7
  mortgage crisis 69–70, 75
  reverse mortgage 270, 274
motherhood 58, 78
Mother's Day 134
multiculturalism 143, 220
  multicultural society 183, 288
Mulvey, Laura 118, 123
musical (genre) 248, 297
Muslims 38, 280
myth, mythology 8, 80 n.5, 179, 213, 286, 289–90
  myth of the West 269–70, 276, 286–7
  success myth 110 (*see also* American Dream)

narrative
  coming-of-age narrative 45
  nonlinear narrative 297, 299, 302–3
nationalism 139, 219, 234, 242, 295
  ethnonationalism 184
  post-nationalism 241
  white nationalism 47, 184, 193
  xenophobic nationalism 167, 214, 220
nationhood 8, 134

Native Americans 144–5, 234–5, 256, 268–9, 272–4, 282, 284. *See also* Indigenous peoples
naturalism 35–6
Nebraska 209
neoliberalism 2, 9–10, 32, 36, 47–8, 71, 83–5, 88, 91, 95, 96 n.2, 96 n.4, 167, 176, 214, 217, 219, 242, 248, 265, 271, 277, 305. *See also* ideology, neoliberal ideology
  competition and 84–8, 91, 94–5, 178
  critique of 252
  democracy and 232
  emotions and 227
  financial crisis and 266, 269, 293–4
  impact of 2–3, 31, 297, 301
  neoliberal geographies 163, 165, 168
  space and 237, 241–2
  values of 54, 65–6, 78, 87, 91, 241, 276
  violence of 9, 266, 268
  women and 165
neo-neorealism 164
New Queer Cinema 71
The Newsroom 101
Nichols, Mike 55, 101
Nightcrawler 8, 83–6, 88–9, 93–5
Night of the Living Dead 150
nihilism 6, 290
9/11 attacks 1, 31, 38–9, 47, 68, 134, 165, 167, 187, 190
  post-9/11 society 38–9, 114, 124, 131–2, 134, 163, 165
1984 (novel) 26
Nine to Five 55
99 Homes 75
No Country for Old Men 281–2, 286
Nomadland (film) 178
Nomadland (novel) 178
El Norte 35
North American Free Trade Agreement (NAFTA) 294–7, 299, 301, 305, 305 n.5
nostalgia 69, 73, 219

Obama, Barack   105, 134, 150, 156, 199, 218, 267
On Thermonuclear War   107
opioid epidemic   143, 175. *See also* drugs
optimism   198
   "cruel optimism"   80 n.5, 200, 204, 206
The Other Side   220
Out of the Furnace   220

Panic Room   134
The Parallax View   105
paramilitary organization   142
Paranormal Activity   35, 153–5
Paranormal Activity II   35
parenting   169, 173
patriarchy   69–71, 75, 78–9, 115–23, 173
Patriot Act   114
patriotism   187, 193, 195
Peele, Jordan   8, 148–50, 152, 155, 158, 161
performativity   8, 58, 115, 121, 123, 125, 275
pessimism   6, 16, 199, 202, 208–9
police state   132
political correctness   108, 194
pollution   3, 248
Poltergeist   149
popular culture   59, 70, 135–6, 281
populism
   ethnopopulism   9, 184
   right-wing populism   214
pornography   119, 148, 153
postcolonialism   140, 240–1. *See also* colonialism
postindustrial economy   266. *See also* service-oriented economy
postindustrial society   31–3, 42, 46–8, 266, 268, 272, 275
poverty. *See also* underclass
   chronic poverty   143, 172, 207, 214
   criminalization of   166, 171
   cycle of   3, 207, 214, 218
   extreme poverty   231, 237, 241–2

intergenerational poverty   168
poverty wages   219
rural poverty   231, 237–8, 240–2
precariat   3, 19
precarity   31, 66, 70–1, 80 n.5, 171, 270, 276
   economic precarity   169, 171, 209 (*see also* economic precariousness)
Precious   220–1
Pretty Woman   63
prison. *See* incarceration
The Purge franchise   2, 8, 131–4, 140, 145–6, 220
   The First Purge   133, 140, 142–3
   The Purge   132–5, 138–9, 141, 144–5, 154
   The Purge: Anarchy   132, 140–3, 145
   The Purge: Election Year   133, 140, 142–3

race   55–6, 60, 66, 70, 123, 137, 139, 143, 149–51, 154, 156, 158, 190, 195, 201, 241, 245, 280
mixed race   143
multiracial community   240–1
post-racial era   44, 161
race relationships   150, 168, 195
racial bias   122
racial disparities   44, 70, 155, 186
racial fears   199, 280
racial horror   161
racial memory   255–6
racial politics   153, 185–7, 190, 193, 282
racial quota   64
racial revenge   188, 192
racial slurs   156
racial tensions/conflicts   179, 189, 195
racial threat   123
racial violence   8
racism   4, 94, 151, 153–6, 161, 186, 193, 210 n.4, 240, 242, 282, 295
   systemic/structural racism   131–2, 190

Raíces de sangre 35
Rambo series 9, 282–4, 289
  Rambo 283–4
  Rambo: First Blood 283–4
  *Rambo: First Blood
    Part II* 283, 289
  Rambo III 284
  Rambo: Last Blood 279, 282–90
Random Acts of Flyness 35
Razvi, Ahmad 37–8
Reagan, Ronald 47, 210 n.6, 269, 283
realism 34, 36, 43, 206, 240
Red River 271, 275
Reichardt, Kelly 33, 42, 164, 220, 269–70
religion 136, 248, 273
resilience 43, 177, 273–5
Rich Hill 220
The Rider 270
right-wing discourse 283, 285
right-wing extremists 191
The Road 6, 231
Roma 295, 305 n.6
romance 37, 54–6, 58, 63–4, 66
romantic comedy 54–5, 63–4, 295. *See also* rom-com
rom-com 55, 64. *See also* romantic comedy
Rosemary's Baby (book) 158
Rosemary's Baby (film) 158–9
rural communities 32, 232, 237–8, 240–1

Saludos Amigos 25
Saw series 1
Scorsese, Martin 35, 84, 105
The Searchers 271–2, 287, 290
Second Act 53, 55–61, 63–5
service-oriented economy 219, 266, 271
Shane 269, 290
The Shining 151
Sideways 209
The Silence of the Lambs 148
Simón Bolívar 25
Sinister 154
slavery 149, 151–2, 158, 240–1

enslavement 154
sex slavery 287
slave trade 153
slow cinema 8, 164
Snowden, Edward 114, 125
social cohesion 178, 209
social fragmentation 199
social isolation 37, 41–2, 276, 289, 301
social justice 59, 214–15, 219–20, 227
social media 8, 21, 61, 100–4, 108–9, 111, 203. *See also* digital media
  Facebook 80 n.5, 100–12
social mobility 57, 149, 299
The Social Network 8, 99–103, 105–7, 109–11
social programs 4. *See also* welfare, welfare programs
social realism 240
social services 16, 170, 225, 233, 235
solidarity 9, 25, 138, 177, 214, 216, 232, 237, 239–41
  female solidarity 173
Sólo con tu pareja 294–5
Songs My Brothers Taught Me 35, 220
Sorkin, Aaron 100–4, 107–9, 111
Sorry to Bother You 35
space
  metropolitan areas 159, 237
  public space 157, 170
  rural spaces 32–4, 48, 167, 231–2, 285
  space of isolation 222
Spa Night 33, 35–6, 43, 45–7
Spencer, Octavia 161
Spielberg, Steven 26, 151
Stagecoach 270
The Stepford Wives 158
stereotypes 152, 201, 235, 279, 281–2
Steve Jobs 103
stock market 15, 21, 103
  crash of 1929 22, 74, 78, 266, 270
Straw Dogs (2011) 134
suburbanization 19, 22, 270

supremacism, supremacists 33, 44, 133, 144, 161 n.9, 258, 280, 289
surveillance 8, 104, 106, 113–26, 126 n.1, 132, 135–6, 138, 166, 168, 171, 250
　surveillance capitalism 3, 8, 99, 101
　surveillance culture 102, 115
Syriana 1

Taken 285
Take Shelter 35
Tea Party 204, 218
terrorism 1, 146 n.1, 184, 255, 260 n.5, 269. *See also* 9/11 attacks
The Texas Chainsaw Massacre 156
The Thing 150
The Three Burials of Melquiades Estrada 281
The Three Caballeros 25
thriller (genre) 1, 40–1, 132, 134, 158, 201
　prison thriller 201
Time Out of Mind 220
Too Big to Fail 47, 80 n.1
Top Gun 26
torture porn 1
Touch of Evil 287
Traffic 287
trailer home 41
trailer park 175, 177–8, 235–7, 243 n.1
　trailer-park community 178, 236–7
transgender people 114
Trespass 134
Trump, Donald J. 83–4, 99–100, 106–11, 131, 133, 143, 150, 161, 167, 170, 183–4, 196 n.3, 198, 213–14, 219, 227, 279–85, 288–90
　Trumpism 131, 199, 204, 210
21 Grams 35, 296

underclass 41, 166, 169–9, 172. *See also* class

unemployment 2, 16, 32, 70, 71, 136, 143–4, 172, 185. *See also* employment
　female unemployment 54
Union Maids 34
United States-Mexico-Canada Agreement (USMCA) 294
Upham, Misty 41, 48
upper class 60, 73, 132, 139, 156, 185, 295
　upper middle class 54, 156

vigilantism 9, 146 n.1, 195, 206, 282
　vigilante films 285, 287
　vigilante militias 281–2
violence
　domestic violence 7, 168, 275
　economic violence 9, 164, 266–76
　graphic violence 139–40, 184–5, 190, 192, 201, 290
　racial violence 8, 151–2, 155, 160, 269
　regeneration through 9, 145, 289
The Visitor 209

Wall-E 6
Wall Street. *See* stock market
Wall Street: Money Never Sleeps 5, 69
Wanda 35
war
　home front 132, 134, 165, 168
　Iraq War 267
　war veterans 139, 168, 170, 234, 243, 254, 283–4, 286
　War on Terror 1, 114, 132–3, 139, 163–8, 171, 176, 255
Warrior 163
welfare
　curtailment of 166–7, 213
　welfare programs 4, 47, 171 (*see also* social programs)
　welfare queen 171, 213
　welfare state 1, 166
Wendy and Lucy 33, 35–6, 40, 42–3, 46–7

Western (genre)   9, 236, 265–7, 269–70, 272, 275–7, 281–2, 287, 290
  classic Westerns   9, 269, 271–2, 276, 282, 287, 290
  conventions of the   273, 282, 287
  horror in the   184, 201
  masculinity in the   175
  post-Westerns   269–70, 282, 284
  Western hero   275, 284, 286, 289
The West Wing   101
What's Your Number?   54
white-collar workers   31–2, 37, 45, 47
The Wild Bunch   272
Wind River   272
Winter's Bone (film)   2, 34, 164, 169, 172, 176, 178
Winter's Bone (novel)   168
The Wizard of Lies   80 n.1
The Wolf of Wall Street   8, 83–6, 92–3, 95
workers
  neoliberalism and   8, 271
  rural working class   219, 237
  white working class   219, 267, 272
  working-class location   158–9
working men   8, 70, 170, 295
working poor   41, 171, 218
working women   8, 54–56, 61, 65, 78
working class   19, 45–6, 163–5, 185, 204, 214, 218–19, 267, 295. *See also* blue-collar
Working Girl   55, 65
World War Z   6

xenophobia   36, 187, 195, 202, 210 n.4, 279, 288. *See also* nationalism, xenophobic nationalism

Ya no estoy aquí   9, 293, 296–304
Yellowstone (TV series)   272
Y tu mamá también   295, 303, 305 n.5

Zahler, S. Craig   9, 183–7, 189–95, 196 n.4, 199–202, 206, 208–9, 210 n.3
Zhao, Chloé   35, 178, 220, 270
Zuckerberg, Mark   99–103, 105–11

www.ingramcontent.com/pod-product-compliance
Lightning Source LLC
Chambersburg PA
CBHW052146300426
44115CB00011B/1535